Ethnicity, Security, and Separatism in India

Ethnicity, Security, and Separatism in India

Maya Chadda

COLUMBIA UNIVERSITY PRESS   NEW YORK

Columbia University Press
Publishers Since 1893
New York   Chichester, West Sussex

Library of Congress Cataloging-in-Publication Data
Chadda, Maya
    Ethnicity, security, and separatism in India / Maya Chadda.
      p.   cm.
    Includes bibliographical references and index.
    ISBN 0–231–10736–6 (cloth). — ISBN 0–231–10737–4 (pbk.)
    1. India—Politics and government—1947–   2. India—Foreign
relations—1947–1984.   3. India—Foreign relations—1984–   4. India—
History—Autonomy and independence movements.   5. India—Ethnic
relations.   6. Ethnicity—India.   I. Title.
DS480.84.C45   1997
327.54—dc21   96–48962
                                          CIP

Casebound editions of Columbia University Press books are printed on permanent and
durable acid-free paper.
Printed in the United States of America
c 10 9 8 7 6 5 4 3 2 1
p 10 9 8 7 6 5 4 3 2 1

For my father
the late Gopalrao Ramchandra Kulkarni
whose life has been a source of strength and inspiration to me

Contents

❧

Preface

꽃

This book is about domestic conflicts—particularly those that emanate from conflicting ethnic nationalities—and their impact on the formulation of a country's foreign policy. The focus is South Asia, particularly India. I have concentrated on ethnic conflicts that seemed to pose the greatest threat to the Indian nation-state during the 1980s. In the early 1980s, the violence in Punjab and Assam had frustrated policy makers in New Delhi. In the 1990s the Kashmiri insurgency broke out. All three were border states and in the case of Assam and Kashmir, ethnic nationalities extended into Pakistan and Bangladesh. Similar separatist challenges from the Tamil nationality in the 1980s had engulfed Sri Lanka and by transborder ethnic connections, the southern state of Tamil Nadu in India. Most agreed that these events challenged India's integrity and territorial unity. Most observers of the South Asian scene agreed also that the problem originated in the failures of leaders to make their nations congruent with their state. Involvement of neighboring countries—Pakistan in the case of Punjab and Kashmir and India in the case of Sri Lanka—came after the conflict had festered and then deteriorated into a dangerous threat. Yet, in the previous decades, India had succeeded in winning loyalty and commitment of these nationalities to the idea of a single nation-state of India.

What went wrong? And why did leaders begin to look beyond the national border for succor and support? That hostile and ambitious neigh-

boring states would take advantage of such "domestic" turmoil was not surprising in the least. In this book I have tried to look beyond the obvious and
into the deeper connections between ethnic conflict and foreign policy.
The purpose is to unravel the operational mechanism by which India
responded—at times successfully and at other times less successfully—to
such challenges. In so doing I have reinterpreted events and policies from
a new ethnically sensitive perspective.

My book has been a long time in gestation, almost seven years, during
which I have learned a lot about myths and mythologies of nation and nationalities, about hate and passionate commitments, about the dangerous gap
between public discourse and political reality. Almost every action or policy
of the Indian government during the past decade and a half was shaped by
these contradictory pulls and pressures. The pattern of these contradictions
was however far from clear. to discover and mod it into a coherent frame was
an intellectual challenge I could not resist.

The journey since then has been arduous and often frustrating but never
dull. It took me to Punjab, Kashmir, and Sri Lanka several times. I was fortunate to have had some friends in high places who introduced me to others
responsible for the difficult decisions facing them in Jaffna, Amritsar, and Sri
Nagar. I was struck by the incredible depth and detail in which public officials and leaders understood the problem, the surprising degree to which
they took account of the cultural and emotional dimension of the conflicts.
Policies they pursued did not unfortunately reflect the wisdom of their
analysis. The gap was all the more surprising because many of these decisions
had backfired again and again. This led me to ask whether there was an objective set of conditions that forced policy makers into repeat response even
when they knew it would fail. This search for patterns led to historically
shaped perceptions, myths about the Indian nation-state, and the Indo-centric understanding of regional problems.

Similarly, I was struck by the tragic repetition of the kind of "assertions"
many separatist militants felt forced to make. They deliberately courted violence to keep their cause alive. But the state did not budge on the question
of separation. Even the small and weak Sri Lanka remained whole and carried on with the regular business of elections despite the violence of the civil
was, a fact that has received less scholarly attention than it deserves. One has
merely to look at the proliferation of failed nation-states around the world
since the 1990s, and the wars of national debilitation that has contributed to
their collapse to appreciate Sri Lanka's valiant struggle to remain whole. (of
the eighty-six conflicts recorded by the United Nations since 1989, only

three involved armed conflicts between countries. The rest were internal wars caused by ethnic and intercommunal violence.)

The Tamil militant leaders were even a greater surprise. They looked so ordinary and normal in their modest offices in the suburbs of Madras. They were sanguine in the summer and winter of 1986 and supremely confident in their secure positions in Tamil Nadu under the combined blessings of Karunanidhi and M. G. Ramachandran. This was to change within the year. But in that year all seemed well with the Tamil cause. There was a distinct sense of unreality as we sat around discussing the civil war, murder and mayhem in Sri Lanka. Coconut trees gently swayed in the breeze while I heard long speeches listing the past and present injustices, couched in impressive Marxist rhetoric, spoken in unmistakable cadences of Oxbridge English. Only one or two leaders claimed such illustrious intellectual background though the rest were not unfamiliar with guerrilla warfare advocated by Mao, Che Guevera, and the PLO. It was hard to believe that these individuals could take up arms and calmly sacrifice fellow Tamils to the impossible task of winning independence from Colombo.

So also the two militant Sikh "students" I talked with long into the night. Both were thoroughly convinced of the justice of their cause and saw everyone else as unreasonable. The history of persecution was a constant refrain. There were bizarre stories of murder and rape, some straining credibility to the utmost. For instance when I questioned the Sikh students about the poor Hindu refugees in the Durgyana Mandir, they pooh-poohed the idea and said that it was all a government plot. A parallel response came from many officials who in their sober moments carefully distinguished between good and bad Sikhs, Kashmiris, or Tamils. I often thought however that these fine distinctions were more for my benefit and to show up official sobriety in contrast with the mindless responses of the ethnic fanatics. Behind the official line one sensed the anger, frustration, impatience, and ruthlessness. I saw the face of militancy up close, I also saw the ruthless arm of the state wielding its rod without discrimination or restraint. There were personally frightening moments in Sri Lanka and Punjab. Fortunately, as a scholar, I had time to overcome my immediate reaction and reflect on the significance of what I had seen, heard, and experienced.

The desire to find answers to the many questions these experiences raised, to construct the big picture, took me through overextended reading lists. I read through the literature and debates on Indian history to see if there were enduring patterns of integration and disintegration or whether such a quest was merely an unwitting reinforcement of the elite perspective of

Indian history. I have not been able to use the material in this book except to feel fairly confident about the notion of the historic state I have used in the analysis. It did however teach me a great deal about the role of the state in construction of identities. The conflict between the Sikh separatists and New Dellhi concealed the fact that the Indian state in its previous incarnations had contributed to such a construction. Above all the study taught me the differences in the way Indians see themselves, the way others in the region see India, the ways in which different Indians see each other and envision India. Unraveling these strands has been my most difficult challenge.

This book began just as the Cold War was winding down under the imaginative efforts of Mikhail Gorbachev. It ended seven years later when both the Cold War and the Soviet Union were a thing of the past. Many I talked to and interviewed are dead by the assassin's bullet. The list is painfully long (Padmanabha of EPRLF, Amritalingam of the TULF, Prime Ministers Rajvit Gandhi and Indira Gandhi, Premadasa) and growing. Dramatic changes play havoc with books on politics and international relations. Fortunately, the questions raised here survive the new era of commerce-driven global politics. The difficulty of balancing between India's diverse nationalities is as pronounced as ever. The external world has begun to impinge even more forcefully, if in a different way, on the state's control over domestic affairs. The third "wave" of democracy, the now impetus to the ideas of self-determination, easier access to the international bazaar in arms and weapons, and the increasingly intrusive role of the United Nations and the United States in the resolution of regional conflicts has made many countries increasingly vulnerable to international pressures. This is especially true of South Asia. The link between Kashmir, nuclear nonproliferation, trade, foreign private investment, and transfer of technology has blurred the separation between foreign and domestic policies. Will the earlier strategies endure? In this book I have identified what they have been and the elements that shaped them. The question of their future depend on the new configuration of domestic and international connections. This is the subject for another study.

Many have helped me in writing this book. The list over the seven years is too long to be accommodated here, but special mention is due to a number of people. I am grateful to Ainslie Embree, who encouraged me and always gave me sound advice. In fact, it is he who turned me to serious scholarship (and away from the performing arts) and therefore bears some responsibility for my addition to the number of avid students in South Asian studies. He does not, however, bear any responsibility for the views and conclusions offered here. I also ow an intellectual debt to Paul Brass. Discussion with him about ethnicity and nation when we were both participating in the Global Conference on People of Indian Origin was helpful. His works have taught me much that I now know about these issues. Sanjib Baruah and Robert Perimbanayagam went through parts of the manuscript and made valuable suggestions. There were many times when I was drowning in a welter of facts—interviews, speeches, conversations—I had collected over the years. Extracting a cogent narrative from this seemed at times almost impossible. Prem Shankar Jha patiently worked with me through the second draft and made some extremely valuable suggestions that saved the manuscript from being shelved in despair. I owe him a special debt of gratitude for giving unsparingly of his time and effort when his own work demanded all his attention. Susham and Rahul Bedi, close personal and intellectual friends deserve special mention. I "wrote" several sections of this book after long walks during which they patiently and interestedly listened to my arguments. I am grateful to them for their friendship and interest.

I would like to thank Malhotra, late Girilal Jain of the *Times of India*, Ventkataramani of *India Today*, Gursharan Singh, who has served as the director of Kala Kendra in Chandigarh and heads a famous street theater company in Punjab, who arranged meeting with the Sikh militants in Amritsar, and the DMK officials, Mani and his unnamed colleague who introduced me to the Tamil militants. Among the political leaders, I would like to acknowledge Inder Gujral, former Prime Minister V. P. Singh, President Jayewardene, Farooq Abdullah, the late Rajiv Gandhi, and President Premadasa. These leaders gave generously of their time discussing the Punjab, Tamil-Sinhala, and Kashmir conflicts and the rationale of their policies. I am grateful to them all. This book would not have been possible without the sustained support from William Patterson College where I teach. The department gave the release time to write the book. Professor Tina Lesher in the department of Journalism spent long and I am sure tedious hours copyediting my finished draft. I take this opportunity to thank her for her friendship and effort on my behalf. The Rockefeller Foundation gave me a Residency Fellowship at Bellagio to work on the first draft. The beauty and tranquility, not to mention stimulating conversations I had about identity politics with Henry Louis Gates and Samuel Huntington, crystallized some ideas that had eluded me until then. Finally when my manuscript was accepted by Columbia University Press I was fortunate to get the superb editorial guidance of Kate Wittenberg.

The contributions of Vijay Chadda, husband and friend, to this study are far too numerous to be expressed in words. He was unfailingly patient and encouraging, always displaying more confidence in me than I had myself. In many ways this has been his project as well. He read through the manuscript and told me what he felt did not "flow" or make sense, always with a self-deprecating observation that he was not an expert. I found his judgments sound and comments perceptive. In the end, however, the interpretations and analyses with their weaknesses and vulnerabilities are mine alone. I have found this intellectual journey tremendously rewarding. It taught me never to ignore the role of public passions on political life.

Abbreviations and Definitions

卐

Abbreviations

AGP   Asom Gana Parishad, a leading political party in Assam
AIADMK   All India Anna Dravida Munnetra Kazagham, a leading Tamil
         Nadu party
AISSF   All India Sikh Students Federation
BJP   Bharatiya Janata Party, a leading Hindu nationalist party
BSF   Border Police Force
CPI   Communist Party of India
CPM   Communist Party of India (Marxist)
CPML   Communist Party of India (Marxist-Leninist)
CVF   Citizen Voluntary Force (set up by the IPKF)
DK   Dravida Kazagham, predecessor of the DMK
DMK   Dravida Munnetra Kazagham, Another Tamil Nadu Party
EPRLF   Eelam Peoples Revolutionary Liberation Front
EROS   Eelam Revolutionary Organization of Students
IPKF   Indian Peace Keeping Force
ISI   Inter-Service Intelligence (Pakistani intelligence agency)
J&K   Indian states of Jammu and Kashmir
JKLF   Jammu and Kashmir Liberation Front
JVP   Janatha Vimukthi Peramuna

LOC   Line of Control (in Kashmir)
LTTE   Liberation Tigers of Tamil Eelam
NWFP   North West Frontier Province
PEPSU   Patiala and East Punjab State Union
PLOTE   Peoples Liberation Organization of Tamil Eelam
POK   Pakistan Occupied Kashmir
PPP   Pakistan People's Party
RAW   Research and Analysis Wing (Indian Intelligence agency)
RSS   Rashtriya Swayamsevak Sangh
SGPC   Shiromani Gurdwara Prabhandak Committee
SLFP   Sri Lanka Freedom Party
TELO   Tamil Eelam Liberation Organization
TESO   Tamil Eelam Supporters Association, Madras
         (DMK organization)
TNA   Tamil National Army (set up by the IPKF)
TULF   Tamil United Liberation Front, a Sri Lankan Tamil movement
UNP   United National Party (Sri Lanka)
VHP   Vishwa Hindu Parishad

Definitions

Awami League: Leading secular liberal democratic party in Bangladesh.
Akali Dal, Shiromani Akali Dal: Main Sikh party in Punjab.
Chief Khalsa Diwan: Organization of educated Sikhs established 1902.
Dravidadesam: Ramaswamy Naicker's idea of a separate Dravidian country.
Eelam: Independent Tamil state comprising Jaffna and Eastern province of
    Sri Lanka demanded by Tamil militant organizations.
Jana Sangh: Another Hindu nationalist party superceded by the BJP since
    the 1980s.
Janata Dal: A national secular opposition party to the Indian National
    Congress.
Khalsa: Sikh brotherhood, initiated by Guru Gobind Singh.
Lok Dal: Peasant-based opposition to Congress in Haryana, led by Devi Lal.
Mukti Bahini: Bangladeshi liberation force credited with launching the
    struggle against Pakistani armed forces in 1971.
Muslim Conference: Important political opposition party to National
    Conference in Kashmir.
Namdhari: Sikh sect considered heretical by the Khalsa Sikhs.

National Conference: Leading secular political party in Jammu and
    Kashmir state.
Nirankari: Sikh sect also considered heretical by the Khalsa Sikhs.
Razakar: Militant Muslim movement in Hyderabad, 1947.
Sarbat khalsa: Sikh Congregation.
Telugu Desam: A leading regional party in Andhra Pradesh.

Ethnicity, Security, and Separatism in India

Chapter 1

❦

Neither Hegemonic nor Defensive

A Third Perspective on India's Security

In this book I explore the formulation of India's foreign policy in the half century since it gained its independence in 1947. With almost a billion people, India is not only the preeminent power in South Asia and the surrounding Indian Ocean, but is the largest democracy and the second most-populated country in the world. These facts alone make a study of its foreign policy eminently worthwhile. But what makes it especially relevant today is that India is a newly emergent country where the task of nation-building is still incomplete. During the half century of its independence, the formulation of foreign policy has gone hand-in-hand with domestic territorial consolidation, and the two processes have therefore been closely interconnected. There are at least a score of other large, newly emergent countries, wielding considerable influence in their regions, in which the same twin processes are simultaneously at work. A study of the way in which India's foreign policy and security interests have been formulated could throw useful light on the constraints and compulsions within which foreign policy is being made elsewhere.

Studying India has become incomparably more important since the end of the Cold War. The eruption of ethnic violence across Europe, from the former Yugoslavia to the former Soviet Union, has called into question the future viability of the territorial nation-state. Scholars and decision makers are searching for new ways to organize the state in order to end the violence. Such changes will inevitably affect foreign policies as well. A study of an extremely heterogeneous country that has nearly fifty years of experience in nation-state building could provide useful insights for students of post–Cold War Europe and its relations with the rest of the world.

Most of the existing analyses of India's foreign policy suggest that it has gone through three phases. The first phase, 1947 to 1962, was a period of assertive internationalism, in which under the immensely charismatic leadership of Jawaharlal Nehru, India took trenchant, principled stands on a wide range of global issues from decolonization to disarmament.[1] This assertive internationalism became increasingly difficult to sustain as the Cold War encroached into the Indian subcontinent. The Hungarian crisis of 1956, in which India, for the first time, gave priority to its expedient self-interest over principle, brought out the new attitude clearly. However, this phase ended decisively with the Chinese invasion of the Himalayan border region of India in 1962.

The second phase, which lasted roughly from 1962 until the end of the decade, can be broadly categorized as one of retreat wherein India withdrew from its previous involvement in global issues and concentrated on its relations with its neighbors in South Asia. The third phase, which some consider to have begun with the Bangladesh war in 1971, but considered by most analysts to be clearly related to the return of Mrs Gandhi to power in 1980, is considered as India's hegemonistic expansionist phase.[2] The search for hegemony was characterized by India's increasing insistence upon bilateralism in its relations with its neighbors; a willingness to use its armed forces outside its borders, a sharp rise in defense expenditures incurred through modernization of its armed forces and the creation of a blue water navy, and development of nuclear weapons capabilities and short- and intermediate-range missiles. Proponents of this thesis point to India's intervention in Sri Lanka in 1987 and the Maldives in 1988 as proof of hegemonism.

The weakness with such a characterization of half a century of foreign policy is that at no point does it attempt to relate the political and economic challenges that India's successive governments faced at home to its postures abroad.[3] Implicit in this omission is the traditional concept of the nation-state as internally homogeneous and endowed with clearly defined hard frontiers. Implicit also is the notion of power as born from certain fixed attributes of the nation, such as its size, its industrial strength, and the extent of its armed forces.

To say the above, however, is not to criticize this mode of analysis. Until recently, political theorists treated nation-building and international relations as separate fields of study. The former studied the evolution of relations between the individual and the state, and of individuals with each other, as nations evolved and their identities stabilized. The latter studied how states, which enjoyed absolute sovereignty in relation to each other, and therefore lived in a situation akin to Hobbes' State of Nature, arranged their mutual affairs and addressed common concerns.[4] This separation of domestic from international political theory was somewhat artificial even during the early centuries of nation-state formation in Europe. The concept of absolute sovereignty was only the mirror image in international affairs of the notion of the divine right of monarchs in domestic affairs. Each theory conveniently reinforced the other and their common, but not sole, aim was to give the executive authority license to use as much force as was needed to create or reinforce the unitary nation- state.[5] Today, when ethnic loyalties are resurfacing even in European states that have been relatively stable and unified for several centuries, when national boundaries are being redrawn on ethnic lines, and minorities are employing the tools provided by modern technology to demand collective rights that involve a reorganization of the central state itself, and when global economic integration has made severe inroads into the notion of absolute sovereignty, the separation of these fields of study makes even less sense than it did before.

Treating the two as separate fields of study is especially problematic when one applies theories developed on this basis to countries in Asia or Africa.[6] In these areas, the nation state is a recent development. The attempt to impose the European model of unitary state has met with only qualified success and has sparked violent conflicts that, in a small but growing number of new countries has led to or is threatening the collapse of the state itself. At the same time their economic dependence on the rich nations, or international institutions controlled by them, has limited their sovereignty.[7] In addition, global interdependence has made developments within the new nations matters of concern to the industrialized ones, and their economic clout has made it possible for them to influence national policy to an extent that could not be imagined a half-century ago. Therefore the boundaries between domestic nation building and foreign policy are even more blurred than they have been in Europe.

The purpose here is to examine nation-building and international relations in the postcolonial nations within a single coherent framework of analysis. More specifically, it is to understand how ethnically motivated domestic conflicts, particularly those that emanate from the overlapping character of ethnic nationality, become internationalized and shape a state's security perceptions and policies. Even a casual glance at the past decade shows that ethnonationalism is a highly disruptive force, with immense potential for dissolving

sovereign boundaries, precipitating war and intervention, and destroying territorial and political unity of established nation-states. This is not to suggest
that every foreign policy decision is animated by ethnic compulsions. Nuclear
and trade issues are not usually shaped by ethnic considerations. Military
interventions could be a result of miscalculations and opportunism that have
little to do with state formation or nation-building. Ethnic conflicts are not
always a result of external interference. And in the real world, foreign policy
is often inconsistent. Despite these qualifications, we can not ignore the growing importance of ethnic nationalism as a force in shaping foreign and international relations. Two questions need to be asked: why has ethnonationalism
surged to the center of world politics? and how does it influence interstate
relations? This book is meant to provide an answer to these questions, based
on the experience of South Asia.

In many ways, South Asia and India are appropriate places to study the
influence of overlapping nationalities.[8] Here a single ethnic and cultural contiguity broke up to form several independent nation-states. The three major
countries in the region—India, Pakistan, and Bangladesh—were born from
a violent conflict between rival ethnoreligious movements. Even further
back in history, the Mughal and British imperial powers had to contend with
frequent challenges by rebellious local and regional communities to their
central authority. At times, these disparate regions of their empires collabo-
rated with them; at other times, they fought against imposition of central
rule. Always however, power relations between the center and regions
remained the overriding theme of South Asia's subcontinental history. In
other words, despite conflict between regions and the central state, between
the overarching authority and a geographically concentrated, culturally
defined community is a persistent theme in Indian history.[9]

Creation of the separate sovereign states of India and Pakistan and Bangladesh or Sri Lanka has not solved the problem of overlapping nationalities.
Ethnic communities, language and religious affiliations, customs and traditions make South Asia a culturally contiguous entity rather than a sharply
divided subcontinent of separate cultures. Punjabi is spoken in both Indian and
Pakistani Punjab. Urdu is a symbol of cultural heritage and identity for Indian
Muslims, while it is the official language of Pakistan. Tamils of both Sri Lanka
and Tamil Nadu share aspects of culture, history, and literature. Although Sikhs
are confined to India, their historical memories include the Sikh kingdom in
Lahore and places of worship that are today a part of Pakistan.

Two additional features of South Asia have greatly influenced India's relations with its neighbors. First, in size, population, and potential for power,

India is the largest among the South Asian states. Second, most of the countries of South Asia border on India but do not share boundaries with each other. These two conditions have produced fear of Indian hegemony and a deep-seated resentment of India's geopolitical dominance in the region. It has not, however, resulted in a formal anti-India alliance among India's South Asian neighbors.

My focus will be on the three ethnonationalisms—those of Punjab, Kashmir, and Tamil Nadu—which steadily escalated throughout the 1980s and influenced India's relations with Pakistan and Sri Lanka.[10] In what follows, I will seek to unravel the deeper connections between India's overlapping nationalities and its quest for power in the region. In each instance, India faced a different set of conditions and strategic problems with its neighbors. In Punjab and Kashmir, India is vulnerable to Pakistan's interference; in Sri Lanka, India is the source of interference. The history of ethnic nationalism, with its evolution and strength, has varied from Tamil Nadu to Kashmir, but precisely for that reason these movements provide a valuable study in contrast, of success and failures, and of ambitions and fears—elements that are critical to nation-building and national security.

The choice of these three movements has been dictated by greater familiarity and access to primary sources.[11] To gather material firsthand, I traveled several times during the years 1986 to 1990 through Punjab, Kashmir, Tamil Nadu, and Sri Lanka. The most intensive part of the fieldwork—interviews and conversations, meetings with officials, political leaders, journalists, militant organizations and their leaders—were conducted during 1986 and 1989. Three broad lines of inquiry were followed: first, questions about perceptions of specific events, actions, and policies, and the empirical and historical bases that supported such perceptions; second, search for the logic of strategies and actions on the part of individual actors, and the reasons or justifications they offered for such actions; and third, the inferences and conclusions these participants/observers drew from the conflict, and their responses to events or actions, sort of "lessons learnt" from their experiences of ethnic conflict.

Perceptions, strategies, and assessment of impact changed from year to year and from subject to subject. But it was possible to construct a broad pattern of interconnections between these and India's nation-state formation. It was also possible to identify the ways in which these interconnections played into India's relations with Pakistan and Sri Lanka. But this book is not about the history of ethnic movements or political developments since 1947. Nor is it an account of India's relations with Pakistan and Sri Lanka. It is an analysis instead, of ways in which India's relations with these two neighbors have been influenced by the course of the three aforementioned ethnonationalisms. My goal is to construct what might be described as an "ethnonationalistic perspective" to explain India's security and foreign policy toward its neighbors. Although the focus is on India, the line of inquiry has much wider application. It is hoped that what this discussion will reveal in India will illuminate similar problems elsewhere in the world, particularly in other large, heterogeneous multination states.

Briefly, the framework of analysis is as follows: in the newly emergent states of today, the creation of unitary nationhood through the suppression of ethnic and other minorities has become exceedingly complicated. Such attempts have been far from successful and have involved levels of violence and denial of human rights that the world has found difficult to accept. India occupies a special place among the newly emergent countries in that its leaders were educated in the West, were steeped in the ideals of the Enlightenment, and thus aspired to the European model of the nation-state.

When confronted by the task of nation-building, however, they initiated a far different model. From the very start, India has been preoccupied with finding ways of accommodating ethnonationalism within the framework of a modern state. Inherent in this attempt is a conflict between the modernizing impulse of the state and the need to accommodate its constituent ethnonationalities. The tools for building a modern nation-state are economic and social modernization—the creation of a common market, a nation-wide transport system, an information network and education system, and a common legal and political system. These goals are not peculiar to India's supranational State, but are shared by its ethnonationalities as well. Conflict arises because one of the most important consequences of economic modernization is the blurring of cultural and ethnic boundaries. There is a predisposition among the leaders of the ethnonational communities, therefore, to regard the supranational State's modernizing programs as threats to their identity.

In practice, therefore, competition narrows to a struggle for control of the pace and direction of modernization, and to the crucial decisions concerning the allocation and use of the nation's resources, recognition of group rights, and degrees of autonomy. The large measure of overlap between the goals to which the modernizing state and its ethnic components subscribe creates a wide arena for negotiations. The supranational State tries to develop methods for co-opting the elites of the nationalities or controlling them, while the latter look for ways of shoring up their autonomy in various fields. When this process breaks down, secessionist demands can arise.

The need for constant negotiation and accommodation between the supranational State and its ethnonational units makes the former more than usually sensitive to any influence from outside that can disturb the fine balance that is sought. Because the balance is delicate and needs constant adjustment, it makes it possible for an outside power to destabilize the state with relatively little effort. Within the state too, ethnonational units find it possible to shore up their position and strengthen their bargaining power by bringing in extraterritorial powers. The two possibilities combine to make the supranational State highly vulnerable to foreign linkages and influences. The goal of the state is to minimize such potentially destabilizing influences. Thus foreign policy becomes, inexorably, an integral part of the domestic exercise of nation-building. The two are even less separable when the ethnonational communities are to be found on both sides of the international border. In such circumstances, both types of external linkage are much stronger. The potential for destabilizing intervention is therefore much greater.

The three ethnonationalisms focused herein—Sikh, Kashmiri, and in a less marked manner, the Tamil—steadily escalated throughout the 1980s in India. Managing these within the framework of the supranational State has been a main preoccupation of the Indian central government, and has determined, to a large extent, India's relations with Pakistan and Sri Lanka. The purpose here is to unravel the deeper connections between India's overlapping nationalities and its quest for power in the region.

The conventional view of post-Independence India's foreign policy objectives is that it has sought to consolidate its international borders, maintain independence in actions, maximize its options in global politics, achieve self-reliance in military and economic capabilities, enhance India's status in the world, and prevent hostile states (Pakistan, China, the United States, or even the Soviet Union) from undermining any of the above objectives.[12] To this end, India has preferred bilateral relationships, opposed the presence of extraregional states in South Asia, protested against strategic alliances or military relationships of South Asian states with outside powers, built its own military strength, and when necessary, intervened militarily in the affairs of its neighbors. This is the way India's international relations look when viewed from the outside.

That view is misleading, because it focuses too much on the external pressures on foreign policy making. It is argued here that India's behavior toward its neighbors—its insistence on bilateralism in the settlement of disputes, and its strong opposition to any extraregional intervention in the affairs of the subcontinent, is explained in large part by the lack of congruence between the boundaries of the supranational Indian State and its ethnic nations. To understand this nexus, we need first to examine the characteristics of India's modern state that are relevant to its security perceptions. We also need to reach into the process of nationality formation to understand why these have the potential for intruding upon post-1947 India's regional security.

In recent years, several scholars have paid increasing attention to the nexus between domestic and foreign policy.[13] Two broad explanations have been given for it. The first might be referred to as the pluralist explanation of regional hegemony.[14] In the second, India's regional relations are explained from what might be described as the neo-Marxist perspective.

The pluralist explanation is as follows: India's post-Independence policies have been characterized by a relentless accumulation of power by the central state. This power build-up has been used to control the rising tide of demands from an increasingly pluralist nation. The accumulation of political power and coercive capability also has undermined federalism and democracy. Centralization has led to the militarization of the state, and this in turn has led to hegemonism, displayed in India's relations with its neighbors and in the growing use of force to crush domestic dissent. Muted during the first two decades of Independence, the hegemonic quest surfaced with great vigor during Mrs Gandhi's stewardship in the 1970s and early 1980s. The ethnic separatism in Punjab and Kashmir was a direct result of her arbitrary use of power and undemocratic meddling in state level politics. By upsetting the federal equation Mrs Gandhi in a sense reneged on the original bargain between the Indian state and its nesting ethnic nationalities. As the security state expanded, external threats were "discovered" to justify growing expenditures on defense.[15] As a close corollary to this thesis, several observers have stressed the role of growing Hindu assertiveness during the 1980s and 1990s. It is suggested that India's weakened central state had absorbed the newly resurgent ideology of "Hindu Rashtra." the idea of creating a "greater India." These ambitions complicated relations with Pakistan and Sri Lanka in the 1980s and made conflicts in Punjab and Kashmir less amenable to negotiated solutions.

In the neo-Marxist perspective, the Indian state is a Gramscian state, and its main purpose after Independence has been to organize its hegemony by neutralizing or subjugating the dominated, what several critics have identified as the "subaltern classes." For instance, Imtiaz Ahmed identifies centralization and development as the two main strategies for such a project, and correctly argues that the international dimensions of this project are embedded in the "fundamental social relations" within India. He also locates (as do I), in the Indian National Congress and its subsequent incarnations, the main vehicle of the dominant classes. However, it is mainly in the characterization of the foreign policy that my analysis parts company with the neo-Marxist analyses. According to Ahmed, India's ruling classes have pursued the Kautilyan traditions to reproduce its hegemony in the international dimension.[16] It is the Kautilyan strategy that explains India's ruthless crushing of the Communist challenge, the forced integration of Hyderabad and Kashmir into the Indian Union, the war over Bangladesh, and the intervention in Sri Lanka.

Despite their very different starting points, both theories lead to the same conclusion: increasing centralization of power within the domestic sphere leads to growing hegemonism in the international sphere.

The above explanations yield valuable insights into the making of foreign policy, but neither one is able to account for the contradictions with which it is riddled. If India is relentlessly hegemonistic then how does one explain its prompt departure from Bangladesh in 1972, withdrawal from Sri Lanka in 1990, and most particularly its exit from the Maldives in 1989? How does one explain its repeated return of territory captured from Pakistan during their various wars? How does one explain why first the Janata and twelve years later the non-Congress government of V. P. Singh, made no significant departures from the policies laid down by the Congress although both governments were committed to basing India's regional policies on a decentralized, genuinely federalized polity at home? And why, despite a spectacular triumph in the 1971 war with Pakistan, was India unable to settle the Kashmir dispute or to stave off nation-wide challenges that came three years later and forced Mrs Gandhi to impose a national emergency in the country? Last (the conventional frameworks do not adequately explain it) why, despite a formidable expansion in military power, are Indian leaders plagued by a sense of national fragility and fear of political disintegration?

The weakness of the pluralist perspective is that it treats the state, and Mrs Gandhi in particular, as the initiator of political action in the nation-building drama, and the ethnic nationalities as passive reactors. It fails to see that many of Indira Gandhi's actions and policies might be reactions of a central leader increasingly fearful because of the diminution of state power in relation to increasingly assertive ethnic nationalities. It therefore confuses the centralization of power with the quantum of power a state enjoys. It is possible for a state to concentrate the decision-making process in fewer hands and still steadily lose its capacity to reorder society in line with its objectives. A regional and local strengthening of communities and their spokesmen can proceed at the same time as administrative and political decision making is accumulated at the center.[17]

When pluralist analyses have not turned around an excessively central role for Mrs Gandhi, they have tended to do so around the concept of the weak/strong state.[18] The weak/strong state is hegemonistic because it is insecure. It is insecure because it is a young nation, still in the making.[19] According to Mohammed Ayoob, not enough time has elapsed for these countries to develop the intangible ingredients of security such as legitimacy based on mass allegiance of citizens, and national integration based on a shared sense of destiny. Ayoob comments that the process that took centuries to complete in Europe "is now expected to be completed" within a "time bound framework of ridiculous short duration."[20]

The profound flaw in this concept is that it treats the newer nations of the third world as European nation-states in the making. Neither Ayoob nor Buzan (who draw attention to the lack of integration as an important feature of the third world states) envisage the possibility that there might be a different path to integration from the coercive one followed by Europe. This predisposes the pluralists to seeing coercion as the main mode of discourse between the supra-national State and the ethnic nationalities, and makes them insensitive to the extensive use of co-optation and accommodation as methods of integration.

The weaknesses of the neo-Marxists' analyses stem essentially from their attempt to put a country's political developments in a strait jacket of class conflict. The identity of the subaltern classes is vague and shifting.[21] The sub-alterns are identified generally as those in opposition to centralization and the central state. Are the Akalis in Punjab or militant factions allied to the Panthic committees and the All-India Sikh Students Federation to be then included in the subalterns? Since the Sikh militants were killing the Akalis, they both cannot belong to the subaltern category. Yet both include peasants, landless workers, and other depressed classes. In the same way can the regional parties such as the National conference in Kashmir and the DMK or AIADMK in Tamil Nadu to be included among the subalterns?

Imtiaz Ahmed, a leading proponent of this perspective suggests that they are, but then where do we put the militant groups such as the Jammu and Kashmir Liberation Front (the JKLF) and the sympathizers with the LTTE in Tamil Nadu? Ahmed's argument that New Delhi is hegemonistic because of the Congress party's determination to keep the Communists out of power at the center provides the clue to the second weakness of such analyses. Instead of shunning Communist party support, first Prime Ministers Rajiv Gandhi and then V. P. Singh came to look upon the Communists as the central government's ally in fighting separatism in the state as the terrorist violence escalated in Punjab in the late 1980s. The third weakness is that unlike in the pluralist analysis, the international objectives of hegemony remain obscure. Does India want more territory, assured access to resources and markets, diplomatic preeminence in South Asia? And how does this advance the domestic agenda? We are not told what the objectives are except they flow from the purpose of building hegemony within India.

The most serious flaw in neo-Marxist perspective is that it treats the Hindu/Muslim divide as the principal line of conflict in Indian society. According to Ahmed, ever since Partition, India has in reality been little other than a Hindu state. It therefore follows that the Muslims and, where they are recognized, the Sikhs and other minorities, are subaltern classes in their entirety. Typical of this is a statement regarding Punjab: "with the political projection of 'Hindu majority,' particularly within the backdrop of the simultaneous consolidation of the ruling class and caste Hindus, the Sikhs found themselves alienated and reduced to a minority." This ignores the fact that the Sikh community is divided into several factions, by caste, sect, and clan, and that the divide between Sikhs who favored separation, and those who did not, followed, to a considerable extent, class lines within the Sikh community. Ahmed's treatment of the Hindus and Muslims as undifferentiated monolithic blocs is even less enlightening.[22] There is also no place in this perspective for territorial nationalism. This leaves a serious lacuna in understanding the motives and impulses behind India's foreign policy.

Relational Control: An Alternative Framework for India's Security Policy

If the hegemonistic interpretation of India's foreign policy neither explains its actual behavior, nor survives rigorous examination, the opposed thesis— that India is primarily a defensive, status quo– oriented country that has only reacted to threats initiated from the outside—is not a satisfactory one either. A review of India's regional policies since the 1980s suggests that India is neither an expansionist nor a wholly defensive state. The aforementioned seeming contradictions in its behavior stem from the fact that India is as concerned with the maintenance of internal stability as with safeguarding its security.

In South Asia, India seeks a degree of overarching power that would give it "relational control." The objective of relational control is to maximize freedom of action and to widen available options in foreign policy so that outcomes can be influenced in one's own favor. Baumgartner, Buckley, and Burns have developed the idea of relational control to explain the negotiation process and bargaining in social conflict.[23] They suggest that relational control has built within it the notion of reciprocal leverage, and the ability of several players to influence the outcome of events. Relational control (as opposed to direct control) is used by particular groups to promote or stabilize their advantages or dominance over others or to insure the effective functioning of a social system. Relational control constitutes, in part, the "historical forces" underlying the given institutional structure of societies and the dynamics of new institutional forms continually struggling to emerge."[24] The purpose of relational control is "long-term structuring of social process and outcomes."

It may be used to encourage cooperation, or to produce competition or conflict between actors with a view to increase one's power in relation to others. In this sense, India may seek to control the process of fragmentation and integration in South Asia with a view to preventing any adverse impact on the conflict of nationalities within India itself. Relational control aims to secure three objectives:

1. to establish influence over the structure of interaction between players, that is, to have some capacity to set the "rules of the game" in conflict and cooperation.
2. to exercise, if possible, a degree of control over the actions of its neighbors, or at least to control the consequences flowing from such actions, if these are seen to be adverse to India's nation-building enterprise.
3. to acquire a degree of leverage over cultural orientation and ideology in the region.

While these are the objectives of relational control, they are not necessarily its outcome. India may aspire to relational control, but does not necessarily possess the means to ensure it in every instance.

Through relational control India seeks to insulate its nation-building project from any destabilizing development in neighboring countries. India's past leaders were aware that any extraregional power capable of intruding either into the Indian Ocean close to India or the mountainous north wall of the subcontinent had easy access to its heartland. The incongruence between India's legal, national, and cultural boundaries had made it necessary to keep the neighboring regions free of great power conflicts and rivalries. India saw its security closely tied to the neutrality of its neighbors. Political turmoil in the neighboring countries, flight of refugees, displacement of ethnic com-

munities or practice of economic discrimination, threats to the cultural identity of specific ethnocommunities or transborder ethnic conflicts could
destabilize the interlocking balance within India.[25] To maintain its own independence and internal stability, India thus recognized the value of having
neutral neighboring countries.

The nation-building strategies of neighboring states, and the nature of their
regimes determined to a large extent whether or not South Asia became
mired in great power rivalry or became a host to extraregional influences.
Indian leaders had learnt from experience that a drift toward military dicta-
torship or ethnic conflicts in the neighboring countries usually brought arms
and weapons pouring into South Asia and provided the United States, China,
the Soviet Union, and Islamic countries of the Persian Gulf an opportunity to
penetrate the region for their own purposes. The consequences of such intrusions more often than not had undermined India's security, or at least had constrained its domestic and foreign policy options. Indian leaders, therefore,
generally have preferred a neighboring state to be secular, possibly democratic but, most importantly, nonaligned.

Turmoil in the neighborhood has posed yet another danger. Dissident
groups in countries sharing national borders with India frequently linked up
with political groups within India. For example the Nepali Congress party
has drawn support from several political leaders and parties in India. The
Awami League in Bangladesh has looked to the Indian Congress party and
even the left-front government in West Bengal for assistance, money, and
political support. Such support groups in India can wield considerable pressure on the supranational State to intervene or act on their behalf in the
neighboring state. Political leaders in Tamil Nadu, for instance, pressured
New Delhi to intervene in Sri Lanka. India-Lanka relations, a matter of
external policy, thus became entangled in the management of federal balance
within India. This is also true of Punjab and Kashmir and their connection to
Pakistan, Assam's entanglement with Bangladesh, and India's north and east
concerns with China and Burma.

Since the ultimate goal of relational control is an internal one, Indian leaders chose whatever instrument was most appropriate to achieve it. These
instruments have ranged from treaties seeking to mediate the external relations of a neighbor, to giving clandestine support to like-minded opposition
movements in neighboring countries in order to gain a degree of leverage
over its future policies, or even sending troops to determine the outcome of
conflict in those countries. In this sense, India is not a status-quo state. It
entered into treaties of the first kind with Nepal and Bhutan; it gave covert

support to the Awami League in what was then East Pakistan when relations between East and West Pakistan began to deteriorate, and it sent military assistance to Sri Lanka in 1970 and invaded East Pakistan, when all efforts failed to make Pakistan take back the refugees who had come pouring into West Bengal.

It may be argued that the above instruments are also characteristic of hegemonism. Hegemons also enter into unequal treaties in which the weaker party in effect cedes an element of external sovereignty to it. They intervene in the internal affairs of other countries with the aim of shaping or achieving desired outcomes, and they also, when necessary, invade the territories of countries over which they wish to exercise sway. Relational control bears a family resemblance to the concept of hegemony inasmuch as it underlines influence over the policies of a neighbor.

What then is the difference between relational control and hegemonism? Providing an answer is made difficult by the fact that the term "hegemonism" has been used in a wide variety of contexts, and has lost any precision that it ever possessed.[26] Despite this, some differences can be clearly identified, the most important of which is purpose. The concept of hegemonism is intrinsically expansionist. It presupposes the existence of homogenized nation-states with hard frontiers of the European variety that translate growing economic or military strength into an extension of influence beyond these frontiers. Sovereignty is therefore perceived as an intermediate step toward the establishment of hegemony.[27] A "sovereign" state such as India is perceived in Wallerstein's analysis as being dependent on international capitalism in the metropolis. In this sense the concept of hegemony is turned outward, concerned mainly with the structures of domination and dependence. Relational control also permits an unequal relationship. It too incorporates the element of coercion and in its meaning. The crucial difference is that it does not presuppose an European-type nation-state (as the destiny of third world states) and looks at once in both directions, internal and external. It is a more versatile tool for analyzing the external relations of relatively young, heterogeneous states like India.

The ability to map and explain a state's two-directional quest for power makes relational control an apt tool of analysis. It permits us to explore reciprocal influences between neighboring countries, whereas hegemonism is a one-way street. Relational control also emphasizes a somewhat different concept of power than one used in conventional, balance-of-power analyses. Baumgartner et al. write that "Power has been typically conceptualized as ability to gain direct behavioral control. There are other aspects of power, however, such as attempts to structure or restructure the social and cultural matrix within which power activities are to be played out."[28] Power is no longer measured as a capability based on size, population, strength of armed forces, and economic and technological capabilities. The war-making potential of a country becomes particularly significant when that country is prepared to use it. Power exists to the extent that it is used. The difference is not unlike that between the size of a bank balance and the rate at which one is prepared to spend it. The latter in this case depends upon political will and internal constraints.[29] The willingness and ability to use power varies from one situation to another. This leaves open the possibility that a smaller country, on occasion, may have its own way in confrontation with a bigger neighbor, if it is prepared to spend what power it has with abandon (the experience of Vietnam comes readily to mind). Any given amount of power can also be used more or less effectively. A small amount can achieve a great deal if it is focused squarely on the areas of greatest vulnerability of a large state. Guerrilla warfare, the promotion of militancy, and terrorism against civilian populations are clear examples.

Another crucial difference between the two concepts is that relational control is not confined to relations between two states. It encompasses relations between a state and nonstate actors (resistance groups, ethnonationalities, opposition parties, and the like); between nonstate actors themselves (e.g., two or more ethnonationalities within a state; or between elements of a transborder ethnonationality that owes allegiance to two or more states. The conventional analyses of foreign policy have generally tended to ignore the role of nonstate actors.

During the Nehru era (1947–1964), the supranational Indian State established relational control not only with its own ethnonationalities, but also with its neighbors. The extent of control varied, but there was a distinct pattern that resembled closely the layered order of the "historical state" in India. An examination of the various degrees of control exercised within and outside the country shows that there were no less than seven models of sovereign control within the area occupied by the historical Indian state, which was subdivided later into five independent countries in varying stages of modernization. This "layered order" can be illustrated by the following examples.

1. The least amount of influence/control was established over Pakistan, in the Simla agreement, which committed that country to resolving all disputes bilaterally and eschewing the use of force.

2. Next to least, mainly because of greater convergence of interests, a lesser amount of control was manifested in the Friendship Treaty signed with Bangladesh's Awami League government in March 1972.[30] The treaty committed the two nations to consultation on matters of mutual concern in national security and foreign policy and also formalized the convergence of interests, such as in the upholding of secularism and the protection of minorities, while reasserting the equal and sovereign status of the two countries.

3. A level of greater control was embodied in the Treaty of Peace and Friendship signed with Nepal in July 1950. Although the treaty emphasized cooperation and independence of the parties, later statements revealed that secret letters exchanged between the two governments asserted that neither "Government shall tolerate threat to the security of the other by a foreign aggressor. To deal with such a threat, the two Governments will consult . . . and devise effective countermeasure."[31] Nehru had issued a veiled warning to China after the latter had absorbed Tibet, that "Any aggression on Nepal and Bhutan would be considered by us as aggression on India."[32] Implicit in Indo–Nepal relations are constraints on Nepal that require it to defer to India's security interests in matters of defense and foreign policy—giving, in effect, a veto power to New Delhi if it felt that a proposed move by Nepal threatened its security.

4. The fourth level of control is to be found in India's relations with Bhutan. By the 1949 treaty of Perpetual Peace and friendship India would not "exercise . . . interference in the internal administration of Bhutan. On its part, the Government of Bhutan agrees to be guided by the advice of the Government of India in regard to its external relations."[33] Bhutan could not import arms without consulting with India and such arms could not be resold to anyone else—person or state. In 1959, following the growing anxiety about China's intentions regarding Himalayan kingdoms, Nehru declared that the 1949 treaty had made Bhutan an Indian protectorate. India thus took upon itself to lodge a complaint against Chinese maps that had begun to include parts of Bhutan as Chinese territory. India secured United Nations membership for Bhutan. Despite this formal symbol of sovereignty, Bhutan is obliged by treaty to let India mediate its relations with all other countries. This arrangement has loosened somewhat, but endures to this day.

5. The third highest level was the extent of devolution granted to Kashmir by Pandit Nehru, and formalized in the 1952 Delhi Agreement with Sheikh Abdullah, the popular Kashmiri leader. By mutual consent, Delhi took over only defense, foreign policy, currency, and communications, but left every-

thing else to Kashmir. This level later eroded rapidly, but remains important because of its potential to serve as a model for other ethnonationalities now or in the future.

6. The second highest level of control is one in which Kashmir now finds itself, along with Mizoram and Nagaland, two tribal areas in the northeast that were pacified by the Indian army after a prolonged struggle. The most important common feature of all three is the nonalienability of land.

7. The level of most control is the one on which the rest of India is to be found, i.e., ethnolinguistic federalism.

The notable feature of this layered order is that without intention, and despite the shock of Partition, in the context of modern democracy, the Indian state had by 1972 recreated in its essentials something similar to the Mandala (meaning concentric circles) system of the Mauryan state. The relational control sought to be exercised by the supranational Indian State was a scale of graded influence, from the ethnolinguistic federal units of the core to the faint strictures implied by bilateralism at the periphery.

The stability of this entire edifice rested on strength of the base, and that in turn depended on the maintenance of the interlocking balance between the supranational State and the component ethnonations. The high water-mark of relational control over neighboring states was attained in the early 1970s. It is no coincidence that this was shortly after the system of domestic interlocking balance was established and before it came under severe strain. As a tool, the "Relational Control" concept serves equally well to explain the relationship between the supranational State and the component ethnic nations, as between the state and its neighbors. Since 1947, India has been attempting to build a modern, secular, and federal democracy from the historic legacy of a multinational empire state. This has meant consolidating its territorial sovereignty and integrating its nesting nations into a more cohesive polity.

In concrete terms, this involves two interconnected endeavors. First, the supranational State must transform historically formed perceptions and patterns among the nesting nations in the service of modern statehood. This gives rise to fluidity in the identity formation driven by constant negotiations. For the sake of brevity, let us call this a conflict between the historic state and the modern state. The second endeavor involves negotiations of a different kind. As was explained earlier, the elites of the nesting nations are not averse to modernization themselves, but are suspicious of the supranational State's attempts to appropriate control over the process. Thus, a conflict of a different kind ensues. This is over control of the pace and direction of modernization, which, among other things, means over the disposition of resources. As the nesting nations become more politicized, the demands of their elites become more insistent, sometimes aggressively so. The problem for the supranational State then becomes one of maintaining its independence and its capacity to give an overall lead to the State in the face of insistent demands for regional autonomy. In contrast to the first type of conflict, a permanent condition to be found at all stages of the development of the modern state, the second becomes more acute as modernization progresses.

Two aspects of the conflict between the historic and the modern state need to be highlighted. First, India's historic state did not have fixed boundaries—boundaries expanded and contracted in response to the balance of political and military power between ruling dynasties. By contrast, modern India aspires to fixed boundaries. Second, the historic state invested the ethnonationalities with certain narrative histories that were integral to the formation of their identities (though this was not the only source of identity reproduction). In giving a specific shape to the past, these narratives also, to a large extent, predetermine the ethnonation's expectations in the future, in its relationship with the supranational State. They set the limits to the potential for cooperation and conflict between the two. Just as the supranational State lacked fixed boundaries, the ethnonations did not have them either.

India's historic state refers to the nationalist perceptions of the unification model abstracted from the empire states established through India's past. It is not a reference to any one empire state. Each such empire was forged by the partial and selective integration of regions into a single centralized entity. The successive unification of India under historically more proximate empires of the Mughals and the British has left a legacy of memories, symbols, and accounts of conflicts and betrayals (narratives of blood ties and sacrifice) that have helped construct ethnic identities and also embed these identities in the historic rise and fall of centralized subcontinental states in India. Examples of collaboration and mutual support abound in Sikh, Tamil, and Kashmiri narratives, as do accounts of wars and prosecutions by the Mughal and the British state. It is important to note that there are several competing narratives of these relationships and over time these narratives get revised and rewritten.[34]

Such self-stories are written for a variety of purposes. One purpose is to draw boundaries around the ethnonation. The ethnically defined nations seek to exclude those not part of their cultural community, while the supranational Indian State tends to be pluralistic and inclusive. Another purpose is to substantiate claims to parity or equality.[35] "Histories" are used to underscore such demands. A third purpose is to justify prior political, cultural, or territorial claims. Dravida nationalists have "recovered" their history to prove the antiquity of Tamil culture and language. Yet another objective is to support claims to a "homeland" or primary habitat. Tamil histories talk about the rise and fall of Tamil kingdoms in South India and Sri Lanka; while the Sikhs point to glories of the Sikh kingdom of Ranjit Singh. Such histories of dynasties and kingdoms however serve a different purpose in different narratives. For the Indian Tamils, it is a symbol of antiquity and achievement. For the Sri Lankan Tamils, the history of Sri Lankan Tamil kingdom of Ellara is the proof of their rightful claims to northern Sri Lanka.[36] Last, narratives fix identities of the victims and aggressors. These can change, but themes of enduring struggles, of terrible trials, betrayals, and sacrifice persist.

Such narratives are not true accounts of history but are meant to reinforce identities and unify the ethnic community. If audiences change, stories admit new enemies and new supporters. Just as the ethnonations construct historical narratives to buttress their claims, the subcontinental Indian state has produced its own history to claim supranational identity. This history was produced in the course of the nationalist struggle against the British, when the Indian nationalists argued that a larger India had always existed that was more than a sum of is nesting ethnonations. These leaders claimed as their inheritance the legacy of the empire states ruled by the Mauryan, Gupta, and Mughal dynasties. However, the India to which the Independence movement referred was never a strictly territorial concept. The territorial compass of these three empires was different, and the leaders of the Congress were aware of that. For them a unified India did not involve the territorial reestablishment of any one of these empires. What they were referring to was a subcontinental cultural and historic unity that transcended individual ethnic segments of India. Precisely the same, however is true of ethnonational self-assertion in independent India. The ethnonationalists' discourse about their past is not meant to recreate their dynastic kingdoms but simply to buttress their present claims. The first dimensions of interlocking balances are then ideological and perceptual, requiring the state to reconcile the rival versions of India's past, as a single supranation, or, a subcontinent of several nations.

The nation-state building project also involves protection of autonomy and interest of the Indian state from the pushes and pulls of contemporary ethnopolitics. Here, the central focus is on distribution of power, offices, position, legislative dominance and control over political agenda. The autonomy of India's supranational State is best guarded by defining the center-state conflicts in ethnic terms. The turmoil in Punjab is not seen by Indian leaders as a class-based conflict; but as an ethnically motivated conflict between Sikh separatists and the territorial nation of India. The state claims its superior supranational status by appropriating the symbols and slogans of secularism and modernity. In contrast, the conflict in Punjab, Kashmir, or Tamil Nadu is portrayed as works of narrow and parochial ethnonationalists. This "ethnically rooted perspective" of the Indian leadership is shaped by a certain reading of history and the need to control the current distribution of political and economic resources. It is easier for the post-Independence state of India to appropriate and represent ethnic interests then it is to defuse class based or economic antagonisms.[37] It can co-opt the leaders of a community. If that fails, it can isolate them and try to create an alternative leadership. If even that fails, it can seek to mobilize the rest of the nation against the community. The last weapon in the supranational State's armory, if all the others fail, is to deploy force to regionalize a conflict and contain it within manageable geographic area while carrying on the task of governance in the rest of India.

India's experience has demonstrated that this approach can be a double-edged weapon. Relegating intra-ethnic class or economic conflicts to the background means treating the entire community as an undifferentiated whole. Any measures adopted by the state against the ethnonation then becomes an action against all of its members. It consolidates the ethnic identity and makes the challenge to the modern state more serious. The attempt to make the nation and the territory congruent can very easily jeopardize the central state's autonomy. By contrast, agreeing to share decision-making power with the ethnic elite can ease the confrontation between the historic and modern state. But it might weaken the state's control over pace and direction of the modernization agenda. India's recent history also has examples of the latter kind.[38]

The complex weaving of negotiation, accommodation and coercion described above creates a shifting, never entirely stable equilibrium in which, unless the supranational State loses control of the integrationist agenda altogether, it moves toward greater coherence and convergence between the goals of the nesting nation and those of the supranational state.

When the balance of interlocking interests is lost, the state correspondingly loses the ability to negotiate the "rules of the game" and may compensate by greater application of coercion and force. The causes of such disruption might be exogenous and not internal to the balance at any given time. Expansion of democracy, entry of new strata into politics, change in the distribution of income and wealth, or access to opportunity within an ethnic community or geographic region may disrupt the balance. The shifting, unstable nature of the internal balance goes a long way to explain the seemingly contradictory tendencies exhibited by India's foreign and defense policies. The central unswerving goal has been to shield the interlocking internal balance from rude exogenous shocks, which can make either of the two types of conflict described above more difficult to manage. The Indian state has adopted whatever method has seemed most appropriate in the given circumstances to achieve its aim. These methods have ranged from great accommodation at one extreme to decisive military intervention at the other.[39] In all cases of the latter type however, Indian troops have withdrawn once the threat to the internal balance is perceived to have been ended. It is this that distinguishes relational control from hegemonism.[40]

For a variety of reasons, the balance of interlocking interests was fairly easy to maintain in the first two decades after Independence. Led by Nehru, the Congress government centralized administration and increased the state's regulatory power over society. However, after Nehru's death, a number of developments that had been incubating in the first two decades rapidly made their presence felt and complicated the task of maintaining the balance. The spread of democracy and growing politicization of the populace increased ethnonationalist self-awareness. Modernization and industrialization began to integrate the country and heightened the competition between the supranational and ethnonational elites as well as between ethnonational elites themselves for the distribution of resources and power.

Throughout the 1970s, India therefore experienced a growing challenge to the dominance of the Congress system. Its cooptation and appropriation strategies were less and less effective. As the quantum of real regulatory power diminished, the state responded by further nominal centralization of power. Politics by negotiation and consensus gave way gradually to abuses of the constitution and increasing use of coercion to deny autonomy to ethnic communities. In the few cases where this too failed to restore the balance, the state resorted to increasing coercion.

As confrontations between state and ethnic nationalities led to violence, the three arenas of conflict, between ethnic communities, between communities and the supranational State, and between the state and its regional rival became interlinked: disputes over Chandigarh led to conflict between Haryana and Punjab that was transformed into Hindu–Sikh estrangement, and soon enough, Pakistan became a safe sanctuary for separatist Khalistanis (those advocating a separate Sikh state of Khalistan) from which they waged their struggle against New Delhi. The strength of an ethnic community to resist the state depends on possession of long history and rich heritage, sizable numbers, strategic location, internal coherence and political awareness, quality of leadership and organization, and last but not least, a level of dependence on the central state. The state has all the conventional advantages of force, size, "national" authority, and sovereign legitimacy on its side.

The growing global interdependence and revolution in technology and communications apparent in the 1980s have tilted the balance somewhat in favor of the ethnic separatists. They have gained easier access to international media, forums such as the United Nations, support from human rights organizations such as Amnesty International and Asia Watch, and most important, access to arms bazaars. These connections have reinforced the power of the separatists to resist the state. More often than not, protracted conflicts, as in Punjab, Kashmir, and Sri Lanka have led to mobilization of support from beyond the borders of the state.[41] Aspiring nationalities have reached across territorial boundaries in quest for support from fellow ethnics, or hostile states have pushed the country's boundaries inward by fomenting insurgencies. Overlapping nationalities therefore have created opportunities for reverse leverage against the neighboring states.

The above framework leads to a different view of transborder ethnic conflict from the conventional one in which ethnic nationalities are perceived as independent in origin and locked in a continuous struggle with an "oppressive" state. Relational control permits one to factor in the episodic nature of ethnonationalism. Such nationalism surfaces when other methods of maintaining the balance between the historic state and the modern state have failed. It dies down when a new accommodation is reached. That accommodation may result from a change in the supranational state's tactics (for instance, ceding a part of the control over the modernization agenda to the ethnic elite) or because of changes within the ethnic group that make the continuation of conflict redundant. It also offers a single framework within which we may understand the specificities of individual ethnic conflict.

It is necessary to underline at this point what the book is not meant to do. It is not meant to pass moral judgement on the desirability of relational control strategy. Nor is it intended to explore the consequences should the vision of India's separatist ethnic nationalities become a reality. I have not intended this study to recommend policy. India's unity is envisaged as a function of a proper management of relational control. This study admits that the need to use such a balancing strategy would decline as India becomes increasingly confident of her unity and stability. It does however claim that India's diversity is irreducible and therefore a balance between her ethnic nationalities and the supranational State would always remain an enduring necessity.

Definitions in Brief: Ethnicity, Nation, and State

The definitions of terms such as ethnicity, nation, state, and nationalism have been a subject of growing controversy among social scientists.[42] Some have argued that ethnicity and nationalism are modern concepts; others see them as primordial notions. Nor is there a consensus on the precise markers of ethnicity. A review of these debates is beyond the scope of this book. The following paragraphs, however, will briefly outline the ways in which these terms are used here.

This study subscribes to the description of *ethnicity* by Paul Brass as "any group of people dissimilar from other peoples in terms of objective cultural criteria and that contains within its membership either in principle or in practice the elements for a complete division of labor and for reproduction."[43] Ethnic groups, communities, and nations cannot be distinguished by any single and separate criterion, though these do connote different stages of self-awareness and political consolidation. Nations might eventually emerge from the "transformation of an ethnic group in a multiethnic state into a self-conscious political entity. It can be also created by "amalgamation of diverse groups and the formation of an inter-ethnic, composite or homogeneous national culture."[44] Ethnic identities need to be separated from identities based on class, caste, race, religion, or interest group. A large number of scholars have defined ethnic identities in these terms, but for the purposes of this book, ethnic nationalism and conflict have not been subsumed under any one or more of these categories. Ethnic identity is treated as a separate category. This is because ethnic groups may take any of the cultural symbols and use them to achieve solidarity and internal cohesion. These same symbols or clusters of symbols permit them to create an identity distinctly different from other culturally defined groups.

Scholars of ethnicity and nationalism also disagree whether ethnic ties are primordial or variable and whether both ethnic and state-centered nationalism is of modern origin. My fieldwork and research in Tamil Nadu, Sri Lanka, Punjab, and Kashmir supports neither the extreme instrumentalist conceptions of ethnic identities nor their primordialist definitions. It is true that politicized identities are spawned by collective "imaginings," that the truth or falsehood of their claims is less important than the fact that, at that point, these are seen to be necessary for cohesion and solidarity. It is also true that such imaginings take place within the conditions of existence—in life as it is lived—that define a group and its place in the scheme of things. Over a relatively short time frame, cultural and economic conditions remain constant or at least might not change drastically.[45]

Drawing on works of Breuilly and Brass, and my conversations with Tamil and Sikh militants, in this study I prescribe to the premise that ethnic nationalism is "constructed" mainly in the political sphere and for purposes of political power.[46] Here the "political" is not confined to formal competition of parties, elections, or control of political institutions. Rather, it includes efforts to redefine the rules by which political competition is played out. The politics of identity formation or ethnic conflict is more about who will control and shape the rules of the political competition, and what resources, symbols, issues, and ideas will become its focus. Such conflicts tend to redefine the civil society and its relations with the state. These continually remake the supranational State and recast its political capabilities. The conflicting sides might resort to violence, or use literary forums, or convert temples into armed fortresses, or turn protest meetings into covenants to pledge loyalty to the ethnic nation.[47]

It is also important to distinguish between the nation and the state, because nations can be in conflict with the state. Here, I draw on Walker Connor's definition of nation: a *nation* can be identified by the "psychological bond that joins a people and differentiates it, in the subconscious conviction of its members, from all other people in a most vital way." This is why foundation myths and history play such a critical part in making and dividing nations. Loyalty to the state is defined by several authors as patriotism, while nationalism is the ideology of the nation. The Indian nationalism was a response to colonial domination by the British.

In the interest of clarity, the central *state* is referred to as the supranational State throughout this book and is distinguished from India's federal units, i.e., the state of Punjab or Tamil Nadu. Generally, three separate perspectives can be identified in the scholarly debate on the question of the Indian state: the political-institutional approach, followed by Robert Hardgrave, Rajni Kothari, Lloyd and Susanne Rudolph; the political economy approach, followed by Marxist and neo-Marxist scholars, such as Hamza Alavi, Imtiaz Ahmed, and Sudipta Kaviraj; and the cultural perspective, favored by historians such as Ravinder Kumar, T. K. Oomen, T. N. Madan, Partha Chatterji, and Ashis Nandy.[48] These scholars differ sharply on the elements that constitute the Indian supranational State, its objectives and characteristics, but seem to generally agree that the Indian state enjoys a measure of autonomy from contending domestic and external forces. The liberal pluralist perspectives tend to define the state in terms of its behavior, while the Marxist-oriented approaches look to the constituting elements of the state, such as class.[49]

These questions are not resolved here, nor is the state seen as an arena of group conflict alone, or exclusively as a reflection of class interests. Instead, I subscribe to the approach outlined by Nettl: "The concept of the State is and ought to be treated as a variable in social science, as a reflection of the varying empirical reality with which social conscience concerns itself."[50] It is possible then to talk about the variable qualities of statehood or "stateness." England has a lower order quality of statehood than France where as the collective notion of the State was much more depersonalized. Countries like the United States and India might appropriate the notion of statehood but "where the notion has . . . remained remarkable by its absence or . . . transformed into a very different meaning."[51]

The different meanings of stateness are to be identified by empirical observations, such as the actions and policies of the Indian state, i.e., its military interventions and withdrawals and inability despite superior military capability to prevail over its overlapping nationalities. Nettl says the European stateness evolved by implosion —a narrowing of sovereignty into ethnically homogeneous or at least ethnically defined states. The third world states, on the other hand, have emerged out of a process of explosion—extension of sovereign authority and territorial state "across ethnic boundaries and . . . hitherto "sovereign" communities. Like their European counterparts, these states have also sought "self-definition, integration, and even domestic viability by emphasizing their international role."[52] But this is hardly the European type of state. The more or less stateness is a useful idea for understanding the distinctive integration paths of different kinds of states.

In other words, the identity of the state is defined by what it does. And what it does, its outcomes, might call into question set assumptions about the Indian state and its role in the region. The Indian state has identifiable interests, some of which have been described as relational control and balance between its heterogeneity and unity, which are determined by the competition for symbols of power—resources, office, and ideology.

Chapter 2

आईं

FORGING RELATIONAL CONTROL

Security in the Nehru Years

How did India's security come to depend upon establishing an interlocking balance of internal interests and relational control? What events shaped its logic? What view of the past permitted Indian leaders to make their historical legacy compatible with their conception of modern India? And how did these interpretations shape the relations with Pakistan and Sri Lanka during the first decades after Independence?

The precise nature of India's nationhood has been a subject of enduring debate, marked by at least three broad claims and counterclaims. India's British colonial administrators believed that "India was not a political name, but only a geographical expression like Europe or Africa," and that "there is not and never was an India, or even a country of India, possessing according to European ideas any sort of unity . . . no Indian nation, no 'people of India,' of which we hear so much."[1] Such a view was anathema to the Indian nationalists, who took every opportunity to claim India's glorious past and great achievements as a single civilization. The nationalists argued that, although Indian history was studded with prolonged periods of disunity, vast spaces of the subcontinent had been unified again and again under a single imperial rule and a single ruling dynasty. In their view, India would have evolved on its own had it not been colonized by the British. Contemporary ethnic nationalists hold a third view. Several scholars have argued that "India is best studied as a subcontinent with several historical distinctive national entities rather than as an area inhabited by people who share in the same cultural logic or a common, unitary model of social conceptualization."[2] Theories about a single Sanskritic tradition—whether defined as Hinduism or Brahminism—are essentially meant to justify the state-centered subcontinental nation of India. Indian and Hindu civilizations are not verifiable facts but colonial constructions.[3]

The British colonial view, most vividly articulated by John Strachey, was meant to justify the British rule of India. Indians were deemed incapable of writing their own history or creating unity unless it was imposed from without. The Indian nationalists rejected such a view of India's past and painstakingly recovered and reconstructed the history of India. This reconstruction went through subtle shifts of interpretation over time. But whether we take the views of Bankimchandra Chattopadhyay (1838) or the later nationalist leaders such as Nehru and Gandhi, they all regarded India to be a single civilization with diverse impulses. The Nationalist interpretation of history was inclusive—the opposite to what the ethnonationalists were trying to prove. For the ethnonationalists, the reconstruction of history consisted of separating each ethnic strand from the others. By contrast, the nationalists did not deny India's ethnic plurality but asserted that the whole was greater than the sum of its parts. This view came to dominate the freedom movement during the last years before Independence and was defined most explicitly by Jawaharlal Nehru.

A review of Nehru's speeches and writings reveals the elements of his concepts of national unity and international security.[4] First, he believed that independent India had to selectively retain those elements of its past that made its unified existence possible. This meant respecting its ethnic plurality. Second, its foreign policy had to play a crucial role in ensuring its future as an integrated, industrialized modern nation state. Third, the above compulsions had to require that India carve out a distinct path in domestic and foreign policy—one that avoided ideological straight jackets and nurtured its particular genius and its civilizational strength.

In a remarkable passage entitled "Importance of the National Idea, Changes Necessary in India" in the *Discovery of India*, Nehru writes that one of the imperatives of his time and circumstance was the rediscovery of the past. To forget the past, he said, was to build without foundations and cut off the roots of national growth. He faulted the Communist party of India for being completely ignorant of national traditions. He also derided those "who talked glibly of modernization and . . . essence of western culture" while being ignorant of their own culture. He concluded that

National progress can, therefore, lies neither in a repetition of the past nor in its denial. New patterns must inevitably be adopted but they must be integrated with the old. Sometimes the new, though different, appear in terms of preexisting patterns, and thus create feeling of a continuous development from the past, a link in the long chain of the history of the race. Indian history is a striking record of changes introduced in this way. . . . Because of this there is no sense of cultural break in it and there is that continuity, in spite of repeated change, from the far distant days of Mohenjodaro to our own age.[5]

What is this continuity to which Nehru is referring? Clearly for him, the continuity was of historical and cultural forms even while "the inner content continued to change." In the 516 pages of *The Discovery of India*, Nehru reconstructs, for his own understanding, the political forms and changing content of India as a single unified civilization, created by diverse streams of ideas and people but unified in themes and culture from the days of ancient empires of Asoka Maurya and Samudragupta in the third and fourth centuries B.C. to the more recent centralized empires of the Mughals and the British.[6] What is remarkable is that Nehru and India's leaders managed to rescue these "lessons of history" from the body blow dealt them by Partition, the communal holocaust that followed, and war. The million and more deaths, and the five to ten million people who lost their homes and had to start afresh on both sides of the line of division, should have destroyed their faith in the design for a democratic, secular, federal, India. Instead, it reinforced the faith. The leaders did not choose the authoritarian variant nor did they accept the notion of a fragmented India divided into several separate nation states. From each new challenge, the Indian leadership 'reasoned' their way back to the ideas that had nourished its understanding of India's nationhood.

Nehru abstracted four broad principles on which to unify and govern India:

1. Historically each unified formation in India, whether termed a paramount or an empire state, had created a universal order that transcended specific ideologies and beliefs but did not seek to eliminate or merge them. Instead the empires created an overarching ideology that was both tolerant and inclusive.[7]

2. The legacy of history to the modern Indian state was the notion of layered order, and a central state that limited itself to the public domain. Nehru saw that each empire state explicitly recognized the extant social order.

Separate caste and religious communities were accommodated within the broad framework of the overarching ideology, where each maintained its distinctive identity but derived it, in large part, through reference to the whole. The early empires were tributary systems organized as *mandalas* or spheres of influence, at the center of which was the *Chakravartin*, the paramount king. The regional kingdoms maintained a large degree of freedom in domestic and foreign policy.[8]

3. The third principle, derived from the first two, was that each imperial ruler, king, or authority enjoyed a degree of autonomy from India's existing social order. The overarching ideology of the state meant that it could transcend particular interests; it neither represented such interests exclusively nor allowed such interests to claim the state.[9] This ability of the subcontinental state was the most important gift of the imperial formations of the past. Autonomy gave the state the flexibility that it needed to integrate the nation, develop the economy, create new economic and political opportunities, and to equalize society. The notion of an autonomous state that he could show to be deeply rooted in past permitted Nehru to claim such a state to be an authentic expression of India's civilizational unity. He argued that India's history had repeatedly produced such a state and that Indian people had flourished and achieved greatness under its aegis.

4. In contrast to the previous three, Nehru's fourth principle was not derived from earlier Hindu and Muslim epochs, but from the period of British rule. Until the advent of the British, the external boundaries of all subcontinental empires tended to be amorphous. In the early empires the mandala system forestalled the fixing of concrete boundaries. To the Mughal rulers, territorial sovereignty meant ability to collect revenue and command the loyalty of local chieftains in wartime. The British broke with the past in this respect. They introduced the notion of fixed boundaries that were clearly demarcated on the ground and drawn in maps. The purpose was to give an exact definition to the term "India."

The British desire to establish frontiers was driven by the need to expand their empire to the natural geographical limits of the subcontinent, to establish clear lines of control and jurisdictions in case of internal dissensions or regional revolts, and to prevent rival imperial states such as Russia from encroaching on what the British had clearly defined as their possession. It is important to note that the British quest for fixed boundaries was not dictated by racial, linguistic, and religious considerations. The frontiers of British India cut across ethnic entities with an imperial disregard. Independent India inherited these frontiers and was to follow these broad rules of international security. It sought, however, to eschew the imperialist and expansionist element from this strategy. In Nehru's view, the making of modern political India had to be based on principle of territorial unity. This was to be the first cardinal rule of India's foreign policy.

However, fixed boundaries, inherited in this way, could not resolve the problem of making India's nation and state congruent. And inherited boundaries were not without problems as evidenced in disputes with China and Pakistan. India's leaders recognized that in the "historic" state (or an "imagined state" according to Benedict Anderson), the definition of domestic as distinct from "foreign" had altered with the contraction and expansion of the central or paramount state. When boundaries ran through single culturally defined communities, relations with neighbors became even more complicated.

The problem would not have arisen if ethnic groups had been dispersed as, for instance, Muslims were throughout South India during the British period and are today. But that was the exception rather than the rule. Over time, ethnic nationalities had acquired a distinct geographical identity. Periods of imperial disintegration had encouraged the geographical consolidation of culturally defined identities. These tendencies persisted into the next epoch of imperial consolidation and often gained a higher order of coherence. Periods of tranquility led to cultural, literary, and artistic advances within the autonomous regions; temples and monuments were built, and these provided people with tangible and intangible symbols of ethnic identity.

Successive imperial epochs however witnessed different levels of integration. For instance, the Islamic polity of the Mughals required individual kingdoms to pay tribute and contribute troops toward the maintenance of their centralized rule, but the Mughals were not anxious to economically integrate their empire into a single boundless market as were the British a century and a half later. The response of the ethnonationalities was in large part a reflection of the demands made on them by the centralized state. While each succeeding imperial formation brought greater administrative centralization and placed subcontinental unity on a more advanced stage, the contrary trends also set in and consolidated further the regional loyalties and cultural identities. India's nationalist leaders had inherited this contradiction and needed to solve it while modernizing and strengthening India's economy.

The legacy of history therefore provided Nehru with a distinct model of the supranational State. This consisted of a clearly identifiable central authority; an overarching liberal, i.e., nonintrusive, ideology, and a layered order based on regional and cultural autonomy. This historical interpretation of the Indian state provided the basis for Nehru's vision of a democratic, federal, secular India. India was to be secular not in the Western sense of an agnostic state, but in the sense of the Mauryan polity, in which the state was required to be impartial and to respect all religions; the layered order of the past was to be translated into the federal State of the future, one that embodied unity in diversity and that not only permitted, but created political space for the latter. "The diversity of India is tremendous" Nehru wrote in the *Discovery of India*, yet with all the differences "there is no mistaking the impress of India on the Pathan as it is on the Tamil." At another place he noted: "it is fascinating to find how the Bengalis, the Marathas, the Gujaratis, the Tamils . . . the Punjabis, . . . the Kashmiris . . . and the great central block comprising the Hindustani-speaking people, have retained their peculiar characteristics . . . and yet have been throughout these ages distinctively Indian, with the same national heritage and the same set of moral and mental qualities."[10] In his view, India's culture and civilization gave shape to all things Indian. He also talked about "some kind of a dream of unity" that has occupied the mind of India since the dawn of civilization." This unity was not imposed from outside; "it was something deeper. And within the fold, the widest tolerance of belief and custom was practiced and every variety acknowledged"[11] The overarching ideology of the historical state, which required the separation of the public and private domain, found its modern expression directly in liberal democracy.

However, the historical model of the state did not resolve two problems: how to offset tendencies toward fragmentation and how to do so within fixed and internationally recognized boundaries. For solutions to these problems, Nehru turned to modernization and nonalignment. In his vision of India, the congruence of the modern nation with the supranational State was to be achieved through modernization—the extension of the market, industrialization, trade and transport, and the creation of a single vast arena of opportunity for future generations—bound together by a common administrative, legal, judicial, fiscal, and monetary system. Similarly, the need to endow India with fixed boundaries, and the fact that these had largely been inherited and did not follow ethnic fault lines, made him opt for nonalignment in foreign policy. Nehru felt that India needed time and freedom from external influences. Nonalignment was designed to give India both.[12]

This interpretation of India's nationhood as forged by Nehru and the first generation of leaders of free India is the cornerstone of the strategy of maintaining interlocking balances between India's supranational State and its ethnonations, and of exercising relational control over these ethnonations and the neighboring states. The subcontinental formations of the past had achieved unity by implementing such tactics. Although the states of the past were authoritarian, Nehru saw democratic possibilities lurking in their womb. A political order based on explicit recognition of diversity and layered order bespoke a limited state. India's nationalists could build on this while transforming India into a modern nation. The common feature of the paramount state of the past and the modern Nehruvian state was their quest for autonomy. The former needed autonomy for precisely the same reasons as the latter. Both needed it to forge unity through impartiality, and to fend off external threats. The Nehruvian state, furthermore, was committed to achieving these goals within the framework of democracy and modernization. Nehru said, "Any part we want to play in world affairs depends entirely on the internal strength, unity and conditions of our country." The world, he said, "will attach importance to our voice only in proportion to the strength they know we have (internally)."[13]

The Demand for Partition

Even before India became independent, the Nehru/Gandhi vision of the future was gravely imperiled by the Muslim League's demand for a Pakistan. The two-nation theory on which it was based threatened the elements of the historical state that Nehru and the Congress party leaders wished to incorporate into their design for modern India—its secularism, its many layered federalism, and its democracy. The most immediate effect was to drive a wedge between the ethnonationalities of British India on the basis of religion and ethnicity. It set off a chain reaction among the most affected communities that came close to scuttling the attempt to set up a federal democratic state. The worst affected were the Sikhs, rulers of the Punjab until only a hundred years earlier. They owned more than half the arable land but comprised less than a fifth of the population; now they faced the loss of a large part of their homeland.

As the Muslim League's demand for a separate state for the Muslims of British India became increasingly strident and the possibility of Punjab's division became real, the main Sikh party, the Akali Dal, began to mobilize their community to agitate for a separate Sikhistan.[14] But the Alkalis had to compete for power with the Muslim League, the Congress party, and the Unionist party in undivided Punjab. The Sikh community was itself divided between the Unionists, the Congress party, and the Alkalis. Therefore, despite religious appeals, the Akali support for a separate state remained marginal. As the movement for Pakistan gathered momentum and communal tensions mounted, the Akali Dal entered into an alliance with the Congress for the 1946 provincial elections. But this did not give them the requisite bargaining position to persuade the British authorities to yield on Sikhistan. Instead the British advised, even encouraged, the Akalis to negotiate an arrangement with either the Congress party or the Muslim League. But Akali–League talks failed. In contrast, their negotiations with Nehru led to his famous statement about "setting up an area and a set-up in the north where the Sikhs can also freely experience the glow of freedom."[15] In March 1947, the Congress leaders accepted the inevitability of partition and formally asked for the division of Bengal and Punjab. At this point the Akali strategy focused on getting the line of division moved west to the river Chenab, so as to include their rich and fertile lands in the Indian Punjab.[16] The boundary commission did not accede to the Akalis' demands and placed the border more or less along the river Ravi, thus dividing the Sikhs in half.[17] The outbreak of the Muslim Sikh rioting, in which the Sikhs in the fertile settlements of west Punjab became the main targets for Muslims, followed as an inevitable outcome, and foreclosed all options but one for the Sikhs: massive and wholesale migration across the border into India. The trauma of that surgery, however, lingered on and came back to haunt Indian leaders a decade later.

A demand for a separate state also came from other nationalities not on the sensitive border of India. In 1939, Ramaswami Naicker, leader of the Tamil movement that consolidated the Tamil political identity, organized a "Dravida Nadu Conference" to mobilize southern India behind an independent Dravidadesam (Dravida Nation). Such a demand had been put forward in 1940, at the same time the Muslim League had also resolved at Lahore to create a separate Pakistan.[18] Naicker had in fact supported the demand for Pakistan and even sought to enlist the Muslim League's support for his cause. However, his separatist agenda did not have too many takers. Naicker enjoyed immense popularity but the provincial wing of the Indian national Congress continued to claim electoral power. The stature of Nehru and Gandhi, and support of highly respected Tamil leaders such as Rajagopalachari, kept the Congress party at the center of politics in that state. The competitive strategies of nationalist leaders are a subject for the next chapter. Here it is enough to note that religious differences and linguistic diversity did not deter the nationalist leaders from claiming India, even after Partition, to be a single nation state.

When the British announced the lapse of paramountcy and transfer of power in June 1947, several princely states declared that they would assume independent status. The princely states of Bhopal and Junagadh in the north and Travancore and Hyderabad in southern India announced their intention to set themselves up as sovereign states.[19] Nehru argued that withdrawal of paramountcy did not mean total independence for all states nor a complete severance of relationship with successor states. On the other hand, Jinnah had argued that every princely state was fully entitled to choose between India and Pakistan. According to V. P. Menon, secretary of the Ministry of States, who supervised the gigantic task of integrating the princely states of "British India," Pakistan was trying to get some of the border states to join it.[20] Menon mentions the ruler of Jodhpur, Jaisalmer, and Hyderabad. According to him, Jinnah had given an unconditional guarantee to the ruler of Jodhpur if he chose Pakistan over India. Muslim League leaders had been similarly busy with the nizam of Hyderabad, who had adamantly refused to join India.[21] As negotiations stalled, the nizam threatened to refer the issue to the United Nations, purchased a large amount of arms, and secretly encouraged Razakars' (many among these were fanatic Muslims) insurgency against the pro-India forces in his state.[22] The situation was further complicated by the Communist-led uprising of poor peasants mobilized because of the collapse of the old order to protest against economic domination by landed oligarchy favored by the nizam.

The greatest challenge to the new Indian nation-state came in Kashmir. The ruler of Kashmir, Maharajah Hari Singh, also dreamed of retaining his independence from India and Pakistan. He had faced serious political opposition to his rule since 1931. Had the demand for Pakistan never arisen, or had it not been conceded, Kashmir would have become a part of the new independent state without much fuss. But the emergence of the religious factor and the communal violence that erupted all around the state in British India put the Maharajah in a very difficult position from which he sought to extricate himself by remaining independent. It is enough to note here that the Muslim League's success in getting the British and the Congress to accept its demand caused a shift in the locus of Kashmiri politics. Earlier, the split between the older Muslim conference and Sheikh Abdullah's National Conference had been over personal rivalries and a sharp difference on the extent to which the movement would be democratic, i.e. active mobilization of the ordinary people for a program of social and economic reform.[23] After the League voiced the demand for Pakistan, and even more, after it was conceded, the fault line shifted to whether to join India or Pakistan if independence, the preferred option of both parties as of the maharajah, was not attainable.

The National Conference, which dominated Kashmir Valley to the virtual exclusion of the Muslim Conference, preferred autonomy within India if independence proved not to be an option, but the Muslim Conference, whose various factions collectively enjoyed the support of the majority of the Muslims of districts of Kashmir that adjoined west Punjab, and the North West Frontier, wanted to join that country.[24] In Jammu, the main political party, the Hindu-dominated Praja Parishad was largely a pro-maharajah party, and wanted what he wanted. The British administrators, to a man, saw little of Kashmir's ethnic and political plurality and stressed the contradiction involved in a Hindu maharajah choosing to join India when the majority of his subjects were Muslim.[25]

Partition, when it occurred, came close to destroying the goal of creating an impartial, secular Indian state, irrespective of geography and ethnicity. By June 1947, everyone had accepted the inevitability of partition. The Congress leaders came to the reluctant conclusion by then that the League was unlikely to yield on its demand, and would continue fanning the fires of communalism till the polarization of Hindus and Muslims was complete.[26] The Congress wanted to minimize the schism and loss of life; it also believed that the refusal to partition India would delay Independence. However, instead of averting communal violence, the division of the subcontinent led to a holocaust. By June 1948, some five and half million Hindus and Sikhs had crossed from West Pakistan into India and about an equal number of Muslims had moved the other way."[27]

Pakistan, when it came into being, was perforce a unitary state.[28] The extreme bitterness that the communal riots engendered came close to making India one, too. Partition had frustrated the Congress's objective of creating a loose but united federation. Not surprisingly, therefore, many persons began to question the need for any federation at all. K. M. Pannikar, state minister in the princely state of Bikaner and an important voice in support of integration, sent a strong note of dissent to the Union Constitution Committee in the summer of 1947. He was convinced that India's strategic security could not be separated from the internal arrangement of power. "a federal center" he said, "postulates the protection of a major power, which will hold its iron ring around us, to enable India to develop peacefully. This was the conception of the Government of India Act of 1935, and all negotiations that preceded it. It was to be a protected India enjoying self government, where the defense power was to remain mainly with Britain." The British dominion had ended. Clearly then, India's leaders had to step in and build a self- reliant India that could forge an iron ring around itself without depending on others to do it. Given the "weak and insecure national integration," India could be "courting disaster" if it were to "now create a Center limited by legalism and cramped by the indefensible rights of provincial units," said Pannikar. He believed that federation would leave "the national government with but limited powers, weak and consequently incapable of dealing with national problems" He advocated a unitary constitution that permitted limited power to the provinces.[29]

Nehru did not wholly agree with Pannikar but he fully appreciated the latter's crucial argument: the need to insulate secular and democratic India from the threats generated by its ethnic and religious diversity. This became apparent when, within a year after Independence, Mahatma Gandhi was assassinated by a fanatical former member of the Rashtriya Swayamsevak Sangh (Militant Hindu nationalist organization). This was a terrible blow to India's aspirations to build a modern nation-state. It was the most extreme manifestation of the backlash against secularism and plural democracy that swept the Hindu nationalist organizations at that time.

Nehru and the Congress averted the threat in a variety of ways. Under the stewardship of Vallabhbhai Patel, the deputy prime minister in the interim government, the integration of the states was completed rapidly. The Constituent Assembly reaffirmed India's federalism and created an instrument that proved sufficiently flexible to accommodate the rise of ethnonationalism in later years. Nine years later, in 1956, Nehru completed the design for ethno-federalism by conceding the demand for the linguistic reorganization of the states. In Kashmir, after the Maharajah acceded to India, the government moved rapidly to repel the Pathan raiders sent in by Pakistan, and later pushed back the Pakistan army from two-thirds of the state.

Following Gandhi's assassination, the government moved swiftly to reassert the secular nature of the polity by banning the Hindu Mahasabha (the political front for the RSS) and including strict prohibitions against any incitement of communal passions in the constitution and the Indian penal code.[30] Within the Congress party, Nehru exerted all his immense authority to beat back the Hindu nationalist challenge, by securing in 1951 the ouster of Purshottamdas Tandon from the presidency of the party in 1951, after he had been in that post for just one year.[31] Over the succeeding years, Nehru was mainly responsible for forging a special relationship between the Congress and the Muslims that lasted until the late eighties.

However, Partition brought forward to the top of Nehru's agenda, the issue of India's territorial boundaries and integrity. Had India remained united, this issue would have been of peripheral importance. United India would have inherited the borders created by the British, a policy that had been honed over more than a century, and a core of administrators well versed in implementing it. But Partition created a whole new set of boundaries, and these cut through the heart of more than one of British India's ethnonations. Under Nehru, the government sought to give India the clearly defined territorial boundaries that befitted a modern state. But at no point did he forget the need to establish ethnonational identities that were embedded in the historical state. The strength of Nehru's integrationist impulse was demonstrated by his treatment of the princely states and by his impulse to accommodate genuine ethnic differences. Nehru also perceived the potential for disruption embedded in Sikh and Tamil ethnonationalism. But since these were dormant, he adopted a method of keeping them in check within the modern Indian state—by appropriating a large part of their platform so as to isolate their more extreme leaders. The variety of, and the contrast between the methods he used illustrates the way in which interlocking balances and relational controls were established during his long stewardship of India's future.

The Princely States and Indian Integration

According to the 1947 India Independence Act, the five hundred-plus princely states of British India were, in theory at least, free to choose between the two dominions of India and Pakistan or remain independent. But to the Indian nationalists, as distinct at least from the formal position taken by the Muslim League,[32] the third option was simply not on the cards. In *Discovery of India* Nehru wrote, "the right of well-constituted areas to secede from Indian federation or union has been put forward, and the argument of the USSR advanced in support of it. That argument has little application, for conditions there are wholly different and right has little practical value."[33]

He had been utterly opposed to the partition of India on the basis of religion, having pointed out that "if this or any other criterion were to be used, India was not two but several nations. What is more, it was impossible to draw clean boundaries around them since they overlapped and were intermixed"; it was not clear if the majority in one or other nations wanted to secede. On the basis of what he had seen in the North-West Frontier Province (NWFP), Punjab, and Bengal, Nehru was convinced that religious sentiments were artificially whipped up by extremists on both sides and did not represent the dispassionate and objective views that the same people would take when not in the grip of violent emotions. Last, but for him the most important was, partition, which he feared would threaten the very "beginnings of freedom and [the] formation of [a] free national state. . . . Disintegration will be in the air, and all . . . who are otherwise agreeable to . . . unified existence, will claim separate states for themselves, or special privileges that are encroachment on others." In any case, "it is difficult to conceive of any free state emerging from such a turmoil." In effect, a properly functioning free India must exist before right to secession was exercised. Only then was it possible to consider the question objectively.[34]

If Nehru did not accept religion as a basis for secession, he could hardly have been expected to take the claims of various princely states seriously. He saw no justification in history, although history is precisely what the rulers of Kashmir and Hyderabad were using to legitimize independent existence. As Nehru saw it, the British were taking a narrowly legalistic position on this question. "How did these states come into existence?" Nehru asked and then proceeded to answer his own question. Some of the states were quite new, having been "created by the British; others were vice-royalties of the Mughal Emperor, and their rulers were permitted to continue as feudatory chiefs by the British; yet others, notably the Maratha chiefs, were defeated by British armies and then made into feudatories. Nearly all this can be traced back to British rule; they have no earlier history. If some of them functioned independently for a while, that independence was a brief duration and ended in defeat in war or threat of war."[35]

Nehru cited specific states: the Rajput and Marathas would have disintegrated even in the absence of British intervention, the dominion of Oudh and Nizam in Hyderabad was "bogus"; even in Kashmir, Nehru distinguished between claims to autonomy based on ethnicity, and the maharajah's claim to independence, based supposedly on history. Kashmir, he wrote, was sold by "the East India Company after the Sikh wars to the great-grandfather of the present ruler. The only truly independent kingdom was Nepal, which held a position analogous to that of Afghanistan." These (Indian) kingdoms and princely states survived only because they were deliberately sustained by a single "dominant power which protected them." These same perceptions animated the thinking of other nationalist leaders, notably in Vallabhbhai Patel and K. M. Pannikar's perceptions about India's unity and defense.

Nehru's reference to Nepal is of significance, for it sums up his entire philosophy of nation-building. The fundamental drive toward the creation of a unified nation-state could be modified or qualified only on the grounds of ethnicity. To Nehru, ethnicity did not spring from (although it could include) religion, but rather from that special fusion of language, custom, tradition, and culture that distinguishes one group of people from another. Since distinctions like these take time to develop, history has an important role in shaping ethnicity. All these together constitute identity, which does not by itself provide a sufficient ground for independence. For that, a nation should have existed already as an autonomous unit, with all the attributes of statehood. Nehru felt that Nepal genuinely had these attributes, but the princely states of India did not, their sovereignty having been reduced more than a century earlier to an empty show of pomp. Nehru was aware that Nepal did not only consist of the ethnically distinct montane regions, but that a large part of the population lived in the submontane "Terai" in the Indo-Gangetic plain, and were indistinguishable from the Indians living alongside them to the south of the border. Exercise of sovereignty by Nepal had to accommodate India's need to build a modern nation-state and protect its territory from outside interference. It is this that explains the Indo-Nepal treaty in the 1950s. Once India's interests had thus been secured, Nehru was prepared to extend the same opportunity to Nepal as he wanted for India—the opportunity to make the boundaries of the nation and state congruent, through concerted development and modernization.

Nehru was thus only too aware of the variety of ethnonationalities that existed within the territories directly administered by the British. He also knew that in the final analysis, it was largely a matter of the accident of non-birth[36] that determined which parts of the country remained nominally independent and which came under British rule. Nehru employed a variant of the system of interlocking balances, which he had developed in dealing with Kashmir. This did not evolve all at once, but gradually, in response to the increasing assertiveness of the ethnonations that made up British and then modern India.

As noted, Nehru, Patel, and the Congress had little patience for the pretensions of the princely states. Within a few years of their signing the instrument of accession, the government had merged them into larger contiguous provinces, in which the rulers lost whatever little power they had enjoyed in British days. Their armies and civil services were merged with the Indian army and the All-India civil services, and they were in effect pensioned off with handsome privy purses. In the transitional phase, some among them were appointed the rajpramukh, i.e., governor, of the province. But the significant feature of even this transitional phase was that the consolidation was done roughly on the basis of ethnicity.[37] Thus the Sikh-ruled states of eastern Punjab were merged to form PEPSU (Patiala and the East Punjab States Union); the states of central India were merged with the extant Central

Provinces; those spread in a patchwork quilt throughout Orissa became Orissa; those in Gujarat, Kathiawar, and Kutch became a part of what was then Bombay province; the princely state of Travancore and Cochin became a part of Madras, and so on. This pattern was repeated throughout the country. The immediate result was the strengthening of ethnonational identity within the new Indian state.

Having made this necessary concession to ethnicity, Nehru imposed control on the agenda of the states in a wide variety of ways. In politics, the Congress had already developed strong links with democratic movements against the princes; these movements had sprung up in nearly all the large states before Independence. A States Peoples' Conference had been set up; Nehru served as president at the time of Independence, having taken over the position, again significantly, from Sheikh Abdullah. After India became independent, the Congress formally absorbed the state movements into itself, and thereby appropriated their democratizing, modernizing agenda.

Harnessing Ethnonationalism

The challenge to India's modern nationhood did not end there. Within only a few years of Independence, ethnic self-assertion swept large parts of the country. Beginning with one Potti Sriramulu's fast unto death to demand the creation of a separate Andhra province that spoke Telugu, ethnolinguistic demands all over India burst forth in 1953. Nehru initially refused to give in to the ethnolinguistic redrawing of boundaries and adamantly held onto the idea of administrative boundaries. Undoubtedly his response was shaped by the experience of Partition but there was also his understanding of India's past in it. The ethnic and regional demands were for the Indian leaders a resurfacing of the traditional India although within a modern context.[38] Nehru feared empowering ethnic and religious identities by providing them with political structures within which to operate, but by consolidating the princely states with adjoining provinces more or less on the basis of ethnicity he had already done this to a considerable extent. Nehru and others could not ignore the fact that ethnic consolidation was a direct result of democracy and electoral expansion.

Not without some misgivings, Nehru bowed to the rising clamor and agreed to reorganize the Indian provinces into linguistic states (the change of nomenclature, although perhaps influenced by the United States, was not without significance). This took place in 1956. Having done so, he again sought to impose control over the agenda of ethnic self-assertion by appropriating the platform of the ethnonational leaders. In Punjab, for example, he brought in Partap Singh Kairon, a charismatic and energetic Sikh leader, to head the Congress government. Under Kairon, Sikhs (only two-fifths of the population) gradually came to dominate the local level administration and the police. Since most Sikhs who had lost their lands in West Punjab had already been resettled in East Punjab or adjoining west Uttar Pradesh by these institutional and administrative means, Kairon completed the process of reconstituting a Sikh homeland in much the same way.[39]

In Tamil Nadu, Nehru promoted Kamaraj Nadar, a homespun leader of a low caste, economically humble origin, few words, and remarkable shrewdness and administrative capability. Kamaraj transformed the Congress party from the predominantly upper caste and eclectic party it was under its earlier leaders, and gave it a distinct non-Brahmin, Dravida flavor.[40] In both states, therefore, the strategy Nehru followed was to appropriate the appeal of the ethnic leaders and weaken them and their parties sufficiently to ensure that power remained in the hands of the Congress party.

Consolidating the Supranational State

The above analysis of Indian nation-building also gives us a fair idea of how the accommodation of ethnonationality within the modern Indian supranational State shaped India's approach to the establishment of its own security within the region. The perennial preoccupation of the supranational State was the maintenance of its autonomy to determine the future course of the nation. Above all, this required the continual maintenance of control. New Delhi could negotiate the way power was shared with the ethnonations. But this negotiation had to be done within a framework that ensured that the direction in which the State as a whole moved was controlled firmly by it. This system of interlocking balance and relational control was forged by Nehru and began to unravel only in the later days of his daughter, Indira Gandhi.

Nehru was far less tolerant when demands for separation were instigated by external forces, whether it was Pakistan or the Soviet Union. India's right to integrate Hyderabad has been contested by Pakistan since 1947 and has been a matter of serious controversy among scholars. For instance, Lamb and Ahmed argue that India's position in Kashmir was inconsistent with that in Hyderabad where the nizam had opted first for independence and then belatedly toyed with the idea of joining Pakistan.[41] India had accepted the right of rulers to choose between India and Pakistan. By forcibly integrating Hyderabad, these authors argue, the nationalists had exposed their pro-Hindu bias and hegemonic designs.

This accusation does not stand up to scrutiny. The nizam's ardent desire was to remain independent. He even entered into discussions with the Portuguese in Goa for port facilities, with the objective of securing a corridor between Hyderabad and Goa.[42] He was dissuaded from pushing his claim by Louis Mountbatten and the British government. The president of his Executive Council and the leader of the delegation that negotiated the Standstill agreement with India, the nawab of Chhatari, urged him to accede to India. The nizam was on the point of signing the Standstill agreement with India, a precursor to accession, when he heard that Pathan raiders had invaded Kashmir. Assuming that Pakistan would seize Kashmir and become a much larger state, he reneged on his decision at the last minute, thus provoking the resignation of the nawab of Chhatari. Only then did the nizam bring in Laik Ali, who was closely aligned to Kasim Rizvi, head of the Razakars, as the point man and principle adviser, and begin a flirtation with Pakistan. The nizam obviously was aware that neither the condition of contiguity nor the wishes of the people allowed him to accede to Pakistan. But the fact that the Nizam was a Muslim ruler did not automatically make India's action pro-Hindu, just as the fact that the nawab of Chhatari was a Muslim did not automatically make him advise accession to Pakistan.

As for the people of the state, the previous two years had seen a militant agitation against the feudal rule of the nizam. The nizam knew that the Congress was far more a grassroots organization than was the Muslim League, and far less likely to continue the privilege and powers of the princes. The Congress also had extensive relations with the antimonarchy democratic movements in the large princely states. Ironically, the nizam's real reason for wanting to remain independent was exactly the same as that of the Hindu maharajah of Kashmir—his distrust of the Congress's populism, and especially of Nehru. The nizam's desire to join Pakistan, his second option, was fueled by the Muslim League's willingness to pander to it.

Nehru had little patience with the demands of the nizam, but was prepared to give him time to come around. What made the former decide to send in the army was the growing evidence of Pakistani activities and interference by the Muslim League in Hyderabad. There were indications that the nizam was aided and abetted by Jinnah and that the Razakar insurgency of militant Muslims in Hyderabad had received arms from Pakistan.[43] In the view of Indian leaders, this external intervention justified the use of force.

Nehru's treatment of Kashmir reflects the same 'Congress' sensitivity to grassroots populist, antimonarchic sentiment on the one hand, and the same refusal to countenance foreign intervention on the other. Where it differs significantly from his attitude to Hyderabad is in his sensitivity to Kashmir's distinct ethnic identity. There can be no doubt that Nehru desperately wanted Kashmir to join India. When Mountbatten sternly rebuked him on July 27, 1947, for wanting to go up to Srinagar against the maharajah's explicit wishes to see the imprisoned Sheikh Abdullah on August 4, and risk being himself thrown in prison just eleven days before he became prime minister of free India, Nehru broke down during a stormy meeting with Gandhi and Patel and said that Kashmir was more important to him than "anything else." In this he was almost alone in the cabinet and among the leaders of the Congress party, who were too preoccupied with the turmoil in the rest of India to worry about Kashmir. But Nehru wanted to ensure certain conditions before making Kashmir a part of India. As Jha has demonstrated in his recent book, based on the correspondence and reports in the India Office Records library in London, the truly extraordinary lengths to which Nehru went to make sure that Kashmir would not be allowed to accede to India until the accession had the full backing of Sheikh Abdullah—support that the sheikh could only give if he were free and at the helm of the government.[44] Nehru wanted Kashmir, and did everything in his power to keep Sheikh Abdullah on his side. But if, after coming out of jail, Abdullah had advised the maharajah to accede to Pakistan, there was a strong possibility that Nehru and Patel would have accepted his decision.

Nehru continued to demonstrate his sensitivity to ethnonationalism when he accepted Mountbatten's suggestion that the accession should be ratified by plebiscite. He was able to do this because he was aware that the bulk of the Kashmiris were bound together not by religion—for the state residents included orthodox Sunnis, Sufi Sunnis who were Sunnis in name only, Shias, Ismailis, Hindus, and Buddhists—but by ethnicity. He felt confident that as long as Sheikh Abdullah was at the helm of affairs, Kashmir would opt for India in a two-way choice.

Nehru's decision in the 1947–48 war to stop the army from going beyond the Jhelum gorge at Uri into Muzaffarabad district, when it had the Pakistan army in retreat, thereby starting a chain that has left a third of the princely state of Jammu and Kashmir in the hands of Pakistan, has been criticized by succeeding generations of Indian leaders and publicists, particularly after Kashmir was gripped by a violent movement for independence in 1989.[45] But even this decision reflected his sensitivity to ethnicity. Beyond the Uri, as in most of Poonch district, which also stayed with Pakistan, the population was overwhelmingly Muslims who were ethnically part of the Punjab, and had very little in common with the Muslims of the Kashmir valley. In these areas of Poonch, Sheikh Abdullah's National Conference was relatively weak, while the pro-Pakistan Muslim Conference was strong. The decision to stop there was dictated by the convergence of both the ethnic and political fault lines at the Uri gorge.

The balance that Nehru was striving toward in shaping Kashmir's relations with New Delhi was formalized in the 1952 Nehru–Sheikh Abdullah agreement. Abdullah and the National Conference renounced the claim to independence in return for a special status in India's federal structure. Article 370 of the Indian constitution grants Kashmir a large degree of internal autonomy, keeping only defense, finance, and foreign affairs in the hands of New Delhi. The agreement reflected a tacit understanding on part of each that the National Conference would contain and channel Kashmiri nationalism while the Congress would refrain from political meddling in the state. Article 370 thus formalized the idea of layered sovereignty as the basis of Indian unity. The Indian state would be the paramount state and would permit regional autonomy.

The desire to accommodate ethnonationalities, that is, to mediate between the historic nations of India and the modern supranational state, does not explain all of Nehru's actions. Why was he prepared to accommodate Kashmiri ethnonationalism but adamant about crushing the Communist uprising in Hyderabad? A simple explanation would be that the uprising challenged the recently established merger of Hyderabad with India. But this is only half the answer. The peasant agitation of 1948 had been launched in response to a call from Stalin just as the world communist movement switched in the late 1940s from a collaborative to revolutionary strategy toward the indigenous bourgeoisie in newly independent countries. Stalin had sent out the signal for the shift, once the Cold War had replaced the wartime alliance and ordered Communist parties in other countries to oppose the nationalists and work toward their overthrow. Stalin had specifically criticized Gandhi and Nehru, calling them the running dogs of imperialism.[46] Such an externally instigated movement was anathema to the Indian nationalists.

Integration of Kashmir and Hyderabad underscored the fact that Nehru did not eschew the use of force. But while the modern Nehruvian State relied upon accommodation for reconciling the ethnonations inherited from the historical state with the modern Indian state, it brooked no rivals in dictating the agenda for modernization. The Communist challenge in Hyderabad was precisely of this nature.

The Internal Equation and Foreign Policy

Nehru's treatment of Hyderabad and Kashmir in 1947 contained within it the seeds of what was to become the enduring foreign policy of India. It was the compulsion to maintain control that was to form the bridge between domestic and foreign policy. What was the central state to do if popular disaffection and turmoil in India's neighborhood seemed likely to spill over into India, or disaffection in an Indian ethnonational community threatened to involve external actors? Under such circumstances, the security imperative took precedence over all considerations. India would use force a) to repel foreign influence on the domestic interlocking balance, and b) to prevent the domestic turbulence from spilling across and involving a neighbor. While the security apparatus held the boundaries, the national leaders were required to seek political settlements. In other words, the need to safeguard the ability of the national leaders to achieve such settlements determined India's security response in South Asia.

These two imperatives shaped Nehru's attitude to the vexed question of overlapping ethnonationalities, specifically the Tamils in Sri Lanka, and the large Bengali Hindu population in East Pakistan. Consistent with the attitude that he had adopted toward Nepal, Nehru believed that 'Indian ethnic elements in neighboring countries should identify with and be accepted by those countries and not keep claiming an Indian identity. In Sri Lanka, this issue did not arise with regard to the large Tamil minority of Jaffna and the northern districts—that conflict was a decade away—but it came up immediately in connection with the plantation Tamils, who had been imported into the southern part of the Island at the end of the nineteenth century to work the tea plantations. During Nehru's time, India insisted that these Tamils had to be given Ceylonese nationality and refused to consider Ceylonese requests to repatriate most,[47] if not all of them. It was only after Nehru's death that his successor, Lal Bahadur Shastri, partly conceded to Sri Lanka's demand. Nehru took the same approach toward the Hindus in Pakistan. On April 8, 1950, he signed an agreement with Pakistani Prime Minister Liaquat Ali Khan which reaffirmed that "the allegiance and loyalty of the minorities is to the state of which they are citizens, and it is to the government of their own state that they must look for the redress of their grievances."[48] He also took the same position with regard to people of Indian origin in Burma, South and East Africa, and Fiji.

Success in such a negotiated settlement depended on how the ethnonational leaders perceived actions by the national leaders. Perception that it was impartial reinforced the supranational State's authority. It provided the central leaders with greater autonomy and insulated their decisions from intra-ethnic struggles for ascendancy. Nonalignment reflected in external policy what impartiality reflected in domestic policy: the attempt to balance between competing claims in order to maximize supranational State's room for maneuver. The nonalignment posture sent two messages. To India's neighbors and the big powers it said, "Stay away; let us resolve our problems by ourselves. Do not upset the delicate balances that we are trying to establish." To the ethnonations within India it said, "We can arrive at an accommodation; don't bring in anyone else. If you do, it will make accommodation more difficult, and will leave us with no option but to use force."

Nonalignment was not rooted, as many have contended over the years, in the logic of the Cold War.[49] It was based in the desire of Indian nationalists to make India into a strong, independent modern nation-state on the world stage. The Cold War certainly gave an added impetus to this policy. Nonalignment was meant to free India from entanglements, offer no opportunity for others to threaten its security, promote its economic and technological development, and provide maximum freedom of action to pursue its national interest. Nehru explained that this was not a passive or neutral pursuit of interest. India intended to retain flexibility and autonomy to define its interests independent from external pressures, to win the goodwill of neighbors, and to earn prestige by contributing to world peace. Although nonalignment claimed moral high ground, Nehru insisted it was embedded in a realistic view of India's power and requirements.

Nehru's decision to adopt nonalignment did not go unquestioned even in the early days of Independence. Many in the Congress party and the country felt that alignment with the United States would have been a better course given the hostility of Pakistan and the Soviet Union. More recently, nonalignment has been subjected to severe criticism for being too idealistic and for failing to protect India from Pakistan and China.[50] The Kashmir issue was not resolved. Pakistan moved into the U.S.-led military alliance and continued to seek a change in the status quo in Kashmir. Nonalignment therefore failed to keep the Cold War out of the subcontinent. It did not convince China that India was not an enemy. After the 1962 Sino-Indian border war, the doubling of defense expenditures also restricted the freedom to pursue modernization through economic development.

These setbacks to India's security have led many to argue that Nehru ignored the region and did not build up an Indocentric foreign policy. What this means is that Nehru ignored military defense and focused excessively on building an impregnable moral position through the exercise of impartiality to shield India from external pressures and incursions. Nonalignment landed India in a predicament where it was left alone to suffer the consequences of its weakness. India would have been better off building its defenses simply to reduce the possibility of war with China and joining one of the two sides in the Cold War rivalry.

Nehru could hardly have been unaware of the risks inherent in his policy, and the alternatives to it. He could hardly have failed to recognize that there is not one but two ways to secure complete immunity from external intrusion into domestic affairs: 1) to stay away from everyone, or 2) to go completely under the umbrella of one superpower (preferably the stronger one) and rely on it to shield India from intrusion. This, after all, is what Japan and Taiwan and most of Southeast Asia did with complete success. Why did he not do the obvious: join the Western alliance and gain arms and developmental assistance?

A large part of the answer is that the option was never there. Files of official correspondence from Lord Pethick Lawrence, secretary of state for India, to Lord Wavell, the viceroy in the India office record's library in London, show that once Partition had been decided, Britain quietly decided that Pakistan was the essential component in its policy of containment of the Soviet Union—a policy that it transferred in its entirety to the United States.[51] Had India joined the Western alliance, it is more than likely that Pakistan would have turned to the Soviet Union. This would have unacceptably damaged the Anglo-American grand design, by giving the Soviet Union access to the warm waters of the Indian Ocean.

However, an important part of Nehru's reluctance to explore this possibility stemmed from his belief that nonalignment was a surer way of shielding India, because the high profile it enabled him to acquire for his country abroad increased his autonomy in subjugating ethnonational impulses at home, thus preserving the internal balance. Nehru was loathe to go down the path that many accused Indira Gandhi of following in domestic politics two decades later. He was aware that joining a military alliance would mean militarization. This would eat into resources for development and, if India joined the Western alliance, would increase the possibility of conflict with China.[52]

Militarization and the need for increased control on India's borders could lead to political centralization and increasing rigidity in dealings with India's ethnonational entities. The room for accommodation would decrease. This would jeopardize the nationalist leadership's vision of a stable and democratic India.

The state-centered nationalism of Nehru and Patel permitted use of force and coercion to consolidate India but force had to be used sparingly. A country of India's size and diversity could be managed only by persuasion and negotiation, occasionally backed by coercion. The Congress movement had been the dominant cohering force for more than seventy years. The subcontinental spread and organization of the Congress party, as well as the vitality of its regional leaders and activists, could be deployed to create a political steel frame that would bind India's disparate nations together.

Chapter 3

✻

NARRATIVES OF ETHNIC NATIONS
The Sikhs, Kashmiris, and Tamils

How have India's ethnonationalists interpreted their inheritance from history? Do these narratives complement or oppose the concept of a multinational India? And what role have these divergent narratives played in defining relational control and balance of interlocking interests? It has been argued so far that formation of India's policy in South Asia has been shaped by the domestic objective of making India a modern nation-state. This task, which Nehru and his colleagues set themselves, did not go unopposed.

The partition of the subcontinent, and the way this sowed the seed of Sikh and Tamil separatist demands, has already been described. Subsequent measures to integrate India, by building institutional structure to give shape to her unity, temporarily defused these demands but did not eliminate them. In 1953, Sheikh Abdullah began to raise the issue of independence for Kashmir, and had to be removed from office. By the mid fifties, only a few years after India's Independence, Sikh and Tamil ethnonationalism surfaced again, this time as a demand for greater autonomy. Since then, the tides of ethnonationalism have ebbed and flowed in Indian politics. This chapter will provide a brief sketch of the three nationalisms to juxtapose them with the nationalist vision of a unified India. Of particular importance is the way history has been used to construct opposing narratives that empower ethnic communities against the supranational State.

Such "narrativization of history" has several purposes: to provide a coherent story of origin and evolution to the community, to inculcate pride and provide an ideological anchor, to consolidate and unify the ethnic community around a particular objective or program, and to claim a specific social space for ethnic community in relation to the larger space of other ethnonations and the supranational State. The theoretical chapter has stressed that the truth or historical accuracy of these narratives are not important.[1] What is relevant for our purposes, is the Tamils' belief that they are a "unique nation"; the Sikhs' belief that they are not Hindus; and the Kashmiri Muslims' belief that they still have a right to self-determination. These perceptions have had a profound impact on the nationality formation among these communities.

Do narratives create the sense of unique peoplehood or do cultural markers—differences in language, custom, or religion—create the impetus for distinctive ethnic narratives? Scholars disagree about what came first. Some have argued that narratives are created because of objective differences of culture, economy, and place in the larger society. Others suggest that such objective distinctions are not important in themselves. Perceptions of differences in relation with others, whether that other is the state or a rival ethnic community, is what shapes ethnic identity. For the purposes of this study, their origins are less important than the fact that their narratives reinforce and shape responses to challenges from outside the community. Narratives then set ethnic boundaries, the lines that separate one ethnic community from its cultural rival. These self histories are emphasized in this chapter because they shape one dimension of the interlocking balance, the interaction between an ethnic nationality and India's central state. The narrative of the central State was discussed in the previous chapter.

The relationship between ethnic nation and territorial nation-state is dialectical. Each phase of conflict and cooperation leads to further "thickening" of ethnic identity that change the subsequent interaction. Objective distinctions that define an ethnic community—language, origin, religion, or traditions—do not by themselves explain the tensions that exist between two proximate ethnic communities or between the supranational State and its nesting nationalities. Nationality formation generally passes through three stages:[2] in the first stage, the group is distinguishable from the outside because of its obvious cultural markers but members of that group do not perceive these markers as politically significant. Such groups are "ethnic categories." In the second stage, groups become conscious of distinctions, and use them to demand superior or equal share of economic goods and political status. Brass uses the term "communities" to distinguish these groups from the less self-conscious ethnic categories. The third stage is reached when the ethnic community demands a right to self-determination, based on recognition for the group as a whole. Ethnic communities become, at that point, a distinct nationality. The Sikh and the Kashmiri nationalism had reached the third stage in the early and late 1980s respectively

Whether one begins with the colonial period or the postcolonial period, the central Indian state has been pivotal in transforming ethnic categories into self-conscious ethnic nationalities. Urmila Phadnis makes this point in regard to South Asia. According to her, a state which arrogates more and more legislative, executive, judicial, and coercive powers to itself, and attempts by preemption of such powers to homogenize the population within its domain, will unleash countermobilization of ethnic identities.[3] One might point out that the Sikh identity was forged on the anvil of the hostile Mughal state. The nineteenth-century struggles to acquire control of the Gurdwaras (the Sikh religious temples) in the teeth of opposition by the Hindu Mahants and the British authorities were subsequently critical to the formation of Sikh identity. The British policy of recruiting Sikhs to the Indian army for their "martial spirit" and characterizing them as a warrior race had much to do with the later popular image of the Sikhs as fearless and brave people. Sant Bhindranwale, the Sikh militant leader in the 1980s, drew on these popular images of martyrdom and sacrifice to recruit Sikhs to his separatist cause.

Much the same can be said about the struggles for power between the Dogra kings in Kashmir and the Kashmiri Muslims. The British preference for Sri Lankan Tamils in civil service and Indian Tamils on the plantations was an important cause of later Sinhala-Tamil conflict in independent Sri Lanka. Structural causes of conflict are always important; that cannot be denied. But they have to be interpreted as such and linked to the struggle for separate identity of ethnic communities. Histories of struggles are central to nationality formations. And almost always, struggles are against a dominant political authority and rival ethnic community.

Nevertheless, there is a qualitative difference between modern and premodern conflicts between Tamils and Sinhalas, Kashmiri Muslims and Hindus, and Hindus and Sikhs. The quest for ethnic recognition is properly a part of the era of nationalism, the transformations that have swept South Asia in its encounter with the West. All three ethnonationalisms—Sikh, Kashmiri, and Tamil—have been wrought by colonial transformations of the Indian subcontinent: the introduction of modern education, competition for the civil service and armed forces and, most importantly, growing awareness of ideas of equality, political rights and representation.[4]

Nationalist Themes in the Sikh Narrative

The Sikh identity has evolved largely around two historical axes.[5] The first is spiritual and begins with the founding of the Sikh faith by Guru Nanak (1469–1538) and his nine successors. The religious pillar of Sikh identity was based on the founders' teachings and establishment of congregation (Sangats), by their setting up of sacred points such as Govindwal and Amritsar, and by the compilation by Guru Arjan, the fifth Guru, of the anthology that ultimately became the Granth Sahib, the sacred scripture of the community.[6] The Sikh confessional identity became sharply defined in the period of the tenth Guru, Gobind Singh. He abolished the institution of the Gurus and vested power and responsibility for the protection of the community in the Khalsa, the Sikh brotherhood. He also established a new code of conduct, initiation rites and oath of allegiance to the Khalsa. This codification of the Sikh beliefs, glorification of the sacrifice and martyrdom, the tradition of Miri-Piri (the identity of the religious and temporal), was the distinct contribution of the last Guru.

The Mughals had subjected the Sikhs to relentless prosecution and pogroms. The massacre of thousands of Sikhs in the Chotta Gallughara (the small holocaust) of 1746 and Vadda Gallughara (large-scale killings sixteen years later) underline the themes of valor and shahidi (the martyrdom). Wars with the Mughals and later the Afghan invaders were the crucible that formed the Sikh identity and response: Sikh attraction for theocratic militarism. The second axis of Sikh identity was temporal, provided by the founding of the Sikh kingdom in 1801 by Maharajah Ranjit Singh, who abolished the Misl system (a confederacy of twelve mutually warring petty Sikh kingdoms) and established the first unified territorial states of the Sikhs.

Several themes of this early history have embedded themselves in the collective consciousness of the Sikhs and ipso facto placed them in a position of potential confrontation with the Indian nation-state. The most significant among these is the theme of "Raj Karega Khalsa," the destined rule of the orthodox Sikh brotherhood. Two meanings have been attached to this slogan. In one the "rule" is not meant to be temporal and territorial, but is a reference to the spiritual triumph of the religious belief, of the true believer over heretics and apostates. The second is interpreted to mean establishment of a separate Sikh state, a culmination of the theocratic militarism embedded in the Guru Gobind Singh's call to the Sikhs. This ambiguity provides the Sikh leaders with room for maneuver but is also a source of serious misunderstanding and confusion between Hindus and Sikhs in Punjab. For instance, the Anandpur Sahib resolution passed by the Shiromani Akali Dal in October

1973 states that "the Sikhs of India are a historically recognized political nation ever since the inauguration of the order of the Khalsa in the concluding years of the 17th century." It goes on to claim juridical status by asserting that "this status of the Sikh Nation has been internationally recognized." What stands between the Sikhs and full nationhood is the "brute majority of India" which imposed a "constitutional arrangement" that "denuded the Sikhs of their political identity and cultural particularity" and as a consequence "liquidating the Sikhs politically and exposing them to spiritual death." The resolution further proclaimed that "the Sikhs are determined, by all legitimate means, to extricate and free themselves from this degrading . . . situation" and assert their "birth right to influence" the "world history" of the Sikhs.[7] This resolution could be interpreted as a clarion call for secession or as a claim of a nesting nation to equal social and cultural status within the framework of the federal India.

During the 1980s, many Punjabi Hindus began to reinterpret the events of the 1940s and found in the present demand for Khalistan a continuation of the past demand for a separate Sikhistan. Many believe the demand for a separate state in the 1940s was an attempt to fulfill the promise of the Gurupanth; others reject this and argue that the call for Sikhistan was merely an attempt to rally the Sikhs around their nishan (flag) and their Gurdwaras, so they would be able to withstand the tragedy of partition. A strict adherence to the Khalsa, the path of the pure, has frequently meant exclusion of rival Sikh sects—of the Namdhari and Nirankaris—from the Sikh religious mainstream. The first step in Bhindranwale's movement for Khalistan was to attack the Nirankaris because, according to him, they were heretics, even worse then Hindus. The Nirankari sect was founded in the early nineteenth century and was a midway order between Hindu and Sikh religions. According to a pamphlet published by the Shiromani Gurdwara Prabhandak Committee (the SGPC) on the Sikh–Nirankari conflict, the sect fell into corrupt ways and began to undermine the Khalsas. The SGPC pamphlet claimed that the government of India deliberately encouraged the Nirankaris to pollute the Pure Khalsa. In the Akali Dal and SGPC discourse, the Nirankaris were "yet another element in the Hindu conspiracy to destroy the separate identity of Sikhism, and thereby prevent the emergence of a true Khalsa Raj."[8] The notion of Khalsa was meant to impose religious orthodoxy, to homogenize the Sikh community, and to eliminate or marginalize challenges from within the religious tradition.

The second theme is that Khalsa must always be ready to fight injustice and persecution[prosecution]. The lives, experiences, and martyrdom of the Gurus, and the tradition of Miri-Piri are frequently cited to exhort the Sikhs to stand up against perceived oppression. The Sikh doctrine of Miri-Piri upholds the indivisibility of the religious and political power. This belief is represented in the Sikh emblem (nishan) in which the double edged sword signifying the purity of faith is shielded by two protecting swords (kirpans). The doctrine implies the supremacy of religion and an absence of autonomy for political things. Government is legitimate so long as it remains just.

This convergence of the religious and political immediately places the Sikh community in potential conflict with the official policy of secularism espoused by the Indian nationalists. If the Indian national government was perceived as just, conflict could be avoided. But the Sikhs' penchant for interpreting politics in religious terms made separation extremely difficult, once government's actions were seen to be, or interpreted as, oppressive and anti-Sikh.

This became the principal hurdle why the Sikhs remained inconsolable after Mrs. Gandhi sent the Indian army into the Golden Temple on June 6, 1984. In interviews/discussions I had in Amritsar, Sikh leaders and militant students made continuous references to the Shahidi of Guru Arjan and Gobind Singh—their brave defiance of the mighty Mughals. It was impossible to ignore their use of history as metaphor. They meant to convey that the past was somehow repeating itself, that the Sikhs have known such oppression from New Delhi before and had the strength and determination to struggle until they were free.

There was also considerable drawing on the folklore and legendary exploits of the other martyr figures in Sikh history. Robin Jeffrey and Joyce Pettigrew also confirm this heavy hand of history on the collective consciousness of the Sikhs. Jeffrey comments how "astonished" he was "at the ways in which Sikh politicians found it especially necessary to invoke the past—and to portray past events in a way that did not correspond to any documentary evidence I had seen." Jeffrey distinguishes between what he calls the academic history from rhetorical history of Punjab. His definition of the latter echoes the belief in this book, that such narratives need not stand up to the test of historic accuracy.[9] That is not their purpose. The student informants in Amritsar found it easy to move between the past and the present. It was clear that they were using the imagined past to justify the present, and to reconstruct their identities in the context of new developments. But such construction had to return again and again to the two historical axes of their Sikh identity.

The texts of various resolutions passed by segments of the radicalized Sikh community throughout the 1980s—at the December 1985 Gurumata of the Shahidi Samagam, at the Sarbat Khalsa (meeting of all Khalsa Sikhs) called by the All India Sikh Student's Federation (AISSF) at Akal Takht (seat of Sikh power in Amritsar) in January 1986, and the April 13, 1986, declaration on Khalistan (also passed at the Akal Takht), describe the present in terms of the themes of the past. The resolution on Khalistan opens with the reference to the founding of the Khalsa in 1699. and Guru Gobind Singh's "dictum, Raj Karega Khalsa" (the Khalsa's shall rule forever) and declares that, in announcing the creation of Khalistan, the panthic committee was "fulfilling the most cherished dream of the Sikhs."[10] "We have to act; words are not enough," said Jarnail Singh Bhindranwale in one of his taped speeches sold outside the Golden temple. Elsewhere he wrote, "Here you raise your sword but tomorrow you may dust the chappals of Bibi Indira."[11] He frequently made references to the Nehru family's Brahmin Hindu origins in order to tap the traditional Sikh suspicion of caste Hindus. In the Punjab countryside, these two castes are regarded as devious and exploitative. These references recall the egalitarian anti-caste beliefs of the Sikhs and their history of struggle against rulers in New Delhi.

The third theme derived from history is the belief that bravery and martyrdom are the hallmarks of a true Sikh. Pettigrew reports a conversation with Bhindranwale in which he calls on Sikhs not to fear reprisals and not to succumb to the lure of office. "Unless you are prepared to sacrifice your own life, you cannot be a free people."[12] The fourth theme identified the main enemy of the Sikhs: Since the days of the Mughals, it was the "throne" of Delhi that had been the main source of "treachery" against the Sikhs. The resolution passed at the Sarbat Khalsa (the congregation of the Sikhs) at the Damdami Taksal (Gurdwara at Damdama) and the All India Sikh Students federation (AISSF) on April 13, 1986, noted that "today the Sikhs are shackled by chains of slavery . . . To smash these chains Sikhs . . . by . . . reasoning and . . . force . . . have to defeat the communal Brahmin-bania combine that controls the Delhi Darbar. This is the only way of establishing the hegemony of Sikhism in this country."[13] This hegemony was defined as a combination of India's poor led by the Khalsa. The stress on Brahmin- Bania combine and Delhi Darbar was a sarcastic reference to the dominance of the Brahmins in the government and the fact that all the first four prime ministers of India were Brahmins.

As mentioned earlier, the territorial claims of Khalistan or Sikhistan are highly problematic. Raja Ranjit Singh's kingdom was headed by a Sikh ruler. Sikhs gained in power and positions during his reign, but the boundaries of the empire included several other nationalities and cultural communities from areas that were overwhelmingly Hindu (in the cis-Sutlej region), to others, that were overwhelmingly Muslim (in the trans-Jhelum and Multan

regions).[14] Ranjit Singh's rule replicated the model of unification and governance practiced by all the subcontinental empires in India. This was apparent
in his choice of key advisers, many of whom were Hindus. Sikh historians disagree about how to interpret the contribution of the Sikh kingdom.
Khushwant Singh believes that Ranjit Singh "took Sikhism back towards
Hinduism by making obeisance to Brahmin priests, worshiping in Hindu
temples, and going on pilgrimages to Hardwar."[15] Leftist Sikh scholars criticize the kingdom and Ranjit Singh for breaking with the tradition of Sarbat
Khalsa or collective decision making.[16]

Although Ranjit Singh's kingdom laid the material and territorial basis[17]
for the notion of the Sikh homeland, the Sikh principalities (Misls) in the Cis-
Sutlej territories, had remained outside his jurisdiction. By no stretch of the
imagination is it possible to claim the rule of Khalsa to be identical with the
kingdom. It neither established dominance of the Khalsa nor provided a compact, coherent territorial base for the ethnically defined Sikh community.
Nevertheless, it played a critical, symbolic role in the confrontational discourse between the contemporary nationalists and Sikh separatists. For
instance, during the 1985 election campaign, Rajiv Gandhi taunted the Sikh
militants by reminding them that the seat of the Sikh kingdom was in Lahore
and they were welcome to establish a separate state there.

Ranjit Singh's kingdom disintegrated shortly after his death. Following
the Anglo-Sikh wars, the British annexed it in 1849. The construction of Sikh
identity during the colonial era (1849–1947) is decisive from our point of
view, not only because in many ways it differed from the self-images in the
earlier eras, but also because this identity remains intact to this day. Harjot
Oberoi writes that at "the start of this period it was possible to be an Udasi,
Nirmala, Suthresashi, . . . or a votary of a Muslim Pir . . . and still be considered a Sikh."[18] He stresses the tolerance accorded to a heterogeneity of
religious beliefs, rituals, and diversity of lifestyles within the community. In
the same passage Oberoi writes, that a variety of mediums such as "myths,
texts, narratives, folklore and plays -produced by non-Sikh authors were
accorded a firm place within the Sikh cosmology." By the closing decades of
this phase, successive waves of Sikh reform, spearheaded by institutions like
the Singh Sabha, Chief Khalsa Diwan, and Akali "combatants of the 1920s,
had expelled most of these older conventions and practices."

The British had emerged as the paramount power in the subcontinent by
1900, Sikh temporal power had collapsed, and its adherents were rapidly
merging into the larger Hindu society. The economic and political transformations—the introduction of new agrarian system of ownership, settle-

ment, revenue, and irrigation—demanded a new response from the Sikh community. It came in terms of reform movements that drew sharp boundaries around the Sikhs and established the modern institutional framework to consolidate this identity. The twentieth century brought the devolution of power to Indians by the British colonial authorities. It also saw the beginning of nationalist movement. English-educated Sikhs and Hindus scrambled for posts in the newly formed provincial administration. The competition for political patronage and office brought with it the beginning of communal politics. This was a new element in the definition of Sikh identity in Punjab. It was being defined in context of the we/they dichotomy in which the Sikh leaders were stridently claiming that they were not Hindus ("Hum Hindu Nahin"). But they did not share the Muslim political world view either. To that extent then they found some common ground with the anti-Muslim platform of the Hindu communal organizations in Punjab. The whole issue had become critical because the British had recognized the Muslims as a distinct community, - but their position on the Sikhs was ambivalent. At stake were separate electorates, jobs and recruitment to the armed forces. This added further fuel to the fire of ethnic and religious tension in Punjab.

The 1920s saw a sharpening of the Sikh self-image and a further distancing of the community from the Hindus. This process also divided the Khalsa from the non-Khalsa Sikhs. Although a younger generation of Sikhs joined the nationalist movement, Sikh participation initially was eclipsed by concerns over management and control of the Sikh temples or Gurdwaras. Many Gurdwaras had been under the control of non-Khalsa Sikhs and Hindu Mahants (managers) who nominated their own successors. There was considerable misuse of funds and abuse of trust, and this provided a convenient focus for the Khalsas who made a bid for control on the grounds that they wanted to purge their places of worship of such hypocritical elements. The activities of the Hindu Arya Samajists in Punjab, including their aggressive shuddhi movement in which they urged Sikhs and Muslims to come back to the Hindu fold, increased Sikh self-awareness and created tensions between them and the Arya Samajis.[19] This period witnessed the creation of Shiromani Akali Dal, the political wing of the SGPC. The most notable success of this new phase of Sikh mobilization was the enactment of the Sikh Gurdwara act of 1925 which ceded control of the temples to the SGPC. Henceforth, Sikh ethnonationalism had a sound financial base and its longevity was assured.

Had Punjab not been partitioned, the balance between Muslims, Hindus, and Sikhs might have proved durable. The Sikhs were the fewest in number, but compensated for this by holding a disproportionate share of economic power as the principal landowners. This balance between Hindu, Sikh, and Muslim communities was reflected in the Unionist party, which dominated Punjab politics in the 1940s. But the unionists were brought down by a burst of Muslim League inspired communal violence in March 1947. Partition followed, and approximately half of the Sikhs found themselves uprooted from their homeland that was now a part of Pakistan.

Partition changed the demography of Indian Punjab radically. The Sikhs in Indian Punjab formed 33 percent of the population against their previous 20 percent, but the Hindus increased from their earlier share of around 30 percent to 66 percent in Punjab. More important was the fact that a three-way equation had been turned into a two-way Hindu-Sikh equation. The Sikh could no longer safeguard their position by playing the balancing role, as they had done before, in the Unionist Party in undivided Punjab.[20]

A short while after Partition, the demand for a Sikh homeland resurfaced. After great reluctance, Nehru conceded to the demand for linguistic states in 1956, but the Linguistic Reorganization Commission actually enlarged Punjab by including within it Himachal Pradesh and the remaining princely states. Paradoxically, the enlargement of Punjab increased the Sikhs's sense of being a minority, and strengthened the demand for Punjabi Suba, requiring yet another redrawing of the boundaries to give Sikhs a majority in the new state. This was eventually conceded in 1966.

Things should have ended here but the after shocks of partition continued to reverberate. In the early 1970s, the Akalis began to put forward fresh demands for a Sikh homeland. These demands were partly in response to government mishandling of the situation in Punjab and Congress party's machinations against the Akalis who were grappling with a fundamental shift in power from the traders to Jat peasants in their community. This shift had been caused by the previous decade of Green Revolution in agriculture. A more detailed examination of government mishandling is presented in chapter 6. Here it is enough to note that history was rewritten once again to accommodate these changes. The SGPC and Sikh communities abroad (in the United States and Canada) began to argue that the Akalis had agreed to the union with India only because the Congress had promised to give them special status and a large degree of autonomy within Punjab. Others argued that contemporary Sikh politicians were misinterpreting the statements of Nehru and the Congress leadership. The Akalis retorted that the British government had offered Sikhs a homeland but the Sikhs nobly refused the offer after assurances from Nehru and the Congress. Robin Jeffrey says that he found the details of this "rhetorical history" (the account of Sikh acquiescence) inaccurate and without documentary evidence.[21]

Several inferences can be drawn from the above brief sketch of the Sikh history: First, the ethnic story of the Sikhs is inextricably tied to the events in the subcontinent, particularly the policies of the colonial and the independent Indian state. It is not possible to separate the elements—the chain of cause and effect in Sikh nationality formation—that are external (i.e., decisions of the supranational State) to the community, from those that are arguably internal (i.e., factional fights and personality conflicts within the Community) to it. The Mughals, the invading Afghan raiders, the British, the Indian National Congress, the Arya Samaj (a nineteenth-century Hindu reform movement that got large numbers of converts among Punjab Hindus), and the Muslim League—all shaped and contributed to the Sikh political identity.

Second, this identity does not easily separate religion from politics. The religious heritage is capable of producing diverse responses. Sikhism contains a quietist, devotional, pacifist tradition associated with Guru Nanak and the first five Gurus. But there is also the theocratic militancy associated with Guru Gobind Singh. It is this theocratic strand—the Khalsa, the order of the pure—that has prevailed in shaping the modern Sikh ethnonationality.

Third, the notion of the Khalsa is not territorial but doctrinal, rooted in the community and faith, not the state. According to Joyce Pettigrew, a relationship between land, territory, and people does not exist in Sikh theology in the way one finds them in Judaism. "Territory," she says, "cannot be a focal point of nationalist movement" for the Sikhs. "Sikhism does not lend itself easily to the formation of the state, and it is very difficult to equate peoplehood and nationality in their case."[22] Harjot Oberoi concurs with this interpretation.

Fourth, if the territory is problematic, so is the notion of the Khalsa. The Khalsa does not include all the adherents of the Sikh faith. "Their numbers were fluid, their numerical strength derived from converts from the Hindu community, and they relapsed into the Hindu community from time to time. Besides, even as members of the Khalsa, Sikhs followed many of the practices, customs, and traditions of the Hindus and continued to be bound to the Hindus by ties of kinship and marriage."[23]

The Sikh identity is then variable. The precise origins of Hindu–Sikh tensions remain indeterminate in history although we know the elements that shaped them. On the basis of caste, religion, language, and regional variations, the Sikhs are divided from within. The conflict between Nirankaris and Khalsas has already been mentioned. Although the Sikh faith rejects castes, the Sikh community is divided in terms of Jats, and lower castes of Mazhabis, Ramgharias, and untouchables. These lower castes preferred the Congress to the Akalis in numerous electoral contests until the Operation Blue Star in June 1984, and the sudden rupture that followed between the Congress and its Sikh constituents. The internal diversity of the Sikh community has been exacerbated by competitive party politics and divergent economic interests. It is extremely difficult to realize the cherished dream of "Raj karega Khalsa" if this is to be interpreted in territorial terms.

Given the nature of Sikh ethnonationalism, the supranational State could, in theory, have followed one of two approaches to its absorption into the modern state. One possible approach was to concede most of the economic and social demands of the community, share power in Punjab, and concentrate on persuading the community leaders to separate politics from religion, at least in practice. The second approach was to divide the community, co-opt a large segment into the Congress fold, and thereby weaken the base of the more hard-line advocates of ethnic separatism. When neither approach worked, negotiations gave way to confrontations. However, such confrontations did not have to spill over into the international arena. The movement for Punjabi Suba launched by the Akali leaders in the 1960, and the protests against centralizing policies of the Indira Gandhi government during the 1970s enshrined in the Anandpur Sahib resolution, did not involve Pakistan. Only in the '80s did the Sikh struggle for self-assertion became internationalized, with Pakistan intruding in what until then had been a two-way encounter.[24]

The Sikh historical narratives have nurtured the quest for a separate identity, but the precise identity of a homeland has continued to elude the Sikh separatists, because a majority of the Sikhs in Punjab have never seriously entertained the prospects of separation from India. These contradictions have, nevertheless, posed a permanent challenge to the Indian state and its strategy of relational control.

Themes in Kashmiri Nationalism

There are at least three different versions of Kashmiri history that have shaped the substance and direction of its nationalism.[25] In one, Kashmiri culture is perceived as unique, distinctive, and separate from that of its neighboring regions. Kashmiri Islam is totally different from the practice of Islam in Pakistan, as the former's origins are to be found in the Sufi and Rishi traditions and not in the Wahaby Sunni tradition of the Islam of Pakistan and large parts of India. The nationalist movement against Dogra rule, led by Sheikh Abdullah and the National Conference party and, half a century later, the movement for self-determination led by the Jammu and Kashmir Liberation Front, drew on this tradition. In the second version, Kashmiri identity is defined by virtue of the majority of the population being Muslim. It is argued by a small but highly vocal and now armed (with the help of Pakistan) segment of Kashmiris that Kashmir rightly belongs in Pakistan and that the partition of 1947 has left this matter unresolved. In the third, Kashmir's common, historic bonds with India and Hindu culture are stressed. In this version, Kashmir's tolerant and humane definition of Islam comes not only from its Sufi origins but from its permeation by Hindu customs and traditions. Kashmir's unique religion and culture can therefore be best preserved in a secular and democratic India. This view is held by Kashmir's Hindu population, some fraction of the Valley Muslims, and the vast majority of people in India. From time to time, it has also been espoused by various National Front leaders (i.e., Farooq Abdullah, J&K's chief minister in 1980s) and those of the Hindu parties in Jammu. For the sake of clarity, the first can be called a Kashmiri nationalist, the second an Islamist, and the third an Indian version of Kashmir's identity.

These conflicting narratives have been fiercely debated since the 1931 popular agitation in Kashmir against Dogra rule, and with greater urgency in 1946 and 1947, when the Hindu–Muslim divide deepened in the subcontinent. They were directly responsible for the armed clash between the emerging states of India and Pakistan on the eve of Independence, and then again in 1965. The Islamist narrative has constituted the subtext of all discussions of Kashmir in international forums ever since India took the Kashmir dispute to the Security Council in 1947. A large number of scholars in the West and a majority of journalists have seen the Kashmir problem as strictly a Hindu–Muslim problem. In this characterization, they have ignored the regional, ethnic, and even religious divisions within the Indian Kashmir. Instead, the paradigm of partition, that asserted the separate identity of the Hindu and Muslim nations, has dominated their thinking about the Kashmir dispute. The insurgency that began in 1989 over the status of Kashmir centered on conflict between the Kashmiri nationalist and the Indian versions of the past. This has been complicated by the conflict between the pro-independence nationalists and the pro-Pakistani Islamist Kashmiris.

The relationship between the supranational Indian State and Kashmir is different from that between it and other ethnonationalities. While the valley of Kashmir, which has slightly more than half of the population of the state, can be identified as an ethnonational unit (of which both the Kashmiri pandits and the Muslim are an integral part), the people of the whole of the state cannot. The Indian state of J&K consists of three distinct regions: the valley of Kashmir, which is predominantly Muslim and accounts for the bulk of the population of the state; Jammu, which has a Hindu majority but also includes a significant Muslim minority, and Ladakh, which is sparsely populated and, unlike Jammu and the valley, is mainly Buddhist. Kashmir is also a multilingual state.[26] Sheikh Abdullah's *New Kashmir* plan acknowledged several languages—Dogri, Punjabi, Urdu, Kashmiri, Balti—as the state languages. There is marked disparity in economic potential and development in the three regions. Kashmir lacks the compact, cultural homogeneity of other regions, i.e., Tamil Nadu. Any single linguistic or religious criterion of nationalism will exclude others who are now part of the J&K. This diversity has required Kashmiri nationalists to construct composite and syncretic accounts of historic and cultural unity.

Kashmir's territorial identity is equally problematic. The kingdom of Kashmir was the creation of the British. After the defeat of Sikh armies in 1846, the British imperial and strategic interests required establishment of regional rulers (under their paramountcy) who would act as a bulwark against revival of Sikh power, maintain stability in the entire tribal zone stretching all across what is now Indo-Chinese border to Baltistan, and serve as a buffer against China, Russia, and Afghanistan. For this purpose, the British separated Kashmir and the hill states from Punjab, from the Indus to the Beas, and transferred them to Gulab Singh as a separate sovereign territory for the sum of 75 Lakhs of rupees. There was no "natural" ethnic or linguistic unity to these territories.[27]

Kashmir's territorial status was altered again in 1947 when the British decided to transfer power to Pakistan and India. According to the India Independence Act of 1947, the princes were free to choose independence or cede to one of the successor states. Maharajah Hari Singh of Kashmir wanted independence but lacked the military and political power to make it a reality. Under the leadership of the National and Muslim Conference parties, Kashmiri masses had been agitating to depose the maharajah since the early 1940s.[28] While the internal situation was unsettled, the partition and the Hindu–Muslim riots made it impossible for Hari Singh to remain independent. Pakistan claimed Kashmir on the basis of its two-nation theory while India was reluctant to help the maharajah without Kashmir's accession to the Union. In October 1947, when Pakistani raiders infiltrated into Kashmir followed by Pakistani regular forces, the maharajah hastily acceded to India in return for military support against the invading forces. At the conclusion of the armed confrontation in 1949, Kashmir was divided by a cease-fire line into the Pakistan Occupied Kashmir (POK) and the Indian state of J&K. Sheikh Abdullah and his National Conference agreed to the instruments of accession with the condition that India would grant the state a large degree of autonomy, an arrangement that was subsequently formalized in the Delhi agreement of 1952 and article 370 of the Indian constitution.[29] In effect, India had recognized that Kashmir would exercise control over all subjects except on matters relating to foreign affairs, defense, and communication; in return for article 370, Sheikh Abdullah would accept the accession as final. But the legitimacy of Kashmiri consent, enshrined in the Delhi agreement was periodically questioned even by one of its chief architects, Sheikh Abdullah.

The post-1950s internal polarization within Kashmir is equally important to the formation of the Kashmir narrative. It must be stressed that with or without Sheikh Abdullah, the National Conference has dominated Kashmiri politics, particularly in the valley, while the Jammu Hindus have been divided between Praja Parishad (closely linked to the Hindu Mahasabha, the RSS, and more recently the BJP in India), and the Congress. Ladakh and Jammu (and not just the Hindu segment of the population) have resented the domination of National Conference and complained of "regional imbalances" in distribution of resources, employment, and educational opportunities. These regions would prefer to be integrated within India and regard the Conference as anti-Hindu and anti-India. By the same token, the Muslim Conference party before and after Partition has had closer links with the Muslim League (in the 1940s) and later Jama'at-i-Islami and other similar forces in Pakistan. The National Conference's position in Kashmiri politics, which can be summed up as "autonomy within a federal India," is defined by the positions of the other political entities in the state: the Islamic pro-Pakistani position of the Muslim Conference in its various incarnations and the pro-integrationist position of the parties in Jammu and Ladakh.

Pakistan's claims regarding Kashmir have not changed since the 1940s, but its enthusiasm for altering the status quo by diplomacy and force has waxed and waned depending on the balance of Pakistan's domestic politics. This too has had a profound impact on the nationalist discourse in Kashmir. Pakistan joined the Western anti-Soviet containment alliance in the early 1950s and 1960s in order to deter India, and to maintain credibility for its position on Kashmir. The Western powers rewarded Pakistan with military assistance and diplomatic support over Kashmir. With the incorporation of Pakistan in the Western military alliance by the 1950s, India found it prudent to nurture its relations with the Soviet Union, which was only too eager to help with economic and military assistance to India. Indo–Soviet relations burgeoned into a close relationship by the early 1970s; they were however at a modest level in the 1950s and 1960s.

This situation was further complicated by the growing friendship between China and Pakistan, particularly after the 1962 Sino–Indian war. Pakistan signed a border agreement with China in November 1963, delimiting their mutual borders between Wakkhan and Taghdumbash Pamir. This agreement adversely affected the talks that had sparked some hope for greater amicability between India and Pakistan. The border agreement brought the talks to an abrupt halt. India claimed that Pakistan had illegally transferred 2,000 miles of territory which though "disputed" had originally belonged to the state of Jammu and Kashmir. The Wakkhan corridor, the strip of border between China and Afghanistan, actually belonged to the later but in the Pakistani seizure of northern territories in 1947, the exact status of this stretch of territory became controversial. Sheikh Abdullah also strongly protested against the Sino–Pakistan border agreement on the grounds that the Wakkhan corridor was originally a part of the kingdom of Kashmir. Since the latter's status was still to be settled, Pakistan had no right, he argued, to cede Kashmiri territory. The validity of these claims and counterclaims remains unsettled and, as in case of all the border disputes between India and its neighbors, subject to rival pre 1947 interpretation of British imperial policies.

Dispute over Kashmir led to a second war between India and Pakistan in 1965. Believing India to be in a state of disarray after Nehru's death in 1964, Pakistan made a second effort to wrest control by force.[30] The third Indo–Pakistani war was not over the Kashmir issue but after Pakistan's military rout in 1971, Indira Gandhi sought to settle the dispute once and for all. Kashmiri leaders were not party to the 1972 negotiations at Simla, where Mrs. Gandhi and Prime Minister Bhutto agreed to resolve Kashmir by bilateral negotiations, and promised to refrain from inviting third party mediation.[31]

Since the mid 1950s, the Indian state has never been wholly free from external pressures to work out a stable interlocking balance with Kashmir. Once India conceded that Kashmir was a disputed territory, Pakistan, China, the Soviet Union, and the United States became involved. India has tried to maintain the territorial status quo established in 1949. Pakistan has tried to undo this status quo by both conventional and unconventional means. It has brought the Kashmir dispute repeatedly before the United Nations to generate international pressure on India. It has enlisted diplomatic support from the United States and Britain to this end. It forged a close strategic relationship with China to intimidate India into a more accommodating stance. Failing in these, Pakistan has sought to foment a rebellion in Kashmir and provided logistical support and arms to Kashmiri separatists across the border. India has adhered more firmly to the status quo, sought to counter pressures from the United States and the United Nations, and progressively consolidated its control of politics inside the state of Jammu and Kashmir. Consolidation has inevitably meant loss of autonomy for the Kashmiris and their gradual integration into the Indian Union. Kashmiri nationalists have had little influence over the course of these developments, though they have been deeply affected by the changing balance of international forces around them. The Kashmiri perceptions of their own destiny has remained in a flux because of the shifting balance of political forces within and around Kashmir.

How have Kashmiri nationalist leaders sought to construct a coherent narrative in the face of such regional and territorial diversity, religious polarization, and international pressures? As mentioned earlier, there is no single narrative. Existing narratives have been recast to accommodate the evolving balance of political and social forces within Kashmir. Nevertheless, one might suggest that Sheikh Abdullah and his interpretation of history and Kashmiri identity represent the master narrative of Kashmiri nation. The salient points of this interpretation can be described as follows.[32]

The first theme is: Kashmir is a distinctive cultural entity that can be traced back to antiquity, but for several centuries it has been enslaved and oppressed by powers surrounding it. The Kashmiri struggle for self-determination and justice reaches back into the distant past.[33] In support of Kashmir's rich cultural heritage, Kashmiri nationalists stress the diverse streams of thought, philosophies and religions—Buddhism in the fourth century B.C., indigenous Kashmiri Shaivism, followed by Vaishnavite influences, and then Islam in the fourteenth century—that fed Kashmir and made it into a preeminent center of learning and arts. As evidence of Kashmir's long history of oppression and subjugation, Kashmiri nationalists stress the loss of freedom under the Mughal, Afghan, then Sikh rule, followed by the rule of the Dogra kings until 1947. The latter are portrayed as usurpers, foisted on the Kashmiri nation by the British imperialists. The Dogra kings are accused of vanity, greed, and indifference to the people. Most importantly, they are portrayed as being anti-Muslim when a majority of their subjects were Muslims. The Kashmiri Hindus, particularly the Pandits, are perceived as the privileged classes in this narrative. The nationalist history is rich with statistics and economic data supporting the charge that they have been discriminated against and exploited by the feudal classes foisted by imperialists and nurtured by its successors. The Hindu Brahmin elite is perceived as the compliant and selfish collaborators of the Dogra court, helping to perpetuate this historic injustice and oppression. The ideas of class conflict and imperialist exploitation find a place of pride in the nationalist discourse. Liberal democracy and the right to self-determination provide yet another source of identity formation. These strains of ideas have greatly impressed the intellectuals and educated among the Kashmiri leaders. Ideas of resistance derived from the Quran complete the circle by connecting their Islamic identity to their present situation. At least initially, the three streams of ideas merged to create a formidable opposition to the maharajah.

The mass upsurge of 1931 led by the Muslim Conference is fixed in the nationalist history as the date when the modern nation of Kashmir was born. The nationalists see the subsequent demand for self-determination and democracy as a natural outgrowth of the movement of 1931. Scholarly studies are however quick to point out that the Dogra state was not as coercive and repressive as the nationalist history suggests. By feudal standards, the Dogra rulers were fairly enlightened and tolerant. The landed Muslim classes were part of and were as supportive of the Dogra state as were its rich Hindu supporters. There was no Muslim "community" of interests nor were Muslim masses perennially alienated and disaffected from the Dogra dynasty. Most importantly, there was no Muslim middle class or a large educated elite that could have caused the 1931 upsurge. According to Zutshi, the causes of the upsurge are multiple, and embedded in the British colonial imperialism. "It is within this framework that a whole cobweb of . . . contradictions, and conflicts developed and resulted in the dawn of political awakening in Kashmir.[34]

If the first theme to nurture the Kashmiri nationalist is the struggle against imposition of outside rule, the second theme is the distinctive nature of Kashmiri Islam. Two arguments are important in this regard: the tolerant, religious humanism of Kashmiri Islam, and the composite nature of Kashmiri culture, which is the natural outcome of a humanist Islam. P. N. Bazaz writes that Kashmiri Islam was deeply influenced by the Sufi mystical, devotional tradition of Central Asia and Iran. According to P. N. K. Bamzai, "Kashmir thus became a meeting place of two . . . traditions—India's monistic wisdom-religion, Saivism and Efran, the wisdom of Quran." This "resulted in the emergence of a remarkable school of order of Islamic Sufis—the Rishis—who exerted enormous influence on the . . . people and set up the ideal of religious tolerance. As in religion so in philosophy, art, and literature Kashmir evolved a composite culture."[35] Kashmiri nationalists often quote Sir Walter Lawrence to show that Hindus and Muslims borrowed and imitated each other's customs and food habits to the point that orthodox Brahmins of India would have been horrified just as orthodox (meaning textual Quranic Islam) Muslims would have considered Kashmiris beyond the pale of their religion.

This theme is central to the construction of Kashmiri territorial nationalism. If the kingdom of Kashmir is to be the home of such a nation, then it must include Hindu and Buddhist populations within its fold. Even after the cease-fire in 1949, Kashmiri nationalism needed to reconcile Muslim, Hindu, and Buddhist claims on J&K's territory. This is the main reason why Sheikh Abdullah changed the name of the Muslim Conference to the National Conference in 1938 and redefined nationalist platform to be secular, socialist, and democratic. He was undoubtedly influenced by Nehru and Gandhi, but his choice was also dictated by the desire to make Kashmir a modern nation-state. The demand for Kashmiri self-determination was not confined to cultural and social freedom, at least not before the accession. Even then, Sheikh Abdullah continued to talk about making Kashmir an Asian Switzerland, independent but neutral. This same nationalistic impulse was evident in his 1946 New Kashmir plan, which defined Kashmir's problems in terms of exploitation of Hindu and Muslim masses and sought amelioration of their condition as Kashmiris. This perception was also one of the bases for two demands that have subsequently shaped the course of Kashmiri nationalism: article 370 of the Indian constitution that bars Indian citizens from acquiring property or settling down in Kashmir and, second, the delinking of Kashmiri Muslims from Muslims in India. Sheikh Abdullah maintained that Indian Muslims had no say in what Kashmiris ultimately decide for themselves.[36]

This interpretation was challenged continually from within and outside Kashmir. The pro-Pakistani, conservative and radical Islamic elements saw in the sheikh's stance a desire for personal power and worse, surrender to Hindu India. Pakistani leaders often called Sheikh Abdullah a "quisling" of India. They changed their assessment once he was arrested but until then Pakistan never forgave him for supporting Kashmir's accession to India. The Jammu Hindus, dominated in the 1950s and 1960s by Praja Parishad and, since the late 1980s, by radical parties such as the Jammu Mukti Morcha, Jammu Mahasabha, and Jammu People Front, also saw in his stance an attempt to deny Hindus any share of power in Kashmir.[37] Ironically enough, they see the National Conference leaders as potential fifth columnists who exploit India's fear of Kashmir's Muslim majority and of Pakistan to bilk New Delhi of large sums of money.

The third theme "explains" the legal basis of Kashmir's original decision and why this legal basis no longer applies. The Jammu and Kashmir Liberation Front (the JKLF) has put forward this justification to launch the armed insurgency against the Indian government. But even moderate leaders like Sheikh Abdullah had argued that the 1947 accession was a "temporary" agreement necessitated by the Pakistani invasion but that India "cleverly" turned that into a permanent situation. Despite this, the Kashmiri nation trusted India because the latter was committed to secularism, democracy, and federalism. Article 370 and the Delhi agreement thus became the basis of that union. This basis was progressively eroded, until only a skeleton of article 370 remained. The Indian arguments that subsequent tests at the polls legitimized the power arrangements are also rejected as fraudulent by the Kashmiri nationalists; they charge that the political parties that participated in the elections to the J&K's Constituent Assembly were dominated by the Congress party. In their view, the Kashmiris never consented to the progressive erosion of their autonomy.[38]

The refrain of betrayal by India, of promises broken, of leaders jailed, and of manipulation and interference in Kashmir's internal affairs, has grown shrill with the passage of time. As a subtext, economic discrimination, anti-Muslim bias in recruitment to central government and private sector jobs, nepotism, cronyism, and large-scale corruption have become part of the nationalist protest. Added since 1989 to this long list of grievances are human rights violations, charges of an indiscriminate search, molestation and rape, and the murder of civilians by the Indian security forces.

Religious identities are particularly significant in the competing discourses about Kashmiri identity. The slogan of "Islam in danger" has the potential for unleashing serious social disturbances within the J&K. This was evident in the 1963 episode involving the holy Mosque of Hazaratbal in Srinagar. The disappearance of the hair of the prophet Mohammed triggered riots and to the formation of the Awami Action committee led by the Mir Waiz of Kashmir, spiritual leader of the Muslims in the valley. More recently, several developments within and around Kashmir have strengthened the Islamic identity of the valley Muslims: the inspiration derived from the Islamic revolution in Iran, the emergence of militant Islamic groups fighting against the Soviet occupation of Afghanistan, and the enormous increase in the schools—madrasa and institutions geared to Islamic fundamentalist propaganda. Rajesh Kadian writes:

> Senior Indian officials began to notice the increasing number of Maulavis [Muslim religious leaders] from U.P. and Bihar in the local mosques and madrasas. These new maulavis did not share the gentle Sufism of their indigenous Kashmiri brethren for most of them were young and educated in the Deoband region of western U.P. They taught of pride in militant Islam and branded Muslim children going to secular schools as Kafirs. Their teachings struck a ready chord in a population already stimulated by Islamic revolution in neighboring Iran."[39]

According to Gull Mohd. Wani, the Jama'at had set up 125 Islamic schools with an enrollment of 17,000 students.[40] Sheikh Abdullah was aware of the political danger in increasing Islamization and tried to stem the tide by banning madrasas (Muslim schools), but there were other political parties, that is, the Awami Action Party led by Maulavi Farooq, which quietly promoted the Islamic cause to weaken the NC and its leaders. Likewise, New Delhi played upon the apprehensions of the Hindus in Jammu about being overwhelmed by the Muslim majority in the state.

Echoing the opinion of many experts, Wani writes that although failure of the democratic and secular forces

> [have] paved the way for the emergence of Islam as an alternative source of inspiration for the masses, it was only after the consolidation of Zia's regime in Pakistan and Islamic revolutionary struggles . . . in Iran and Afghanistan that Kashmir also witnessed Islamic resurgence. It is Jama'at-i-Islami of Kashmir which became a bridge connecting Kashmir with the overall Islamic resurgence . . . the collapse of communism as the leading anti-Western ideology seems to propel Islam into this role.[41]

Both in theory and practice, the Jama'at forces of Kashmir and Pakistan have much in common. Both reject "Indian Colonialism" and "Brahminical Imperialism" and wish to establish an Islamic state in their respective spheres.

One of the best sources of Islamic discourse in Kashmir can be gleaned from the writings of Syed Ali Shah Geelani, one of Jama'at's prominent leaders. Referring to Sheikh Abdullah, he complains that "Since 1931 we have been playing with our blood but the leader in whom we reposed out trust betrayed us." Turning to the youth of Kashmir, he declares, "You, the nation of Kashmiri Muslims, how long will you continue to remain easy-going slaves! Your enemies are bent upon destroying your identity and faith, they are pressing in full strength with their army and weapons. If you ignore this warning, be sure that the history of Muradabad will be repeated here. Like the lands of Bhiwandi, Aligarh, Hyderabad, and Assam, your lands would also be dyed with blood. You are facing a ruthless imperialist power whose Brahminical psyche is bringing new troubles for you every day. If you don't understand even now, you will not find any place in the pages of history."[42]

The Kashmiri Hindus likewise seek to unify the Pandit community in the valley and Jammu around the themes of Hindu identity and Indian national-ism. The communal perception in Kashmir reflects an interesting paradox. The Hindus are a minority in Kashmir but the Kashmiri Muslims see them as the extension of the Hindu majority in India; the Kashmiri Muslims are a majority in the J&K, but see themselves as an oppressed minority that must protect its identity by maintaining a distance from New Delhi. Among these rival discourses of identity the Islamic militant variant is definitely winning the hearts and minds of the people in the state in the 1990s.

A caveat needs to be entered here. Contrary to the portrayals of continu-ous strife and struggle in the nationalist and Islamic accounts of Kashmir's history, there were large periods of relative calm and cooperation in J&K's relations with New Delhi. Kashmir has not been in a state of continuing tur-moil or in a mode of permanent protest, although this is what the national-ist narratives have emphasized. The main purpose of the nationalists was to reconstruct the past to legitimize their power in the future. They were emi-nently successful until the militancy undermined the moderate nationalist rationale for remaining within India. This happened mainly because of the erosion of interlocking balances and New Delhi's failure to democratically integrate the J&K within the Indian union. The story of this failure is the sub-ject of later chapters. Here it is enough to note that contradictions inherent in their ideology have put Kashmiri nationalists on the horns of a painful dilemma. They can mobilize transborder support from POK or Pakistan and raise the stakes in their struggle against the Indian government. But they can only do so at the expense of their Kashmiriyat or "composite nationalism." Since that is also the basis of their territorial claim, Islamization of Kashmiri nationalism challenges the very rationale that supports the nationalist claims to the Hindu- and Buddhist-dominated areas of the kingdom of Kashmir.

The politics of identity in Kashmir is shaped by several pairs of conflicts: between Hindus and Muslims within the state of J&K; between Islamic militants and Kashmiri nationalists, many of whom support complete independence to political autonomy; between India and the Kashmiri nation; between India and Pakistan; and between India and its international friends on the one hand, and Pakistan and its supporters on the Kashmir issue on the other.

Themes in Tamil Nationalism

The quest for autonomy in Tamil Nadu evolved on a very different political trajectory from that in Kashmir and Punjab. Tamil Nadu was not subjected to the trauma of partition; there was no massive migration of people and no communal riots. Nor was Tamil Nadu located on a sensitive and strategically critical border region of India. The assertion of distinctive Tamil identity did not threaten other religious communities in that region nor did it threaten to divide India along religious lines. Caste and language were the principal bases of Tamil nationalism. In this sense, the quest for Tamil identity posed a different kind of challenge to India's supranational State.

The evolution of a self-conscious Tamil identity is rooted in the Tamil literary movement of the early nineteenth century.[43] Western scholarship played a key role in reviving interest in ancient Tamil texts and linguistic heritage.[44] Many Tamil scholars pointed out that Saiva Sidhantha, a specifically Tamil or Dravidian religion, predated the spread of Sanskritic civilization and establishment of Brahminical priesthood in India. The leaders of the Dravidian movement in the twentieth century drew on the Saiva Sidhantha to establish a separate and distinctive identity of the Tamil people and ideology.[45] Eminent Tamil scholars like Sastri launched a Tamil Parity movement and sought to eliminate Sanskritic influences from Tamil.[46] It is against the backdrop of these literary and intellectual quests that the later political thrust of Tamil self-assertion developed.

The origins of Tamil political self-assertion lie in the establishment of the Justice party in 1917. The main purpose of the party, which was active in what was then Madras province and therefore included a large segment of the Telugu and Malayali ethnic community, was to inculcate a sense of pride and self-awareness among the non-Brahmins, to unite them in a common struggle against the Brahmins, and to press the British authorities to provide special quotas to the non-Brahmins in education and civil service. The Justice party propaganda identified Brahmins as the "Aryans" and custodians of Sanskritic civilization and non-Brahmins as the "Dravidians" and heirs to the Tamil civilization.

The Dravidian movement, spearheaded mainly by Tamil leadership, went through many phases, from the narrow anti-Brahminism of the pro-British Justice party to the more militant and radical Self-Respect movement (Suya Mariyathai Iykkam) launched by E. V. Ramaswami Naicker (popularly known as Periyar, Naicker dominated Tamil Nadu from the mid-1920s to the end of the 1940s).[47] In 1944, Naicker established the Dravida Kazagham (DK), or the Dravidian Federation, committed to the idea of a separate Dravida nation consisting of four linguistic groups: Kannadigas, Andhras, Malayalis, and Tamilians. However, by the late 1940s, splits developed and a segment broke free from the DK and established the DMK (Dravida Munnetra Kazagham) under Annadurai's leadership. Annadurai expanded the base of the party by bringing in lower castes like the Nadars and Maravars, and young people mainly from the lower middle classes. He turned the DMK into an effective political organization by extending it to the rural areas, by providing it with a steady and rich source of funds, and by enlisting support from the Madras film industry.

The DMK ceased being a political movement and assumed the responsibility of a full-fledged political party contesting elections, in the late 1950s. It jettisoned the demand for a separate territorial Tamil state in 1963 and instead focused on social and political reforms in Tamil Nadu. This shift in focus and platform coincided with, and may have contributed to, the DMK's ascendancy in Tamil Nadu. This became evident when it swept to power in the 1967 state elections. In the following decades, the main conflicts between Indian and Tamil nationalism revolved around the issues of autonomy, share of federal revenues, status of Hindi over Tamil, and electoral rivalry between the Congress and the two main Dravidian parties, the DMK and the AIADMK. (After Annadurai's death, the DMK split once again: the faction led by M. G. Ramachandran was now called Anna DMK, another split led to the formation of AIADMK.) These rival claims of the Tamil nation have frequently spilled over beyond the borders of the Indian state. For instance, during the 1965 agitation against the imposition of Hindi, the then Tamil Nadu's Electricity Minister S. Ramachndran, warned that imposition of Hindi on Tamil Nadu would lead to a Sri Lanka-type situation. The Tamil secessionist demand in Sri Lanka was also a reaction to the imposition of Sinhalese on the Tamil minority of that country.[48]

Four themes have dominated the Tamil nationalist discourse: anti-Brahminism, anti-Sanskrit and later anti-Hindi sentiments, and a demand for

Tamil political autonomy. The first argument in this narrative is the antiquity of the Tamil language and civilization. In the *Aryan Illusion* Annadurai writes, "It is an indisputable fact that, in ancient times, Tamilians excelled in intelligence, efficiency, and . . . industries. But the Aryans who came . . . polluted the Tamilian culture . . . pushing to the background the Tamilian civilization."[49] At another place he says, "If we believe the customs and practices of the South Indians, we come to know that there was a subcontinent in the South, a major part of which has corroded into the sea, and that in those regions there flourished a wonderful civilization"[50] Although vague, this was perhaps the first attempt to lay some claims to a geographically contiguous region that could be identified as the home of Tamil civilization. Reference to the sea seems to imply Sri Lanka, which is only a short distance from the Tamil coast.

Annadurai identifies the oppressive Hindu caste system to be the main cause of Dravidian decline; the caste divisions held a sway over the Dravidians because they were lulled into "false consciousness" by the devious Brahmins. He called on his fellow Dravidians to abandon the belief in this "Aryan illusion," the hierarchical caste order of Hinduism. Annadurai argued that the only alternative to the oppressive order of the Brahmins was an egalitarian society that would replicate the values and ideals of ancient Dravidian civilization. The first step in this liberation was to reject the Aryan culture, including belief in Hinduism and Aryan (Brahmin) superiority. Dravidians had to be educated in the great heritage of their civilization and its egalitarian values. But more importantly, a separate Dravid Nadu had to be secured where Dravidas could live without fear of Brahmin-Hindu-Hindi domination.[51]

Discovery of the past, claims to exclusive and separate cultural forms, and social organization were crucial to the movement's ideology. Pandian writes that "the fact of their having had a literate civilization in the first millennium B.C. is a cultural premise of great importance" to the Tamils.[52] In his view, the reason why many scholars tend to subsume Tamil culture under the Hindu cultural tradition is because "British scholars introduced concepts such as Brahminization and Hinduization to describe what they considered to be a civilizing process generated by Sanskritic tradition in India. Although Western civilization was thought to represent the apex of evolution, these scholars saw within the non-Western countries the existence of certain ethnic traditions that were superior to or more civilized than others." Following in their footsteps, anthropologists and sociologists focused on "themes . . . of all-India national-cultural integrations." Pandian deconstructs the concept of Sanskritization developed by M. N. Srinivas and writes that scholars such as

Singer and Srinivas "saw themselves . . . as performing an important function in helping the infant nation-state of India, which is composed of various and diverse ethnic, tribal, and caste divisions, to evolve a common all-India indigenous intellectual tradition and thus counteract separatist and secessionist trends. It may be that they accepted the geographical boundary of India . . . as a natural cultural boundary and projected concepts that would legitimize this boundary."[53]

Students of Tamil culture and society, such as Iswaran and Pandian, and founders of the Dravidian movement, such as Naicker and Annadurai, have challenged the notion of territoriality embedded in the Indian nationalism. Their arguments point to a different geopolitical map. In this, Tamil national culture is not a nesting, but a separate and equal territorial entity. Such an entity was believed to extend to all the areas where Tamils had made their home and constituted a majority or were present in significant numbers. This included the Tamil regions of northern Sri Lanka and, to a lesser extent, Malaysia. The history of the great Dravidian kingdoms—the Pandyas and Cheras and Cholas—and their conquest historically mapped the cultural compass of the Tamil nation. The idea of the Tamil homeland with its embedded references to territory was meant to evoke the great past and to unify the Tamil-speaking community behind the Dravidian movement.

Admittedly, the concept of a Dravida nation state is mainly rhetorical, a symbol of a long record of Tamil history as a distinct nation. Nevertheless, it became an important theme of the popular discourse in Tamil Nadu. It is this imagined nation state of Tamil people, whose cause is militantly espoused by only a fringe group of extremists (Nan Thamizar, the "We Tamils" movement in Tamil Nadu but draws sympathetic response among the majority) with an implicit claim to a separate homeland and distinctive culture, that makes Tamil nationalism potentially dangerous to the Indian nation state.[54] The explosion of a more militant variant of Tamil nationalism in northern Sri Lanka has transformed what was once only a theoretical reality into a more plausible one.

The separatist platform does not enjoy much support in Tamil Nadu. It has nevertheless predisposed the people of Tamil Nadu to respond with deep sympathy to the plight of the Sri Lankan Tamils who, for their own reasons, emphasize close cultural and political links with the Tamils in India. The Tamil United Liberation Front (TULF) Manifesto of 1977 states, "Though Ceylon is a single state now, by facts of history, by the languages spoken by its inhabitants, by culture, tradition, and psychology, it is the common home of two nations and consists of two countries." Echoing many of the arguments found in Jinnah's speeches at the time of Partition, the manifesto declares that "though the Tamils and Sinhalese have lived in this country over two thousand years, yet the Tamils have continued to preserve their individual culture based on their language." Here the manifesto resonates the central symbols of Dravidian movement, i.e., sanctity of the Tamil language, and the identification of language with symbols of motherhood and purity. The manifesto goes on to say that Tamil culture was nurtured "even under Portuguese, Dutch, and British imperialistic rule. The vital reason behind this survival was that though the Tamils in Eelam were not strong in numbers, yet they never lost the opportunities of maintaining close bonds with a powerful fountain of Tamil culture across the Palk Strait in Tamil Nadu, South India."[55]

The manifesto reconstructs the Tamil past with references to *Mahavamsa*, the authoritative Buddhist text often credited as the first history of the Sinhala people in Sri Lanka. The main purpose of the TULF manifesto is to lay claim to the territories of Jaffna and the Eastern province as the legitimate homeland of the Tamil Eelam, to underline the history of discrimination and racial terrorism practiced by the Sinhala dominated governments in Colombo, and to justify Tamil rights to independent statehood. As we will see, the charges of racial discrimination are contrary to the nonsectarian founding ideas of Indian nationalism.

The Sinhala chauvinists have developed a counter theory of their Aryan origins and rewritten the Sri Lankan history as a struggle between them and the Tamils. The former are cast in the role of legitimate inhabitants of the island while the Tamils are regarded as the foreign usurpers who invaded from south India and settled down mainly because of the generous and tolerant nature of the Sinhala Buddhists. In the Sinhala nationalist discourse, the conflict between the Tamils and Sinhalas dates back to premodern times when invading South Indian kingdoms sought to forcibly extend their hegemony but were repeatedly beaten back by the Buddhist Sinhala kings and their armies. The interpretation of the current conflict in racial Aryan/Dravidian terms creates dangerous links to the themes of Hindi-Hindu-Brahmin-Aryan hegemony in the ideology of the DMK and AIADMK. The reference to Tamil invasions from across the Palk strait also resonates with the fear of Indian domination of the small and vulnerable Sri Lanka. The nationalist Sinhala narrative then contains themes of interstate and interregional conflicts, that reflects similar themes of war and conquest in Tamil nationalism in Sri Lanka and Tamil Nadu. The central purpose of each nationalism is significantly different, in fact contradictory. It is this dormant link of ideology, culture, and geographical proximity to Sri Lanka that creates a security dilemma for Indian leaders.

India's Indocentric perspective on the region makes her particularly sensitive, even vulnerable, to the enterprise of nation- and state-building in the neighboring countries. There is ample evidence about the role India played in transforming the Tamil–Sinhala conflict into a transborder conflict. India not only extended safe sanctuaries, and arms and political support to the Sri Lankan Tamil militants but also tried to prevent emergence of an independent Tamil state. It indirectly shaped the course of Sinhala Buddhist chauvinism. Initially, India sought to isolate these by supporting the moderate, pro-constitution political parties in Sri Lanka such as the United National party (UNP) and Sri Lanka Freedom party (SLFP). It provided Colombo with military support to crush the JVP (Janatha Vimukthi Peramuna) and the militant Sinhala Buddhist nationalism the latter advocated. It is important to bear in mind that "States necessarily stand at the intersections between domestic sociopolitical orders and the transnational relations within which they must manoeuvre for survival and advantage in relation to other states. The modern state as we know it . . . has always been . . . part of a system of competing and mutually involved states"[56] Nowhere is this more true than in the subcontinent of South Asia where ethnically defined nations do not follow the break and continuity of sovereign boundaries.

Chapter 4

❧

RESTORING RELATIONAL CONTROL
Indira Gandhi's First Term

During Prime Minister Nehru's long stewardship of free India's formative years, the supranational State established an interlocking system of balances between itself and the historic state with its diverse ethnonationalities, and sought to establish relational control over them to determine the course of India's modern state. Nehru adopted three modes of establishing control: co-optation, power-sharing, and confrontation—if the first two methods failed. Having explicitly devolved power on the ethnonationalities through the reorganization of the internal boundaries of the federal Indian state, he relied mainly on co-optation to deal with fresh demands.

Nehru was able to do this because the Congress reigned supreme in the national parliament and the state legislatures. This dominance was assured by the policy of co-opting ethnonational elites. However, by the time of Nehru's death, the potential for containment of such demands through co-optation had by and large been exhausted. In the Shastri period (1964–66) and much more obviously during the initial years of Indira Gandhi's long leadership, co-optation gradually gave way to power-sharing and confrontation. As was the case in the Nehru years, India's foreign and defense policies not only mirrored these internal changes, but contributed to them in so integral a manner that it is difficult frequently to tell where the one began and the other ended.

The dominance of the Congress had begun to fray even before Nehru's death. The crucial factor was India's defeat in the Sino–Indian border war of

1962. The defeat was of little territorial consequence since China vacated most of the new territories that its troops had captured, but its impact on the minds of the Indian intelligentsia was enormous, for it revealed that Nehru was fallible and his policies did not guarantee security. By 1964, shortly before his death, a number of regional leaders in the Congress party had begun to challenge his leadership. Factional conflicts had multiplied while party discipline declined precipitously. Months before his death, Nehru resorted to a drastic purge of fractious leaders in what came to be known as the Kamaraj plan. But this restored neither discipline nor unity. The subsequent deaths of Nehru, and then Prime Minister Lalbahadur Shastri, nineteen months later, confirmed the decline both of the Congress and of party discipline within the Congress.[1]

Even without the humiliating defeat by China, the dominance of the Congress was bound to have declined as the nationalist aura surrounding it faded. There were additional factors at work. The ruling elite was no longer the relatively small and cohesive group it had been in the 1950s. The steady expansion of democracy had widened electoral competition, brought many new groups into the political arena, and intensified the competition for access to the resources of the central state. Following Nehru's and then Shastri's death, an authority vacuum had emerged within the Congress further intensifying the contests for power. It was now difficult to rule by consensus as the Congress had done since Independence. The Congress could no longer count on reliable and powerful operatives able to defuse conflict, arrange bargains between important regional and cultural groups, and cobble such political coalitions to the coattails of the dominant party. Such networking had previously enabled the Congress to claim identity with the central government and even more important, with India's modern supranational State. The weakening in Congress's organizational strength made it increasingly difficult to achieve legislative majorities at the local and national levels. Nor could the party deliver on promises or implement policies that would convince the public of its commitment to their welfare. These developments made the party leadership, now itself divided and fictionalized, unsure and fearful of losing power in individual states. In the days when its dominance was unchallenged, loss of state assembly to opposition parties did not affect Congress' autonomy at the center or its ability to win legislative majorities in the central parliament. This was no longer certain and that made the leadership anxious to secure even greater control to insure party's dominance. These trends were clearly visible in the three years following the 1967 elections.

In 1967, when the party went to the polls, it had an untried prime minister in Mrs. Gandhi and little internal discipline. To make matters worse, there had been severe droughts in 1965 and 1966, which had resulted in unprecedented inflation (32 percent in two years) in postwar India. Furthermore, the steep devaluation of the rupee by 57 percent in June 1966 had weakened the Congress's credentials for retaining the monopoly of the country's modernizing agenda. Its ability to insure the supranational State's autonomy was clearly in jeopardy. This was evident in the government's dependence on American food and economic aid, in the helpless succumbing to the pressure from the IMF to devalue the rupee, in the mortifying conditions attached to the monthly American food shipments, the humiliating step back from its earlier bold criticism of the war in Vietnam. India's supranational State is required to insulate domestic policy from undue outside interference, it is also required to protect its agenda of modernization from perennial domestic conflicts. These the Congress government was failing to do in the 1960s. Indira Gandhi came to head the Congress and the country at a time when both had drifted into a state of disarray. Whatever else she did or did not do, she was required to restore a degree of stability and control at the center.

Much has been made of Mrs. Gandhi's imperious, autocratic temperament to explain the sudden and marked shift to confrontation from accommodation in dealing with India's ethnonationalities. Temperaments of political leaders do determine the course of politics to some extent. She was more autocratic than her predecessors, less tolerant of dissent, and far more inclined to use confrontation and force to get her way. There is no doubt about that. It is important nevertheless to bear in mind that leaders do not operate in a political vacuum, choices made previously narrow their choices in the present, and broader pressures of economy and culture shape their view of what is necessary and "inevitable." Her responses in the late 1960s should be assessed in light of these constraints. Perhaps a degree of correction may not be misplaced—taking into account factors such as the changes in distribution of economic power within India, the declining hold of traditional and entrenched patterns of caste politics, and the historic rhythm of power to and away from the center—when one assess Mrs. Gandhi's responsibility for undermining India's democracy and institutions. Those who blame her for these consequences are not wrong. They do, however, underestimate the role of deeper, more enduring conflicts that have shaped Indian politics. Would a different leader have made totally different choices given the political constraints at that time? Indira Gandhi did not operate under conditions of a dominant Congress. Should she have abandoned the objective of restoring the party to its former position? Does not the logic of competitive politics require leaders to maximize their own and party's power?

The argument here is not about Mrs. Gandhi but about the logic of power in a heterogeneous country that is anxious to become a modern nation state. In India, social heterogeneity produces the impulse to centralize control. On the flip side, such control is dependent on accommodation of heterogeneity. Every decision Indira Gandhi made was not a sociological necessity. Nor was it inevitable. One might debate her decision to split the Congress, destroy the party's old guard and along with it, the party organization. What would Nehru have done to reverse Congress' decline? One might point out that Nehru had strived to identify the Congress party with his government and both with India's supranational State. This was the "nationalist" strategy of unification, partly inherited and partly fashioned by Nehru himself. In splitting the Congress in 1969, Mrs. Gandhi was following in the footsteps of her predecessors. She also wanted to restore the unity of the party (her segment of the Congress) with the central state and government. She stepped up and hastened the process of centralization—which, however, proved fateful to India's democracy.

No matter who had succeeded Shastri, the erosion of Congress's legislative majority suggests that the old method of retaining dominance for the supranational State through the co-optation of regional elites was unlikely to work in 1966. A shift at the very least to power-sharing was inevitable. While Mrs. Gandhi did accept the inevitability of this shift, she did so reluctantly and only after it became clear that policies of confrontation were unlikely to succeed. She used the emergency powers granted to her under article 356 of the constitution to dismiss state governments, although such powers were meant to be used in "the rarest of rare cases" and only when constitutional government was no longer possible. Nehru had used such powers only three times during his years as prime minister. His daughter invoked the constitution at least a score of times between 1966 and 1971.[2] In many instances, she dismissed democratically elected state governments, engineered defections, and enticed legislative support away from opposition state governments. This relentless search for her own and Congress's (at least her segment of Congress's) preeminence was to prove disastrous. As the organizational muscle deteriorated, she was pushed more and more toward populist and personalized means of ensuring Congress's dominance. One might argue that the path she embarked on in 1969 and then in 1975, when she postponed elections and declared an emergency, led from the narrow logic of political survival. But it also led from the pressures and counterpressures of fashioning a modern nation-state out of the heterogeneous subcontinental empire state of India. The Congress and Mrs. Gandhi saw this as their supreme mission.

The declining authority of the Congress became apparent in 1967 when it lost six out of the twelve principal states in the elections and came within ten seats of losing its majority in the national parliament. This compromised not only the party's position but also the supranational State's capacity to perform its traditional functions: mediate support of regional and local coalitions, defuse tensions among and within regional groups, and channel disputes into routine processes of government and politics. Mrs. Gandhi sought to gain the initiative by "helping" to break up the motley coalitions of opposition parties that had come to power in half the country. President's rule was frequently invoked, and at times imposed without just cause, to pave the way for a fresh election. At least at this time, however, the Congress high command did distinguish between opposition governments in areas of the country where ethnonationality was not present or at best weak, and in areas in which it had already assumed a mature form. The striking example of the latter was Tamil Nadu.

So long as the Dravida Munnetra Kazagham (which had broken away earlier from the Dravida Kazagham) espoused full independence, it was not able to make much headway with the public in the state. Nehru's tactics of co-opting and creating a rival Tamil elite within the Congress and of absorbing substantial parts of the DK's agenda had worked. But late in 1962, during the Sino–Indian war, the DMK formally gave up its separatist agenda, and accepted the federal framework of the constitution.[3] Possibly because of this, but more directly because of its success in spearheading an anti-Hindi agitation in 1965, the party won a resounding victory in the 1967 state elections.[4] The Congress recognized the power of this movement and realized that it could not deal with it by provoking defections and toppling the government. It therefore bided its time and accepted the DMK's primacy in the state. In the January 1971 parliamentary elections, Mrs. Gandhi's Congress, which was then uncertain of the extent to which her populist policies had succeeded in weaning voters away from the old Congress party, accepted a minority of the seats in the state legislature in an arrangement with the DMK. It is noteworthy that the 1969 split in the Congress had enabled Karunanidhi, the new chief minister, to forestall not only a showdown with New Delhi but to gain leverage in national politics by throwing the weight of his 25 DMK members of parliament in favor of Indira Gandhi. DMK was one of the opposition parties that helped sustain Gandhi during her struggles with the "Syndicate." When the DMK split in the early 1970s because of internal dissensions, she gained a degree of leverage from the DMK by playing the two fragments of the DMK against each other. But the Congress could not replace the Dravidian parties. In 1977 the DMK and the Congress(I) lost elections. When Mrs. Gandhi returned to power in the 1980s, she promptly forged a power-sharing arrangement with the AIADMK. The arrangement endures until the present, and it is worth noting that the contrast between the way that the Congress high command dealt with Tamil Nadu and the way it dealt with opposition governments in other states mirrors the way in which Nehru and Patel dealt two decades earlier with Kashmir and the rest of the princely states.

The weakening of the center also threatened the supranational State with the loss of its autonomy in the forging of the modern nation-state. Gandhi tried to regain control in a variety of ways. The most important was her attempt to give the party a more leftist (actually populist) orientation.[5] When she met with resistance from the party machine—the "Syndicate"—she broke up the party itself, and for nineteen months headed a minority government that established a temporary and implicit alliance with the Communist party of India, the pro-Soviet wing of the now-divided Communist movement. Her decision to take the Congress leftward was resoundingly endorsed by the electorate in January 1971 when, although Indira Gandhi's Congress did not contest 100 out of the 542 seats, it gained an overall 43.8 percent of the vote.

This strategy was not without cost. To appeal directly to the people, Mrs. Gandhi had to bypass the established leaders of the party. This greatly weakened them and centralized power in her hands. Instead of acting as colleagues and political equals, ministers in her government competed to ingratiate themselves with her. The circle of personalized rule was thus completed, the Congress party was being gutted of its traditional function as a grand mediator of India's multilayered polity and of the multiple divisions of caste, class, language, and religion. In the 1970s and '80s, however, she was to find out that increased centralization did not increase the quantum of power enjoyed by her and her government over its ethnonations, nor strengthen its autonomy in domestic and international arena. Concentration of power did not guarantee greater relational control.

There was a brief reversal of the trend immediately after the Bangladesh war in 1971, reflected in the Congress party's resounding victory in the state assembly elections in 1972. However, after the briefest of lulls, the erosion of the supranational State's political authority continued. Between 1971 and 1975, Mrs. Gandhi sought to stem the erosion by asserting control over the state party units and ruling India directly, almost entirely on the basis of her own charisma. In these four years, she changed the state chief ministers repeatedly.[6] But this only accelerated the weakening of the Congress and thereby the erosion of the authority of the supranational State to push forward with its economic and social reform policies. Rebellions against such excessive centralization began to break out in different parts of the country, notably Bihar and Gujarat.[7]

These and a high court decision declaring her guilty of minor election malpractice, and requiring her to vacate her seat in parliament, pushed her over the edge into declaring a national emergency and suspending democratic rights. This final step in the concentration of decision-making power was an indication of the diminishing control of the Congress over the nation-building agenda. The politically expedient moves—changing chief ministers, bringing down opposition governments by inducing defections, declaring president's rule and finally suspending democracy itself—had exactly the opposite effect. In 1977, when Gandhi lifted the emergency and held another election, the Congress share of the vote fell to 36.5 percent, and it won only 153 seats in parliament.

The 1971 Indo–Pakistani war over Bangladesh was inextricably tied to these domestic developments in India. The first external intervention from across the border in Kashmir in 1947 had forged one pattern of interaction between overlapping nationality and foreign policy in the region, the spillover of the civil war in Pakistan forged yet another pattern of intervention and conflict in South Asia. The war over Bangladesh was rooted in conflicts arising from overlapping Bengali ethnic identity, political oppression of the East Pakistani nation by the West Pakistani ruling elite, and the latter's failure to accommodate Bengali aspirations for ethnic self-determination and autonomy. Still, these conflicts might have remained within Pakistan had millions of refugees not fled into India looking for safety and succor, or, international powers such as China, the United States, and the Soviet Union not tried to influence the war in the final hour. What began as a demand for greater autonomy however turned into a war for Bangladeshi independence.

India had much to gain from intervening on behalf of East Pakistan. It dealt a body blow to Pakistan from which the latter did not recover until the early 1980s. All the same, the conflict would have prolonged and along with it the agony in East Pakistan, had India not committed its military power to tilt the balance in their favor. The consequences of the Bangladesh war were equally significant. The conclusion of the war saw India emerge as the dominant military power in South Asia.

The Bangladesh war is held up as the locus classicus of Indian hegemonism. The conflict did not however originate in India's regional ambitions. What the war actually did was to define the scope and the limits of India's capacity to establish relational control over its own ethnonationalities and of its neighbors. These were to be prevented from jeopardizing India's stability and political unity. It was a classic attempt on part of India's leaders to make its borders congruent with its state and to make the state congruent with its nation. More concretely, because of its victory in the Bangladesh war, India was able to make Pakistan drop its attempts to internationalize the Kashmir dispute, and use the increased room for maneuvering in Kashmir to renegotiate an acceptable set of terms with Sheikh Abdullah. What it failed to do was prevent the agreement from unraveling later and Kashmiri ethnonationalism from turning to full-blown insurgency.

Overlapping Nationality and Indian Security: The Bangladesh War

The events immediately preceding the Bangladesh crisis underline the validity of relational control as a key to India's regional policy. The long history of tensions between East and West Pakistan need not detain us here. It is enough to note that the ten years of military rule under Ayub Khan (1958–1968) in Pakistan had intensified friction and deepened resentment of West Pakistani domination in Dacca.[8] By 1967, the "national question" had catapulted to center stage. East Pakistan's popular leader and head of the Awami League, Mujibur Rehman, had been imprisoned by the Ayub regime for formulating a six-point program for autonomy. The six points challenged the power and dominance of Pakistan's Punjabi ruling elite, who consisted of mainly the rich and powerful among the military/bureaucratic classes and landed wealthy in West Pakistan.[9]

The Pakistani ruling circles generally viewed their Bengali compatriots as timid, inferior and hinduized (therefore not as pure as the Punjabi Muslim) Muslims. The East Pakistani's, on the other hand, saw the West Pakistani Punjabis as arrogant, exploitative, and culturally backward. Conflict over the Urdu language and economy had further aggravated their mutual suspicions. The Ayub government reacted to the six points by denouncing the Awami League as the party of traitors and the rest of the opposition as "enemies of Pakistan." A fake case was invented against some Bengali soldiers, who were accused of "conspiring with India." These actions however boomeranged.

Instead of deterring, the Bengali nationalist sentiment unified in opposition to West Pakistan.

Unable to stem the wave of popular revolt which had been building up in both halves of Pakistan by then, the Ayub government collapsed. It was replaced by the Martial Law government of General Yahya Khan. The latter had announced the intentions to return Pakistan to the civilian rule, holding national elections and abiding by the results of the elections. Yahya Khan had also promised to carefully consider the Bengali demands for autonomy. By then the demand for autonomy had turned into one for a confederal Pakistan in which East Pakistan would enjoy equal status within the framework of a single constitution. Subsequent events were to carry this demand a step further toward total independence.

The December 1970 election took on the character of a referendum on the six-point proposal. The Awami League won by an overwhelming majority. Of the total of 169 seats allocated to the League, it had won 167 in Pakistan's Constituent Assembly and gained 291 out of the 343 seats in the Provincial Assembly. Its 167 seats gave the Awami League an overall majority throughout the country. The election results had truncated the military/ bureaucratic classes in Pakistan. Neither the military nor the Pakistan Peoples Party (PPP), which had emerged with the second largest number of seats in the 1970 elections, felt inclined to follow through on the results because that would have meant accepting the Awami League as a senior partner in government. Nor could they concede to the six-point program because that would have made East Pakistan virtually independent.

The Awami League and Mujibur Rehman had not initially asked for independence. By the same token, they had little, if any, flexibility on the six points. The popular sentiment in East Pakistan was running overwhelmingly in favor of a total separation. The parties to Mujibur's left were pressing for a declaration of independence. In an interview with an Agence France Presse, Mujibur Rehman complained: "Is the West Pakistan government not aware that I am the only one able to save East Pakistan from communism? If they take the decision to fight, I shall be pushed out of power and the Naxalites (Maoists) will intervene in my name. If I make too many concessions, I shall lose my authority, I am in a very difficult situation."[10] In the second week of March, final negotiations were held between Yahya Khan and the leaders of the Awami league. PPP leader Z. A. Bhutto was also present at the meeting. The talks ended on March 25 without any definite settlement. Meanwhile, the Pakistani army had received orders to prepare for an assault on the resistance movement. It struck on March 25, 1971. Mujibur Rehman was arrested along with hundreds of party leaders and cadres. A campaign of terror and killings was unleashed in the months of March and April, from which thousands of unarmed Bengalis fled in search of safety toward India.[11]

Initially, both Muslim and Hindu Bengalis fled across the border but by April, Pakistani forces had begun to target Hindu Bengalis in the hope of turning the civil war into a Hindu–Muslim conflict. The huge influx of refugees, estimated to be around ten million by November 1971, created what India began to refer to as a demographic aggression by Pakistan.[13] Mrs. Gandhi remarked that "had we not opened our door we would in fact have abetted Pakistan's genocide."[14] India had done much the same in response to the 1954 crisis in Tibet and the crushing of the democracy movement in Nepal in the early 1960s. The military crackdown had driven the Bangladeshi resistance underground. It had consolidated the formation of the Mukti Fauj, a militant guerrilla force of Bangladeshi nationalists, later renamed Mukti Bahini. By April, Mukti Bahini had begun to receive weapons and training from India.[15] The core of the Mukti Bahini consisted of the middle-level cadres of the Awami League, along with the elements of East Pakistani Rifles, East Bengal Regiment, and members of the East Pakistani Police force. The Indian government also permitted the Awami League leaders to form a government-in-exile based in Calcutta. Warfare intensified throughout the months between March and December, in which the Indian border force and later the Indian army became increasingly involved. The Mukti Bahini also jelled into a credible guerrilla force, able and willing to soften up targets and carry the fight into East Pakistan.

However, all attempts between April and November to evolve a settlement failed. The Pakistani offer of a compromise came too late and offered too little. The Bengali resistance had gone too far toward independence to abandon its quest. India too saw little possibility of sending the refugees back without a fundamental shift in the power structure. By April 1971, the tide of refugees had become a human flood. The Indian armed forces were ordered to prepare for the possibility of a war in the east. The mobilization of Indian forces sent alarm bells ringing in Islamabad. On December 3, 1971, Pakistan launched a surprise attack on Indian airfields.[16] This was the formal beginning of the war although armed clashes and cross-border incursions had become frequent months before the conflict. The war lasted for about four weeks, at the end of which, Pakistani armed forces in the former East Pakistan surrendered to India and Bangladesh became an independent country.

Tranquility on the borders was restored. The Indian armed forces subsequently handed over power to the Awami league and Mujibur Rehman and withdrew from Bangladesh. The latter signed an agreement of Friendship and Cooperation with India and agreed to take back the refugees. Still the question of some 93,000 Pakistani prisoners of war remained unresolved. The problem was to be settled at the historic Simla summit between India and Pakistan. The 1971 war had however drastically altered the balance of power within South Asia. India had become a preeminent state in the region.

Many India scholars see the Bangladesh war as proof of India's hegemonic ambitions.[17] Pakistan lost, and India won, they argue, because the latter was the bigger and militarily more powerful of the two and used its superiority to establish its unquestioned dominance in the region. Imtiaz Ahmed goes a step further and ascribes this quest for hegemony to Hindu expansionism. The Indian supranational State, he says, is a hegemonic representation of the Hindu majority, which used the Bangladesh crisis to consolidate its domestic and regional dominance.[18] He asserts that the Indian government "succeeded in making the nationalist struggle of Bangladesh into an Indo-Pakistani affair, ensuring thereby India's predominant position in South Asia."[19]

A closer examination of the crisis shows that the charge of hegemonism confuses the outcome with motivation. Although the prospect of defeating Pakistan on the battlefield must have been highly tempting, New Delhi would not have intervened had there been no flood of refugees imposing an intolerable burden on its fragile economy, no fear of losing control of the already volatile northeast and Assam, no anxiety about link up between Naxalite elements in West Bengal and the Bangladesh leftists, no worries about endangering the total demographic balance in the states of Tripura and Assam where the refugees outnumbered the local residents in several districts, no fear of aggravating the communal situation between Hindus and Muslims of India, and no pressures from the opposition or from the Bengali-speaking community within India. These factors weighed equally if not more heavily in the Indian policy decisions. After all, strategic vulnerability of Pakistan's eastern half was not a new opportunity for India. No Indian government had however tried to exploit Pakistan's geopolitical vulnerability during the previous decades.

It was in India's interest to weaken and reduce Pakistan in the region. This is undeniable. But it is equally significant that this interest did not translate into action until after March 1971, when Pakistani armed action had sent a torrent of refugees into India. The steady steam of refugees virtually erased the boundaries between India and Pakistan. India's involvement in the Bangladesh crisis was gradual and measured. Briefly, Indian response evolved through four phases.

The first phase lasted approximately from the last week of March (when the Pakistani army launched an assault on the Awami League) to the end of April. During this time, refugee centers had been set up and the border security force ordered to provide nominal military and weapons support to the East Bengali partisans. Military crackdown in the east was already producing passionate response in West Bengal. The Pakistani actions were seen in West Bengal as an attempt to destroy Bengali culture and identity. Mrs. Gandhi was under mounting pressure to stop Pakistani armed forces from continuing their carnage against the Bangladeshi people. Consolidation of Bengali nationalism on both sides of the Indo-Pakistani border could not but create the most acute anxiety in New Delhi. The Bengali media had embarked with a missionary zeal to publicize every Pakistani atrocity, and to exhort the Indian government to abandon caution.[20] Despite these pressures for action, New Delhi still believed that international pressure and the futility of a military solution might make Islamabad more accommodating. Mrs. Gandhi remained cautious, preferring to wait and watch events instead of rushing into military intervention. Besides, she and her military advisers were not sure of the staying power of the Bengali resistance; the liberation movement was much too divided from within to serve as the lightning rod for independence. India needed to ascertain the ideological inclinations of the various factions and insure that the moderates prevailed over the more radical leaders.

India feared the Marxist elements in the Bangladesh freedom movement because these had the potential to become an extraterritorial rallying point for the Naxalites (radical left elements) operating on the Indian side of the border. In order to escape the Indian army and police, the Naxalites had frequently sought safety across the border in chaotic East Pakistan. These incursions by the radical elements had given Pakistan an excuse to charge that India had begun to intervene earlier than commonly believed and that it had fomented anti-Pakistan rebellion in the east. Sisson and Rose, in their carefully researched account of events write, however, that the "Pakistani allegations of massive BSF intervention were completely fictitious." They reject the charge that India had "arranged the infiltration of Naxalite and other Indian terrorist groups into East Pakistan in the immediate post-25 March period" because no one in New Delhi would have wanted to provide Naxalites with the advantage of safe sanctuaries. The Indian army had launched, during the previous two years, a systematic campaign to root out the Naxalite movement. Both Indian and Pakistani governments "faced serious problem controlling their respective sides" in the spring of 1971. There was no "evidence," however, to support the "elaborate conspiracy theory that became integral to the Pakistani analysis of these developments thereafter."[21]

Ensuring dominance of the moderate element in the Bangladeshi resistance, however, meant acquiring a degree of control over the independence movement and unifying it under the popular and secular but moderate leadership of Mujibur Rehman. Early May saw the end of the first phase. By then over three and half million refugees had crowded into India, with over a million in West Bengal alone. By the beginning of the second phase, the Indian government believed that some 12 to 13 million refugees, mostly Bengali Hindus, would seek sanctuary in India. In anticipation, New Delhi had the Indian army assume control of the border and set up training camps for the Bengali partisans. The purpose was not to encourage secession but to provide leverage over any future settlement of the civil war. There was no other way of ensuring the return of the refugees.

The second phase was also devoted to publicizing in international forums, the gravity of human suffering in the east. India's international diplomacy sought to neutralize Pakistani propaganda and to ascertain the positions of China, the United States, and Soviet Union in the event of a war. Neither China nor the United States, who were friendly with Pakistan, had succeeded in dissuading that country from seeking a military solution. And the assistance the United States had extended was too meager to feed and clothe the millions who had come into India. India was also anxious to keep the United Nations out of the crisis. It feared that Pakistan's supporters in the UN might convert what was a case of genocide into another Indo–Pakistan feud. The latter would have permitted the UN to distribute blame equally. In New Delhi's view, there was no moral or political equivalence in the Bangladesh situation. Early in August 1971, India and the Soviet Union signed a Friendship and Cooperation treaty that included a clause covering mutual military consultations.

The third phase of escalation lasted from August to the end of November. By November's end, it was clear that the international community could not persuade Pakistan to come up with an acceptable solution to the Awami League. Pakistan continued to point to the Indian involvement in training Mukti Bahini and mobilization of armed forces on the eastern Indo–Pakistani border. It argued that the combined forces of Mukti Bahini and the Indian army threatened Pakistan's survival. Mrs. Gandhi traveled to Washington D.C. in a last ditch effort to enlist American support for a negotiated settlement, but nothing came of her visit. The compromise formula that the United States had persuaded Pakistan to offer fell far short of Bengali nationalist aspirations and Indian interests. Gandhi was convinced by November that war could not be avoided.

The fourth phase covers the actual armed conflict and need not detain us here.

The East Pakistani crisis did not then originate in Indian regional ambitions. Nor did India rush to dismember Pakistan. The crisis arose because the Pakistani military leaders failed to cope with resurgent ethnonationalism in what was then East Pakistan. This failure is not surprising. Pakistan had consciously chosen to be a unitary state. It was for nearly the whole of its existence until then, an authoritarian regime. It had deprived itself of every possible means of accommodation with Bengali nationalism. Pakistan's failure was the dark side that mirrored India's relative success in establishing a degree of federal balance. It was a warning, nonetheless, of the dangerous potential of overlapping nationalities, should India ignore their aspirations, as Pakistan had done.

Pakistani officials and intellectuals have often cited statements of K. Subrahmanyam as proof of India's nefarious designs. K. Subrahmanyam, then director of the Institute of Defense Studies and Analyses, had argued that India should abandon restraint because events had presented it with an opportunity "the like of which will never come again." Some in the Indian government agreed with his assessment but there were others even more influential than Subrahmanyam, who advocated restraint. Not everyone in New Delhi was enthusiastic about a liberated Bangladesh. Sisson and Rose also make the point that Subrahmanyam did not speak for the government of India; Pakistan tended to ignore statements that did not fit in its perceptions of Indian designs; and the Indian government "rarely, if ever" revised policies on East Pakistan to suit its critics.[22]

The second crucial element of the crisis was the decision by the Pakistan government to target Hindus for persecution in the hope of fanning communal passions and thereby uniting Bengali Muslim sentiment against the secular Bangladeshi nationalists. In this it miscalculated. Bengali Muslims and Hindus both wished for independence and fought the Pakistan armed forces. They were united in their Bengali nationality and refused to be separated on the basis of religion. This show of ethnic solidarity, therefore, discredited Pakistan's two-nation thesis, that Hindus and Muslims represented separate nations in the subcontinent. But the killing of Hindus threatened communal violence within India and endangered whatever repair work the Congress had done to Hindu–Muslim relations since Partition.

Nor must it be forgotten that by targeting Hindus for killings and expulsion violated, in the most brutal way, the Nehru–Liaquat Ali Pact of 1950, which had specifically committed each country to protecting its minorities. This alone would have justified some extreme action on India's part, but that was not what India argued. India simply asked that Pakistan stop the killing and take the refugees back. Its support for Sheikh Mujibur Rehman stemmed not from its earlier contacts with the Awami League, but from its awareness that Mujib was a safer choice from the point of view of Hindu–Muslim relations. It was not enough for India that Bangladesh gain independence or autonomy. Sisson and Rose stress that the prospect of a radical government in Dhaka worried Indian leaders. Such a regime could forge ties with fellow radicals in West Bengal and the northeast and trigger another exodus of refugees by nationalizing land and property. They argue that India's interest lay in neutralizing Bangladesh as a factor in the defense of its northeast. That goal was best achieved when Bangladesh was a part of Pakistan. Since that was not to be, the next best thing was to insure a secular and stable Bangladesh. The policy of relational control dictated such a strategy. The Indian state sought to structure regional interaction in order to gain influence over ideology and actions of the other players: the radical and moderate East Pakistani nationalists, their fellow ethnics in West Bengal, the Yahya regime in Islamabad, and the fleeing refugees in the Indian camps. The inward orientation of India's motive was only too obvious to be missed.

It has been suggested that Mrs. Gandhi used the Bangladesh insurrection to bolster her own and the Congress party's power within India. A close examination of events does not bear this out. In January 1971, her Congress had won its most spectacular victory of which she was the main architect. Far from jumping at the opportunity that Bangladesh provided, she exhibited patience and restraint. The Indian press even criticized her for too much restraint. *The Statesman* of Calcutta warned the people of Bangladesh not to rely too much on the Indian government which, it said, did not have the courage to recognize Bangladesh. The *Hindustan Standard* observed, "Discretion has played a part, and a very valuable one. But can calculated inactivity be adequate for always?"[23] The crisis in East Pakistan had an immediate effect on the balance between India's supranational State and its ethnonations. Mrs. Gandhi dismissed the West Bengal coalition government in mid 1971. The controversy surrounding the plight of refugees in the state and the need to establish direct control over their movements was the reason for the dismissal. A weak coalition government in which the Congress was but one element was a weak instrument to contain the spillover of the civil war in the east. Mrs. Gandhi was aware that the Communist party of India Marxist (CPM) remained the strongest political force in West Bengal even after it was dismissed from power. It had the ability to whip up local resentment and sabotage the central government's policies toward the refugees. The CPM and CPML, yet another offshoot of the splintered Communist movement in India, opposed the idea of military intervention and instead favored what it called the "people's war." The CPML was worried that strengthening the security apparatus would limit its activities in West Bengal. Mrs. Gandhi wanted the Indian army in control for precisely the same reasons. Although New Delhi wanted to enlist popular support in West Bengal since that was the first destination for fleeing East Bengalis, it did not want to encourage Bengali nationalism to focus on some territorially defined nation of "greater Bengal."[24] India's problem in West Bengal was to restrain excessive ethnic pressures from jeopardizing its flexibility in dealing with the crisis. In the northeast, the problem was somewhat different. There the sudden influx of refugee would have threatened the traditional tribal organization and lifestyle. These dangers strengthened the Indian resolve to insure a speedy conclusion to the conflict and return of the refugees. India's response could hardly have been different, even if the majority who had fled across the border were Muslims.

Mrs. Gandhi and her advisers were also apprehensive about the uncertain international environment. Here we enter the more conventional sphere of foreign policy. The need to insulate the country from destabilizing external influences was growing. Although India had emerged with an edge over Pakistan following the 1965 war, this advantage did not translate into superior strength in dealing simultaneously with its two main adversaries, Pakistan and China. The 1965 war had restored the morale of the Indian armed forces to some extent but Pakistan's growing strategic friendship with China was highly worrisome to New Delhi. China had stated repeatedly that it would support Pakistan in the event India committed direct aggression.[25] Since 1969, the United States was anxious to enlist Pakistan's help to establish a channel of communication with China in order to extricate itself from Vietnam. And Pakistan was willing to oblige Washington in exchange for continued support against India. Pakistan had therefore arranged for U.S. Secretary of State Henry Kissinger's secret visit to Beijing in July 1971. Although the Indian government had not known about the visit, it had watched this convergence of U.S., Pakistani, and Chinese interests with growing apprehension.

Scholars disagree about the extent to which China and the United States mattered in India's decision to sign a treaty with the Soviet Union. Sisson and Rose argue that India had invented the Chinese threat. In their view,

China was unlikely to provide more than verbal support to Pakistan, and Indian officials knew this. China had made no attempt to mobilize forces on the Sino–Indian border and the Indian officials were aware of this. The Indo–Soviet treaty, according to Sisson and Rose, was meant not so much to deter China or America but to bind Moscow more closely to India. Other commentators take the Chinese threat more seriously and see India taking an anticipatory action in signing the treaty. Whatever the nature of the Chinese threat, Indian leaders did not treat it lightly. They saw prudence in buying some insurance since China had issued repeated warning against military intervention.

Indian leaders had been uneasy about the increasingly neutral stance the Soviet Union seemed to have adopted since the 1965 Indo–Pakistani war. They worried that this would mean greater Soviet even-handedness on Pakistani rearmament and the Kashmir dispute. India had come to depend on continued access to Soviet military supplies and weapons to build up India's defense.[26] The treaty then ended the Soviet ambivalence and forced it to chose between ties to India and its budding new ties to Pakistan. After much reluctance, Soviet leaders gave in to Mrs. Gandhi's insistence. Three years earlier the Soviet Union had floated a proposal for an "Asian Collective Security System," but New Delhi was reluctant to endorse the Soviet idea. Instead Gandhi had offered a counterproposal emphasizing economic coop-eration instead of security. The Indo–Soviet treaty of August 1971 did include security cooperation but with one important modification: the idea of the "collective" was replaced by a bilateral security arrangement between India and the Soviet Union.

The agreement facilitated mutual military consultations, and more importantly, pledged each country to come to the other's aid upon request. Once the treaty was secured, and pro-Pakistani powers—China and the United States—thus checkmated, India was free to engage Pakistan in the east; facilitate speedy return of the refugees; and intervene on behalf of Bangladesh. Did India in effect abandon in all but name its traditional posture of nonalignment when it entered the quasi-military agreement with the Soviet Union? It is argued throughout this book that nonalignment, as the West insists on seeing it, never had much relevance in India's dealings with its neighbors.[27] Here, India sought relational control, the freedom to pursue her nation-state project without interference or constraint.

The other controversial aspect of Indian policy was the arms sanctuaries and training offered to the Bengali resistance. This was clearly in violation of international norms. There are at least two important questions here. First, was this support a result of Indian expansionism? And second, was the resistance movement capable of liberating Bangladesh on its own and without the help of armed intervention by India? The first question has already been answered in the foregoing paragraphs. It is enough merely to recall the burden of the refugees and the danger they posed to India's stability and security in the northeast and West Bengal, and the possibility of a Naxalite revival like the one that had been crushed with great difficulty by the Indian police. Each situation threatened to turn the overlapping nationalities into an ethnic entity, separate from India and Pakistan. At the minimum, each was likely to bring turmoil and violence.

In answer to the second, we need to turn to the nature of mutual dependency between Mukti Bahini and the Indian military. India had established collaborative structures to coordinate command and control of the entire operation: the strategic moves planned by the Indian regular forces and the guerrilla assaults planned by the Mukti Bahini. The latter enjoyed considerable autonomy in choice of operational targets, recruitment, and command of its own forces. Such autonomy was necessary if Mukti Bahini was to remain a credible and independent force. But once India had decided to help the struggle, it would have been too much to expect it not to guide Mukti Bahini in the battlefield.

First, the Mukti Bahini was far from a unified force.[27] The whole national liberation movement was riddled with factional conflict. Its more radical and militant factions resented the leadership of the Awami League. Had India's only aim been to sunder Pakistan in two, it would have had no preferences about whom to support. But because it had the longer-term goal of insulating itself from future shocks in its neighborhood, it gave support to the Awami League, the moderate and secular faction of the resistance movement. Rafiqul Islam, a leading figure in the guerrilla resistance, wrote that the Research and Analysis Wing (the Indian intelligence agency often referred to as the RAW) created a special force led by Sheikh Fazlul Huq Moni, the nephew of Sheikh Mujibur Rehman, to countervail the radical elements in the Mukti Bahini. The purpose of the new group was to protect Mujibur Rehman and his interests within the resistance movement. The establishment of the Mujib Bahini gave India greater operational leverage to shape events and exercise restraint on Mukti Bahini, which was otherwise spearheading the guerrilla war against Pakistan.[28] Had India not provided the resistance with weapons, in all likelihood the resistance would have turned to other sources. Although in the 1970s, it had far fewer sources of arms available then the LTTE had a decade and a half later, any international access at all would have undermined the ability to insulate India and the region. This same consideration carried weight fourteen years later in India's clandestine support to the Tamils in the Sri Lankan civil war.

Fully aware that its efforts to make Pakistan negotiate with Mujib were not getting international support where it counted and would most probably fail, India prepared meticulously for an armed intervention. Once the military phase of the operation began, it became importance to control the actual operations. There was no other way to safeguard the safety of Indian armed forces.

Some analysts contend that Indian intervention robbed Mukti Bahini of military success.[29] They suggest that had India not intervened and taken over the military operation, Mukti Bahini would have emerged dominant in Bangladesh. They moreover argue that India's hegemonic designs were evident in its insistence on keeping tight control of the conduct and timing of military operation in the hands of Indian commanders, thereby turning Bangladesh's hour of glory into an Indo–Pakistani affair. In other words, India preempted Bangladesh's struggle to serve its own hegemonic ambitions in South Asia.

The first argument hinges on assessment of Mukti Bahini's military capabilities. Military experts such as D. K. Palit and Captain S. K. Garg, who provide us with an authoritative analysis of the Mukti Bahini operations and India's role in it, point out that Mukti Bahini was not a homogeneous and unified force. The regular guerrilla cadres among them were effective in winning control over the countryside and softening the Pakistani armed forces prior to the intervention but the irregular forces, which were much larger in number, were uncoordinated and lacking in leadership and training. The possible fate of Pakistani POWs was an important consideration. India could not guarantee their safety, had they surrendered to Mukti Bahini. Given the earlier history of West Pakistani atrocities, revengeful actions might have followed. No one except the partisans believed the guerrilla strength was sufficient at the time to quickly and decisively defeat the Pakistani forces. And without such a decisive conclusion, the struggle for independence would have settled down to a protracted conflict, occasionally interrupted by parleys to regroup for the next battle.[30] It is noteworthy that precisely such a pattern of conflict and negotiations was established between the LTTE and the government in Colombo during the late 1980s. Even those Indian military officers who expressed respect for the bravery and dedication of the Mukti Bahini point out that, without the Indian intervention, the civil war would have extended at least another ten months to two years. A protracted conflict so close to

Bengal, Assam, and India's northeast could have jeopardized India's stability in these regions. It is a mix of these domestic and strategic considerations that ultimately shaped India's response to the events in Bangladesh. Once Pakistan declared war on December 3, 1971, the confrontation could hardly be anything other then primarily an Indo–Pakistani affair.

Despite a whole chapter devoted to a discussion of the Bangladesh war as a "Hindu hegemonic representation," Imtiaz Ahmed is hard put to find any Indian government statement or action that showed a desire to mobilize Indians as Hindus. The only citation we have from him in this regard is from members of the Jan Sangh, a recognized Hindu nationalist organization! This was because the Bangladesh war was not an exercise in consolidating Hindu hegemony but an exercise in balancing the overlapping arenas of conflict: between East and West Bengalis, between West Bengali ethnic nationalism and the territorial nationalism of the Indian state, and between India and the interested international actors. The charge that India preempted the Bangladesh independence movement is based on a complete failure to understand the logic of relational control. The purpose of such control is to insure that the choice will be, as far as possible, in favor of an outcome that minimizes destabilizing shocks in the future.

In practice, relational control is exercised by supporting the leader, group, or political movement that broadly subscribes to the same long-term goals as India's. In supporting the Awami League over the Mukti Bahini and its militant Marxist leaders, India was clearly hoping to influence the ideological balance of forces in the new state of Bangladesh. But such choices are not unconstrained, and cannot be equated with putting puppets in power. Mrs. Gandhi and the Congress leaders found Mujibur Rehman ideologically compatible. He was also the most popular national figure in Bangladesh. They did not have any other choice. It was also the reason why India was careful to hand over state power to Mujib alone and to secure his political dominance by signing a twenty-year Friendship and Cooperation treaty with his government.[31] But India had pulled back its military forces and fully acknowledged the independence and sovereignty of its new neighbor. From then on, India's policies settled down to serving its traditional objectives: opposition to military alliances and presence of external powers in the disputes of South Asia, and insistence on bilateral relationships.

This was the second redrawing of the territorial map between India and Pakistan since 1947. Each was a result of the conflict of overlapping nationalities, Kashmiris in the fist instance and Bengalis in the second. The Kashmir conflict had forced Indian leaders to establish the key meridians of its foreign policy: bilateralism, insulation of the region from external interference, integration of its ethnonation in the national mainstream, self-reliance in defense of Indian interests, and maximization of room for maneuver. The last was essential to effect a proper and manageable balance between its domestic and foreign policy interests. The Bangladesh war allowed India to go a step further. It permitted Indian leaders to establish a clearer military and defense component to their regional policy. In popular parlance, this has come to be known as the "Indira Doctrine": India would pursue diplomacy but once that failed, it would use military force to defend, even preempt any adverse fallout of transborder ethnic conflict. India would preserve the choice to use transborder ethnic nations or those that had taken refuge in India to gain leverage on disputes in the region. Its goal was not to expand territory or reduce neighbors to satellites but to exercise selective and limited influence to permit relational control. It is in this sense alone that Indian policies incorporate the impulse associated with hegemony.

Post-Bangladesh Balance: 1972–1980

The Bangladesh war changed the balance of power decisively between Pakistan and India. Not only did it cut Pakistan to half its original size, but when the war ended, India had 93,000 Pakistani prisoners whom the new premier of Pakistan, Zulfiqar Ali Bhutto, had to find a way of repatriating. India took advantage of the situation to secure a new agreement with Pakistan on Kashmir, and to work out a new compact with Kashmiri nationalism within the state. It did the first through the Simla agreement of 1972 between India and Pakistan, and the second through a domestic agreement between Mrs. Gandhi and Sheikh Abdullah in 1975.

The Simla Agreement

At the conclusion of the Bangladesh war, the Pakistani military was in a state of disarray. Its stability was seriously jeopardized by the threat of coup and countercoup. Pakistan was reeling under the psychological shock of losing not only its eastern half but losing it to Pakistan's most hated enemy, India. Since the military junta was discredited, a civilian government led by Z. A. Bhutto had assumed the reins of government. India held 90,000 Pakistani prisoners of war and had concluded a friendship treaty with the new state of

Bangladesh. India, in fact, held all the bargaining cards. It was possible for the Indian leaders to force concessions from Pakistan that the latter might not have been willing to make had the war been concluded along the same lines as in 1965. At Simla, Pakistan had pledged three things: first, to "refrain from threat or use of force against territorial integrity or political independence of each other"; second, to confine bilateral disputes with India to bilateral forums; and third, to upgrade the cease-fire line in Kashmir to a "line of actual control."[32] India linked the delineation of the new line of control in the J&K to withdrawal of forces to the international boundary. It also persuaded Pakistan to vacate Lapa Valley and Titwal, the two posts it had captured in May 1972 in the Kashmir sector after the cease-fire had been already declared.

In practical terms, these concessions meant that Pakistan had agreed to a no-war pact with India, and had promised to settle disputes and differences by negotiation within a bilateral framework, involving no third parties in the process. Since neither country was willing to relinquish claims to the part of Kashmir that it held, agreeing to change the status of that state only through consultations and not the use of force meant agreeing to a permanent partition of Kashmir along the cease-fire line, now renamed the Line of Control. De facto if not de jure, both countries thus agreed to give up claims to territory controlled by the other. If Pakistan adhered to the conditions laid down in the pact, Kashmir's status would no longer be in dispute, in Pakistan, or in international forums. And India could then get on with the task of binding the state more closely to the Indian nation.

There were, however, many loose ends in this new agreement and the fact that India agreed to leave these unresolved is the best proof that it had no design for Pakistan's "annihilation." The existence of these loose ends shows that India was not aiming at a specific outcome of the talks but at creating a more congenial framework for the determination of the future relationship between the two countries. India had not insisted on reducing or capping Pakistani military capabilities or restricted Pakistan's freedom to acquire new weapons and rebuild defense. India had returned the POWs and ignored the Bangladeshi demand for public trials of Pakistani military personnel for crimes against humanity. Even the provision prohibiting internationalization of the Kashmir issue was not binding on Pakistan. There was nothing to prevent Pakistan from bringing the issue back before the United Nations since the opening lines of the pact stated that the "principles and purposes of the Charter of the United Nations shall govern the relations between the two countries." Pakistan could then argue, as it in fact did, that it was not the intent of the pact to exclude the United Nations from the Kashmir dispute.

However the most important loophole, one that India was in an excellent position to close because of its 93,000 Pakistani POWs, was to make explicit the cease-fire line as the international frontier. Did the Indian diplomats overlook these loopholes? Why did they not demand more binding agreements and impose harsher conditions on Pakistan? The real purpose behind the pact has been explained by Mrs. Gandhi herself.[33] She told the Pakistanis "that a bilateral solution was more important than their stress on international law and the UN" and that they should "avoid becoming pawns in a game of big power chess." This was the quid pro quo—the restoration of status quo for a Pakistani promise not to bring a third party into their mutual relationship.

The weakness of the agreement was that it relied only on Pakistani promises to safeguard this quid pro quo. This turned out to be a mistake. The Soviet invasion of Afghanistan seven years later brought the United States back into the subcontinental equation. Pakistan seized the opportunity to extract modern arms and restore the military balance it had lost to India in 1971. As soon as it had done so, it abandoned its commitments to India at Simla.

Perhaps the most important reason for India's "leniency" was Mrs. Gandhi's aversion to Pakistan's military leaders and her marked preference for doing business with a democratic polity. She preferred to negotiate with Bhutto, who was emerging as a popular leader in the truncated Pakistan and was using the same methods that she had used to mobilize the masses behind her in 1969–71.[34] Bhutto thus seemed fully capable of curbing Pakistan's national security state. Gandhi and her advisers at Simla thought it prudent not to weaken Bhutto by imposing onerous conditions on Pakistan. If the Bhutto government fell, the Indian policy makers reasoned, subsequent leaders might not feel obliged to adhere to the pact. Gandhi's goal was stability and not territorial expansion in the subcontinent. She was prepared to make concessions on the legalization of the Line of Control to avoid forcing Bhutto to accept an agreement that would weaken him seriously within Pakistan and give the Pakistani military an excuse for staging a coup. As things turned out, none of her calculations about Bhutto, his popularity, or his intentions and the military, turned out to be correct.

The Indira Gandhi–Sheikh Abdullah Agreement of 1975

The second agreement between Mrs. Gandhi and Sheikh Abdullah echoes in domestic policy what she had sought in Simla: enhanced stability. Her trusted envoys, G. Parthasarathy and Mirza Afzal Beg, a representative and close confidant of Sheikh Abdullah, had begun negotiations soon after the Simla agreement of 1972. The two had signed an accord on November 13, 1974, in New Delhi. This made article 370 a permanent part of the Indian constitution. Sheikh Abdullah was not only released from house arrest but returned to Kashmir to become its next chief minister in March 1975. Gandhi had persuaded the then-Chief Minister, Mir Quasim, to resign and make room for Sheikh Abdullah. She also agreed to roll back certain provisions introduced in the 1960s and '70s that irked the independent-minded sheikh. In return, he agreed to recognize the new political realities in the region (India's new preeminence and Pakistan's humiliating defeat) and refrain from raising the issue of Kashmir's independence. Since the sheikh was the new chief minister of J&K, Mrs. Gandhi did not think he would have any reason to raise the issue of independence. In fact, Sheikh Abdullah made an explicit statement in which he reiterated that his quarrel with India since 1952 had not been about accession but about the extent of autonomy. Although there is ample evidence of his past equivocation in statements that suggested that Kashmir should have a status similar to that of Switzerland, he now promised to treat this as a closed issue. This was particularly significant in view of the fact that Sheikh Abdullah had strongly objected to India and Pakistan deciding at Simla, Kashmir's future without consulting any of its leaders or its people. Article 253 of the constitution as applied to Kashmir has a proviso that "no decision affecting the disposition of Jammu and Kashmir shall be made by the Government of India without the consent of the Government of the state."[35]

Acknowledging the new understanding with New Delhi, Sheikh Abdullah observed that "basically what has been achieved is a reestablishment of trust and confidence born out of shared ideals and common objectives of the kind which was there all through until 1953."[36] Between 1953 and 1972, he had remained under detention of one kind or another. Mrs. Gandhi explained to the parliament on February 24, 1975, why she was now willing to trust the sheikh. "Nobody had denied Sheikh Abdullah the previous role. In between he seemed to have changed his mind and there was disagreement and estrangement. [Now that] he is again expressing his willingness to work for unity, for secularism, we welcome him."[37]

The two agreements together—the Simla pact and the Kashmir accord—were meant to establish India's relational control, that is, its ability to structure relations among all the actors that had the ability to damage or influence it. This included Sheikh Abdullah and his followers in the valley, the Hindu nationalists in Jammu, members of the ruling Congress party in Kashmir, the national opposition to the Congress(I), and most importantly,

Pakistan. Pakistani Prime Minister Z. A. Bhutto acknowledged as much when he said to a post-Simla delegation of visiting Indian journalists that "Pakistan was not in a position to pursue the policy of confrontation, that it wanted consultation and negotiation on the Kashmir question, that it was up to the people of Kashmir to fight for self-determination, that the people of the subcontinent wanted to turn their back on the past animosities and desired peace."[38] Mrs. Gandhi used both the agreements to wrest a promise from Pakistan and from Sheikh Abdullah. Pakistan would refrain from meddling in J&K while Sheikh Abdullah normalized and neutralized the situation there. Each provided the supranational State with greater domestic and foreign policy autonomy to pursue its primary objective: making India's nation congruent with its territorial state.

The year 1972 was the high point in India's nation-building efforts. Over a period of twenty-five years, step by step, first Nehru and then Mrs. Gandhi had constructed a system that attempted to balance and harmonize the aspirations of India's emerging ethnonations with its supranational State, established a level of autonomy for the latter in determining the course of modernization, and secured a degree of influence over the policies pursued by the neighboring states. At Simla, the Kashmir dispute seemed more or less resolved and the state of J&K was back under a popular administration that retrospectively gave its sanction to the accession and the subsequent integration of its economy with that of India; Bangladesh was under a popular administration that was friendly and secular; Pakistan had reconciled itself to the status quo in Kashmir and was busy repairing the economic and psychological damage done to it by the loss of Bangladesh, and Punjab was calm, the Sikh ethnonational impulse seemingly absorbed by the creation of Punjabi Suba.

The request by the Sri Lanka government for military assistance in quelling the revolt by the JVP in the south of the country seemed to underline the success of the Indian strategy. But, this was not to last. Within India, the steps that Mrs. Gandhi had taken to establish her personal preeminence in the Congress party set off a chain of political consequences that were to end by severely compromising the autonomy of the supranational State. In India's neighborhood, too, the arrangements mediated by Mrs. Gandhi did not last. Sheikh Mujibur Rehman was assassinated in 1975; two years later, the Bhutto government was overthrown by the armed forces in Pakistan. Thus, the 1980s saw the Indian model of achieving nation-state congruency come under increasing strain as accommodation and co-optation gave place to confrontation and coercion.

Chapter 5

꙼

THE EROSION OF THE SUPRANATIONAL STATE

India Under Indira Gandhi and Rajiv Gandhi

In 1972, Indira Gandhi was at the height of her power. Three years later, the Congress was a beleaguered party, Mrs. Gandhi was under attack and had to declare a national emergency to stay in power. By 1977, when elections were held once more, the Congress was thrown out of office for the first time since Independence. The causes of this precipitous decline are a subject of considerable debate.[1] But as pointed out in chapter 4, most of them were rooted in the manner in which Gandhi secured supremacy for herself in the Congress party between 1969 and 1971. Finding herself in a fight with the organizational leaders of the party over her attempt to take the Congress sharply left in its programs, Mrs. Gandhi, in July 1969, went over members' heads to establish a form of direct rule based on populist appeal and personal charisma.[2]

This weakened the party organization even more, and reduced the ability of regional and local leaders to serve as the intermediaries between the party and its top leaders on the one hand, and people and the government on the other. Subsequent events—the declaration of a national emergency in 1975, the defeat of Mrs. Gandhi and the Congress party in the 1977 elections, and then the collapse of the Janata government—show that this form of personalized politics was intrinsically less stable than the one it had replaced.[3] It pushed popular movements and regional dissent increasingly away from regular channels of electoral politics and in the direction of violent protest and even armed insurgency. This is what eventually happened in Punjab and Kashmir in the 1980 and early 1990s respectively.

Why did the weakening take place and how did it undermine the Nehruvian model of interlocking balances between ethnic nationalities and the central state established in the 1950s? What impact did this have on India's relational control over the overlapping nationalities it shared with its neighbors? This chapter outlines the ways in which Mrs. Gandhi and then Rajiv Gandhi unwittingly weakened the authority and popular legitimacy of India's supranational State. Scholars are divided about who or what to blame for this growing crisis of governance and democracy. One explanation focuses on Indira Gandhi and her authoritarian personality; another concentrates on the breakdown of traditional patterns of economic and political power in wake of modernization; a third blames the uneven development and growing gap between the haves and have-nots in India; while yet another explanation sees the root cause of this crisis in democratic overload, i.e., undisciplined expansion of the electorate without the corresponding growth in institutional capacity. It is beyond the scope of this book to sort through these diverse explanations.

Two caveats, however, need to be stated at this point. First, India's crisis of governance has multiple causes, although this chapter focuses on the weaknesses of party politics. It distinguishes between personality factors and larger sociopolitical trends in a modernizing, large, and heterogeneous state such as India. Since India's heterogeneity is an irreducible given, her leaders, whatever their personal preferences, have to reconcile the imperatives of unity with those of democracy. In the post-Nehru period, broadly two visions for achieving unity amidst diversity have emerged: one came to be represented by Mrs. Gandhi, who sought to centralize power based on her general distrust of regional and ethnic movements. The other was represented by regional movements (the DMK in Tamil Nadu, the Samyukta Maharashtra movement in Maharashtra) initially and then by the coalition of forces supporting the Janata party. This second vision saw national unity through greater regional and cultural autonomy. Although Jawaharlal Nehru had managed to reconcile the two conflicting trends by conceding the 1956 linguistic reorganization, he had done so reluctantly and only because of great popular pressure. Lacking the base of a unified and dominant Congress, an advantage Nehru had that his successors did not, Mrs. Gandhi reacted with greater anxiety to the demands for regional autonomy. Arguments about her personal culpability in undermining the democratic processes must be corrected by taking into account the pressures arising out of India's heterogeneity. This is not to defend Mrs. Gandhi or her successors but to emphasize the compelling logic of interlocking balances and relational control located in the nationalist project of making India into a modern nation-state.

The second caveat, this chapter has a limited objective: to show the ways in which Mrs. Gandhi responded to Congress's loss of dominance, and how that in turn undermined the strategies of balance and ethnic representation essential to India's unity. Distinctions were drawn in chapter 1 between the concept of centralization of power and quantum of power. The latter refers to a state's ability to resolve conflict without violence and move ahead with its modernization agenda. Centralization of power, on the other hand, means concentration of administrative power at the top.

To keep a personal hold on the electorate, Mrs. Gandhi felt compelled to exercise increasing control over the state units of the Congress party. She did this by replacing chief ministers (who had come up through the party machine) with her personal nominees, and frequently passing over the legislative and organizational leaders of the Congress in the states.[4] This disrupted the party organization in the states just as her "rebellion" against the organizational leaders had disrupted it with the Congress split in 1969. But personal control of party organization did not give her freedom from the gnawing anxiety that the Congress was losing authority—an anxiety that began to mount when by-election results began to go against the party.[5] In her quest for direct control, Mrs. Gandhi changed chief ministers no less than fourteen times in these five years. Twelve of the fourteen were Congress chief ministers, including the highly regarded H. N. Bahuguna of Uttar Pradesh (1976), and V. P. Naik of Maharashtra (1973). Bahuguna was widely considered one of the best chief ministers Uttar Pradesh had, and Naik had been the chief minister of Maharashtra for more than a decade. After the latter was ousted, Maharashtra was plagued by weak and unstable leadership.

The effect this had on the states was disastrous: Congress leaders got the message that their tenure depended less on how well they governed their states than how Mrs. Gandhi viewed their performance. What was worse, governing well was almost as dangerous as governing badly, for any chief minister who developed an independent base in the state became a threat to her supremacy in the party. The end result was that, within a short period of time, there was a decisive break in the link between the party and the people. The provincial leaders of the Congress ceased to represent ethnonational aspirations in their dealings with the central state. This robbed the Congress party of its ability to deal with emerging ethnonational sentiment by either co-opting its emerging leaders, or appropriating a large part of their agendas and isolating them, as Nehru had done on more than one occasion. Neither option remained feasible because both required leaders to come up from below and not be thrust on people from the top.

For the supranational State that left only one way of maintaining the balance between itself and ethnonational sentiment—an explicit decision to share power in such a way that while Congress supported the dominant ethnonational party in the state, the latter supported the Congress and through it the agenda of the supranational State at the center. This was the arrangement that Nehru had made with Sheikh Abdullah in Kashmir in 1947–1952 and Mrs. Gandhi had struck with the DMK and then the AIADMK in Tamil Nadu. But for reasons explained below, this was no longer possible for the Congress after the mid-seventies.

After the brief interlude of rule by the Janata party, from 1977 to 1979, the Congress came back to power in December 1979 with 351 parliament seats; it seemed on the surface that the model the Congress had been pursuing since Independence was again ascendant.[6] But the Congress victory was based on a very different reality. During the Janata interregnum, the Congress party had split for a second time. As in 1967, the organizational leaders of the party were once more combined against Indira Gandhi. Whatever organizational base the party had left after its first split in 1969 was also lost to the ruling Indira Gandhi Congress. Even more than before, the party had lost its grassroots and begun to rely for its success on the almost mythic proportions of her personal charisma. The party could not however survive on charisma alone. To meet its daily expenses and to fund the elections, it had to collect money. By now the amount needed to meet electoral expenses had risen to levels that were unthinkable a decade earlier. The separation of parliamentary elections from elections to the state assemblies in 1971 had doubled the expenses, and inflation and mounting political competition had almost doubled it again. When the Congress party banned corporate donations to political parties in 1970, it did not create any alternate legal way of funding political activity. This opened the way for criminal elements and economic offenders with unaccounted income to make political donations in cash and acquire influence within the party.[7] According to reports published in the press and conversations with members of Delhi's political elite, even these funds were no longer sufficient to finance an election or meet day-to-day political expenses. New ways had to be found for raising large sums of cash. The favored new method was to load front-end commissions on large government purchases of arms, aircraft, power plants, and the like.

Considering their impact on the general public, the stories of corruption in high places had the most disastrous effect. What everyone could see was that political parties, above all the Congress, were spending huge sums on electoral battles, and on meeting day-to-day expenses, but without any visible source of funds. By the early 1980s, after more than a decade of blatant corruption, the political system as a whole (and mostly the Congress) had been severely delegitimized. This played a powerful role in eroding the moral authority of the Congress and its strategy of national integration. Ethnonational appeals began more and more to reflect moral outrage against a corrupt Center. With this there was a decline in the central state's capacity to maintain the interlocking balance with India's nationalities.

By the early 1980s, the paradox implicit in these developments had become obvious. Mrs. Gandhi's attempts to centralize power had led to a corresponding decline in the quantum of power enjoyed by the government in its dealings with the states. This erosion became apparent in three ways:

1. The habit among aspiring politicians to look toward New Delhi instead of the people of their own states for legitimation proved difficult to break. It became next to impossible for the central Congress leadership to stay out of factional squabbles in the states where the ruling party was in power. It is by no means certain that Indira Gandhi ever wanted to separate herself from these squabbles, but Rajiv Gandhi, who succeeded her in 1984, certainly did, at least initially.[8] Until 1988, he made it a point to support the incumbent chief ministers, and discouraged dissidents from traveling to the capital to see him. In the end, he too embraced the practices of Mrs. Gandhi

2. Growing political awareness in the people and intensifying competition for economic resources made it more and more difficult for the central government to deal separately with each state. Chief ministers of Congress states often felt their economic interests to be linked with those of their neighbors, and insisted that they be consulted before the center arrived at any accommodation with their neighbor.[9] They threatened that if the central government insisted on going ahead without consulting them, the state unit of the party would be adversely affected. Such threats began to be made over the allocation of investable funds by the planning commission, over the amount of power that a state government allowed to flow through its part of the regional grid to a neighboring state, and, most contentiously, over the sharing of canal and river waters. As such threats multiplied, the supranational State found it increasingly more difficult to maintain its autonomy in dealing with the ethnonational units.

3. The above two problems related mainly to those states that ruled by the Congress. But a parallel development arose in states that were ruled by

the four main parties of the opposition that had jointly formed the Janata government. The experience of reconciling their differences and working together made it possible for many of the state governments to forge lateral alliances and present a common front to the center. This further reduced the capacity of Mrs. Gandhi's government to deal with each in isolation from the others. There was a corresponding decline in the autonomy of the supranational State.

Of the three ways, the first was to have the most serious impact on the authority of the supranational State. Put schematically, the way in which the Congress central leaders' involvement in the internal squabbles of the state parties eroded the State was somewhat as follows:

a) To increase her control over the state unit of the party, Indira Gandhi would replace an independent-minded chief minister with one of her own choice;

b) Dissident factions within the local unit soon would realize that the way to power would be to gain Mrs. Gandhi's support in toppling the incumbent chief minister. So they would make many trips to Delhi and woo powerful leaders at the center to get a hearing from Mrs. Gandhi. If these central leaders were from their own state, then so much the better;

c) The resulting central intervention, no matter in whose favor, would increase the intrusiveness of the center in the affairs of the state unit. This would have two consequences. It would cost the center the impartiality on which a large part of the authority of the supranational State rests and in the state it would further divorce the Congress party from the people.

d) Where states whose territorial boundaries reasonably approximate ethnonational boundaries, and consequently where political mobilizations on ethnonational lines were fairly well advanced, this would leave the field vacant for the rise of an ethno-based political party to challenge the dominance of the Congress. In nation-building terms, since the Congress was seen by many in it as the instrument of the supranational State, co-optation and isolation as methods of exerting relational control over the ethnonational unit would be ruled out. This amounted to a further loss of autonomy of the supranational State. Henceforth it had to negotiate the quantum of its autonomy with the representatives of the concerned ethnonation.

e) However, the developments that shut out co-optation and isolation as techniques of relational control also made it very difficult for the party to accept power-sharing along the above lines. For by this time the central unit of the party would be so completely enmeshed in the affairs of the state unit, that it would be unable to stand up to the anger and sense of betrayal that its attempts to deal with the ethnonational opposition aroused in the state party members. The fact that by now these state party members had powerful patrons within the central leadership in Delhi complicates matters further, because they knew that their position in Delhi depended on their capacity to act as intermediaries between the center and the state unit of the party.

f) The center therefore would resort to the only method left in dealing with the ethnonational opposition: it would attempt to break it, either by encouraging defections from it to the Congress or, where this was impossible, by promoting an even more extreme form of ethnonationalism to discredit the moderate representatives within the opposing political party.

These problems surfaced within months of Indira Gandhi's return to power in January 1980. Two months later, she resumed the practice of toppling opposition governments and declared President's rule in no less than nine states. Several commentators have defended her action by saying it was the Janata party, which ruled from 1977 to 1979, that set the precedent for such wholesale evictions by throwing nine Congress governments out in May 1977. This underlines the general point made by several scholars that by the 1970s, no government in New Delhi could hope to establish a stable rule unless it also controlled a significant number of state legislatures. This does not justify the arbitrary dismissals of elected state governments in which Mrs. Gandhi indulged so frequently but underscores growing interdependence between regional and central politics. Such intertwining was a sign of growing national integration in the sphere of politics but it underlined also the diminishing autonomy of the central state from its constituent units. In any event, it highlighted the growing difficulty of managing the twin burdens of governance and democracy, a task at which Janata leaders had failed while Mrs. Gandhi had succeeded by strengthening the security apparatus of the central state.

Mrs. Gandhi and the Congress, however, were not solely to blame for the decline in the governing ability of India's central state. The opposition parties and ethnic leaders bear a large responsibility for undermining the interlocking balance between India's security and its stability. Ambitious leaders within the opposition—the Akali Dal in Punjab, the National Conference in Kashmir, and the DMK and the AIADMK in Tamil Nadu—had also discovered the power of patronage and profit from ministerial positions. They too were beset by factionalism and prone to using arbitrary, undemocratic tactics. In their quest for power many of these leaders appealed to religious and ethnic separatist sentiments and turned to criminal elements to wrest away office and power from their rivals.

Atul Kohli comments on this peculiar characteristic of India's political mobilization. "Leaders have mobilized socioeconomic groups more as power resources in intra elite struggles and less to satisfy group aspirations." Thus, "Indira Gandhi discovered India's poor when she was pressed politically by other members of the Congress elite. Devraj Urs and Karpoori Thakur similarly discovered the backward castes when they desperately needed to establish new ruling coalitions. The Akalis began stressing issues of Sikh nationalism only when thrown out of power." He remarks that such coalitions are not wrong or bad, since democracies tend to produce all manner of leaders and parties. What is wrong in his view is "the disregard" these show for the "consequences of such mobilization." And what are these consequences? The very constituencies that catapulted leaders to power were ignored in the end. This is why he says, "Indira Gandhi basically ignored the poor," although she was elected because of the promise she made to eliminate poverty from India. "Both Devraj Urs and Karpoori Thakur offered little more than tokens to the backward castes. The Akalis have been willing periodically to sell their nationalistic claims for state power." Once mobilized, unorganized groups stay in the public arena and contribute to political instability.[10]

It should be pointed out that the Janata had some moral justification for dissolving the state governments. These were in their sixth year in office under a constitutional amendment that Mrs. Gandhi had passed (during the emergency when 31 members of parliament were in jail and many others were in hiding) to lengthen the term of the parliament and state legislatures from five to six years. With no constitutional excuse and on a flimsy political basis, Mrs. Gandhi threw many state governments out when they were only in their third year of office. One of those governments was the Akali/Jana Sangh government of Punjab. Whatever effect this action may have had elsewhere, in Punjab, where this was the third Akali government to be brought down prematurely by Mrs. Gandhi, it convinced the Akalis that the Congress simply would not tolerate a non-Congress government. It shut the door on power-sharing and made the Akalis even less disposed to stand up against the militants of Bhindranwale. That prompted the Akali Dal to pass the

Anandpur Sahib resolution in 1973 demanding control of all branches except defense, currency, and communications.

Punjab was not the only state in which Mrs. Gandhi's partisan actions consolidated ethnonational sentiment and reduced the supranational State's autonomy. This happened in that most unlikely of places, the neighboring state of Haryana. The latter is a part of the much larger Hindi-speaking heartland of India (which is spread over five states), and also shares with Punjab a powerful Jat landowning community that has dominated politics in Haryana since its creation in 1966. In the days before Punjab was split to create the present day states of Punjab and Haryana, the Sikh Jats had backed the Akalis. The Hindu Jats had backed the Congress. This had continued undisturbed until 1977 when, for the first time, the Hindu Jats in Haryana backed the Janata party. In 1982, when elections were again held in Haryana, a pre-election coalition of the land-based, Jat-dominated Lok Dal and the BJP, similar in caste composition to the Akali-BJP combine in Punjab, secured the largest number of seats. However, acting on the instructions of New Delhi, the governor insisted on treating the two as separate parties, and on asking the Congress to form the government. As a result the Congress became the largest single party in the state. To provide sufficient time to wean legislators away from the other parties with promises of ministerial berths and more, the governor gave the Congress leaders a full month to call the assembly and prove their majority. There followed a low comedy in which the Lok Dal and the BJP spirited away their legislators to a farmhouse to prevent the Congress from getting to them, and the Congress filled the pages of newspapers with complaints that the leaders of the opposition were keeping the members of the legislative assembly imprisoned. In the end, the Congress had its way and wooed away enough BJP and Lok Dal members to form a government. This left the Jat voters deeply embittered, and facilitated the emergence six years later of a distinct Haryana Jat ethnonationalism under a charismatic ex-Congressman, Devi Lal. However, the immediate effect of the estrangement of the Jats from the Congress was to reduce the central state's capacity to deal with growing unrest in Punjab. Mrs. Gandhi was soon to find out that she could not take Haryana for granted, and therefore could not afford to make concessions to the Akalis that, had those concessions been made in time, probably would have averted the ten years of insurgency in the state that followed.

Between 1980 and 1983, the central state's loss of impartiality lead to the birth of another full-fledged ethnonationalism. This took the form of the rise of the Telugu Desam (the Telugu nation) party in Andhra Pradesh.[11] Although Andhra Pradesh was not located on a strategically sensitive border of India and claimed no fellow ethnics beyond India's borders, the policies that caused the erosion of the supranational State were most clearly visible in this instance. In much the same way as she ousted V. P. Naik in Maharashtra, Indira Gandhi had ousted Brahmananda Reddy, an extremely able Congress chief minister in 1972, who had led the party there for almost a decade. A succession of chief ministers followed, with progressively shorter tenures, and the once stable Congress party in Andhra Pradesh progressively lost its links with the people.

In 1982, following a public insult by Rajiv Gandhi delivered to the then chief minister, T. Anjaiah, a wave of humiliation swept through Andhra. Within weeks the new party, Telugu Desam, came into being, under an aging film star, N. T. Rama Rao. Nine months later, in state assembly elections held in January 1983, the Telugu Desam swept into power. For the first time since Independence, the Congress found itself out of power in Andhra Pradesh. To make matters worse, the Congress also suffered its first-ever defeat in neighboring Karnataka, at the hands of the Janata party. Clearly, the logic that drove Indira Gandhi in Punjab and Haryana, Andhra Pradesh and Karnataka, was not shaped by prejudice against any particular ethnic nation.[12] The similarity of responses in such diverse instances shows that she saw herself at the center of the nation-state, entrusted with keeping the nation and the state together. It is true that this perception was narrowly focused on ensuring her political survival and accumulation of power for that purpose, but these endeavors also enabled the supranational State to dominate the political agenda.

These twin defeats in what the Congress had always thought of as its own special preserve—in Haryana and Andhra—brought home to Mrs. Gandhi the full extent of the party's declining authority. Her subsequent actions showed that she could neither accept the loss nor learn from it. Instead of changing tactics and accepting the need to share power as she had done so readily in Tamil Nadu a decade earlier, she struggled incessantly to break the two governments by triggering defections from them to the Congress. She failed in Karnataka, but for a short while, it seemed that she had succeeded in Andhra. In August 1984, offended by Rama Rao's imperious ways, a sizable group of Telugu Desam members sought to defect. Thinking that the party was on the verge of disintegration, Mrs. Gandhi virtually ordered the governor, a former Congress chief minister from Himachal

Pradesh, to dismiss the government. N. T. Rama Rao still had an absolute majority in spite of the defections. Mrs. Gandhi was sure that, once the Rama Rao ministry fell, more defections would follow. This did not happen. After a humiliating week in which Rao repeatedly paraded his majority before the Governor and the press, Mrs. Gandhi was forced to give in, pin the blame on the governor for having acted out of turn, and get him to reinstate Rama Rao.[13]

The loss of center-state balance in Haryana and Andhra made governing India more difficult for the Congress. But it did not impinge on India's relations with its neighbors, and put India at a disadvantage in the region. In Punjab and Kashmir, however, similar mistakes threatened India's national unity and territorial security. These are border states with fairly well-developed ethnonational personalities (see chapter 3). Both border on Pakistan, which had felt wounded by its humiliating defeat in the 1971 war. In different ways, both were transborder ethnonationalities, with a significant connection to Pakistan. In the case of Punjab, this was not through the presence of Sikhs in Pakistan—there were few left—but because to Sikhs consolidating their ethnonationalism by harking back to the past, Pakistani Punjab was a part of the lost homeland where they had lived and ruled in the not-too-distant past. Lahore was the capital of that homeland and Guru Nanak's birthplace at Nankana Sahib was located in Pakistan. Despite the grim legacy of Partition, and the exchange of populations that caused it, Sikh pilgrims went to Nankana Sahib by the thousands every year on pilgrimage, a practice that Pakistan, for its own reasons, never discouraged. In the case of Kashmir, the transborder ethnic connection was much more apparent. Although the Muslims of the valley were not ethnically of the same stock as those of Azad Kashmir, social interactions and intermarriages had created a host of links between the people of Muzaffarabad, Poonch, and Mirpur districts, which had fallen into Pakistani Kashmir, and the Muslims of Kashmir valley and Jammu. Pakistan never ceased to lay claim to Kashmir; it insisted that Kashmir was a disputed territory, something that India had acknowledged at the Simla summit but which in the view of Mrs. Gandhi's many associates had not been altogether prudent or wise.

Thus in Punjab and Kashmir, the Congress's progressive loss of control over its state units translated not only into the supranational State's loss of relational control over India's ethnonations, but also into India's loss of relational control over its neighbor in foreign policy, and its growing vulnerability to superpower politics and the cold war. The way in which this happened is discussed in the following chapters.

Rajiv Gandhi's Failure to Regain Interlocking Balance of Interests

There can be no doubt that Mrs. Gandhi's long reign saw a determined effort by her to centralize power in her hands. There also can be no doubt that if her aim was to acquire greater power, then she failed. Every increase in centralization led to a corresponding decrease in the quantum of actual power enjoyed by New Delhi. Were there structural causes that forced her to pursue a course of action that reduced her real power to govern and consequently weakened the supranational Indian State? Rajiv Gandhi's five years in office suggest that there was another way to restore the authority of the supranational State—by going back to the model of accommodation constructed by Nehru. However, by 1980 if not earlier, the Congress had already passed the turnoff point on the road to this alternative. Rajiv Gandhi therefore abandoned the attempt to restore regional autonomy and instead recommitted himself to the course of centralization followed by Mrs. Gandhi. One is led to this conclusion because he tried to initially change the course of Congress politics, and failed.

Following Mrs. Gandhi's assassination on October 31, 1984, Rajiv Gandhi and the Congress were returned to power with the largest vote that the Congress had ever obtained—49.1 percent of the total—and an unprecedented 401 seats, that swelled over a number of by-elections to 413 seats in a parliament of 544 members. By then, ethnic and religious nationalism of various hues had not only staked a claim to different parts of the Indian nation, but Hindu nationalism was making its collective muscle felt in mainstream politics. This had been evident in the conscious wooing by the Congress of the Hindu chauvinist vote in the 1980 and 1985 elections, in the history of violence that had led to the assassination of Mrs. Gandhi, in the widespread perceptions that the Congress would lose the 1984 elections, and in the series of regional political revolts that had culminated in the Janata rule in Karnataka and the birth of the Telugu Desam in Andhra. By the end of 1984, the Congress had lost the south and all state governments there had passed into the hands of regionally based political parties. These could not and did not compete for national power with either the Congress or the Janata party, but they made Indian politics unpredictable and highly volatile.

Three factors in particular contributed to the return of the Congress to the helm of affairs. The first was the "sympathy" factor. Shocked and bewildered by the brutal assassination of Mrs. Gandhi, many voters had switched their support to the Congress. Second, the Congress(I) and Rajiv Gandhi deliberately and consciously set out to appeal to the "Hindu" vote. The RSS Hindu extremist organization, which had on previous occasions campaigned for the Jan Sangh and BJP candidates, had on this occasion swung heavily and openly behind the Congress(I). Nana Deshmukh, a top RSS leader had endorsed Rajiv Gandhi's candidacy in November 1984, a month after Mrs. Gandhi's death. The RSS wanted to show the country that "it was the majority community that elected the government."[14] James Manor writes that this "widespread RSS support for the Congress-I became apparent" to him "from numerous interviews with BJP and Congress-I activists in several Indian states during December 1984 and January 1985."[15]

The appeal to the "Hindu" constituency was meant to undermine parties that stood to the right of the Congress (I), mainly the BJP, but also the Lok Dal, which appealed to elements that were sympathetic to the anti-Muslim or Anti-Sikh ideology of the Jan Sangh. The Congress campaign poster plastered on the walls of cities and villages of India read "Give Unity a hand," while its subtext made pointed references to the Sikhs.[16] Although violence against Hindus made the "Hindu Rashtra" ideology a factor in the elections, it also had triggered deep anxiety about the unity of India. This was the third factor that had contributed to Rajiv Gandhi's victory. At every campaign stop, he attacked the opposition for having supported the Anandpur Sahib Resolution. He charged that the Janata Party, the BJP, and the Dalit Mazdoor Kisan Sabha had links with Sikh extremists living in Britain.[17] The anti-Sikh themes surfaced continuously in the campaign speeches by Congress (I) leaders and in the full-page advertisements published in the leading newspapers.[18]

Rajiv Gandhi's stunning victory at the hustings showed that the vision of a unified, strong India had dug deep roots in the popular imagination. The blatant appeal to communal vote had nevertheless underlined the erosion and uncertainty within the ruling party and its loss of control over national agenda. The popular wave in favor of the Congress hid the growing rift between India's heterogeneous segments and the central state. The Congress (I) leaders and Rajiv Gandhi believed, as had Mrs. Gandhi before them, that the communal-minded constituency was safer in their hands than in the hands of committed chauvinists of the RSS and the BJP variety.

It is not surprising then, that Rajiv Gandhi should drop the highly emotive stance he and his colleagues had adopted soon after the Congress was securely in place. Since 1982, he had been talking about rebuilding the party at the local and provincial levels and restoring the idealistic image it enjoyed during the days of Nehru. He enthusiastically turned to reforms. Rajiv wanted to strengthen the Congress, restore autonomy to the political institutions, and cleanse the government of corruption. Instead of ignoring members of the opposition, he consulted with them and enlisted their support for agreements in Punjab and Assam. This was a far cry from his election rhetoric that had portrayed every Sikh as a terrorist and an enemy of the state.

Rajiv Gandhi also tried to shed individuals too closely identified with Mrs. Gandhi and her arbitrary rule, to jettison those party members with unsavory reputations or those charged with corruption, and to infuse new and younger blood into the party. He insisted on receiving honest reports on the political events in the countryside, a practice that had almost died out in Mrs. Gandhi's tenure. Rajiv had tried to revive the notion of accountability and responsibility of grassroots organizations and performance. He had launched a blistering attack on his own party. At the celebration of the hundredth anniversary of the Indian National Congress in Bombay (December 28, 1985) Rajiv made pointed references to the "cliques—enmeshing the living body of the Congress in their net of avarice" and to the "self-aggrandizement , . . corrupt ways" of Congress operatives.[19]

Armed with this enormous mandate, Rajiv Gandhi set about rebuilding a working relationship with the opposition parties and reestablishing a minimum of consensus on issues of national importance. Since many of them were in power in various states, this amounted to sending out signals that Rajiv was prepared to share power with them in a layered reordering of the India state through the Tamil Nadu model.

The first opportunity to show that he was prepared to do so came in Karnataka. In the parliamentary election, Karnataka voters again switched sides and returned 23 Congress members in 27 parliamentary constituencies. Local Congressmen immediately rushed to New Delhi and demanded that Rajiv Gandhi throw out the Janata government of Rama Krishna Hegde and hold a fresh election after a spell of President's Rule. Rajiv proved reluctant to do so, and while the matter was being discussed in New Delhi, Hegde resigned and demanded the right to hold a fresh election to renew his mandate. Karnataka Congressmen, backed by their power brokers in Delhi, then demanded that the central government advise the governor not to accept Hegde's demand for another election and put the state under President's Rule. They reasoned that, since Hegde had neither suffered a defection from his party nor lost a vote on the floor of the house, the governor would be obliged to ask him to continue as caretaker chief minister until the next election. They claimed this would give the Janata, in some unspecified way, an advantage in the next election.

Rajiv surprised his party by advising the governor to accept Hegde's resignation and call for elections. Within days of his Karnataka decision, Rajiv
introduced a bill in parliament that was designed to make opportunistic
defections, in pursuit of office or wealth, exceedingly difficult if not impossible. "Defections and floor crossings had plagued the Indian democracy since
1967. Of the 2,700 recorded defections it is noteworthy that the Congress
had attracted nearly 1,900 from the ranks of other parties. The Congress was
then the chief beneficiary of such defections.[20] According to the bill, anyone
who rebelled against his party's whip or changed his party affiliation immediately lost his seat in the legislature. Defections were permitted only if more
than one-third of a party broke away. It was not then deemed a defection but
a split in the party and the "defectors" gained the right to sit as a separate
group in the legislature or join another group.

Subsequent experience was to show that the bill was not as successful in
curbing opportunism and stabilizing the majority of the ruling party as the
framers had hoped it would be. But all that was in the future. Coming on the
heels of the Karnataka decision, this bill, which benefited mainly the opposition, and sought to remove at one stroke the main cause of the embitterment
of politics in the Mrs. Gandhi years, raised Rajiv Gandhi's political popularity sky high. The effect on the opposition and on the intelligentsia country-
wide was electrifying. Suddenly Rajiv Gandhi was the most popular man in
India. Many in the opposition held him in higher esteem than they did their
own leaders.

But Rajiv was not popular in his own party. When Hegde and the Janata
won the March 1985 elections with an increased majority in the state assembly, they openly criticized Gandhi and accused him of "giving Karnataka
away" through his misplaced generosity. Rajiv was not, however, deterred. In
the next nine months he settled longstanding political disputes that had led
to prolonged agitations and insurgencies in Assam and Mizoram. While the
Assamese agitation had been launched by the ethnic Assamese to put a stop
to illegal immigration from Bangladesh and to deny the vote to the immi-
grants who had, over the previous thirty years, raised the Bengali (mainly
Muslim) population of the state to almost half, Mizoram had been in the grip
of a full-fledged insurgency for the previous twenty-four years.[21] Rajiv settled the dispute by negotiating in secret with Laldenga, the head of the Mizo
National Front. Under the agreement, Mizoram obtained a higher level of
devolution than the core states of India. Specifically, people from other parts
of the state were not permitted to buy land in Mizoram. In this, the Mizo settlement followed the pattern that had been set in Kashmir in 1952, and in

Nagaland, another state (composed of sixteen tribes in the far northeast) that had been in revolt for sixteen years until a cease-fire agreement was reached in 1964. In the elections that followed these settlements, the Asom Gana Parishad, the party of the ethnic Assamese, and the Mizo National Front gained resounding victories.[22] Rajiv Gandhi's main achievement was to have brought the two movements back within the fold of democracy. In neither state was the Congress eliminated.[23]

Instead of regarding this as a major achievement, Gandhi's compatriots in the Congress party began to criticize him for costing the party two more states. The rhetoric of their condemnation, not only regarding Assam and Mizoram but also Karnataka, was revealing: they considered President's Rule, which Assam had been under since 1978 and Mizoram for practically two decades, as rule by the Congress. There is no more revealing indication of the extent to which, under the latter-day Congress, India's supranational State had come to be regarded as identical with the Congress party and had as a consequence lost all ability to act with impartiality toward the ethnonations. It destroyed the balance of interlocking forces on which India's stability depended.

Rajiv Gandhi also entered into a pact with Sant Harchand Singh Longowal, leader of the Akali Dal. In the elections that followed, in September 1985, the Congress was soundly defeated in Punjab. These successive losses gave the power brokers in the party the chance they had been waiting for to attack him and his policies. In the Congress, sour jokes became common, that by the time Rajiv finished making his pacts the Congress would have been wiped out of the entire country except New Delhi.[24] The opposition to him came to a head when, in his presidential address to the Congress party during its centenary celebrations in Bombay, he accused the party of having become corrupt and having lost its vigor.[25]

Rajiv began to lose his self-confidence from 1986 onward. His sure touch became uncertain. He distanced himself from his first group of close advisers—Arun Singh, Arun Nehru (a cousin), and V. P. Singh, the finance minister.[26] Listening more and more to the advice of the old guard in the Congress, he reverted to the ways of his mother, Mrs. Gandhi. One of the first signs was the recall of two of Mrs. Gandhi's most faithful and trusted advisers to his side. The first was the former Haryana chief minister, Bansi Lal.

Bansi Lal had been closely identified with the "emergency rule" of Mrs. Gandhi. He did not represent Rajiv's new vision nor did he enjoy a reputation for honesty. Rajiv Gandhi had to appoint Bansi Lal as a counterweight to another potent leader from Haryana, the Congress' chief minister, Bhajan

Lal. Bhajan Lal had resisted accommodation with the Akali Dal. Rajiv however was anxious to settle the conflict in Punjab. The only way to bring Haryana to the negotiating table was to create a countervailing force to Bhajan Lal and his cohorts.[27] The second was R. K. Dhawan, formerly Mrs. Gandhi's private secretary, who returned to the prime minister's house as an adviser. Dhawan was believed to be a past master at reconciling factional fights within the Congress. His return was greeted with relief by the rank and file of the now disenchanted party.

The turning point for Rajiv Gandhi came in 1987. In that year his reformist zeal succumbed to the inexorable logic of a Congress party by now decayed and corrupt. By the end of 1986, the Congress (I) had lost elections in the Punjab, Assam, Mizoram, Kerala, and West Bengal. In June 1987, the ruling party suffered a crushing defeat in Haryana at the hands of Devi Lal, who by then had fully consolidated Jat constituency and the class of peasant proprietors behind him. By the end of 1987, the Congress ruled only twelve of India's twenty-five states, and for the first time since Independence, the whole of South India was in the hands of the opposition parties.

It was in these circumstances that what came to be known as the "Bofors scandal" surfaced and eventually cost him the 1989 elections.[28] Back in 1987, just when Rajiv's stock was falling because of the electoral defeats and his differences with his popular finance minister, V. P. Singh, a Swedish newspaper, *Dagens Nyheter*, published details of kickbacks that had been paid by Bofors, a Swedish arms manufacturer, to middlemen in the sale of $1.2 billion worth of 155mm field Howitzers to the Indian government. Obviously reforms had not stopped the Rajiv government from using public office for personal profit and political gain.

The Bofors deal was awkward, because while the actual signing took place after the October 1985 order, the deal itself had been on the anvil since 1978, and as subsequent exposures were to show, had at least three intermediaries, with commissions (contracted by Bofors) amounting to a mind-boggling 14 percent of the sale price. The contract fell into limbo and commission agreements already made could not be canceled.[29] After immediate and emphatic denials that any such commissions had been paid, the Congress party issued a seven-page resolution charging "foreign forces" in collusion with "parties of the right reaction" of attempting to topple the government "through trickery and fraud and through open incitement of lawlessness and subversion."[30]

But none of this carried any conviction with the public. The rhetoric of paranoia, resurrected for the first time after the 1985 elections, only served to underline how severely the allegations had shaken the government. The awkward timing of the contract was a poor mitigating factor when compared with the enormous crime that any further investigation of the contract might reveal, namely that at the precise moment when the country was slipping into a severe foreign exchange crisis, the government was funding the activities of the Congress party by loading foreign deals with front-end commissions to be paid in foreign exchange in sensitive areas of defense and industry.

Rajiv Gandhi had two choices: to embark on a full-fledged criminal investigation with no idea where the finger of blame would ultimately point, or to try for a cover-up in order to save the party. He opted for the latter. This proved a disastrous decision, because the exposures were not taking place in India, where a cover-up might have been possible, but in Sweden and Switzerland, where the Indian government and the Congress could not control events. The attempted cover-up therefore convinced almost the entire public that Gandhi was a personal beneficiary from the kickbacks. The Indian public saw Rajiv Gandhi as guilty. The sins of Indira Gandhi, whose government banned all legal sources of funding for political parties and forced them to rely on black money, had returned to visit her son.

Following the expulsion of V. P. Singh (highly reputed for honesty) and Arun Nehru (reputed for efficiency and can-do realism) from the Congress party in June 1987, and the resignation of Arun Singh, the minister for defense production and Rajiv's closest friend, the reformist impulse petered out altogether. From then on, Rajiv was guided in all Congress party matters by the old guard. He began to back away from his accord with the Akalis and reverted to Indira Gandhi's methods of retaining control of the other states. This was highlighted in 1988 when, after having sternly refused to listen to pleas from Congress dissidents not to topple the incumbent chief ministers, Rajiv removed no less than eight of the remaining twelve Congress chief ministers, and replaced them with nominees of the Congress organization in Delhi. He also stopped talking about the need to reform the system of electoral finance, one of the principal themes of his presidential address at the Congress centenary in 1985. In sum, Rajiv's brief attempt to restore the interlocking balance between the central or supranational State and the ethnonations by sharing power with them, flickered out after two years and was replaced by the "politics of survival" at any cost.

The most dangerous consequence of this weakening of the interlocking balance was evident in the shortsighted compromises Rajiv Gandhi made with religiously defined nationalism of the Hindu and Muslim genre. His 1985 campaign rhetoric had focused on themes that had pitted Hindus against Sikhs; the latter were cast in the role of terrorists and secessionists. A large number of RSS cadres had worked in this election for Rajiv Gandhi. According to several scholars, the Hindu nationalist constituency had switched its support in favor of the Congress in the 1985 election. During the years immediately following the electoral victory, the 1986 Shah Bano case, and Rajiv Gandhi's political maneuvering around it, finally exposed the desperate tricks to which the Congress and Rajiv Gandhi, the legate and heir to Gandhi and Nehru, had sunk.

In brief, the Shah Bano case involved a Muslim woman, Shah Bano, who had filed for maintenance after she had been divorced. Her former husband argued that, under the Islamic law, he was not obliged to provide maintenance. The supreme court of India handed down the decision that civil law superseded Muslim personal law, particularly since Shah Bano had sought protection under civil law. A highly vocal segment of conservative Muslims protested the decision and argued that the secular court had no jurisdiction over religious matters. They turned the divorce case into a challenge to the supreme court and supranational State's authority to prevail in such matters.

Rajiv Gandhi initially supported the court. Then to soothe the Muslim community, which was highly agitated over the issue, he put through legislation in the parliament that made the Shari'a superior to the civil law in family matters.[31] This provoked a fierce response from the Hindu nationalists. To counter Hindu sentiments, Rajiv Gandhi opened the Mosque Temple site at Ayodhya to Hindu pilgrimage. This political quid pro quo was hardly designed to retain religious equidistance, or maintain the image of impartiality that is so crucial to the balance of interlocking forces in India.

"If it is alleged" writes Varshney, "that the state is moving toward one particular religion, the state, to equalize the distance, can subsequently move toward the other religion. Each such equalizing step may be aimed at soothing the religious communities. But the state gets more embroiled in religion. An unstable equilibrium results, breeding distrust all around."[32] This is precisely what happened in Rajiv Gandhi's attempts to appease the Hindu nationalist and Muslim fundamentalist sentiments during the second half of the 1980s.

While the Muslim challenge to the courts was serious enough, the retaliatory Hindu challenge to the supreme court's jurisdiction to rule on the dispute over the Mosque Temple site at Ayodhya proved disastrous to India's stability. The Mosque was located in Ayodhya, a small town in Uttar Pradesh. The Hindu nationalists led by the VHP, the BJP, and their family of organizations claimed that the mosque was built on a site where a temple celebrating the birth of Ram had existed before 1528. The invading troops of Babur, who later established the Mughal dynasty and the second Muslim empire in India, destroyed the temple and built a mosque in its place. The Hindu nationalists were impervious to the arguments by archeologists and historians that question the VHP construction of events. According to local stories, attempts were made several times in the past to "liberate" the birthplace of Ram, but the most significant episode occurred in 1948. Fearing Hindu–Muslim riots, the courts padlocked the site. It remained closed until 1986 when it was reopened at Rajiv Gandhi government's direction. Ever since then, the Babri Masjid–Ram Janma Bhoomi dispute has repeatedly thrown India into a state of turmoil. In 1990, it became a catalyst in bringing down the V. P. Singh government. In 1992, the BJP and its ideological cohorts mobilized the mass sentiments to lead a protest march to Ayodhya and destroy the mosque. Such an attack on religious monuments were unprecedented in post-Independence history. Retaliation for destruction followed soon. There were Hindu–Muslim riots in many cities, and lethal bomb blasts in Bombay that demolished the stock exchange and brought India's financial center to a halt. More Hindu–Muslim riots and killings followed, often in complicity with the local politicians and police who looked on as frenzied Hindu mobs led by hired criminals destroyed Muslim homes and murdered innocent civilians for belonging to a different religion.

The growing polarization between Hindu and Muslim communities within India, reflected in the aforementioned disputes, catapulted the BJP and its family of political-religious organizations (all belonging to the loosely defined categories of Hindu nationalist advocacy or what is popularly known as the Sangh Parivar) to the center of Indian politics. These same organizations had contributed to the Hindu–Sikh polarization in Punjab and sought to answer Sikh militancy with Hindu militancy. The BJP and its supporters take the most hard line positions on center-state relations and foreign policy. For instance, they oppose any negotiations with Sikh and Kashmiri militants, advocate a use of force to eradicate what they call secessionists, urge a tough stance toward Pakistan, and support acquisition of nuclear weapons. They constitute a formidable challenge to the more moderate, secular, and relatively more liberal vision with which the Congress was associated.

A variety of economic and cultural explanations are made for the rise of Hindu nationalism. Some see it as a natural outgrowth of the expanding electoral democracy in a traditional society; others see it as a result of economic failures, particularly of the ruling bourgeois classes to transform India. Political explanations center around India's weakening institutions.

The Hindu nationalism certainly presents an alternative to the Congress-led version of Indian nationalism. And it has grown in the vacuum of power created by the near collapse of relational control and interlocking balance between India's supranational State and its diverse ethnonations.

Rajiv Gandhi's attempts to appease the most regressive segments of Hindu and Muslim community were rooted in the belief that he, like his predecessors, might be able to retain control over India's diversity by practicing equidistance. Given the extent to which Congress's legitimacy and authority were already eroded, it was not surprising that he failed to do so. Instead, his decisions strengthened his rivals (both to his right and left), who succeeded in defeating him in the 1989 elections. These developments had a profound impact on India's relations with her neighbors, Pakistan and Sri Lanka.

It could hardly be otherwise. Any contest over India's national identity—which conflicts in Punjab, Kashmir, and over Babri-Masjid Ram Janma Bhoomi fully reflected—could not but spill over into the neighboring states that also shared some of these identity problems. The most obvious instance of this was the extension of the Hindu Muslim polarization within India into Indo-Pakistan tensions over Kashmir. It is to this we turn next.

Chapter 6

ॐ

FROM PROTEST TO MILITANCY

Punjab and Kashmir

Chapter 5 was devoted to describing how the progressive deterioration of the Congress and the attempts by Mrs. Indira Gandhi and Rajiv Gandhi to centralize power in their hands destroyed the interlocking balance between the center and the states and reduced the actual quantum of power that the first was able to exercise over the second. As long as this occurred in the interior of the country, it did not translate into a problem for India's foreign policy. But in Punjab and Kashmir, this condition did not hold. The loss of relational control over these two ethnonational regions made India vulnerable to Pakistan and altered the balance that Nehru and then Mrs. Gandhi had built in relations with that country until 1972. The declining capability of the supranational State first became apparent in relation with Punjab.[1]

Punjab

Earlier I characterized the Sikhs of Punjab as an ethnonation without a territorial homeland. Their uprooting was a direct consequence of the partitioning of India in 1947. Much that is obscure about the behavior of the Sikhs in the subsequent four decades becomes comprehensible when it is viewed as an attempt to find a new homeland.[2] In post-Partition Punjab, the proportion of Sikhs to total population changed from 18 to more than 30 percent.[3]

Punjab thus fulfilled the need for a "home" for those displaced from Pakistan, but did not meet the need for a political habitat they could call their own. This became the first demand of the Akalis in the 1950s. The fact that the Hindus of Punjab refused to acknowledge Punjabi as their mother tongue in the 1951 and 1961 censuses, and wrongly insisted on saying that it was Hindi, fueled the Sikh demand for a Punjabi Suba (province).

In 1966, the central government conceded the demand and split Punjab to form modern Punjab and Haryana. In the new Punjab, the Sikhs were nearly 60 percent of the population, but because of internal differences, often based on caste, the community remained split in its loyalties between the Akalis and the Congress.[4] Thus, the Akalis were able to come to power only in coalition with the Jan Sangh. This made Akalis' claim to represent Sikh enthnonationalism somewhat tenuous and left them open to attacks from the more radical flank of Sikh ethnonationalism. The insecurity of Sikhs also made the proponents of ethnonationalism among them more than normally sensitive to modernizing developments, like the green revolution or employ-ment opportunities. Availability of nationwide economic opportunity acted as a strong incentive for the aspiring Sikhs to merge their identity into the mainstream Indian nationalism. The fact that Sikhs and Hindus had continued to intermarry throughout the period of incubation of Sikh ethnonationalism in the twentieth century made some elements of the Akali Dal even more sensitive to the loss of identity.

It is not surprising that when the nine-month-old first Akali-Jan Sangh government was brought down in November 1967 by the Congress, which promised to make the leader of the defectors the next chief minister, and the second also collapsed in 1972 after being in power for three years, Akalis began another round of ethnonational self- assertion. They sought to consol-idate the Sikh vote behind the Akali Dal.

These tensions surfaced within a short time after Mrs. Gandhi's return to power in 1980. Frequent confrontations took place between the Akalis and the Congress (I) during the second half of 1970s, especially during the period of the "emergency," but these were not secessionist challenges. There were no clandestine connections between any element of Sikh ethnonationalism and Pakistan, nor was there communal violence between Hindus and Sikhs in Punjab. Sikh ethnonationalism had continued to become consolidated after the formation of Punjabi Suba in 1966. This became evident when the Akali party passed a resolution at its meeting at Gurdwara Anandpur Sahib in October 1973.[5] According to the then Akali president, Longowal, the reso-lution emanated from the growing fear that "like Buddhism and Jainism, the

Sikhs might also lose their identity in the vast ocean of overwhelming Hindu Majority." The resolution pronounced that "the Shiromani Akali Dal is the very embodiment of the hopes and aspirations of the Sikh nation and as such is fully entitled to its representation."

The Anandpur Sahib resolution set forth three broad categories of demands.[6] First, it demanded that Punjab be given full jurisdiction over its own administration and law and that the central state be restricted to the management of foreign policy, defense, currency, and general communications. Second, the territorial conditions set forth in the resolution demanded that the Sikh-populated Punjabi-speaking areas that were outside though contiguous with Punjab should be merged with Punjab state. This included Chandigarh, areas in Haryana, Rajasthan, and Himachal Pradesh. Third, the cultural demands in the resolution set forth regular recitation of Gurubani on government broadcast facilities, instruction of Sikhism in the schools, and enactment of an all India-Gurdwara act. The last was meant to provide control of all the Sikh Gurdwaras and their funds throughout India to the Akali Dal. The earlier act gave control only over the Gurdwaras in Punjab. The economic conditions demanded that commercial agriculture in Punjab be made more profitable. The resolution called for fixing a favorable price for agricultural produce, for giving the Punjabi farmer access to the "entire country as a single food zone" for providing increased and cheaper irrigation facilities, and for demanding more capital investment.

The demands of the Anandpur Sahib resolution remained within the framework of the Indian constitution; they did not raise the question of a separate Sikh state. But many observers in India asked: "What did the Akalis mean by the term 'Sikh nation' "? The Akalis explained that the term *nation* was a translation of the term *qaum* in Punjabi which denotes a community rather than a nation. Some ventured to ask, "Was this explanation the truth or just a cover-up?"[7] M. J Akbar, a well-respected pro-Congress commentator answered that "the word *qaum* was deliberately used by the drafting committee, with everyone fully aware of the capacity for different interpretations. Its use was an implied threat—that if the demand of the Akalis was not met, they would openly begin to use the interpretation less palatable to Delhi."[8] Akbar raised further questions about the real intent of the Akalis in their announcement to establish the political preeminence of the Panth and of the Khalsa. He questioned what the Akalis meant by "Raj Karega khalsa?" Rule over whom or what? Did the Akalis want a separate country?

The most serious issue raised by the Anandpur Sahib resolution was the demand for the restructuring of the constitution to insure "real federal principles, with equal representation at the Center for the states." The demand for limiting the functions of the central government was a disingenuous reference to the terms spelled out in the 1946 Cabinet Mission plan that had envisaged a loose federation of Hindu and Muslim nations under a limited central government. The Akali Dal's view of Mrs. Gandhi's foreign policy, as expressed in the resolution, denied her any credit for the conduct of the Bangladesh war. Instead, the resolution said that the "foreign policy of India framed by the Congress Party . . . is worthless, hopeless, and highly detrimental to the interests of the country, the nation. and mankind at large." It pledged to "support only . . . that foreign policy of India which is based on the principles of peace and national interests. It strongly advocates a policy of peace with all neighboring countries, especially those inhabited by the Sikhs and their sacred shrines."[9]

Such statements led to interesting interpretation of what the Akalis were suggesting. "Simply put" Akbar comments, "the Akalis were asking for a soft Indo-Pakistani border at a time when 90,000 Pakistani prisoners of war had just left Indian camps. Was the Akali foreign policy . . . the first step toward a deal with Pakistan by which the latter would help in eventual war against Delhi for Khalistan? After all, Sheikh Mujibur Rahman's Awami League had been friendly to India, even at the risk of being called treacherous, for many years before the need arose to seek the help of Indian troops for the creation of Bangladesh."[10] The strategic and ethnonationalist connections in Akbar's biased, but highly provocative discourse, are instructive. At the minimum, it underlined the dilemma Akalis faced in mixing religion with politics in a secular India.

What the Anandpur Sahib resolution represented was a list of Sikh grievances. It was not a secessionist document and was not regarded as such by the Indian government. Its language was certainly ambiguous and lent itself to the kind of interpretations in M. J. Akbar's commentary. Viewed in the theoretical perspective presented in this book, the Anandpur Sahib resolution was a perfect paradigm of the kind of tension that is permanently embedded in the interlocking balances. Such tension might remain confined to the supranational State and its constituent ethnonations, or, it might spill over into relations between India and a neighboring state. This had not happened in Punjab.

Implicit in the Anandpur Sahib resolution was the notion that Sikhs were a people with a distinctive identity; Punjab was the natural territorial habitat of the Sikhs; and Sikhs had a right to make territorial claims based on their religious identity. The resolution was in a profound sense Janus-faced, in that it looked simultaneously at the past and into the future. The reference to Punjab as a homeland for the Sikhs harkened back to the continuing trauma of partition, in which the Sikhs had lost their original homeland. The fear of the future stemmed from the rapid pace of modernization and the social and economic changes that were being effected by the green revolution. These changes had created fears that the separate Sikh identity might become submerged into the larger "Hindu" India.

The meaning and intent of the Anandpur Sahib resolution have been subject of fierce controversy. At least three versions of the document exist, each associated with a factional leader and his followers within the Akali Dal. The Talwandi Dal's version asserts that Sikhs of India are a "historically recognized nation" ever since the founding of the Order of Khalsa, and that this nation has been oppressed since the 1950s by the "brute majority of India." The Sikhs are perceived to have been "denuded" of their identity, "shackled and enslaved" by Hindus who reneged on solemn promises made at the time of Independence. The resolution implies that the Sikhs had not agreed to India's constitution and were resolved to "extricate and free themselves" by all "legitimate" means. These means were not spelled out.

Also included was a demand for an "autonomous region in the north of India" in which "Sikh interest would be dominant" and would have the power to frame its own constitution, except foreign relations, defense, and currency. The resolution further demanded "preeminence" and "self- determined political status" for the Sikhs so they can control their own history and forestall absorption into the "saltish sea waters of inchoate Hinduism." These phrases framed the demand for greater autonomy and more favorable investment and agricultural pricing policies.

The economic demands in all three versions reflected the new prosperity and agrarian transformation brought about by the green revolution. It also reflected the growing political dominance of the class of peasant proprietors in the rural Punjab, such a phenomenon was shared by Haryana, parts of Uttar Pradesh, Madhya Pradesh, and Rajasthan. Although experts disagree about the impact of the green revolution, most have argued that the agricultural transformation had sharpened ethnic consciousness among the Hindus and Sikhs in Punjab,[11] and the new economic stratification had strengthened the Jat Sikhs within the Akali Dal and the SGPC. The Akali Dal had always remained almost exclusively the party of Sikhs in Punjab. Not all Sikhs however, voted for the Akali Dal. A significant number favored the Congress(I). The latter party was particularly popular among the non-Jat castes of Mazhabis, Ramgarias, Khatris, and Aroras. A small number of Sikhs regularly supported the

Communist parties. A similar divide characterized the Hindus in Punjab. A large number preferred the Jan Sangh and its aggressive Hindu nationalist platform, but a significant number of Hindus voted for the Congress(I). This meant that the Congress(I) was the only "secular" nonethnic party that could straddle the Hindu–Sikh constituencies in Punjab.

For the same reasons then, the Congress(I) could not be defeated unless the Akali Dal formed an alliance with Jan Sangh. Between 1967 and 1972 and again from 1977 to 1980, several Akali–Jan Sangh coalition governments were formed in Punjab; these did not offer a stable alternative to the Congress, partly because of factional quarrels within the coalition and partly because in its bid for power, the Congress made relentless effort to break them. Other factors were at work as well. The more ideologically sensitive members of the Akalis Dal found accommodation with the Jan Sangh difficult; the more pragmatic Akalis found it hard to accept a compromise on the issues of Hindi and distribution of office and ministerial positions. According to one scholar, the coalition governments were destined to collapse because the only thing holding them together was the desire for "capturing power."[12] The Jan Sangh members of the coalition were reluctant to support the Akali demands for Chandigarh and division of the river waters. Nor did they fully endorse the demand for greater autonomy. The Akali Dal remained a Sikh party, and the Jan Sangh a Hindu party; only the Congress(I) had the ideological flexibility and electoral support from both Hindus and Sikhs to span the gap.

The Congress(I), however, failed to take the high ideological road in Punjab. It embarked on a strategy to destroy the coalition government by splitting the Akalis. When first such coalition government was formed under Gurnam Singh in March 1967, the Congress leaders in Punjab "persuaded" Lachman Singh Gill (a key leader in the Gurnam Singh cabinet) to defect from the Akali government. In return, the Congress promised to support him in his bid to become the chief minister of Punjab. Subsequently, the Congress withdrew its support and the Gill government collapsed. During the 1971 national and 1972 state elections, the Congress once again swept the polls.[13]

The spectacular victory in the Bangladesh war easily won Mrs. Gandhi and the Congress(I) 11 out of 12 Lok Sabha seats and 66 of the 104 assembly seats in Punjab. The Akalis again found themselves floundering in political wilderness. Their immediate response was to move into the protest mode and pass the Anandpur Sahib resolution in 1973. The 1977 national elections returned the Akali Dal to power in Punjab and their alliance partners, the Janata Dal, to power in New Delhi.[14] In subsequent years, the pattern of fragmentation and collapse was to repeat itself all over again but this time it bore violent results. The Congress leaders began to look for ways to undermine the Akali appeal and recapture power in Punjab as part of a larger plan to defeat the Janata government in the elections and reinstate Congress at the center. Defeat and loss of legislative majority, however, had reduced the Congress from a party to a conglomeration of caucuses held together by narrow self-interest and electoral arithmetic.

The previous chapter has outlined how the Congress leaders sought to hold on to their power base by resorting to ruthless and often undemocratic means. Not only did they use the standard practices of divide and rule, pitting faction against faction and engineering defections, but in a bid to beat the Akalis at their own game, the Congress began to employ religious themes and symbols against the Akalis.[15]

The growing communal consciousness among the Sikhs had its counterpart among the Hindus in Punjab. The green revolution not only had transformed Sikh politics, but it had transformed the politics in the entire Hindu-Hindi belt of north India. It had empowered peasant proprietors and trader-merchant classes all across Haryana, western Uttar Pradesh, and parts of Bihar and Rajasthan. Instead of welding such classes across religious and ethnic lines, agricultural prosperity added a new edge to old grievances and reinforced parochial identities. For instance, the green revolution increased the demand for water by farmers both in Punjab and Haryana. It lent a sharp new edge to the simmering canal waters' dispute between the two states. Since the farming community in one was predominantly Sikh, while it was predominantly Hindu in the other, the water dispute predisposed the Jat Sikh community in Punjab to accepting a communal anti-Hindu interpretation of any compromise suggested by the central government. For the Congress, Punjab was important because of its political ripple effect in the Hindu-Hindi belt states and not because of its legislative seats in the Lok Sabha. Punjab commanded only 12 seats in parliament/the national legislature.[16]

It is against this background that one needs to see the significance of Jarnail Singh Bhindranwale and his rise in the politics of Punjab during the 1980s.[17] The Congress(I) leaders Giani Zail Singh and Sanjay Gandhi, the initial sponsors of Bhindranwale, had hoped he would put the Akali Dal on the defensive and undermine the support it got from the Sants and preachers associated with the Sikh gurdwaras. Bhindranwale was not particularly effective in undermining the Akalis by conventional means. It was only when he applied violent means to make his point that he became an important actor in Punjab politics. One of the first measures he took to shape the political scene was to launch a murderous attack on the Nirankaris in 1978, a sect of Sikhs considered to be heretics by the Khalsas.[18]

In 1978, the Akali Dal/Jan Sangh government was in power in Punjab. It had given permission to the Nirankaris to hold their 1978 convention in the city of Amritsar. Legally, the Punjab government could hardly deny the Nirankaris the right to preach and organize processions on a religious occasion. But more importantly, the Nirankari traders had links with the Hindu traders supporting the Jan Sangh, their coalition partners in government. Denying them permission would have angered the Jan Sangh. But the Akali acquiescence incensed Bhindranwale, who organized a protest march against the Nirankaris. In the ensuing clash, twelve Sikhs and three Nirankaris were killed.

This episode provided Bhindranwale with a cause that catapulted him a few years later to the center of Punjab politics. It provided the Congress leaders Sanjay Gandhi and Zail Singh, who were masterminding Mrs. Gandhi's return at the center, with an opportunity to break the Akali Dal/Jan Sangh government.

For the Akalis, the Nirankari agitation posed a serious problem: As the defenders of Sikh orthodoxy, they could not disassociate themselves from the movement against a heretical sect. But as coalition partners in the Punjab government, they could not permit or overlook violence against lawful processions.[19] The Akali Dal split and made it possible for the Congress(I) to ride back to victory. The Congress strategy was truly Machiavellian.

When Mrs. Gandhi returned to power in the 1979 general elections and dismissed the Akali-Janata coalition government in Punjab (along with other state governments), the Akalis again moved to agitate and protest against the arbitrary policies of the central leaders. Now there was a noticeable hardening in the Akali's rhetoric. They had been ousted from power by an attack from the radical flank of Sikh ethnonationalism led by an obscure priest who had been secretly aided by their arch rival, the Congress. They felt that their claim to be the only representative of the Sikhs had been undermined. The first order of requirement was to launch an agitation. The Akalis resurrected the Anandpur Sahib resolution of 1973, added several new conditions to it, and presented Mrs. Gandhi with a list of forty-five specific demands. An All-World Sikh Convention, held in July 1981, had already authorized Longowal to start a Dharma Yudh (Righteous struggle) against New Delhi.

The Akalis found another reason: on April 6, 1981, Mrs. Gandhi laid the foundation stone of the Sutlej-Yamuna link canal at Kapuri, near Patiala. According to a 1981 award she had granted, the government should have

waited until 1983 to open the canal. Akali leaders claimed that the Congress
was deliberately deflecting Punjab's share of water to Haryana. They argued
that this gave the Congress electoral advantage in Haryana but left parched
the farmlands in Punjab. For a variety of reasons, the Kapuri protest failed to
generate popular support. In desperation, the Akalis moved the protest to
the Golden Temple. Preparations began with having every district unit of the
party headed by a jathedar (head priest), who was urged to provide volunteers and transport them to the Golden Temple. At this point, the SGPC took
over and sent the volunteers into protest marches where they were promptly
arrested by the government.

During 1981 and 1982, Bhindranwale and his growing number of followers embarked on acts of murder and targeted violence. In April of the
previous year, Baba Gurbachan Singh, the guru of the Nirankari sect, had
been murdered; September 1981, Lala Jagat Nrain, the proprietor of a
chain of newspapers published in the Punjab city of Jullandur, was shot
dead; and in December 1981, Santok Singh, the president of Delhi Gurdwara Management Committee, was killed. Despite the growing lawlessness
and violence, Bhindranwale received continuing support from Congress
leaders Zail Singh and Sanjay Gandhi (until Sanjay Gandhi was killed in a
plane crash).[20]

Why did the Congress leaders in Delhi consider Bhindranwale useful?
Most political commentators agree that Zail Singh, a former Akali Dal politi-
cian-turned Congress leader, wanted to preserve his base in Punjab but saw
the newly appointed Darbara Singh, Mrs. Gandhi's choice for the chief minister of Punjab, as an obstacle to his ambitions. Politically, the two men were
poles apart. Darbara Singh was firmly secular and committed to left-wing
political ideas. Zail Singh was a home-grown, deeply devout Sikh who did
not separate religion from politics. Mrs. Gandhi wanted neither of these
individuals to exercise independent influence in Punjab and therefore
encouraged, or at least did not stop, their plotting against each other. The
consequences were disastrous. Whenever Chief Minister Darbara Singh took
a tough stance toward Bhindranwale and ordered his arrest, President Zail
Singh countermanded the orders.

By July 1982, the turmoil and violence were beginning to worry Mrs.
Gandhi. The central government's stance began to harden visibly against
Bhindranwale, although no overt move was made to stop his campaign for
Khalistan. Bhindranwale announced that he would lead a protest march to
demand the release of his close comrade in arms who had been arrested by
the government. Jacob and Tully write:

If Bhindranwale's morcha (demonstration) had been allowed to
flop it would have been a fatal blow to his prestige. But the Akali
Dal, cynical as ever, had other ideas. They wanted to launch their
own morcha which had failed in the east. They believed it would
succeed if it was launched in Amritsar a second time where Akali
support was strong and where, of course, there were the required
religious overtones. The way to guarantee success, Longowal
thought, would be to take up Bhindranwale's cause too.[21]

In August, the Akali Dal and Bhindranwale merged their efforts. The new
movement was a great success. Each day hundred of the volunteers would
set out from the Golden Temple to protest against the Congress policies.
Within two months of the launching of the morchas, the government jails
were overflowing.

This tactic got results. Mrs. Gandhi ordered the release of all Akali
demonstrators and sent a special envoy to Amritsar to reopen negotiations.
Several rounds of talks took place in 1982 and 1983 between Akali leaders
and Mrs. Gandhi and her advisers. Meanwhile, Bhindranwale continued his
campaign to undermine the Akalis and generate support for Khalistan.
Fearing that Akali protests would spoil the planned Asiad games in Delhi,
the government decided to step up negotiations. An agreement was reached
on November 18. The government agreed to refer the water dispute to a
supreme court judge, consider the Akali conditions regarding the enactment of an all-India Gurdwara act, accede on other religious demands contained in the Anandpur Sahib resolution, release Bhindranwale's men from
jail as demanded by the Akalis, and refer the entire territorial dispute over
Chandigarh and Fazilka and Abohar to a commission.

This agreement was never implemented, mainly because Haryana's chief
minister refused to the transfer of Fazilka and Abohar, in return for Chandigarh. Talks again resumed on June 11, 1983, but nothing came of them. Mrs.
Gandhi, however, had announced two unilateral awards: she had accepted all
Akali Dal religious demands and decided to set up the Sarkaria Commission,
named after the retired Sikh supreme court judge, R. S. Sarkaria. This commission was charged with studying the constitutional arrangement between
the central and state governments. Both Jacob and Tully, as well as Nayar and
Khushwant Singh, believe that if the concessions had emerged from the talks
with the government, the Akali Dal could have claimed them as victory for
the morcha. This would have strengthened the Akali Dal against Bhindranwale, who had opposed all Akali negotiations with New Delhi. Bhindranwale

had stepped up assassination of Sikh and Hindu leaders in the hopes of derailing the talks.

The failure of the 1983 talks boosted Bhindranwale, while Akali Dal leader Longowal faced humiliation and loss of stature among his own followers. Longowal sought to reestablish his leadership by announcing yet another demonstration (called Rasta Roko, meaning "block the roads") against the government. This time the Sikh community responded in large numbers. Having regained his prestige, Longowal challenged Bhindranwale openly. He ordered Bhindranwale to take an oath of loyalty to the morcha and implicitly to the goal of nonviolent agitation. Bhindranwale complied, only to break his oath twelve days later when one of his followers was ordered to assassinate deputy Inspector General A. S. Atwal. Atwal's murder on the steps of the Golden Temple produced an immediate outcry and public demand for forceful measures to stop the terrorists.

Some in Mrs. Gandhi's circle of advisers favored a more reasoned response, however. Several well-respected leaders in the Hindu and Sikh community suggested that she strengthen the Akalis, who could force Bhindranwale and his men out of the Golden Temple, but Mrs. Gandhi seemed unable to move. As the Akalis weakened, Bhindranwale's popularity began to spread among Sikh youths, many of whom came under his spell and saw "a great deal of truth" in his portrayal of "Sikh oppression by Hindu India."[22] Nayar and Khushwant Singh report a conversation with Bhindranwale around this time in which he stated that "to be armed is the birthright of every Sikh . . . a Sikh without a weapon is naked." Indira Gandhi, he said, "is a very clever woman. She is full of double standards . . . she either wants to liquidate all the Sikhs or make them lick her chappals . . . born in a Brahmin family, what does Mrs. Gandhi know about the problems of the Sikhs?[23]

As tension mounted between Sikhs and Hindus, a whole phalanx of Hindu militia-type organizations began to emerge. The RSS became active; new organizations such as Hindu Suraksha Samiti, Bajrang Brigade, and Shiv Sena were established to protect the Hindus in Punjab.[24] The Dal Khalsa, an organization closely associated with Bhindranwale, held a convention under the presidency of Ganga Singh Dhillon, a Sikh ex-patriot living in the United States. The convention passed a resolution demanding a United Nations membership for the Sikhs.[25] Until October 1983, the targets of Bhindranwale's cohorts were Hindus, who were known to be hostile to the cause of Khalistan, or Sikhs, perceived to be pro-government. After the murder of Deputy Inspector Atwal, however, the killings became indiscriminate. Innocent civilians were pulled out of buses and shot because they were Hindus.

The spate of killings had confounded the Akalis, who had pursued the more conventional path of protest and negotiations. In the growing communal polarization, the Akali leaders found themselves becoming more and more irrelevant. Bhindranwale and his men were increasingly in control of the situation in the state. Akali leaders like Prakash Singh Badal and Longowal repeatedly called for Hindu–Sikh unity, but they were unable to control Bhindranwale. A vicious circle had come into being: killings multiplied; the government grew adamant and then sullen, treating Punjab as a law-and-order problem; and the Akalis could not deliver on their promises to the Sikhs that, in turn, strengthened Bhindranwale and his cohorts who became increasingly bold in fixing their targets and carrying out assassinations with impunity. From the information that came to light subsequently, a small connections had been established between the Khalistanis and Pakistani intelligence agency.

Reaching the point of desperation, the Akali Dal began to espouse Bhindranwale's political rhetoric. Since the Sikhs had been inspired by Bhindranwale to maintain their distinct character, Longowal demanded an amendment to the Indian constitution's article 25, clause 2, which lumped Hindus and Sikhs together. The Akalis decided to burn the constitution.[26] This act was however perceived by a majority of Indians as an affront to the Indian nation.

Taunted by the press and the opposition for the failure of President's Rule, which she had imposed after dismissing the Darbara Singh government in 1983, Mrs. Gandhi increasingly turned to confrontation and coercion. With the general election looming in a few months, she had to resolve the Punjab crisis quickly in order to reestablish her government's credibility in the eyes of the public. On June 2, the army surrounded the Golden Temple. The government tried to negotiate with Bhindranwale, who by then had acquired a veritable arsenal of small arms and guns and had entrenched himself and his followers in the temple. The alternative to laying a protracted siege to the temple was ruled out because of the fear of an uprising in the Punjab countryside. The only other choice was to raid the temple and flush out the militants who had taken refuge there in the belief that the government would never order an army to storm the holy shrine. They were obviously mistaken. On June 6, 1984, the Indian army launched an assault on Bhindranwale and his adherents.

According to the government's figures, the militants already had killed 165 Hindus and Nirankaris in the twenty-two months since the launching of the Akali morcha. They had also killed 39 Sikhs for opposing Bhindranwale.

The total number of deaths from assassinations, encounters with the police, riots, and morchas was 410 by June 1984. This number was to escalate dramatically in the months following the armed assault, code-named "Operation Blue Star." In the assault itself, 700 soldiers were killed. According to one estimate, approximately 3,000 people were killed in the confrontation between militants and the soldiers. Clearly a large number of civilians had been caught in the crossfire between the militants and the Indian army.

The armed assault on their holiest shrine stunned the Sikh community. As the news spread, Sikh soldiers in the Indian armed forces mutinied in several places, notably in the Sikh regiment stationed near Ganganagar on the Pakistan border, and at Ramgarh, in Bihar. This marked the first instance of mutiny in the Indian armed forces since Independence. (The Indian military has a strong tradition of noninterference in politics and deep loyalty to elected governments.) The crisis in Punjab had dealt a blow to one institution of the supranational State that had remained relatively untouched by the struggle for political survival that had weakened the rest of its political institutions.

The government's white paper, issued after Operation Blue Star, squarely blamed the Akalis for aiding and abetting Bhindranwale's extremist movement and for failing to control his campaign of terror. As noted, the events that led to Operation Blue Star, were quite different from their portrayal in the government's white paper. Mrs. Gandhi and her Congress colleagues also blamed a "foreign hand" for stoking the fires of hatred in Punjab. The "foreign hand" was obviously a veiled reference to Pakistan and the United States. There is some evidence of arms smuggled from Pakistan and extension of training facilities and safe sanctuaries to the militants but at this point Pakistani involvement was small and sporadic. It cannot be blamed for causing the turmoil and violence in Punjab. References to external involvement, however, helped justify the decision to storm the Golden Temple. Clearly, the Indira Gandhi government was trapped by its own weakness and paralyzed by the widening circle of Bhindranwale's violence. Disunity among Akali's made them poor partners in restoring peace. The impending general elections however made it politically necessary to restore control. Coercion was then the only alternative. India's supranational State had lost all political leverage to affect a balance between Hindus and Sikhs in Punjab or between Punjab and New Delhi.

The crisis in Afghanistan and the militarization of the Indian Ocean might also explain to some extent, Mrs. Gandhi's anxiety about the loss of control in a border state. These concerns are more properly the focus of the following chapters. It is enough to note here that the Indian leaders were beginning to see a sinister design in Pakistan's renewed status as the U.S strategic ally in South and Southwest Asia.

Throughout the summer and fall of 1984, the Indian security forces combed through villages in Punjab to gather up the remaining militants who had escaped from the Golden Temple complex before the Indian army launched its attack. The search spread more fear in the Sikh community. Many young Sikhs fled to Pakistan to escape the police dragnet. In November 1984, Mrs. Gandhi was shot dead by her two Sikh bodyguards. The act of revenge was followed by a three-day carnage in Delhi and several other cities of north India. There are no reliable estimates of how many Sikhs might have been killed in these deliberately orchestrated riots but by all accounts the numbers exceeded 4,000.[27]

Within months of assuming the premiership, Rajiv Gandhi realized that failure to distinguish the Akalis from the militants had pushed them into the latter's arms. He therefore released the detained Akali leaders—Badal, Tohra, and Longowal—from jail, and appointed Arjun Singh, until then the chief minister of Madhya Pradesh and a trusted political confidant, as governor of Punjab. Singh and others carried on secret negotiations with Longowal, the president of Akali Dal, and mediated an agreement between him and Rajiv Gandhi; the pact was signed in July 1985.[28]

Accordingly, Chandigarh was to be transferred to Punjab, the Hindi-speaking areas of the state were to go to Haryana as a compensation for the loss of Chandigarh, and Punjab was to retain its existing share of river waters until another commission could decide on a permanent allocation. Most important, from the point of view of Sikh sentiment, those guilty of riots that took lives of hundreds of Sikhs after the assassination of Mrs. Gandhi, were to be prosecuted and punished. On July 26, twelve years after the passage of the Anandpur Sahib resolution, the accord was ratified by the Akali Dal at Anandpur Sahib. The Akali quest for autonomy and power had come a full circle.

Predictably, however, the Sikh separatists rejected the Rajiv–Longowal agreement—a month after it was signed, they assassinated Longowal. This could have unraveled all that had been achieved. But Rajiv Gandhi kept his word and proceeded with the promised elections in Punjab. He remained determined to give the Akalis a fair chance to come to power, and to work with them to isolate the extremists. On September 25, elections were held for the Punjab Assembly. The Akalis won an absolute majority for the first time and Surjit Singh Barnala became chief minister of the state. Rajiv Gandhi had purposely kept the Congress wing of Punjab in the background, and in effect, permitted the Akalis to win the election with ease. His strategy was in marked contrast to that of his mother. He had acknowledged the Akali's claims to be the sole representatives of Sikh ethnonationalism and worked to establish a new balance with them.

It is commonly believed that this political strategy floundered because of terrorist violence and the inability of the Akalis to take a hard line against it—this is partly true. An equally, if not more important reason is Rajiv Gandhi's failure to make the Congress party fall in line with his strategy. He met opposition from disgruntled leaders of the Punjab Congress, and from Haryana's chief minister, who belonged to Gandhi's party. Their combined opposition delayed the promised transfer of Chandigarh to Punjab.[29] This highly symbolic failure rekindled mistrust among the Akalis, and made them ascribe base political motives to Rajiv Gandhi, even where none might have existed. For example, the reports of the judicial commission on sharing of river waters was delayed for procedural reasons, but the Akalis believed that Rajiv Gandhi was dragging his feet. Their mistrust weakened his position still further within his own party, and forced him eventually to concede the hardliner's demands to dismiss the Akali government and deal with the terrorists exclusively through the use of force.

According to many political observers, Barnala's dismissal was triggered by the up-coming elections in Haryana. After his dismissal, Barnala remarked bitterly that the central government had succumbed to the "lobby that wanted to play the communal card in Haryana elections."[30] The Indian daily *Statesman* saw Rajiv Gandhi desperate "to retain Haryana, making intemperate commitments that will further alienate moderate opinion in Punjab."[31] Why was it so important that Haryana remain in the hands of the Congress? The answer is to be found in the declining ability of the supranational State to accommodate ethnonational sentiment. The prime minister of India could no longer override ethnonationalist (Haryana Jat identity) sentiments within his own party, much less its full-blown presence in the opposition. This was part of the decline of the supranational State's autonomy and its ability to balance the diverse demands of Sikhs and Hindus in Punjab and Haryana.

The twelve months that followed the dismissal of the Akali government in May 1987 saw a quantum jump in violence in Punjab. Many observers concluded it was largely the result of New Delhi's shift to an all-out confrontation.[32] In a succession of planned massacres in which militants boarded passenger buses, forced the drivers to drive to deserted by-roads, separated Hindu passengers out from Sikh passengers, and killed them. The militants took communal relations in Punjab as close to the brink of civil war as they were ever to get. (Such massacres took place at three different places in a short space of time and included Hissar in Haryana and a village called Lalru, on the main road between Delhi and Chandigarh.) In response, the security forces staged faked "encounters" and summarily executed those known or suspected of terrorist activities. These strong-arm methods of search, inter-rogation, and seizure deeply embittered ordinary Sikhs. The growing polar-ization of anti-Delhi sentiment cut still more ground from under the feet of the moderates. The Akali party was the first and most important casualty. Within months of the dismissal of the Barnala government, it found itself splintered into at least four groups that disagreed with each other over how to deal with the militants and the police.

In 1987 and 1988 Rajiv Gandhi had two more opportunities to defuse the crisis in Punjab—resurrect the Sikh middle ground, and isolate the extrem-ists. But the loss of autonomy of the central state was so far gone that he was unable to take advantage of either. In May 1987, even as the hard-liners in the Congress party in Delhi and Chandigarh were missing no chance in their efforts to get the Akali government dismissed, Darshan Singh Ragi, the new jathedar of the Akal Takht (the center of religious and secular power in the Sikh community) was using his good offices to bring about a rapprochement between Akali leaders and the militants. Ragi was consulting with a Jain ascetic, Acharya Sushil Muni, who had the full backing of New Delhi.

Sushil Muni and Ragi were able to announce an agreement on a four-point plan to end the violence in Punjab that had the concurrence of all but a small fraction of militants in Punjab.[33] The plan was announced from the Golden Temple on May 7, but the resolution did not suit the hard-liners in New Delhi. Anxious to replace Surjit Barnala with his own supporters in Punjab, Home Minister Buta Singh disowned the Ragi-Muni agreement next day on the floor of the parliament, without consulting fellow members of the gov-ernment. Ragi was immediately discredited by the militants. The extremist faction supported by Pakistan (which had stayed out of the talks) gained vastly in standing. Torn between opposing sides and anxious to retain unity within the Congress, Rajiv Gandhi succumbed to the hard-liners. The Barnala government was dismissed, and three months later, Ragi was himself a fugitive from militants' death threats.

Rajiv Gandhi's second opportunity came with the success in flushing out the terrorists from the Golden Temple in May 1988. The inflow of Ak 56 automatic rifles from across the border gave the militants an edge over the Punjab police. With their confidence bolstered, the hard core among them began to congregate once more in the Golden Temple, using it both as a sanctuary and as a nerve center for planning and coordination. The Punjab government suddenly laid siege to the Golden Temple, cutting off water and power supply to the entire complex. After two weeks, the militants surrendered. Unlike the heavy-handed assault of June 1984, in which a large number of civilians had been killed in the cross fire, the operation code named "Black Thunder" of May resulted in only a few casualties. There were no civilian deaths and the security forces were able to recover a large volume of correspondence that helped them to map the terrorist network and locate its sympathizers in Punjab. Militarily, the blow was a crushing one for the militants but its more important effect was to embolden a section of the Akalis into condemning the militants and making another bid to consolidate the party.

Home Minister Buta Singh again intervened. He immediately put the Akali leaders in preventive detention. A few weeks later, the government attempted to establish direct negotiations with the militants and bypass the Akalis altogether. The common strand that linked the central government's misadventures in Punjab was the Congress party's unwillingness to concede, that after Operation Blue Star, the Nehruvian method of controlling Sikh ethnonationalism by taking over its platform, was no longer feasible. To restore the interlocking balance between the supranational State and Sikh ethnonational sentiment, New Delhi needed to accept and even bolster the Akalis as the representatives of the Sikh nation, as it had done with the AIDMK in Tamil Nadu.

Had party discipline within the Congress been strong, Rajiv Gandhi would have had no difficulty in implementing the Nehruvian strategy or continuing with policy he had adopted toward the Akalis in 1985. But by 1987, the Congress was little more than a coalition of caucuses centering on powerful leaders. Buta Singh had been one of them. Each leader depended on his following in the Congress party of his or her home state to maintain power and status in New Delhi. Any attempt to deal with the Akalis alone and neglect the Sikhs in the Congress party was seen by them as a severe threat to that power, to be restored at almost any cost. The inability of the prime minister, who is the custodian of the supranational State, to make his own party accept the layered order, that ceded the custodianship of Sikh ethnonationalism to the Akalis, destroyed the interlocking balance of power between New Delhi and Punjab. After that, only direct armed confrontation with the militants remained.

Kashmir

The growing violence in Punjab had begun to cast a shadow over Kashmir.[34] By 1984, Bhindranwale's hit squads had specifically begun to target Hindus for killing in Punjab. Operation Blue Star had been fairly popular among the non-Sikh Hindus in Punjab as well as in the rest of India. Perhaps buoyed by this, senior Congress ministers and leaders had begun to charge Farooq Abdullah's government with secret support for the Sikh extremists, collaboration with Bhindranwale, and establishment of training camps on Kashmiri soil. The central government formally complained that Farooq Abdullah (chief minister of J&K and head of the National Conference party) had refused to arrest Sikh extremists in Jammu and Kashmir, even though the union home minister had sent him a specific list of such persons. The Abdullah government categorically denied these charges.[35]

By July 1984, following the defection of twelve members from the National Conference party, Governor Jagmohan, who had earlier replaced B. K. Nehru, dismissed the government of Farooq Abdullah. In his place, the Congress installed the leader of the defectors, G. M. Shah, as the chief minister of J&K. These machinations by New Delhi must be seen in the context of weakening of the Congress party, and the numerous setbacks it had received since 1983. The Kashmiri leaders of the Congress party were still bitter about 1983, when Farooq had rejected the idea of a Congress–National Conference alliance.[36] This had cheated many aspiring politicians of ministerial positions and state patrimony that accompanied such positions. Ever since, they had pressured Mrs. Gandhi to dismiss Farooq Abdullah. Initially, she had resisted the suggestion, partly because of the sensitive geopolitics of Kashmir, and partly because the only rival to Farooq Abdullah in the National Conference, his brother-in law, G. M. Shah, was even less acceptable to the Kashmiri people.

Nevertheless, Farooq Abdullah had imprudently approached the Mir Waiz Maulavi Farooq, leader of the Awami Action Committee and a known advocate of an independent Kashmir. Although Mrs. Gandhi overlooked this, she had made a mental note of Farooq Abdullah's attempt to use the Mir Waiz to counteract the Congress(I)'s standing in the state. Approaching the Mir Waiz had been clearly an expedient move for Farooq. If he seemed to be making common cause with the Islamic platform of the Mir Waiz, it was because in the early 1980s, Sunni Wahabi Islam had begun to gain adherents among the Kashmiris. Farooq Abdullah's election speeches of 1983 (for the J&K Assembly) clearly appealed to Islamic sentiments. Farooq might have appealed to religion, perhaps to keep the Jama'at-i-Islami at bay, but the tactics exacerbated tensions between Hindus and Muslims in the state. Abdullah's campaign rhetoric had lumped the Jammu Hindus and Congress together and portrayed each as having betrayed the Kashmiri Muslims. Not to be outdone, the Congress leaders in Kashmir charged that the Resettlement bill sponsored first by Sheikh Abdullah and then by his son, Farooq Abdullah, was an attempt to erase the boundaries between the Indian and Pakistani Kashmir. It was, they charged, a stab in the back of the Indian nation. The political atmosphere in the state had become progressively embittered by sectarian charges.

The total rout of the Congress(I) from the valley in the 1983 elections proved to be a turning point. It made Farooq overly confident and the Congress leaders overly suspicious. Convinced that the defeat in Kashmir was the beginning of Congress(I)'s defeat in the impending national elections of 1984, Farooq Abdullah began to tilt toward parties that opposed the Congress. He was present at the anti-Indira rally organized by N.T. Ram Rao in Vijaywada in May 1983. Five months later, Farooq organized in Srinagar an impressive conclave of fifty-nine leaders representing non-Congress parties on the sensitive issue of center-state relations. It might be argued that, in extending himself beyond Kashmir, Farooq was violating the tacit understanding that had since 1947 governed Kashmir's relations with the central state. Even Sheikh Abdullah, who had more reason to be confidant of his popular base in Kashmir, had never involved himself in this way. By the same token, one might make an opposite case that, as a loyal member of the Indian union, Farooq had every right to take sides on issues relating to the rest of the country, and that he was doing so because he considered Kashmir an integral part of the Indian Union.

Indira Gandhi did not see it that way. In her view, Farooq's confabulations with the opposition were dangerous, particularly since the demand for decentralization in the center state ties had emanated from Srinagar. Professor Ralph Buultjens, who was a member of the close circle of Mrs. Gandhi's advisers at this time, explained to me in an interview, that Mrs. Gandhi did not regard the opposition to be antinational or unpatriotic, but she believed it to be singularly "inept and weak." In his view, Mrs. Gandhi was convinced that the opposition could not govern India and had to be prevented from "messing up" Kashmir.[37] The new developments beyond Kashmir's borders required New Delhi to stay on top of events in the state.

In retrospect, the armed insurrections that broke out in 1989 can be traced back to this monumental blunder. Why did Mrs. Gandhi commit it?

The answer lies in the declining autonomy of India's supranational State in the 1980s and its progressive failure to control the course of events in its eth-nonations. Kashmir was no different from Tamil Nadu, Assam and Andhra, or Karnataka. What made Mrs. Gandhi throw democratic norms overboard in Kashmir was its status as a disputed territory, Pakistan's never-ending claims to it on the grounds of religion, and the close military cooperation that had developed between Pakistan and the United States. In the face of these unsettling developments, New Delhi simply had to have control over the J&K.

Mrs. Gandhi sought it first through a coalitional arrangement between the Congress and the National Conference on the line of the Tamil Nadu model. But she failed to understand that ethnonationalism was much more consolidated in Kashmir, and therefore the Kashmiri Muslim sentiment would not accept a coalition arrangement. She had no option but to fall back on the creation of the layered order in Kashmir and entrust the National Conference with the articulation and control of Kashmiri ethnonationalism. She might have settled for cooperation with the National Conference as a means of retaining control had Farooq Abdullah played his cards better, had Mrs. Gandhi not been so suspicious, and had communications between the two been more cordial. But this communication and trust, always rather fragile, was steadily undermined by Kashmiri detractors of Farooq in the Congress party in Delhi and within Mrs. Gandhi's own household. She therefore threw democracy overboard in a desperate bid to retain control.

In 1986 and 1987, the troubles in Kashmir were still some years away. The dismissal of Farooq Abdullah had sown the seeds of future insurgency, but there was nothing inevitable about its taking root. That was to happen after the elections in 1987. Early in March 1986, G. M. Shah's government had fallen and Kashmir had been placed under President's Rule. Governor Jagmohan, an appointee of Mrs. Gandhi, had gained a measure of popularity in Kashmir by exposing corruption and getting a number of developmental and other public works completed. Rajiv Gandhi was keen to end President's Rule and return Kashmir to an elected government, but by late 1986, the political instincts which had given him signal successes in restoring the internal balances in 1985 had begun to desert him. Under attack from Congress diehards who disingenuously held him responsible for the party's defeats in state elections in the areas he had pacified—Punjab, Assam, Mizoram and Karnataka–Rajiv Gandhi hesitated to hand Kashmir back to the National Conference. Unlike his mother, Rajiv Gandhi enjoyed an excellent rapport with Farooq Abdullah but many among his circle of advisers kept bringing up Abdullah's playboy tendencies to dissuade him from taking this step.[38]

As a result, Rajiv Gandhi made what turned out to be the fatal error. He insisted that the National Conference enter into an overt electoral alliance with the Congress to form a coalition government in Kashmir.[39] Rajiv Gandhi may have been misled, as indeed Farooq was, by their mutual esteem, into believing that it could be made to work this time but, in the interim period, internal developments in Kashmir had made this even less likely than it had been in 1984.

Islamic fundamentalism had taken a much firmer root, and was taking a dangerous turn: unemployment of the urban-educated was far more widespread, and the dismissal of Abdullah in 1983 continued to rankle and be cited as an argument against continued association with India. Most serious of all, by 1987, Pakistan's intelligence agency, the ISI (Inter Service Intelligence), was also training "Kashmiri" youth to foment discontent and enforce the tenets of Wahabi Islam in the valley.[40] The news that the National Conference was entering into a coalition with the Congress was popularly regarded as a betrayal of "Kashmiriyat." Within weeks the Congress–National Conference coalition faced a self-proclaimed Muslim United Front that wanted an "Islamic" Kashmir separated from "Hindu" India, and that campaigned with the Holy Qur'an in one hand and the Kashmiri flag in the other. Thus, in his attempt to establish relational control over Kashmir (via a coalition) that suited a less consolidated ethnonationalism, Rajiv Gandhi had completed the destruction of the interlocking balances between Kashmir and India, and in the process lost control over the situation. After that, only brute force, that last resort of the supranational State, remained.

Looking at the 1980s, one sees that during the four years of Indira Gandhi and the five years of Rajiv Gandhi the supranational State had lost that which it required the most—its autonomy in determining the progress of the historic Indian state toward the modern nation-state. It did this because both mother and son violated at least two fundamental principles of India's political unity. They sought to replace the National Conference in Kashmir and played fast and loose with the supranational State's commitment to secularism. From the accession in 1947, India's control over Kashmir had been predicated on the premise that the National Conference would act as a vehicle for local aspirations and as a buffer between Kashmiri nationalism (of both secular and religious variety) and the government of India. The Congress had never attempted to form a government in Kashmir. However, concern over growing violence in Punjab and Afghanistan, and Farooq Abdullah's ineffectiveness in dealing with the rising tide of Islamic fundamentalist sentiments, propelled Mrs. Gandhi to initiate the idea of a coalition government. Although this failed, it had violated the principle of interlocking balances that required the center to deal with a mature ethnonationalism through negotiation and power-sharing.

Yet another fundamental principle of Indian unity had been visibly violated in Punjab. While competitive party politics might drive the Congress to opt for partisan advantages, it needed to refrain from weakening the constitutional neutrality and secular temper of the supranational State. Mrs. Gandhi had not refrained from such a practice, nor did the opposition when it came to power briefly in 1977. Both the government and the opposition repeatedly used state institutions to tilt the election outcome in their favor and abused clauses of the constitution, such as arbitrary imposition of President's Rule in a state, to throw their rivals out of office and power. Democratic politics involves some compromises, but these need not have sunk to the level of sponsoring known religious fundamentalists like Jarnail Singh Bhindranwale as the Congress(I) did in 1978 .

The consequences of these policies were disastrous. In the short term, they deepened alienation and encouraged separatism, terminated the political process in Punjab and Kashmir, and jeopardized India's national security. In the long term, these compromises weakened the union and helped to polarize India along ethnic and sectarian lines. The Hindu nationalists, represented by the BJP and the RSS as well as a phalanx of local organizations affiliated with the first two, drew on the violence in Punjab and Kashmir to strengthen their appeal in national politics. While the votaries of the Hindu Rashtra thus enlarged their following by harping on the breakdown of law and order in Punjab and Kashmir, Pakistan found a ready handle with which to hasten India's descent into violence. In the final analysis, the abandonment of Nehru's principle of interlocking balances caused a loss of relational control. This led to more departures from the model and a further weakening of India's supranational State. Mrs. Gandhi, not unlike the figures in a Greek tragedy, was driven to actions that led to her own demise. Rajiv too fell victim to a similar spate of ethnonational violence.

Chapter 7

桜

COLLAPSING FRONTIERS

Indo–Lanka Relations Since the 1980s

The 1983 outbreak of violent confrontation between the Sri Lankan government and the Tamil separatists spilled over into Tamil Nadu and rapidly drew
New Delhi into a conflict for ascendancy between Colombo and the Tamil
militants who were demanding a separate state of Tamil Eelam.[1] Observers
of South Asia have attempted to explain the 1987 Indo–Lanka Accord and the
introduction of the Indian Peace Keeping Force (the IPKF) as a bid by India
to establish hegemony over its smaller neighbor.[2] Disparity in size and military power between these two countries certainly fits the hegemony argument, but as I will show, Indian policies were far more complex than those
portrayed by the proponents of the hegemony thesis.

The most important flaw in the hegemony thesis is its inadequate explanation of the contradictions in Indo–Lanka relations during the 1980s. If
India is a hegemonic state and possesses overwhelming military, economic,
and political advantage, why was a nonstate actor such as the LTTE (Liberation Tigers of Tamil Eelam) able to defy and frustrate India? If Sri Lanka is a
subservient state, how was it able to order the Indian IPKF out of Sri Lanka,
and, even more puzzling, why did India comply with it? Far too often and
with misleading consequences, the hegemony thesis relied on size and military power to explain dominance. This chapter seeks to explain these contradictions, not in the context of accumulated military capabilities, but in the
framework of shifting balance of conflicting interests and the changing "rules

of the power game" in which outcomes are results of bargaining between actors with fluctuating capacities to influence the game.

The question still remains, particularly in regard to a small country like Sri Lanka, whether the desire to dominate is incompatible with the need to establish relational control. Relational control certainly presumes a measure of power to shape Colombo's external policy, an Indian ability to limit the kind of options Sri Lanka might pursue in its quest for security and survival. This is a relationship of superior power and as pointed out in the first chapter, relational conrol bears a degree family resemblance to the notion of hegemony. It is however different from hegemony in terms of purpose and intent. India does not seek enduring control over Sri Lanka's economy, culture, and politics. The course of India's Sri Lanka involvement in the 1980s suggests instead a limited objective, episodic interest, and a purpose shaped by her own domestic stability. These distinctions are important because they establish a different base line of motives and actions for India's policy toward its smaller neighbor. Had India wished to expand into Sri Lanka, it would not have fought a two year war with the LTTE, would not have waited to be invited into Lanka to restore order, nor would it have patiently pursued five years of diplomacy to bring about a negotiated solution to Lanka's civil war. New Delhi also extended clandestine support to the Tamil resistance, and a strong argument can be made against such interference but this support was not intended to extend India's territorial or political boundaries. It was meant to protect India's own political boundaries. Support to the Tamil resistance provided India with a degree of leverage over the course of events in Sri Lanka which had spilled over into Tamil Nadu. The Indian strategy of relational control in Sri Lanka meant that:

1. India would have to acquire a degree of leverage over the process of bargaining and negotiations among several players: the Sri Lankan Tamil militants, the nationalistic Jatiya Vimukthi Peramuna (JVP) representing the Sinhala Buddhist chauvinist forces, the highly vocal Dravidian political parties in Tamil Nadu, and the governments of Sri Lanka;
2. Continued threats to national unity were likely to drive Sri Lanka to seek out military and economic assistance from countries that could be unfriendly to India;
3. Such intrusions in the region, particularly in a wake of the intensifying Cold War in the 1980s, were likely to militarize the Indian Ocean and adjacent areas, and threaten India's security and stability.

Sri Lanka's geostrategic importance increased in Indian security perceptions as the superpower tensions escalated in Afghanistan. Traditionally,
Indian defense analysts and political leaders have regarded Sri Lanka's as an
integral part of India's oceanic defense.[3] In the years following Independence, the Indian governments had accepted the British naval (in Trincomalee)
and air bases (Katunayake) in Sri Lanka. At that time, India had neither the
naval strength nor the necessary resources to undertake a joint defense of its
own and Sri Lanka's security. Nehru had remained preoccupied with Pakistan
and China, as had his successor, Prime Minister Lal Bahadur Shastri. Once the
United States embarked on the policy of containment and included Pakistan
in its network in the 1950s, Indian leaders began to worry about military
bases in countries close to or bordering on India. Since Sri Lanka is only about
ninety miles from the coast of Tamil Nadu, Indian leaders were particularly
concerned about Sri Lanka's foreign policy orientation. In those early years,
sharp differences had developed between the two countries over the issue of
nonalignment.[4] Sir John Kotelawala, prime minister of Sri Lanka at that time,
shared Pakistan's fear of Indian dominance and looked for a countervailing
support against its large neighbor. These differences gave way to a greater
convergence by 1956 when S. W. R. D. Bandaranaike assumed the reins of
government in Colombo. Between the mid 1950s and early '80s, Indo–Lanka
relations remained friendly and amicable.[5] Sri Lanka managed to maintain
India at arm's length by adopting an anticolonial, mildly pro-socialist, nonaligned posture in foreign policy. In its own national interest, Sri Lanka had
chosen voluntary finlandization, a policy of self-imposed limits.[6]

The fear of Indian hegemony diminished as it became evident that India
had no desire to interfere in Sri Lanka's internal politics. Conclusion of the
Lanka–China maritime agreement in 1963, and grant of air passage by
Colombo to Pakistani planes during the Bangladesh war, caused minor irri-
tations but did not disturb the cooperation and general good will between
India and Sri Lanka. In April 1971, Mrs. Gandhi sent five frigates to seal off
the approaches to Colombo and ordered troops and arms to guard airports
in response to a request from Sri Lanka. Prime Minister Bandaranaike feared
that the Lankan forces might not be able to crush the violent insurrection,
led by the radical Sinhala Buddhist JVP. Mrs. Gandhi wanted a stable, secular, and democratic Sri Lanka. In her judgment, the chances of stability were
greater under Mrs. Bandaranaike than under a sectarian Buddhist regime
committed to social revolution. At that time, the Indian government believed
that the JVP had received assistance from China and North Korea. That, and
the fact that the JVP was also virulently anti-India influenced the decision to

help the Sri Lanka government crush the JVP rebellion of 1971. Although there were no security problems from shared nationalities during the 1950s and 1960s, India was not indifferent to the changes in the domestic and foreign policy of governments in Colombo.[7] These concerns were greatly heightened in the late 1980s when ethnic conflict besieged Sri Lanka and gave its policies a markedly pro-Western tilt.

The central issues in Indo–Lanka relations until then revolved around the legal status of Indian Tamils in Sri Lanka. India had argued that these "estate Tamils" (as the Tamils who had migrated to Sri Lanka to work on the plantations since the nineteenth century were called), belonged to Sri Lanka since they had lived there for many generations. Sri Lanka, however had denied them citizenship. Nehru had held adamantly to this early position that the people of Indian origins in the neighboring countries were not India's responsibility. His successors, Prime Ministers Shastri and Indira Gandhi, agreed to divide the stateless Tamils and grant a portion among them the right to return to India as its citizens.

By the time Mrs. Gandhi was reelected in the 1980s, the Lankan drift toward the West had picked up speed. Jayewardene had been quick to assure India that Sri Lanka's opening to the West was not anti-India in intent, but Mrs. Gandhi remained unconvinced. New Delhi watched visits of American officials to Colombo with growing unease. In early 1980s, the United States extended $37 million in economic assistance to Sri Lanka and invited President Jayewardene to Washington.[8] These developments produced some anxiety in New Delhi. Indian officials refrained from any retaliatory steps. Mrs. Gandhi remained preoccupied with the situation in the north, the acquisition of arms by Pakistan, and the conflict in Afghanistan.

In the last week of July 1983, massive ethnic riots plunged Sri Lanka into a civil war. The long history of Tamil–Sinhala relations need not detain us here since that is not the focus of this study.[9] It is noteworthy, however, that the unitary structure of Sri Lanka's political system and the growing strength of the sectarian Sinhala Buddhist nationalism had led Sri Lanka into political turmoil. By the early 1980s, the situation was well beyond the meager capabilities of Sri Lanka's weak and mostly symbolic security forces. Pressed by circumstances, President Jayewardene turned to outsiders for help but he pointedly ignored India in this quest for arms and assistance.

The violent politics of identity in Sri Lanka could not but involve the 50 million fellow Tamils across the Palk straits in India.[10] The intensification of the ethnic strife in Sri Lanka had welded Tamil nationalism on both sides of the Indo–Lanka border. Although the Sinhalas constitute a majority in Sri

Lanka, a growing number who have turned to Buddhist nationalism do not see Tamils as a minority. Instead, they see them as an extension of the 50 million Tamils in Tamil Nadu, backed by the subcontinental power of "hegemonic" India. On the other hand, the Lankan Tamils draw on the strong cultural and familial ties to India and share in the Dravidian identity (particularly the linguistic identity), but regard their struggle to be separate from the Dravidian politics in the state of Tamil Nadu. Tamil cultural affinities make the Lankan Tamils, however, suspect in the eyes of the Sinhala chauvinists, particularly of the JVP variety. Until 1980s, neither the DMK nor the AIADMK ventured beyond moral and rhetorical support to the Tamil cause in Sri Lanka. India's strategic concerns remained free from the pressures of identity politics in Jaffna and Tamil Nadu.

This situation changed in the 1980s. The Indian government watched with concern as the Sri Lankan diplomats fanned out to foreign capitals to seek assistance on the plea that India had supported the Tamil terrorists. This was more fiction than fact. There is no evidence of such support to Lankan Tamils before 1983. Sri Lanka enlisted Mossad and Shin Bet, the famous intelligence agencies belonging to Israel, and a private mercenary agency called Keenie Minee to train and equip its security forces. The Keenie Minee was rumored to have been financed by the British Ministry of Defense.[11] Sri Lanka had also sought Pakistan's help. The latter had contributed ten million rupees toward training and arms to Sri Lanka. There were several exchanges of visits between Sri Lankan leaders and Pakistani officials.[12] During an official visit to Pakistan in March 1985, President Jayewardene equated the situation in Kashmir to that in Afghanistan and urged that Kashmiris be given the right to self-determination. He also stated that South Asia should be made a nuclear- free zone although India had rejected the idea because China was not included in such a zone. President Zia returned Jayewardene's visit in December of that year. Reflecting a widely held sentiment in New Delhi, one Indian official described the newly found friendship between Sri Lanka and Pakistan as neighbors "ganging up on India."[13] Sri Lanka also received sizable and cheap military supplies from China. In 1981, President Jayewardene asserted that the defense pact that Sri Lanka had signed with Great Britain in 1947 was still valid. This assertion was frequently repeated after 1983.[14]

Jayewardene had agreed to permit visits by U.S. naval vessels for refueling and crew rest in return for western support, particularly from the United States. He had granted contracts to a Singapore based private consortium (known to have close links with the United States) to renovate and expand refueling facilities at the Trincomalee harbor and agreed to build a powerful

Voice of America transmission facility near the Katunayake airport. Though seemingly innocent of strategic intent, the extension of naval facilities could be a cover for an unofficial U.S. naval base at Trincomalee. A number of Indian officials believed that America's sudden interest in Sri Lanka had this hidden purpose.[15] They were even more suspicious of the proposed transmission facilities. I was told by several Indian officials that the transmission station was to be managed by American personnel. Sri Lankans were excluded from top management in the agreement.[16] These officials feared that the construction of six powerful transmitters would permit the United States and its friends (i.e., Pakistan) to monitor land communications and military movements in the entire region, including India.[17]

From India's point of view, Jayewardene was seeking a military solution to the Tamil problem that India did not countenance, at least not at this point in the conflict. Even more important, he was inviting military presence of extraregional forces that might, as a quid pro quo, demand a permanent presence close to India's southern borders. These perceptions explain India's apprehensions about Sri Lanka's pro-Western tilt, but they do not explain why the small amounts of arms Lanka had received until then should cause it to feel threatened. Clearly, Western assistance was limited in scope. The United States had given Sri Lanka a small grant against arms sales in 1982–1983. The Western states—the United States and Great Britain—were aware that India would react sharply to any military intrusion in its vicinity.[18] They had no compelling interest at stake in Lanka to become deeply involved in its civil war, at least not enough to jeopardize their relations with India. Pakistan was too preoccupied with the Afghan war, and China with domestic reforms, to take on additional responsibilities in Sri Lanka.

The answer lies not so much in the quantity or type of assistance to Sri Lanka but in India's fear that this could be the beginning of Lanka's progressive absorption into the Western strategic network for the defense of the Indian Ocean. According to one official, the temporary, military assistance from outside the region could turn into a permanent threat to India's domestic and strategic interests.[19] Many officials argued that the flow of arms to Afghanistan and Sri Lanka was a part of the overarching strategy to establish U.S. dominance in the Persian Gulf and Indian Ocean. Although the American arms grant was small, it came close on the heels of massive arms and weapon transfers to Pakistan, the expansion of the military base in Diego Garcia, and the search for additional bases and harbors to facilitate U.S. pre-positioning of weapons in the region. The United States withdrew its offer of arms sale to Sri Lanka when the Tamil–Sinhala clashes escalated and Lanka descended into civil war. But the suspicions spawned by the earlier overtures—the Voice of America station, the facilities granted to U.S. naval ships, and the oil farm contract—continued to linger.

Indian officials saw these as the first steps to incorporate Sri Lanka into the strategic consensus led by the United States. India had vehemently opposed such a consensus beyond its northern borders into Pakistan; it could do no less than discourage its extension beyond the southern borders into Sri Lanka. India's leaders have argued that Pakistan and Sri Lanka constituted the outer rim of India's defense perimeter. Each country had the ability to destabilize India from within. In retrospect, it is apparent that such fears were exaggerated. What mattered was not the truth or accuracy of these contentions but the construction of India's security narrative and the way in which Sri Lanka's civil war began to fit into it.

The continued warfare between the Tamil militants and the Lankan security forces in the north had sent a flood of Tamil refugees into India. By 1986, there were at least 150,000 Tamil refugees in Tamil Nadu and surrounding areas. The spectacle of fleeing refugees and violence against fellow Tamils in Jaffna produced a wave of sympathy and widespread anger in Tamil Nadu. The Tamil militants quickly became the figures in the DMK and the AIADMK pantheon of heroes. The ruling AIADMK vied with the DMK, its arch rival, to pre-empt slogans and symbols of "greater Tamil nation."[20] A flurry of legislation was moved in the Tamil Nadu state assembly. The AIADMK supported the central government and attenuated DMK's attempts to mobilize public opinion in favor of military intervention.[21] In the summer of 1986, the DMK leader, Karunanidhi, told me that New Delhi should accord the same importance to liberating Tamils as it had accorded to the Bangladeshis in 1971 wars with Pakistan. In his view the situation was similar. He was not surprised, however, at New Delhi's tardiness. In his opinion, the anti-Dravidian bias of the Brahmin-Bania ruling classes that dominated the Indian government was responsible for New Delhi's indifference to the Tamil's suffering.[22]

Indira Gandhi's Response to Sri Lanka, 1983–1884

Mrs. Gandhi did not want to seem unresponsive to the clamor in Tamil Nadu, but her policies had to reflect the larger considerations of national security. She wanted Jayewardene to know that efforts to exclude India would not be without cost and that India did not countenance his attempts to build closer military relations with the West. Although less of a burden than the ten million that had fled East Pakistan in 1971, the growing problem of Lankan Tamil refugees was still a grave concern for India. Mrs. Gandhi did not want to endanger Sri Lanka's territorial integrity by endorsing demands for a separate Tamil state of Eelam. What Mrs. Gandhi wanted most was to see Jayewardene accede to negotiations, refrain from use of unwanted force, and return to a policy of strict nonalignment.

How was India to persuade Sri Lanka to negotiate with Tamil leaders? How was it to achieve the contradictory objectives of strengthening the Tamils (in response to pressures of Madras) while at the same time dissuading them from destroying Sri Lanka's unity? And what could India do to wean Lanka away from the temptation to join the Western economic and strategic network? The answer lay in acquiring a measure of control over the Tamil self-determination movement, in developing mechanisms by which India could reward Sri Lanka's adherence to the Indo-centric perception of South Asia, and in pressuring Colombo when it strayed from it. Mrs. Gandhi told the Indian parliament in 1983 that

> We have made it clear . . . that India, does not pose any threat to Sri Lanka, nor do we want to interfere in their internal affairs . . . we want the unity . . . of Sri Lanka to be preserved. At the same time, the developments in Sri Lanka affect us also. In this matter India cannot be regarded as just another country. Sri Lanka and India are two countries who are directly involved. Any extraneous involvement will complicate matters for both our countries.[23]

Sri Lankan officials could hardly miss the veiled warning in Mrs. Gandhi's statement and were quick to point to this as more saber-rattling by New Delhi.[24] Mrs. Gandhi's approach, however, did not include military intervention.[25] Her reasons for excluding such an intervention are not hard to see. Indian intervention might have jeopardized relations with the United States. Indo–U.S. ties had improved significantly since Mrs. Gandhi's visit to Washington in 1982. Military intervention would have made others (notably China) uncertain about India's intentions, possibly strengthened Pakistani and American resolve to forge unity of purpose in South Asia, and brought forth charges that India was doing in Lanka what its close ally, the Soviet Union, was doing in Afghanistan, i.e., trampling underfoot the sovereignty of a small and weak neighbor. Most important, military intervention could have served no strategic or political purpose. Who would be the target of the Indian intervention? India could hardly target the Lankan Tamils. Nor could it send its forces against

the Sri Lankan government. For its own reasons, India was anxious to preserve Lanka's territorial integrity. There were no political grounds to justify
intervention; no precise objective could be fixed for it. The only real option
was to use diplomacy and urge the two sides to find a political solution.

Accordingly, Mrs. Gandhi offered India's good offices to facilitate direct
talks and put forward a compromise formula known as the Annexure "C" that
tried to meet the basic aspirations of the Tamil people, as well as the reservations of the Sri Lankan government.[26] India's efforts had not remained solely
confined to official diplomacy. Mrs. Gandhi had established other, nondiplo-
matic avenues for regaining a measure of relational control over Sri Lanka.
These included frequent expression of sympathy for the Tamil cause and clandestine support for militant organizations like the PLOTE, EPRLF, LTTE, and
EROS. New Delhi excoriated the Lankan security forces for their brutal suppression of the Tamils and joined with the Tamil Nadu government in declaring
a strike to protest Colombo's repression of Tamils. Mrs. Gandhi did not prevent Tamil militants from gaining a free access to parties and politicians in Tamil
Nadu. The Indian Intelligence agency, commonly known as the Research and
Analyses Wing (RAW), was directed to train and supervise the militants. The
latter were granted safe sanctuary, some arms, training, and small amounts of
weapons.[27] Tamil militants could therefore plan their activities, carry them out
in Sri Lanka (which was only a short distance from India's coast), and return to
safety of Tamil Nadu and the protection of that state government. It was apparent to me that, by 1986, Madras had become their extraterritorial headquarters, and the state of Tamil Nadu had become a base from which to conduct
propaganda and armed campaign into Sri Lanka. The availability of a sanctuary
in India proved invaluable to the guerrilla movement. It gave Tamils easy access
to media, arms, and connections with the outside world.

It needs to be stressed that India did not extend training and arms to the
militants before 1983; there is no evidence to suggest that it had done so.[28]
Until then, the Indian involvement had remained modest. The Indian purpose
was political rather than military. During the summer of 1988, several Tamil
militant leaders complained to me about the limited nature of Indian involvement. A. Selvan, top leader of the PLOTE, remarked that the Indian involvement was just sufficient to keep New Delhi informed about the militant activities while providing Mrs. Gandhi some means to influence the course of the
ethnic conflict. Depending on how they responded to Indian proposals, she
could reward or punish Colombo and the militant groups. The extension of
sanctuary ensured that these groups did not become a host to elements that
were dangerous to India's regional interests. Officially however, Mrs. Gandhi

supported Amrithalingam, the moderate leader of the TULF, to represent Lankan Tamils in the proposed talks with the Jayewardene government.

Mrs. Gandhi then mixed diplomacy and threat in equal parts to structure relations between Colombo, Tamil militants, and Tamil leaders in Tamil Nadu. She hoped to use the leverage (diplomatic and clandestine) to restore greater autonomy to the supranational State so that it could preserve better control over its overlapping nationality, the Tamils. It should be noted that the Annexure "C" envisaged fundamental reordering in the structure of ethnic relations in Sri Lanka. It was not limited to finding a common ground between the disputants. In this sense, the proposal reflected the objective of relational control ("long-term structuring" of social process and outcomes) to achieve congruence between India's ethnic and territorial boundaries.[29] The success of this strategy depended on retaining tight control over the Sri Lankan militant. Mrs. Gandhi did not succeed in the first objective of the peace plan, but according to most Sri Lankan Tamil leaders, India had tightly controlled their activities during her tenure as prime minister.[30] Failure in this regard led to tragic results in the late 1980s.

Rajiv Gandhi's Perceptions and Policies, 1985–1989

Initially, Rajiv Gandhi made three tactical changes in the policies his mother had pursued toward Sri Lanka. First, he categorically ruled out the use of force and stepped up the search for a negotiated settlement. He seemed to lean more favorably toward Colombo than the militants. Second, he insisted on direct negotiations between the militant groups and the Sri Lankan government. He therefore legitimized the militants and undermined the relevance of the more moderate TULF. Third, unlike Mrs. Gandhi, who had relied on Parthasarthy, Rajiv Gandhi personally took over the formulation of policy for Sri Lanka. He frequently changed envoys assigned to Sri Lanka. These individuals did not possess any particular knowledge of Lankan politics or the maze of Tamil–Tamil connections across the Indo–Lanka border. This led to errors of judgment about motives of actors in Lanka's violent ethnic conflict.

The Parleys at Thimpu, 1985

To promote consensus and accommodation, Rajiv Gandhi sponsored two rounds of talks at Thimpu on the ethnic crisis during July and August 1985.

It took much persuasion, even a bit of arm-twisting on part of Foreign Secretary Romesh Bhandari to get the disputants to the negotiating table. Sri Lanka agreed because, at this time, it was under great pressure from international aid donors to end the violence and settle with the Tamils.[31] The Tamil groups went along because they wanted to be recognized as the legitimate representatives of the Tamils in a regional forum, particularly one endorsed by India. According to *India Today,* "Rajiv's attitude was that he is all for the Tamils in Sri Lanka getting their legitimate rights in a fair and just manner. He also respects their demand for autonomy. But he made it clear that what he wants is a solution to the problem within the framework of a united Sri Lanka and a radical separatist movement within India's borders was no longer tolerable."[32]

The Indian government had promised Jayewardene that it would keep the Tamil groups in check. Indian naval vessels started intensive patrolling of the Palk Straits to discourage traffic of militants and arms between Jaffna and Tamil Nadu.[33] At Thimpu, Rajiv let it be known that he did not support the key militant demand for a Tamil homeland by merging the Eastern Province of Lanka with Jaffna.[34] The first set of discussions ended without any conclusions being reached. Under pressure from the Indian government, both sides agreed to reconvene in August 1985. But even the second round did not break the impasse. In retrospect, neither Jayewardene nor the militant leaders were serious about negotiations at that time.

Colombo's lack of sincerity was evident in the composition of the delegation it had sent to Thimpu. The delegation consisted of lower level officials who did not have the power to make political decisions. The militants also contributed to the failure at Thimpu. The four preconditions they had attached to the talks were more in the nature of declarations of absolutes than positions of negotiation.

The fact that India had invited them for direct negotiations (a status accorded only to the TULF leaders thus far) underlined the new approach in New Delhi. It was an important departure from the "rules of the game" laid down by Mrs. Gandhi. In Rajiv's diplomacy, the militants had become more than a mere ploy to pressure Colombo. But their increased importance was to be offset by a tougher stance toward their independent activities. The whole purpose of this "carrot and stick" policy was to spur them on to channel Tamil nationalism through New Delhi. If they did not comply, he could withdraw extension of sanctuaries in India.

Rajiv Gandhi had hoped that dependence on Indian arms would make militants more pliable. It is important to recall that in 1985 he had negotiated several agreements with India's own ethnic nationalities in Punjab and Assam. He was also assured of international support. The Western countries, notably the United States and Great Britain, had come to the conclusion that Sri Lanka was best left in India's care. Rajiv Gandhi represented the promise of a younger leadership in New Delhi; he was far more committed than his mother to economic liberalization at home and peace in the neighborhood. Western leaders did not want to discourage these trends in India.

The failure of Thimpu led to a hardening in India's stance toward the militants. The Rajiv Gandhi government ordered deportation of three top Lankan Tamil Front leaders—A. S. Balasingham, S. Chandrahasan, and N. Satyendra—to show that refusal to cooperate with India would be punished.[35] But in ordering these measures, Gandhi had reckoned without the transborder reach of Tamil nationalism. The DMK and AIADMK mobilized huge rallies to protest against the deportation order. Karunanidhi led a six-kilometer march in which more than 15,000 people participated. The DMK collected ten million signatures to petition the United Nations to grant Tamil Sri Lankans the right to self-determination. The DMK's general secretary resigned his post in protest against the failure of Tamil Nadu Chief Minister M. G. Ramachandran (henceforth MGR) to pressure the central government to take a more pro-militant stance. The DMK formed an association (TESO: Tamil Eelam Supporters Association) to coordinate help for the Sri Lankan Tamils. DK, the other opposition party, went as far as to warn the Rajiv Gandhi government that "if orders are not withdrawn, Gandhi will face agitations like Punjab and Assam and we (DK) will not allow any north Indian to set a foot here."[36] MGR immediately moved to counter the DMK propaganda while secretly continuing the crackdown on the Sri Lankan militant groups in Madras.

K. Mohandas, deputy inspector of police in Madras at that time, wrote that "[Ramachandran] informed me that Central agencies like RAW and the IB should not be informed about the operation and that even the state's top officials like the Chief Secretary and Home Secretary should be kept in the dark about the details of my plan."[37] The reported exclusion of the central intelligence agencies and Tamil Nadu officials from consultations is particularly significant. MGR wanted to keep his DMK and DK rivals off balance by championing the militants' cause, but he also wanted to protect his role as a mediator between the Lankan militants and the central government.

The Tamil Nadu political parties had developed a client-patron relationship with specific militant groups. The DMK promoted the TELO, while the AIADMK supported the LTTE led by Veluppillai Prabhakaran.[38] According to Marguerite Johnson, by early 1987 there were 39 rebel camps and about

3,300 guerrillas in the state of Tamil Nadu.[39] The LTTE used the crackdown as a cover to eliminate several guerrilla leaders belonging to rival Tamil groups known to have close relationship with the RAW. This gave the LTTE greater control over the situation in Jaffna and parts of Sri Lanka's Eastern Province. It also gave them greater independence from India. As Dr. Balasingham, the LTTE's principal ideologue, told the *Financial Times* of London that the LTTE was trying to shift "the balance of military power in" its favor so that it "can negotiate with the government on our own terms."[40] By mid 1986, the LTTE was too well entrenched in Tamil Nadu politics for Rajiv to risk its expulsion. The crackdown had led to contrary results. The transborder Tamil ethnic connection had defeated its purpose.

After the collapse of talks at Thimpu, the Lankan security forces launched a major offensive against Tamil's guerrillas in the north, but this failed to crush the Tamil movement. The Sri Lankan economy was groaning under unbearable pressure. The Tamil movement itself had fragmented into several rival groups. The unity achieved at Thimpu had proved ephemeral. In the opening months of 1986, violence in Lanka escalated beyond control. The tragic specter of petty rivalry, personal feuds, and fratricidal killings among the Tamil groups, particularly the brutal elimination of the entire leadership of the TELO by the LTTE, had dampened the ardor of many Tamil Nadu politicians in mid 1986.[41] Tamil Nadu had become disenchanted with the "brave Tamil heros" from Sri Lanka. In fact, I frequently heard people in Tamil Nadu refer to the militants as "the arms-toting uneducated thugs and smugglers." The time then seemed ripe for another attempt at a negotiated settlement.

The December 19 Proposals

The Indian government sent a team headed by P. Chidambaram (a cabinet minister from Tamil Nadu and a close aide to MGR) to pave the way for discussions on the composition and powers of the proposed provincial councils and devolution package for Jaffna and the Eastern Province. In mid-December, Chidambaram and the minister for state, Natwar Singh, visited Colombo once again. These visits produced what is commonly referred to as the December 19 proposals. Throughout these months, there had been no letup in the violence in Sri Lanka. Thousands had been killed in the confrontation that sent waves of new refugees into Tamil Nadu.

Details of the December 19 proposals need not detain us here. India had worked out a formula that required a structural alteration in the balance of interest within Sri Lanka, and reflected the minimal requirements of the Sri Lankan government, the Tamil militants, and India's own security concern. By 1986, India was no longer just an impartial broker, it had invested in the diplomatic efforts and had staked its prestige to restoring peace in Sri Lanka. In view of Indian officials, the December 19 proposals were the best compromise solution to a tough and seemingly intractable conflict.[42] If the talks had succeeded, India would have automatically stood as a witness and a guarantor to the agreement. However, the Sri Lankan government abruptly changed its mind about the December 19 proposals.

Gandhi's inclination for diplomacy instead of force raises an important question. Why did he not withdraw the safe sanctuary and political support to the militants? That would have been consistent with India's commitment to preserving Sri Lanka's unity and territorial integrity. The hypocrisy of aiding and abetting the militants while condemning Pakistan for similar deeds against India was drawing worldwide criticism. The Indian government argued that disengaging from the Lankan militants would not stop the violence in Sri Lanka. India might lose important means of influencing Colombo and the militants, and in all likelihood anger the 50 million Tamils on its side of the Palk Straits. It would have reinforced Colombo's diplomatic intransigence, making future negotiations with all parties even more difficult than before.

Underlying this reasoning is the logic of relational control and its attempts to protect the balance of interlocking interests among the Lankan Tamils, the Sri Lankan government, the pro-militant public of Tamil Nadu, and the Rajiv government in New Delhi. It highlights the key domestic imperative of India's security—the need to preserve the autonomy of the supranational State. This same reasoning had propelled Mrs. Gandhi to follow the two-track policy of preventing the creation of a Tamil Eelam while supporting the Tamil cause, and preserving leverage over Colombo while nudging disputing parties toward a settlement. The Thimpu and then the December 19 proposals were predicated on a parallel two-track policy. All three proposals—those at Thimpu, those contained in the Annexure "C," and those outlined in the December 19 formula—reflected a rearrangement of power within Sri Lanka. Indian leaders argued that such a rearrangement would restore peace in Sri Lanka that would translate to stability and security for India. But in the final analysis, all three proposals were formulas for discussions. They were not backed by threat of intervention. Unfortunately, the December 19 proposals also failed to produce meaningful dialogue between the Tamils and Colombo.

In retrospect, it is possible to argue that Rajiv Gandhi's failures centered in permitting militants to become too deeply entrenched in Tamil Nadu politics. They also lay in following contradictory policies toward the Tamil militants. The tough stance toward the militants, i.e., the arrests and deportations, pushed them to search for greater independence from New Delhi. Militants began to seek alternative sources for weapons and financial support; they also began to exploit the inherent tensions between New Delhi and Tamil Nadu and between the Congress and the Dravidian political parties. The LTTE and the EPRLF turned the rivalry between DMK and AIADMK to their advantage.

Rajiv Gandhi also failed to dovetail the activities of the intelligence agencies with his diplomatic efforts. The intelligence agencies lost control over the Tamil guerrilla groups; the former frequently became willing participants in the internecine struggle of the Sri Lankan Tamil's groups. His mercurial changes in directions —sometimes pro-Colombo, and at other times pro-militants—confused officials charged with implementing his policies. Strangely enough, Rajiv Gandhi and his immediate circle of advisers continued to retain the illusion of control when, in reality, it had slipped away. This gap between perception and reality led eventually to the IPKF's unfortunate embroilment in Sri Lanka.

The Intensification of Civil War: The Growing Effect of the Spillover from Sri Lanka

Early in 1987, Prabhakaran had left Tamil Nadu and returned to Jaffna. Having physically eliminated many leaders of rival militant groups, the LTTE had emerged the dominant militant group by mid-1986 and proceeded to take over the civil administration in Jaffna. The Sri Lankan government retaliated by imposing an embargo on many essential commodities, particularly fuel and gasoline, and by moving swiftly to crush the militants. The number of deaths of innocent civilians mounted. As the situation in Jaffna deteriorated, Rajiv Gandhi sent Dinesh Singh, his personal emissary, to Colombo in March 1987. He urged Jayewardene to declare a cease-fire and return to negotiations, and conveyed to him, in the strongest possible language, India's opposition to Lanka's proposed military assault on Jaffna.[43] These representations did not dissuade Colombo. Violence escalated in April 1987.[44] India could find no purchase for its diplomacy in the midst of renewed war.[45] This chain of events had been implicit in Prabhakaran's decision to return to Jaffna. After the crackdown in Madras, he had come to believe that access to the sanctuary in India would no longer be available and that the Rajiv government could not be depended on to support his cause.[46]

Jayewardene had used the talks—first the Thimpu and then the December 19 parleys—to prepare for war.[47] As the situation deteriorated, he turned to the United States and England for help. Sri Lankan government had already sought help (for training its security forces) from the mercenaries from South Africa, Mossad (Israeli Intelligence), and aid from the Pakistani government. In the last week of May 1987, the Sri Lankan security forces launched an all-out offensive against the Tamil groups. The goal was to secure Vadamarachchi and crush the Tamil insurgency. Tamil Nadu instantly responded to the launching of the offensive. In a telex sent to Rajiv Gandhi, the chief minister of Tamil Nadu indicated that he was convinced that thousands of civilians would be killed "at the hands of the Sri Lankan Army—notorious for its undiscipline and cruelty." He condemned the Sri Lankan government's attack on Jaffna as "inhuman, uncivilized and . . . a serious violation of fundamental human rights." There were demonstrations in Tamil Nadu and all political parties swung into action. MGR collected Rs. 4 crores in relief material for the beleaguered Tamils of Sri Lanka.[48]

The Rajiv Gandhi government could not ignore the tide of public sentiment in the south. But there were other questions to consider. Sri Lanka's resolve to make this a "fight to the finish" could end in one of the three possible outcomes. The militants could win. In that event, India would have to cope with a separate Tamil state close to the border of Tamil Nadu. Mrs. Gandhi had forestalled this outcome, and Rajiv Gandhi wanted to do the same at all cost. Second, the Sri Lankan security forces could subdue the militants and retake Jaffna in a decisive victory. This could strengthen Colombo's ability to continue repression of the Tamils and, more important, its search for ways to countervail India. Third, the civil war could drag on, alternating between stalemates and renewed violence. This could confront India with the same dangers that had compelled it to become involved in the first place. It was then important to prevent total defeat of one side and propel both toward a compromise settlement. The only way to evolve such a formula was to restructure the distribution of power in Sri Lanka. India would have to abandon the stance of a distant mediator and become an active third force in the power arrangement inside Sri Lanka.

Still, India remained reluctant to militarily alter the impasse in Lanka. It is noteworthy that Jayewardene had requested assistance in August 1986 to curb "terrorism" and to help Lanka conduct elections for the provincial councils in the Tamil areas. At that time, India hoped that its diplomacy might bear results.[49] When the Sri Lankan army moved toward Jaffna and fighting intensified in early 1987, Indian thinking about military intervention changed. New Delhi informed Jayewardene that it would not countenance the fall of Jaffna. In retrospect, it is doubtful if Lankan security forces would have succeeded in taking Jaffna. But no one could have known that in advance. In February 1987, about four months before the Indo–Lanka pact and the induction of Indian armed forces in Sri Lanka, India had begun seriously to assess the pros and cons of military intervention. The growing clamor in Tamil Nadu and the strident demands by Tamil politicians to stop the assault on Jaffna had spurred the Rajiv government.

J. N. Dixit, Indian high commissioner to Lanka and subsequently foreign secretary, told me in the summer of 1988 that the fall of Jaffna to the Sri Lankan forces would have led to a massacre of Tamil civilians. Whether or not this would have actually come to pass, the Indian officials seemed to believe that it would. India therefore decided to insert itself in the conflict and cited humanitarian reasons to do so.[50] Colombo turned down the Indian request to send food to Jaffna, and on June 3, 1987, the Lankan navy intercepted nineteen Indian boats carrying food and medicine there.[51] The Indian vessels returned to Rameshswaram, but the next day, Indian transport planes escorted by four Mirage 2000 fighters parachuted twenty-five tons of food into Jaffna.

These Indian attempts to breach the Sri Lankan embargo had little humanitarian value; it was an assertion of India's larger interests in South Asia.[52] Within ten days after the airdrop, India and Sri Lanka signed the pact that laid the basis for induction of Indian armed forces, designated as the Indian Peace-Keeping Force (IPKF) in Sri Lanka. Within 48 hours after the flight of the Mirages, India had presented Sri Lanka with a fait accompli: India would send more relief with or without Lanka's consent. This was an unambiguous assertion of its self-declared right to look after the interests of Tamils whether they were in India or Sri Lanka. It was also a warning that India would not allow domestic conflict in the neighboring states to pose a threat to its own domestic tranquility, and that New Delhi would remove the cause preferably by diplomacy, but failing that, by force if necessary.

Jayewardene had signed the agreement for a variety of reasons. In the course of a lengthy conversation with me, President J. R. Jayewardene admitted that the signing of the accord was a painful but necessary decision in view of the extreme threat to Sri Lanka's territorial unity. "I had consulted my political colleagues and apprised them of the stalemate in the north," he said.

He also talked at length about the JVP-inspired violence and insurgency in the south. Although Jayewardene demurred about the danger of a military coup, he did not deny the possibility. Many in Sri Lanka seemed to think that to be the main reason why Jayewardene had invited the Indian armed forces into the country. Colombo's military options against the Tamils had been exhausted by May 1987. Jayewardene had tried to secure support from the United States and Pakistan but, as he told the editor of *Hindu*, "no one was willing to lift a finger."[53]

Jayewardene had then gambled on India to be the mediator and a benefactor, able and willing to use its superior military strength to protect Sri Lanka from disintegration. He argued that "if Sri Lanka's independence had to be compromised, better that it was compromised by India," a country that could deliver the Tamils to the peace table.[54] India had not then forced Sri Lanka to accept the IPKF, although it did not permit Jayewardene to escalate the conflict to the point where New Delhi might have had no alternative but to intervene. The fall of Jaffna, the flight of refugees, and the possible massacre of the Tamil civilians could have brought India to such a point.

New Delhi's reasoning in agreeing to the accord was presented by J. N. Dixit in a candid speech to the United Service Institution in New Delhi on March 10, 1989. The talk provides a clear and unambiguous clue to Indian motives—the mix of fears and ambitions that led India to commit troops to Sri Lanka. In his various official capacities and as the chief tactician of India's Lanka policy between 1986 and 1988, Dixit played a key role in events before and following the accord. "We went to Sri Lanka to preserve our own unity" and "to ensure the success of a very different experiment that we have been carrying out ourselves," Dixit explained. He was referring to the Indian federal democracy and the strategies that had bound its disparate ethnic nationalities to the Indian union. This same model was to be made available to Sri Lanka.

Did the spillover from the Sri Lankan civil war pose a threat to India? Dixit said "the first voice of secessions in Indian Republic was raised in Tamil Nadu in the mid sixties." Tamil insurgency in Sri Lanka therefore had "implications for us," he noted. Between 1978 and 1986,

> the strength of the Sri Lankan army was raised approximately from 12,000 to 35,000 . . . Sri Lanka signed informal confidential agreements with the governments of the United States of America and United Kingdom to bring their warships to Colombo, Trincomalee, and Galle . . . Sri Lanka invited British

mercenaries into its intelligence services. Sri Lanka invited Shin
Bet and Mossad . . . Sri Lanka sought the assistance of Pakistan
to train its Home Guards, and its Navy, Sri Lanka offered broadcasting facilities to the Voice of America, which would have
enabled the United States to install highly sophisticated moni-
toring equipment on Sri Lankan soil which would have affected
our security.

Last but not least, "Sri Lanka was an important domestic political factor," he
said, particularly since doubts were being raised among "our Tamils" and
questions were being asked about the "relevance or validity of our (Tamils)
being part of a larger Indian political identity."

Geographical proximity was the other critical factor in shaping India's
policies, Dixit said. "Had Sri Lanka been 15,000 miles away with seas in
between, like Fiji is, perhaps our involvement could have been less, but it is
not. There is just 18 miles of water between us and that is also very shallow.
"With the rise of sea power," Dixit explained, "with the increase in capacity
for communications, free of limitations of land, our strategic thinking has to
take into account potential danger which a country can face. It need not necessarily be direct military intervention; it can be a creation of circumstances
in neighboring countries generating political, social trends in those countries
which can have a ripple effect on our policy and disintegrate us. That is why
I think, the IPKF is in Sri Lanka."[55]

Dixit's tone is polemical and his justifications could be interpreted as self-
serving, but conversations with a number of individuals in New Delhi's policy community suggest that Dixit's views were widely shared by others in
Rajiv Gandhi's government. Dixit's exposition also reflects a particular
understanding of the complex interaction between the Indian, Tamil, Sri
Lankan, and Buddhist Sinhala nationalism. It reveals the intuitive grasp of
relational control and its domestic foundations, i.e., balances between India's
ethnic nationalities (the Tamils in this instance) and the supranational State.

However, it would be foolish to ignore the opportunistic elements in this
policy. In 1987, the Indian government was facing separatist militancy in
Punjab, Assam, Kashmir, and Gorkhaland. There were no immediate military
or politically visible solutions there and the agreements in Punjab and Assam
had already unraveled. There is also an obverse side to this anxiety about
instability and disintegration. It is pride. Indian leaders felt confident that
India's military forces would disarm the Tamils and restore Sri Lanka's political sovereignty over the affected areas. The subsequent events were to belie

this confidence. Rajiv Gandhi had promised what India could not deliver. The asymmetry of size and power, and India's vastly expanded military capabilities were thought to be sufficient to meet its obligations in Sri Lanka, but military capabilities could not end the ethnic violence. Power turned out to be issue-specific. Force could not substitute for parleys. India could not persuade Tamil nationalists to reintegrate into the nation of Sri Lanka.

The Indo–Lanka Pact of 1987

According to the main provisions of the Indo–Sri Lanka accord of 1987, both countries sought to preserve the "unity, sovereignty, and territorial integrity of Sri Lanka." India had agreed to assist Sri Lanka militarily to disarm the separatist, secure a cease-fire, and help conduct the referendum. In the pact, India also promised to deny the Tamil separatists use of Indian territory as a launching pad for any secessionist activities, and jointly patrol with the Lankan navy to halt free movement of the militants to and from Tamil Nadu. Sri Lanka agreed to take back the Tamil refugees and to merge the Northern and Eastern provinces, subject to a referendum to be carried out after the merger. In the interim, the two provinces were to be linked by an administrative council that was to have wide-ranging powers. Maintenance of law and order remained with the government of Sri Lanka as did the power to postpone the referendum. The entire process of a merger and elections—creation of an interim administrative council, its mandate, and its composition—depended on everyone's adherence to the terms of the pact. If perceptions changed, or the political equation tilted, the pact would be in jeopardy. In the December 19 proposals, the merger of the two provinces was to follow the referendum. In reversing the sequence, the pact had favored the Tamils.

In a separate letter attached to the pact, Lanka agreed to several provisions that addressed India's security interests: 1) India would not employ foreign military and intelligence personnel that would prejudice Indo–Sri Lanka relations; 2) India would not to make Trincomalee or other ports available to other states for any purposes that might endanger Indian interests; 3) India and Sri Lanka would jointly undertake operation of the oil-tank farm at Trincomalee; and 4) Voice of America or any other broadcasting company's facilities would not be permitted for military or intelligence purposes. Sri Lanka had officially abandoned its quest to enlist outside support. The letter had reestablished the status quo ante that predated Colombo's gradual drift away from the Indocentric conception of South Asian security.

This letter has been cited as evidence of India's hegemonic ambitions. But the interpretation is misleading because it divorces the letter from the context of the previous five years of negotiations between Colombo and New Delhi, and Sri Lanka's dependence on Indian support to settle the conflict with its Tamils. The letter should be read as a part of the overall attempt toward restructuring relations between the Sri Lankan state and its own nesting nations.

Jayewardene had offered India similar assurances prior to the signing of the pact, but these were invariably tied to endorsement of coercion against the Tamils. India could not agree to this. There is ample evidence to suggest that India had intended the IPKF to moderate the conflict; the pact was not a cover for a military takeover of Jaffna. Rajiv Gandhi had not expected the LTTE to resist the attempts to disarm nor had he expected the IPKF's stay to be protracted. He had certainly not envisaged an armed conflict between the IPKF and the LTTE that began in October 1987. For these same reasons, President Jayewardene and Tamil leaders had welcomed the pact. After some criticism for the manner in which India had sought to break the embargo, Western countries had also endorsed the Indian role. The U.S. reaction was unusually mild.[56] South Asian states, however, reacted sharply, but that was expected.

The pursuit of relational control propelled India from a bystander to a mediator, and from that role to an active third force in the conflict. The pact restored New Delhi, at least temporarily, as the arbiter of ethnic and regional conflict in Sri Lanka. The militants lost their demand for Eelam, but gained guarantees of autonomy and political equality; Lanka was promised peace, and Tamil Nadu was appeased. India's supranational State had secured the right to represent Tamil aspirations abroad; it had regained the ability to reward or punish actions by the militants and the Sri Lankan government. Most important, India had secured the power to restructure Indo–Lanka relations in ways that would block military and political influence of elements from outside the region.

For the accord to succeed, several conditions had to be fulfilled: the IPKF induction should have received full and tacit support from of all the subnational groups involved in the conflict; it should not have been perceived as tilting in favor of militants or the security forces, and the IPKF should have impressed on the LTTE that the cost of breaking the agreement would be greater than the price of complying with it. Although this chapter does not focus on the Sri Lankan opposition parties or on the JVP, these too had the power to undermine the accord. Colombo's cooperation with the provisions of the pact was vitiated by Jayewardene's domestic weakness. He had hoped that the IPKF would be able to free up his security forces from the north so that these could be redeployed to subdue the JVP-led rebellion in the south. However, the induction of the Indian troops exacerbated the rebellion. Sri Lankan leadership became badly split. Prime Minister Ranasinghe Premadasa vehemently protested the presence of the Indian military forces in Sri Lanka. Jayewardene's ability to deliver on the pact had depended on his ability to win over dissident forces in and outside his government. The proliferation of actors willing and able to sabotage the IPKF mandate greatly complicated the Indian task.

A number of observers in India and abroad have charged that Rajiv Gandhi never properly consulted the LTTE in forging the Indo–Lanka pact. This too is offered as an indication of India's real purpose: establishment of an unchallenged dominance over Sri Lanka. The LTTE was not, it is pointed out, invited to sign the agreement. This had almost insured that the pact would fail. Since there are several versions of the meeting between Gandhi and Prabhakaran before the signing of the pact, it is difficult to make a judgment about this charge. The controversy over this issue boils down to the question of what might be considered adequate consultation. LTTE leader Prabhakaran would have liked to see all his demands fulfilled before approving the agreement. The same would be true of the Sri Lankan government. On balance, Indian officials had adequately consulted the Tamil militants, but as subsequent events showed, that did not guarantee their cooperation. While the final draft of the pact was being formalized, Indian officials had met all the militant groups in Madras. On July 24, under instructions from Dixit, Hardip Puri of the Indian high commission had contacted Prabhakaran in Jaffna to apprise him of the pact. Subsequently, all the important Lankan militant leaders were taken to New Delhi for further consultation.

On July 28, 1987, Rajiv Gandhi met with the representatives of the Sri Lankan Tamil groups. This meeting was followed the same evening by a separate meeting with Prabhakaran at the Asoka Hotel. Rajiv Gandhi was accompanied by P. Ramachandran and K. Narayanan. No other officials from the Indian foreign office were present. Although there are several versions of what actually transpired at this meeting, it is now clear that the LTTE leader had accepted the accord on the condition that the Indian government would permit him to keep back some weapons for personal safety and ensure LTTE's leading roles in the interim council (although the TULF and EROS would also be allowed to be represented). New Delhi was to compensate the LTTE in cash, ostensibly for rehabilitating its members. It is not the lack of adequate consultation that doomed the 1987 agreement. There were other reasons for the accord's failure, not the least of which was LTTE's refusal to share power with other Tamil groups in the interim council.

The success of the pact also depended on the continued belief that the IPKF was genuinely impartial. This could not be sustained. Tamil militants were convinced that the IPKF had been brought in to shore up President Jayewardene's failing government; the JVP also believed this. Both believed that Colombo would use the IPKF to contain and pacify the Tamils while the Lankan forces crushed the Sinhala nationalists in the south. Neither movement thought the IPKF to be an unbiased and neutral force. Each thought it had a hidden agenda. There was certainly a kernel of truth in these perceptions. Thirty minutes before the accord signing, Jayewardene told Gandhi that the situation in the south was serious and that he would have to move Sri Lankan forces from Jaffna to the south. The two planes which had brought in Rajiv Gandhi, his security staff, and car, made four trips that night to Galle, in south Sri Lanka, when Gandhi was still in Colombo.[57] Similarly, the settlement of Sinhala people in the Eastern province continued after June 1987 although Jayewardene had agreed to stop it. The LTTE saw this as a breach of the accord because such settlement altered the distribution of ethnic balance in the government's favor.

The success of the pact also required India to keep the political and military initiative in its hands. This meant speedy implementation of the terms of the accord: disarming of the militants, setting up the administrative council and holding the referendum, and restoring law and order in northern Sri Lanka. The IPKF should have been provided with sufficient fire power, adequate preparations, and a clear set of objectives. The available account of the IPKF operations in Sri Lanka suggests that it was not prepared for the battles it was ultimately forced to wage. The IPKF was never given a clear set of objectives and its operations were confused by the mercurial changes in directions from New Delhi.

These flaws in India's strategy underline what has been pointed out before, that the IPKF was not meant to be an occupational force, nor was it sent with the purpose of expanding India's borders or preempting economic resources for India's use. The IPKF commitment is best understood as an extension of the political restructuring envisaged in the accord. The commitment permitted New Delhi to maintain a degree of control over the battlefield, and in the forum of negotiations.

The accord ran into trouble within two months after it had been signed. In keeping with the provisions of the agreement, the Sri Lankan security forces returned to the barracks in August 1987, but the Tamil guerrillas did not surrender their weapons. Some arms were handed over, but the bulk of the LTTE's weapons and equipment remained hidden in caches.[58] Other stipulations also faced obstacles. Sri Lanka refused to merge the Eastern and Northern provinces until the militants had been disarmed.[59] By October 1987, the IPKF had launched the 'Operation Pawan' to disarm Tamil guerrillas.

India was anxious to make the interim council work and but LTTE intransigence was obstructing its efforts. In June 1988, the LTTE accused the IPKF of having committed greater atrocities than the Sri Lankan security forces, and called the 1987 accord a "charter of servility for the Tamils." Prabhakaran stated that the "enormous sacrifice made by the Tamil people and martyrdom attained by thousands of Tamil youth was not to affect a temporary merger and elections for powerless provincial councils. What is described as north and east is the motherland of Tamils and that is indivisible." The LTTE had rejected the accord and closed all possibilities of a negotiated settlement.[60]

This placed New Delhi in a serious dilemma. It could not get out of Sri Lanka without fulfilling its promises; staying on meant confrontation with the LTTE. In retaliation for LTTE's intransigence, India disclosed to the press that Prabhakaran had accepted cash payments for endorsing the accord.[61] It pointed out that Prabhakaran had ordered elimination of rival Tamil leaders and groups. In November 1988, Gandhi urged President Jayewardene to hold elections to the provincial councils in the Northern and Eastern provinces. Following this, an interim government for the two provinces was formed. But the LTTE refused to enter this arrangement. The battle for control, this time with considerable communal violence, continued in Trincomalee and Batticaloa. Clearly, the IPKF mandate had changed once it became evident that the accord could not be fulfilled unless the LTTE was subdued. IPKF's subsequent military victories in the battlefield did not translate into LTTE's political acquiescence. New Delhi was never able to resolve this dilemma.

The decision to wage a war against the LTTE was not an easy one for Rajiv Gandhi. Nor was he oblivious to the cruel irony in being forced to crush the very elements he and Indira Gandhi had nurtured with care and money. Rajiv Gandhi's speech to the Indian parliament on November 9, 1987, provides a clue to his thinking. India had spared no effort, he said, to bring the LTTE into the political mainstream. "It had accommodated their demands in the composition of the Administrative Council for the Interim government in Jaffna and the eastern province" although Sri Lanka was loath to accept them. "But within hours the LTTE went back on their commitment. The LTTE chose to adopt a course of violence . . . While they promised us to support the agreement, they started a propaganda campaign against India . . . They threatened all Tamil civilians who disagreed with them. They hunted down and massacred 100 members of other Tamil militant groups . . . They publicly repudiated the agreement and started armed attacks on the IPKF . . . There was no alternative to disarming the LTTE." Rajiv could abandon neither the Tamils nor could he support its chief representative, i.e., the LTTE.

Confrontation with the LTTE had followed from the need to maintain relational control and to restore balance of forces between the various actors in Indo–Lanka relations. That the balance was in danger is clear from the account of the IPKF operations by field Commander Sardeshpande: "We gathered credible intelligence through smugglers, boatman . . . about exact bungalows, lanes, hospitals, beds, towns, cities and helpers of the LTTE cadres, convalescing Tigers, gunrunners and manufacturers of explosive devices and grenades and gave it to the Tamil Nadu police, only to be told that there were no such individuals, no such activities! We told them that the LTTE cadres after enjoying India's shelter and medical treatment were returning to Sri Lanka and killing IPKF soldiers . . . All this made no impression on the Tamil Nadu government and the police. Some of our own MPs (members of parliament) and political figures in the country were adding insult to injury by decrying us, the IPKF, as killers of the Tamils in Sri Lanka and lionizing the LTTE as great fighters who were fighting us. This was the tragicomedy played out in our own country."[62] Facing an impasse in Tamil Nadu and fearing its deleterious impact on the IPKF role in Sri Lanka, the central government on January 1988 imposed President's Rule in the state.[63]

That the Lankan militants should enjoy such a privileged position in India while Indian soldiers were being killed in direct action with the LTTE was indeed ironic. It underscored the gap between Rajiv Gandhi's policies and the political realities on the ground. It also underlined the contrast between the immensely richer emotional reserves and symbolic imagination of Tamil nationalism, and the relatively limited imagination of the supranational State. The former possessed larger social space to stage protests and demonstrations, to transform ethnic sentiments into weapons of war and propaganda, and fellow ethnics into an instrument against the supranational State. The IPKF operations lacked the social base, the symbolic and emotional power that the Tamil liberation forces enjoyed in northern Sri Lanka and Tamil Nadu. Preservation of an accord could not evoke the same response as the call to liberate the Tamil homeland. In a revealing passage, J. N. Dixit remarks that "in moments of introspection, they (the IPKF) were always wondering.

This is not China, this is not Pakistan, why are we in Sri Lanka? We are originally supposed to come and protect the Tamils." Why is it then the IPKF was
being shot at, asks Dixit, and was now compelled to shoot back. The contrast
with India's Bangladesh operation is obvious. There, India's success had
depended on her ability to control an ethnic actor and their fellow compatriots both within and without India. In Lanka, the IPKF could not count on
local Tamil support.

The Premadasa Government in Colombo:
Growing Differences with India

Loss of control over the activities of overlapping nationalities was followed
by loss of friendly government in Colombo. In the 1988 presidential elections in Sri Lanka, Jayewardene lost his office to Premadasa, who had vehemently opposed the accord and the introduction of Indian armed forces into
Sri Lanka.[64] Premadasa believed in a different method of settling with the
LTTE. In two conversations during June 1988, he told me that he was willing to give the LTTE a free hand in Jaffna and a share in power in the Eastern
Province. Conceding Jaffna was meant to convince the LTTE of the advantages in entering into a dialogue with Premadasa.

This bargain with the LTTE was totally different from the terms of the
1987 accord. India had no role in Premadasa's scheme of things. He wanted
to talk directly to the LTTE. He had constructed this scenario on the assump-
tion of a weakened LTTE that would have lost a lot of its cadres in battles
since it had been defeated by the IPKF in Jaffna. The LTTE was on the run
from the IPKF and was even more anxious than Premadasa to see Indian
forces gone from Sri Lanka. A settlement with the LTTE then required a
simultaneous withdrawal of the IPKF.

This strategy was possible because Premadasa knew that the Rajiv Gandhi
government was facing increasing criticism at home, not only because of the
Sri Lankan embroglio but also because of charges of rampant corruption, the
failure to settle Punjab and Assam, and the declining morale within the
Congress(I). Application of reverse leverage was therefore possible. Premadasa
demanded in March 1989 that the accord be replaced by a treaty of friendship.
This kept the security provisions intact but altered the terms of the agreement
to reflect greater reciprocity. Colombo established links with Prabhakaran
through LTTE's London office, and on June 1, 1989, in what India regarded as
an ultimatum, asked the IPKF to withdraw by the end of July 1989.

Rajiv Gandhi found the demand for withdrawal embarrassing and abrupt. The manner in which it had been made suggested to him a deliberate slight to New Delhi. Premadasa's insistence on withdrawal had eliminated the legal basis of IPKF presence in Sri Lanka. Between June 1 and July 7, 1989, seven letters were exchanged between Gandhi and Premadasa on the question of IPKF withdrawal. This exchange took place at the same time as Premadasa was conducting secret negotiations with the LTTE that included provision of some arms and transport to the LTTE.[65]

Having sacrificed Indian soldiers to pacify the LTTE and form the interim administrative council of merged provinces, Rajiv Gandhi could not simply withdraw the IPKF and abandon the accord in haste. In a letter of June 2, 1989, he reminded Premadasa that "when the situation seemed headed inexorably toward the break up of Sri Lanka," India had sent the IPKF. "The IPKF will not stay in Sri Lanka a day longer then necessary. But we cannot be unmindful of the responsibilities and obligations of the two countries under the Indo–Lanka Agreement and to join the democratic process within the framework of a united Sri Lanka . . . Our two governments are, therefore, morally and legally bound to ensure that the Tamils are given the autonomy they were promised, . . . as also in the additional areas promised in the agreement signed between former President Jayewardene and myself on the 7th November 1987."[66]

In a desperate attempt to save face and to retain some leverage, in the event it was forced into an untimely withdrawal, the IPKF began to set up the Tamil National Army (TNA) as an alternative to the LTTE in the northeast. This involved bolstering the Citizen's Volunteer Force (CVF).[67] The TNA was to provide the muscle for the interim government that had been created since the merger and elections of November 1988. The TNA was a doomed force from the beginning. If the IPKF could not remain in Sri Lanka without the accord, and the pact could not be implemented without the cooperation of the LTTE and the government of Sri Lanka, the TNA, which was entirely the creature of the IPKF, had no hope of surviving its withdrawal.

Several things are clear in the exchange of these letters. India had no intention of permanently staying in Sri Lanka; Rajiv Gandhi's reluctance to withdraw in a precipitate manner had to do with retaining some leverage in a situation where the overlapping nationality could endanger India's stability and security. Domestic political considerations also played a part. The Tamil Nadu public had begun to show signs of disillusionment with the LTTE. It was then possible to discredit the LTTE while championing the Tamil cause. For the first time since 1967, the Congress(I) seemed to stand a chance of gaining a majority and returning to power in Tamil Nadu. At least, this is what Tamil Nadu Congress party had begun to tell Rajiv Gandhi in January 1989.

Some have argued that the creation of the TNA and reluctance to withdraw were proofs that India sought regional dominance. Others are of the view that Rajiv Gandhi was compounding the original mistake by committing a new one. They argue that he should not have sent in the IPKF in the first place; having failed to disarm the LTTE, he should have withdrawn the IPKF immediately. Yet another line of argument in India in the late 1980s was that he had been duped first by Jayewardene and subsequently by Premadasa.[68] Premadasa had used anti-India rhetoric to defeat Jayewardene. Then he had tried to cut a deal with the LTTE behind Gandhi's back. And while the IPKF waged a war in the north, Premadasa had sent his security forces to wipe out the JVP in the south. Having crushed the JVP, Premadasa was then anxious to bypass India and deal directly with the LTTE.[69]

It is not without significance that both Premadasa and his army chief, General Hamilton Wanasinghe, had asked the IPKF to slow down its phased withdrawal when the JVP violence in the south could not be contained and was threatening to accelerate during the March 1989 parliamentary elections in Sri Lanka. Once the elections were over, Premadasa had renewed the demand for IPKF withdrawal. New Delhi was as much a pawn in Lanka's internal political game as the Tamil cause was in India's nation-state equation.

All of which shows that the introduction of troops, the battles against the LTTE, the creations of an alternative force (the TNA), or the reluctance to comply with Premadasa's timetable for the IPKF withdrawal, were not motivated by desire for territorial expansion or Indian military dominance over Sri Lanka. Nor do the four long years of patient diplomacy (1983–1987) to find a solution to the ethnic conflict fit the charge of Indian hegemony. New Delhi made serious attempts to hammer out acceptable formulas for talks, detailed several devolution packages for consideration, and unequivocally upheld Sri Lanka's territorial unity. None of the three proposed formulas suggested or hinted at intervention. Given the ethnic overlap, Lanka's unity could not be separated from domestic stability, or from the autonomy of her supranational State. Involvement in Lanka was not based on altruistic motives but on perceptions of self-interests determined by India's own nation-state relations. The Indian commitment to Lanka developed in stages, and by bits and pieces. There were no grand designs or blueprints for policy. What evolved was in response to developments on ground, and because of the fear of Lanka's imminent collapse. In New Delhi's view, the Tamil–Sinhala conflict had the potential to undermine India's efforts to maintain the balance of interlocking interests between Jaffna, Colombo, Madras, and New Delhi.

In January 1990, the Indo–Lanka political scene dramatically altered. Rajiv Gandhi and the Congress(I) were defeated in the 1989 general elections and the V. P. Singh-led National Front (NF) government came to power; Jayewardene had lost the elections to Premadasa in Sri Lanka; and, last but not least, the Congress(I) and AIADMK had been defeated and the DMK had formed a government in Tamil Nadu. These changes tied the course of Indo–Lanka relations even more closely to the politics of overlapping nationalities in India and Sri Lanka.

The National Front government agreed that it would unconditionally pull out the IPKF from Sri Lanka in March 1990. Implicit in this decision was a new set of policy priorities. V. P. Singh did not see India's interests served by defending the cause of self-determination for the Sri Lankan Tamils, at least not with India's military power. It was a signal to the Sri Lankan Tamils that they would have to fight their own battles, and that India would coerce neither Colombo to implement the devolution package, nor would it coerce the Tamils to abandon their armed struggle against the Sri Lankan government. India would have no role in restructuring the ethnic equation between the Sinhala and the Tamils of Sri Lanka or in redesigning Sri Lanka's power structure.

In V. P. Singh's view, the cost of maintaining the IPKF in Sri Lanka far outweighed the dangers emanating from a continuing civil war in that country. He believed that Rajiv Gandhi had exaggerated the dangers from the Tamil irredenta. In any case, the National Front government believed that its domestic policies—devolution of power and autonomy—would bind ethnic nationalities more closely to India's supranational State and deny other countries a chance to exploit India's ethnic divisions. The NF seemed not to worry particularly about the future presence of foreign powers—China, Israel, Pakistan, or the United States—in Sri Lanka. For V. P. Singh, India's security concerns stopped at the Indian borders. The international situation in the 1990s certainly warranted a correction and change in assessment of security threats to India. The collapse of the Soviet Union in 1989 had ended the superpower rivalry in the Indian Ocean. The V. P. Singh government had extracted reassurances from Premadasa that he would be careful about not stepping on India's security interests. Such promises could not be enforced.

India withdrew the IPKF in March 1991. It had no fallback in the event the ethnic conflicts in Lanka were to once again engulf Tamil Nadu.[70] One could not discount the possibility that step-by-small-step, India might yet again get drawn into the Lankan civil war. Such ominous signs had begun to appear even before the V. P Singh government brought its short tenure to an end. Encouraged by a sympathetic state government, Tamil militants returned to India. By mid 1990, violent clashes between the LTTE and various other militant groups in Tamil Nadu was a commonplace occurrence.[71] The V. P. Singh government had left it up to Karunanidhi to manage the Tamil Nadu politics, in the interest of federal autonomy and to ensure continuing DMK support for the National Front, and to control the traffic of militants from Sri Lanka. The problem had however grown beyond the abilities of the Tamil Nadu chief minister.[72] In the midst of the campaign, in a small village near Madras, a woman later identified with the LTTE, blew herself up with a powerful bomb—in which Rajiv Gandhi and eighteen other people lost their lives.

Rajiv Gandhi's solution to the Sri Lankan problem was based on a particular vision of the quadrangular balance between New Delhi, Tamil Nadu, Colombo, and Jaffna. Implicit in this vision was the attempt to protect the elements that had preserved the stability and unity of India's supranational State. Gandhi had provided one answer to the question raised by Pannikar about the trade-off between autonomy and centralized authority. V. P. Singh had an alternative vision and an alternative answer to the problem of quadrangular balance. The Rajiv Gandhi approach laid a trap for New Delhi from which it could not extricate itself without abandoning relational control and interlocking balances within India. The V. P. Singh vision permitted India to cut its losses but not without the risk of losing control altogether over the course of politics in Tamil Nadu and India.

Chapter 8

✵

COLLAPSING FRONTIERS

India–Pakistan Relations Since the 1980s

In the wake of the Bangladesh war, India seemed to have established a degree of relational control at Simla, over its most fractious neighbor, Pakistan.[1] The agreement had removed Kashmir from the international arena and made it an exclusively bilateral issue. Pakistan had forsworn any future attempt to unilaterally change the status quo in the area through the use of force, and the cease-fire line had been turned into a de facto, if not as yet a de jure, international border, a fact signaled by the change in nomenclature from "Cease-Fire Line" to "Line of Control."[2] But this state of affairs proved too good to last, from India's point of view. Two developments coincided in the 1980s to rob India of relational control over Pakistan and put the two countries back on the path to military confrontation. The first was the Russian invasion of Afghanistan in December 1979. The second was Mrs. Gandhi's and then Rajiv Gandhi's attempts to control Punjab and Kashmir by increasingly intrusive methods that destroyed the interlocking internal balance between the supranational Indian state and these two border states.

The Russian invasion of Afghanistan was a continuation of a set of events throughout the Persian Gulf and Indian Ocean that steadily narrowed India's foreign policy options in the 1980: the fundamentalist revolution in Iran in 1979, the U.S. hostage crisis in November of that year and the eruption of the Iran–Iraq war in 1980, and election of an aggressive anti-Soviet, virulently anti-Communist Ronald Reagan to the White House.[3] President Reagan had eschewed all pretense at detente and renewed the anti-Communist, security orientation in U.S. policy. During the first two years of the 1980s, the United States stepped up its military presence in the oceans adjacent to the region, renewed its 1959 treaty commitment to Pakistan, and extended a substantial military and economic aid package to that country and to the Afghan resistance movement. The purpose was to counter, if not roll back, the Soviet occupation. Pakistan's inclusion into the new U.S.-led "strategic consensus"[4]—based on military cooperation among pro-American countries such as Saudi Arabia and the smaller Gulf states, and including Egypt and Pakistan— added to the fact that Pakistan had already developed close security ties with China over the previous decade. India was apprehensive about the combination of unfriendly powers on its northern borders.[5]

In exchange for allowing its territory to be used as a sanctuary, training ground, and arms depots for the Afghan Mujahideen, Pakistan was able to enter into a financial aid agreement with the United States that promised it $3.3 billion worth of supplies between 1981 and 1987. In March 1986, the United States agreed to a second $4.02 billion aid package consisting of $2.28 billion in economic aid and $1.74 billion in military sales (on credit at favorable terms) for the six years beginning in fiscal 1988.[6] In return for Pakistan's willingness to serve as an arms conduit to the Afghan Mujahideens, the Reagan administration ignored Pakistan's clandestine efforts to acquire nuclear weapons capabilities. The Congressional Research Service warned the U.S. Congress that Pakistan had stepped up its search for nuclear weapons.[7] But the Reagan administration was more anxious to nurture Pakistan's role in containing the Soviet Union, than in containing the spread of nuclear weapons.

The conflict in Afghanistan had brought the global powers back into South Asia but this time they were unevenly balanced. The USSR was clearly on the defensive. The United States had little time to pay attention to the conventional and nuclear arms race between India and Pakistan. This was certainly not a situation where India could protect its room for maneuvering by off-setting the U.S.—Pakistan alliance with its own close ties with the Soviet Union. Although its criticism of Soviet intervention was muted, New Delhi was profoundly disturbed by the Soviet action. India's super power ally had violated a nonaligned country and intruded militarily into a region vital to India's security.

The greatest danger for India from the Afghan crisis was the changes it wrought in Pakistani perceptions of its own military and psychological power. Nearly all the U.S. military aid extended to Pakistan took the form of equipment that was meant to modernize its armed forces. The importance of this new injection of arms in making Pakistan go from the defensive to the offensive in its relationship with India (as Indian government saw it) cannot be overestimated. At least, this is what mattered to India in the short run. Pakistan's military planners concentrated on selected pieces of equipment (force multipliers) that amplified the military capability of all its equipment and widened the range of tactical options. Among such equipment was forty F-16 multi-role fighter bombers, the most versatile attack airplanes in service at the time; three U.S. destroyers on lease; the Harpoon ship-to-surface ballistic missiles; artillery-locating field radar units that could track back artillery shells and locate and silence the enemy battery within two minutes of its opening fire; and 155 mm, self-propelled field howitzers, which were far more powerful than anything that India had at the time.

Even more important, the United States helped Pakistan upgrade its command and control systems for air warfare. Pakistan had asked for and was on the point of getting the latest American Awacs (Airborne early warning and fire control systems) for this purpose, when exceptionally vigorous protests by India made the United States back off at the last minute. In the 1980s India also expanded its defense capabilities by acquiring Anglo-French Jaguar fighter-bombers, Soviet MIG 23 combat aircraft, and Soviet T-72 tanks.

Despite the acquisition of matching weapons, Indian defense analysts continued to worry about the narrowing in the "margin of safety" that was necessary to maintain an edge over Pakistan. They justified such a margin of safety by pointing to the history of conflict between the two countries. According to them, three additional factors had to be taken into account— terrain, duration of conflict, and training.

As to terrain, Pakistan had a decided advantage. According to Raju Thomas, a noted defense expert, a land war does not favor India whether it is against Pakistan in Kashmir, or against China along the borders with Tibet in Ladakh and Arunachal Pradesh. "India has recognized that defense of Indian Kashmir against Pakistan must entail opening other fronts in Punjab and Rajasthan."[8]

As to duration, military superiority offered by quantity of weapons, Thomas writes, is of little significance in short-duration wars, particularly if the advantage of surprise is with the adversary. Indian defense analysts have stressed that all wars between India and Pakistan were of short duration. In Thomas's view, the important question was not how many combat aircrafts India had but what they could do against matching aircraft deployed by Pakistan. The F-16 could tilt the balance in favor of Pakistan, if India did not acquire matching weapons. In the view of Indian military experts, Pakistan could even the advantages of India's size, and military strength by carrying out a preemptive lightening strike (with conventional weapons) across the border.[9] By most accounts, however, India possessed 3:1 advantage in conventional arms.[10]

As to training, Pakistan armed forces are generally known to be disciplined and trained to handle modern weaponry with competence. A significant number of air force personnel received on-the-job training when they were deputized to various Gulf Kingdoms in the 1980s. Pakistan military was part of the Saudi–U.S. strategic defense against the Soviet Union and Iran. Pakistani officers were regularly exposed to sophisticated defense equipment and strategic planning as a part of the exchange program with the U.S. military establishment.

The notion of maintaining a margin of safety against Pakistan has been interpreted in a variety of ways. Advocates of a military buildup in India have justified it on the grounds that Pakistan's inclusion in the U.S-led strategic consensus required acquisition of weapons. They also argue that maintaining such an edge had kept South Asia free of wars since 1971. It was Pakistan that sought to change the territorial status quo in South Asia and not India, therefore they argue, India had little choice but to maintain sufficient deterrent capabilities. Their opponents argue that India is not so much responding to the changing strategic environment as creating that change through acquisition of new weapons.

These arguments ignore the role of domestic factors in shaping perceptions of threat. In this regard, we might do well to look at the analysis of an expert who is neither an advocate nor an opponent of Indian military buildup. Writing under the auspices of SIPRI, Chris Smith observes that by the early 1980s, "India perceived three key areas of threat to its security—China, Pakistan, and a more nebulous threat from the Indian Ocean . . . there were perceived problems from Afghanistan, the renewed and much resuscitated relationship between Pakistan and the USA and . . . developments in the Persian Gulf." Although these changes meant a different balance of strategic forces, they did not, according to Smith, constitute a direct external threat to India's territorial integrity. Pakistan posed little threat to India because any Pakistani attempt to forcibly alter the territorial status quo in Kashmir jeopardized its arms and economic relationship with the USA. And in Smith's view, Pakistan could not afford to do that. A territorial threat from China had receded because of the preoccupations of post-Mao leadership with political and economic reforms. Smith admits that Pakistan's role in the defense of the

Persian Gulf and in encouraging fundamentalist forces in Afghanistan was of concern to India, but these did not endanger India's offshore oil resources. In conclusion Smith states that the Indian military build up was politically motivated and was not a result of careful calculation about India's defense.[11] Among political considerations, concern over Pakistan's support for the Sikh and Kashmiri separatists figure quite prominently in this assessment.[12]

One might question the ease with which Smith dismisses the Pakistani and Chinese threat but that is not at issue here. What needs to be stressed is that the eroding control over Punjab and Kashmir had redefined the notion of threat for Indian policy-makers. Their generalized notion of threat underlined the extended security concern that includes not only South Asia but also the overlapping ethnonations that culturally extended beyond, and into India. India's defense meant more than holding to the territorial status quo, it meant securing a measure of control over such ethnic connections, and achieving influence over the consolidation of overlapping nationalities. The threat perceptions that drive India's defense expenditures or her security policy, extend beyond the narrower, albeit critical concerns about Pakistani military build up. This generalized, nonspecific threat perceptions do not spawn territorial ambitions or desire for total dominance. It produces the desire to maximize the state's autonomy and secure as much relational control in the region as possible.

Undoubtedly, the infusion of new and sophisticated arms gave Pakistani generals a new confidence and put them in a different frame of mind from that in the 1970s. But the opportunity for Pakistan to take the offensive against India—in what the Indian government has in the 1990s characterized as a proxy war—was not created by Pakistan. It was created by India, particularly by Mrs. Gandhi, and later by Rajiv Gandhi, who failed to work out an accommodation with ethnonational leaders in Punjab and Kashmir. Their reasons have already been discussed in the previous chapter.

When Pakistan entered into a strategic understanding with the United States, India responded with a twofold strategy: it intensified diplomatic efforts to persuade Pakistan not to get involved in the Cold War. When this failed, it intensified the arms buildup and a modernization program that had already been scheduled for its armed forces in the "80s. In July 1981, Mrs. Gandhi sent Foreign Minister, P. V. Narasimha Rao to Islamabad to urge Pakistan to steer clear of such involvement. Rao urged the Zia government to keep the Cold War out of the subcontinent, and to join India in forging a common position on the Russian invasion. In their joint communique, Rao conceded Pakistan's sovereign right to acquire arms for self-defense, a concession that meant a good deal more than appeared on the surface, because it implied drawing a distinction between defensive and offensive weapons. But Pakistan was by then fully committed to a policy of lending the United States a helping hand in Afghanistan in exchange for arms that would strengthen it against India. Three days after Rao's visit to Islamabad, the United States announced the sale of F-16s to Pakistan.

Despite the rebuff, India continued to seek a resolution of the outstanding problems with Pakistan. So great were the differences between Pakistan's and India's methods of seeking security that no progress could be made. India kept striving for bilateralism in its relations with Pakistan. Pakistan actively sought closer relations with the United States to build a counter-vailing power to India. Some features of the Afghan struggle gave India further cause for anxiety. The first was the increasingly Islamic character of the struggle against the Soviet occupation. Pakistan was not only the main conduit for the transfer of arms to the Mujahideen, but had become the headquarters of the Hizb-e-Islami, the most fundamentalist of the Sunni factions, under Gulbadin Hekmatyar. Several high-level Indian officials in the Ministry of External Affairs told me in the mid-1980s that they feared Pakistan was instigating or enlisting the Islamic states—notably Iran and Saudi Arabia—to undermine India's territorial integrity and stability.[13] All but two divisions of the ten divisions of Pakistani armed forces continued to remain stationed on the Indo–Pakistani border. This was the second disturbing feature for India's leaders in the 1980s. President Zia often talked about his country's "front line" status as it faced the hostile Soviet forces across the Durand line in Afghanistan, but this Soviet danger had not persuaded him to shift the focus of Pakistan's own armed forces away from India.

The tussle over the terms of a nonaggression pact proposed by Zia in the early 1980s revealed the main difference between India's and Pakistan's approach to national security. President Zia-ul-Haq proposed a No-War pact in 1982, but Mrs. Gandhi rejected it and proposed in its place a more comprehensive treaty on friendship and cooperation. Zia's proposal was intended to simply guard his flanks and leave him free to deal with Afghanistan while his army refurbished its weaponry. Mrs. Gandhi's proposal was meant to bring Pakistan into a much closer relationship with India, which automatically meant fewer ties outside the region and strict adherence to nonalignment. Such a treaty would have meant that Pakistan would have to forswear military bases to foreign states on its soil and promise instead to resolve its differences with India by negotiations within a bilateral framework. The friendship treaty was quintessentially an exercise in retaining relational control, and an attempt to return to the 'rules of the game' established at the conclusion of the Simla summit. But for those very reasons, Pakistan could not agree to Mrs. Gandhi's proposal. It saw the treaty as an attempt to establish Indian hegemony.[14]

The friendship treaty had envisaged expansion of trade, cultural exchange and greater flexibility in permitting visits of families, journalists, and academics. Indian diplomats had argued that such cultural and economic relations would broaden contacts between nationals of the two countries and lessen the suspicions that had so bedeviled Indo-Pakistani ties in the past. President Zia was not interested in a friendship treaty at this point. Pakistani diplomats argued that Pakistan might never want any foreign power on its soil but they could not forego the right to make such decision on their own. Talks on these proposals did not progress beyond expressions of a desire to prevent escalation of tensions in South Asia.

It is important here to recall the tension in Punjab throughout 1983. Mrs. Gandhi had dismissed the Punjab state assembly and imposed President's Rule in a hope of allowing the Punjab police to keep the terrorists at bay. She thoought Bhindranwale could be used to nudge the Akalis to the negotiating table, and then use them to mop up what remained of Bhindranwale elements. But by early 1984, it became clear that Bhindranwale was beyond control.

Throughout these months, Mrs. Gandhi had been hinting that Pakistan and the CIA might be behind the terrorist killings. Relations with Pakistan had rapidly deteriorated after the talks on the proposed merger of Zia's No-War pact and Mrs. Gandhi's Friendship treaty failed. There were frequent reports of Pakistani troop movements and clashes in the Kotli sector of Kashmir. The Pakistani press repeatedly commented on the situation in Punjab. President Zia's press adviser, Z. A. Suleri, stated in a published interview on April 6, 1984, in the *Pakistan Times*, that "Sikh demand was purely communal as it should be . . . perhaps this may reconcile India to a two-nations theory." The editorials by Pakistani commentators often compared the June 6, 1984, armed assault on the Golden Temple to the Jalianwala Bagh massacre of 1919, when the British troops had gunned down hundreds of innocent Sikhs gathered for a meeting in a compound not far from the Golden Temple. Indian leaders viewed such comments to be offensive and in violation of the principle of noninterference in internal affairs of another country. In April 1984, India officially charged Pakistan with aiding and abetting Sikh separatists. According to two leading journalists close to the Indian Ministry of External Affairs and the prime minister's secretariat, Foreign Secretary Rasgotra had traveled to Pakistan in May 1984 to secure its cooperation while Mrs. Gandhi settled Punjab. This was later confirmed by other observers of the Indo–Pakistani scene.[15]

These developments contradict the argument that India is in relentless pursuit of regional hegemony. It offers instead a more textured perspective on India's strategic security. It reveals that India's responses were shaped not so much by her superior military strength, but by the fears of disintegration, or at least loss of control inherent in the rise of separatism in the border state of Punjab. Mrs. Gandhi wanted Pakistan not to meddle while she restored a measure of control over Punjab. Turmoil there weakened India's ability to defend Kashmir. Sikh militancy could encourage similar anti-India movement in Kashmir and, given Punjab's proximity to Kashmir, it could make India vulnerable all along the Indo–Pakistani border in Punjab and Kashmir.

Following the armed assault on the Golden Temple, India found "evidence" of Pakistani complicity in supplying weapons and equipment to Sikh separatists.[16] There is little doubt that the fear of Pakistani support for the secessionists in Punjab was closely tied to anxieties about Farooq Abdullah's precarious control over Kashmir, the growing Islamic sentiment there, and the barrage of Pakistani propaganda from across the border. Several Indian officials told me that Pakistan was taking advantage of the turmoil in Punjab to weaken India's hold on Kashmir. Pakistan's objective, they believed, was to set up its own satrap there.

The tensions between India and Pakistan over the Siachen glacier should be seen against growing mutual suspicions in India and Pakistan. In itself, the Siachen glacier was of absolutely no strategic or economic importance. The protracted and costly dispute over it was all the more symptomatic of the real problems that beset India and Pakistan: historically entrenched suspicions of each other's intentions and deep-seated fears regarding each one's own political viability. These northern regions had never been properly demarcated. For the reasons given in chapter 2, the British never got around to drawing clear and demarcated international boundaries. After the Kashmir war in 1947, India and Pakistan did the same, simply because this remote and inaccessible region did not interest either country then. The Cease-Fire Line, which had been mapped to a point south of the Siachen glacier, was stated to run "due north" from there, but when the dispute erupted in the 1980s, "north" speedily came to mean different things to the two governments.

India's stand began to harden in the late 1970s when a mountaineering-cum-intelligence gathering expedition sent to the Siachen glacier unearthed evidence that Pakistan had been facilitating American "mountaineering expeditions" there for several years. Fearing that this might be a prelude to link up with the Chinese who were to the northeast of the area, across the Karakoram range, India decided to foil these designs by establishing full control of the frontier in that region. It ordered its northern command to launch an operation to take control over the glacier in April 1984. Lieutenant General Chibber, who had led the April action, confessed later that Siachen should never have assumed the importance it did. In his view, the Indian policy on Siachen was shaped by fears of a conspiracy to weaken and dismember India hatched in Pakistan, China, and the United States, in which each would act to protect its own interests in the region.[17]

Throughout the 1980s, India steadily lost relational control over Pakistan because of the latter's strategic relationship with the United States. But internal conflicts within India made the situation far more dangerous than it need have been. The badly bungled Operation Bluestar marked the low point in the unraveling of the Nehruvian supranational State. The Congress party's growing internal weakness, and Mrs. Gandhi's reckless attempts to maintain control—not by coming to terms with moderate Sikh ethnonationalism but by breaking it—had boomeranged and left the field wide open to extreme forms of ethnonationalism. This had an immediate effect on India's external security, by making it vulnerable to Pakistan in a way that it had not been since the early 1960s. This vulnerability was not alleviated by India's military buildup, which kept pace with and perhaps outstripped that of Pakistan. Both India and Pakistan were acutely aware that Punjab had been the battleground in two previous wars, and that the immense patriotism of the Sikhs had played no small part in securing India's flanks. Thus, if the balance between the two countries had tilted toward Pakistan once more, it was not because Pakistan had acquired the state of the art weapons from the United States. It was because the Indian state was beset by its own domestic failures.

National Security Under Rajiv Gandhi, 1985–1989

The effort to build a new internal balance and a more cordial relationship with the neighboring countries was initiated by Rajiv Gandhi, who won the elections with a landslide majority in December 1984. This gave him considerable confidence to embark on a new search for greater consensus and cooperation in the region.

In his first broadcast to the nation as prime minister (January 5, 1985), Rajiv Gandhi promised that he would strengthen India's ties with the neighboring states and that these ties would be based on strict adherence to mutual respect, equality, and goodwill. He immediately sent the India's foreign secretary to the capitals of the South Asian countries. In 1985 and early 1986, he met Zia-ul-Haq of Pakistan five times, President Ershad of Bangladesh four times, and President J. R. Jayewardene of Sri Lanka three times.[18] The government of India initiated talks at Thimpu, the capital of Bhutan, to find a solution to the violent conflict between Sri Lankan Tamil militants and the government in Colombo. SAARC (South Asian Association for Regional Cooperation) was revived and a series of agreements on communication links, cultural exchange, health research, and medical education were signed with Pakistan. He also concluded the two accords with dissident ethnic leaders in Assam and Punjab.

Rajiv Gandhi's policy of consensus and cooperation improved the atmosphere between India and Pakistan. Talks were initiated between the foreign secretaries of the two countries. The initial goal was to merge the two drafts—the No-War pact Pakistan had proposed and the Friendship treaty Mrs. Gandhi had proposed—to fashion a nonaggression pact. At a meeting in New York on October 23, 1985, Pakistan President Zia and Gandhi promised not to attack each other's nuclear facilities. The agreement was officially signed two months later on December 17, 1985. Gandhi then turned to the settlement of the Siachen glacier dispute. India had occupied a part of it in April 1984. Pakistan had protested against Indian occupation on the argument that the glacier fell on its side of the notional line of control.[19] Two round of talks (first in Islamabad and then in New Delhi) between the defense secretaries had followed this decision.

These initial attempts to improve relations with Pakistan did not produce concrete results, mainly because Pakistan was unwilling to compromise its right to make unilateral decisions on the question of foreign bases.[20] Pakistan had also stepped up its quest for nuclear weapons. To counter this, India had let it be known that it might consider a preemptive strike against Pakistan's nuclear facility at Kahuta.[21] There was a great deal of talk among Indian journalists close to the Ministry of External Affairs about the possibility of India emulating the 1981 Israeli surgical strike against the Iraqi nuclear facility. The persistence of such rumors, obviously encouraged by officials, suggests that if India had not seriously contemplated such a strike, it was in no hurry to correct the contrary impression. There are different theories about why the talks failed, but experts believe that its connection to Kashmir—a conflict that had seen three wars and near permanent state of hostility between the two countries—prevented further progress on Siachen.

Robert Wirsing, an acknowledged expert on the Kashmir and Siachen negotiations, supports this explanation of paralysis in the talks. The boundary question was central to the dispute over Kashmir. Wirsing writes that "Pakistan, the loser in Kashmir and hence a revisionist actor, had generally articulated a 'counter-boundary' policy in Kashmir . . . its legal standing pending the outcome of a plebiscite in Jammu and Kashmir." The Simla pact of 1972 had been a setback to this position. "India on the other hand, the winner in Kashmir and thus the status quo actor, after some initial ambivalence, had moved to implement a 'pro-boundary' policy, one that emphasized the finality of Kashmir's accession to India and the desirability of fixing boundaries in recognition of that immutable fact. For India Kashmir was not disputed but agreed upon territory."[22] India saw Siachen as a dangerous gap, where Pakistan could reopen the dispute over the Line of Control. That is why New Delhi refused to withdraw troops from Siachen until boundaries had been delimited and agreed upon.

While the talks on Siachen were bogged down, Pakistan stepped up its efforts to destabilize Punjab, and foment separatism in Kashmir. There is no longer any doubt that Pakistan's intelligence agencies, particularly the Inter-Service Intelligence Agency (ISI), had actively promoted and aided the secessionist elements in Punjab and Kashmir. Independent reports and scholarly investigations confirmed India's contention that Pakistan was waging a proxy war in Kashmir and, after the armed action on the Golden Temple, had kept the terrorists well supplied in Punjab. During my 1986 and 1988 visits to Punjab, interviews with pro-Khalistan advocates in Amritsar confirmed the latter.

The perusal of a score of detailed interrogation reports of Sikh youths apprehended while recrossing into India in July and August 1986 suggested a low-cost, low-risk involvement of Pakistani intelligence agencies in Punjab. These interviews, together with reports published in 1993 by the Republican Research Service of the U.S. House of Representatives and, in September 1994, by the Arms Control Division of Human Rights Watch in Washington, enable us to piece together a fairly detailed picture of the Pakistani involvement in Punjab—and later, Kashmir.

As already mentioned, Operation "Woodrose" which followed hard on the heels of Operation "Blue Star" in 1984, deeply frightened many young Sikhs in the border villages of Punjab. Several hundreds crossed the border into Pakistan, many swam across the Ravi River at night. Others crossed over in order to, in their words, "fight for Bhindranwale," or to take revenge on India for the desecration of the Golden Temple and the demolition of the Akal Takht. Among the latter were a number of Sikh deserters from the Indian army and some ex-servicemen. Through a network of militants located in the

Gurdwaras, they were contacted by key members of the militant organizations, such as Wassan Singh Zaffarwal, who was based in Lahore, and later became one of the most important members of the first Panthic committee. This is the umbrella organization of the Sikhs created in 1987 to coordinate the activities of all the militant organizations.

These young men were met on the other side of the border by Pakistani rangers, who confirmed that Bhindranwale was alive and well and that they would be taken to him. The rangers took the young men to one or another of several rest houses (for government servants) available in the border areas. Here they were interrogated by Pakistani intelligence officers. All were asked if they were soldiers or ex-servicemen. Soldiers or individuals with some military training were immediately separated and sent away to other places.

The young Sikhs caught while returning from Pakistan confessed to the Punjab police that they never again saw those who had been sent to other locations in Pakistan. After a few days, the remainder were taken by ISI personnel to Faislabad and Kot Lakhpat jails, and housed there in fair comfort. At these locations, they were visited and questioned regularly by members of the main Sikh militant organizations, like Wadhwa Singh of the Babbar Khalsa, Bhai Gurjit Singh of the Damdami Taksal, and representatives of the International Sikh Youth Federation. A second crop of militants was harvested from these interrogations, and presumably turned over to the Sikh organizations. The balance were left to languish in jail for the next nineteen months until, following an attempted jailbreak and a hunger strike in support of demands that they either be trained and given arms, or be allowed to go free, they were given two weeks of training in the use of small arms and in making bombs, and a small sum of money. They were put back across the Indian border with the promise that they would be called upon and given arms when they were needed.[23]

What was done with the servicemen can be surmised from the Task Force Report mentioned above. In 1986, Soviet armed forces conducted a surprise raid of an Afghan training camp at Paktia, presumably close to or just inside the Afghan border. Among those killed were two Sikhs. In addition, Soviet intelligence units collected a large amount of correspondence and other papers that detailed the involvement of Sikhs in the training program. The Task Force Report does not specify where it obtained the information; it no doubt came from the American intelligence sources. Thus, there were even in 1986, at least three layers of training. The most rigorous training was given to those who were already soldiers; this was done directly by the ISI in the Mujahid training camps. A second layer of ideologically committed youth was sifted out of the available recruits by the Sikh organizations and given the military and possibly political training. The rest were an embarrassment. Fortunately for the Pakistani authorities, the wave of Sikh youths crossing the border soon trickled down.

The involvement of the ISI in Punjab was also highlighted in the Arms Report. It pointed out that, of the 2,000 Kalashnikov rifles that came into Punjab till 1993, the overwhelming numbers were Chinese-made AK-56s, the highly portable version with a folding stock that the United States had been supplying to the Afghan Mujahideen.[24] The Report points out that until 1988, the ISI had probably been giving these weapons to the Sikhs. But as commercial considerations became more important, the ISI channeled these to the established market for arms sales at Darra in the frontier tribal agency area.[25] The existence of this market had been reported extensively by journalists.[26] What was not known was that it was kept at least partly supplied by the ISI.

The increasing Pakistani support for militancy was immediately noticed in New Delhi, and caused a rise in tension between the two countries. It is not simply a coincidence that after April 1986, Rajiv Gandhi began to pull back from the accommodative stance toward Pakistan and the Akali government in Punjab. In September 1986, after a gap of four years, Pakistan again raised the question of Kashmir in the UN General Assembly. In October, Pakistan's National Assembly expressed serious concern over the "large-scale Indian troop movements" so "close to Pakistani border." In the meanwhile, the Indian government continued to complain to Pakistan about its support to the separatists in Punjab. Gandhi and his envoys had six "rough" sessions with the Pakistani counterparts on the question of Pakistan offering sanctuaries to the pro-Khalistani elements, but failed to get Pakistani cooperation. In 1986, when Pakistan and the United States agreed to extend the six-year military and economic aid agreement signed in 1981, the search for amicable ties came to an end.

Indo–Pakistani relations plunged to a new low when there was a near clash between the armed forces of the two countries in early 1987.[27] It began when Pakistan came to know that India was planning an unprecedented three-service exercise (a part of the year-long military exercises) code-named Operation "Brass Tacks" in Rajasthan, across from Pakistani's Sindh, a province that has long harbored separatist aspirations, and on the Gujarat coast not far from Karachi. Pakistani armed forces took a series of counter-measures to guard against the possibility of a surprise attack just in case India contemplated making one. When Pakistan moved its strike formation, centered on two armored divisions, to a point opposite to the Punjab border, Indian military planners too were alarmed. The stand-off was eventually defused by urgent, high-level diplomacy, but it underlined the nervous apprehensions with which each side viewed the other.[28]

India's mounting hostility toward Pakistan was summed up by President Zail Singh, who warned Pakistan against meddling in Punjab and claimed that "the escalation of tension on the Indo-Pak border which (had) led to Punjab's border with Pakistan being effectively sealed has aborted the extremists' plan to destabilize the state."The main obstacles to the improvement of relations, he said, were Pakistan's "clandestine efforts to acquire nuclear weapons . . . [and its support of] anti-national and secessionist elements in Punjab."[29] In the Indian perception, terrorism in Punjab, the dispute over Siachen and nuclearization of Pakistan were rapidly becoming parts of the single integrated plan to severely destabilize and weaken, if not balkanize India.

Pakistan followed exactly the same pattern of clandestine support for separatists from the J&K but on an immeasurably larger scale. The pattern of sponsorship, pieced together from credible and confirmed sources by A. G. Noorani, suggests that Pakistan enlisted the services of the Jammu and Kashmir Liberation Front (JKLF) initially, then split that body and established a rival Hizbul Mujahideen organization to better control the course of the "liberation struggle" in the Indian Kashmir.[30] The chairman of the JKLF, Amanullah Khan, revealed in an interview to Zahid Hussain of the Karachi monthly *Newsline* in February 1990, that the planning for the liberation of Kashmir had begun in 1986 and that an actual struggle began two years later in 1988.[31] Amanullah Khan, had been deported from England to Pakistan in September 1986 for illegal possession of explosive substances. Hashim Qureshi (predecessor to Amanullah Khan, the president of the JKLF), who later settled in Amsterdam, revealed that the Pakistani Military Intelligence had started training and arming Kashmiri youth as far back as 1984.[32] Amanullah Khan's interview, published in *Newsline*, February 1990, confirmed Hashim Qureshi's account. Dr. Farooq Hyder, vice-chairman of JKLF, who lives in Rawalpindi, told the *Economist* (London) in June 1990, that at that time, the JKLF was engaged in an urban phase of the guerrilla struggle. He claimed that the Front had 10,000 supporters. Although this might be a gross exaggeration, even a small number of determined operatives aided and abetted from the outside would have been, and were in fact, sufficient to plunge the J&K into a state of turmoil.

J&K's Governor Jagmohan also details the terrorist activities and the growing network of various militant organizations during these years. He characterizes this militancy as a "Pakistani supported and inspired urban guerrillas war against India."[33] In any case, it is unlikely that Dr. Hyder and Amanullah Khan could have carried out the planning and organization of these activities from Pakistan without the knowledge and assistance of its authorities. This is evident from the report by the *Economist* correspondent who went with "five Front supporters" and met the Front's armed men in Kashmir. "They said they had been trained years ago, sent back to their villages and told to wait until they were needed." The report states, "For the past two months, they claimed, they had been crossing into Indian Kashmir, carrying on raids and ambushes." Amanullah Khan confirmed the Pakistani role in training arms in an interview to the *Times* (London) on January 30, 1990.

It is difficult to know whether or not Rajiv Gandhi's government by 1988 had pieced together the full extent of Pakistani involvement in Kashmir that is known now. In August 1988, I was provided by Gandhi's secretariat with detailed notes, locations of training camps, figures on arms smuggled into Kashmir and Punjab, and the number of hard-core militants in Punjab and Kashmir. At the time, I believed them to be more in the nature of propaganda. In fact, a majority in the academic establishments and media and press tended to agree with my perceptions and discuss the charges against Pakistan as a flimsy excuse to continue with failed policies in the J&K. In retrospect, there is little doubt that Pakistan had stepped up its support for the separatists in Kashmir although India's failures in Kashmir were a legion.

By 1988, Rajiv Gandhi had lost the earlier enthusiasm to reform the Congress party. The erosion within the Congress could not be reversed. Within two years after his landslide victory in the 1985 election, the Congress had lost power in Punjab, Assam, Mizoram, Kerala, and West Bengal. In June 1987, Haryana was added to the list. Although the losses in Punjab, Assam, and Mizoram were deliberate and meant to restore ethnic peace, the rank and file in the Congress party was extremely critical of Gandhi's strategy.

By 1988, the Congress was beset by internal squabbles, scandals arising from tax frauds, and kickbacks from defense contracts. Rajiv Gandhi had openly quarreled with several close associates who had played a significant role in his 1985 electoral victory. Faced with declining popularity and ebbing confidence in his government, he turned to the tactics used by his mother. He gathered the reins of policy and power in the office of the prime minister, and reduced governance to a close circle of trusted operatives (popularly known as the Rajiv coterie). These about-turns brought confusion. By 1988 the Rajiv Gandhi government was consumed by the need to insure his government's political survival.

Drift and confusion were also visible in foreign policy. In 1988, the IPKF was bogged down in battles with the LTTE and there seemed no early possibilities of settlement in Sri Lanka. India's close ally and trusted friend, the Soviet Union, was in the throes of fundamental change. In keeping with his new initiatives—glassnost and perestroika—Gorbachev had embarked on restructuring the Soviet domestic and foreign policy. He talked about global interdependence instead of the Cold War and about the resolution of regional conflicts in Angola and Cambodia, and withdrawal from Afghanistan. He wanted to resume friendly ties with China and establish a trilateral order in which the Soviet Union, the United States, and China would act to maintain global security. India did not figure in Gorbachev's global scheme. This new Soviet vision was as unsettling to Indian leaders as its invasion of Afghanistan eight years earlier. Both had reduced India's global and regional importance.

There were other signs of marginalization of India's role in international politics. As in war, peace in Afghanistan required Pakistan's cooperation. Rajiv Gandhi had repeatedly tried to find a mediatory role in the Afghan crisis but had failed to impress either the Soviet Union or the United states of the need to use India's good offices. Gandhi's anxiety is not difficult to fathom. The rise of a fundamentalist Islamic regime in place of the Soviet-supported Najibullah government in Kabul threatened to exacerbate India's problem in the region. The new regime of Gulbadin Hekmatyar in Afghanistan was not only pro-Pakistan, but was committed to fundamentalist Islam and anxious to spread Islamic sentiments all over the region, including in Kashmir.[34] The Soviet withdrawal from Afghanistan at the end of 1988 had not therefore eased the pressure on Indian Kashmir or eased relations between India and Pakistan.

But there were other frustrations and disappointments for Rajiv Gandhi to face:

> He had initiated a dialogue with China and wrested a promise of con-
> tinued support on Kashmir from Moscow to offset some of these
> developments. His 1988 December visit to China eased tensions on
> the Sino–Indian border, but there was no breakthrough on the ter-
> ritorial dispute.
>
> He had also established friendlier ties with the United States by step-
> ping up technological and economic exchange. These overtures
> coincided with serious efforts to bring the situation in Punjab and
> Kashmir under better control. However, Congress and human

rights groups in the United States had begun to criticize them for use of draconian measures.

In Punjab, he had encouraged secret negotiations with Bhindranwale's nephew Rode, who had been released from prison, in the hopes that he might convince a sufficient number of militant groups to opt for a settlement. This had failed.

Similarly, he had forged an alliance with Farooq Abdullah's National Conference in 1986. But this too had failed and had enraged Kashmiri public opinion even more. The 1987 Kashmir Assembly elections had proved disastrous. It had been marked by fraud and chicanery, and large-scale rigging of polls, as far as Kashmiris could see in tacit complicity with New Delhi. An increasing number of young educated Kashmiris had begun to turn away from regular channels of democratic politics and instead, search for alternative means to redress their grievances. This led them into the embrace of the militants.

When Zia died unexpectedly in a plane crash and Benazir Bhutto became prime minister in Pakistan at the end of 1988, Rajiv sought her out in hopes of improving relations or at least getting Bhutto to rein in the ISI and Islamic parties from fomenting the separatist militancy in India. Benazir Bhutto had also expressed a desire to reduce tensions and initiate a dialogue with India. Indian leaders believed that she was less encumbered with anti-Indian stereotypes than were older generations of Pakistani leaders and that she was eager to take control of foreign policy away from the generals and bureaucrats, closely identified with the Zia regime.

Talks on the Siachen dispute resumed. In June 1989, a comprehensive settlement of that dispute seemed imminent.[35] In July, Gandhi and Bhutto met in Islamabad and approved the terms of settlement. The differences arising out of age-old suspicions however, confounded progress. According to the Pakistani delegation, India had reneged on its agreement and had tried instead to extend the Line of Control to include Siachen; the Indian delegation denied this and charged that the talks had foundered because of the divisions within the Pakistani delegation. Robert Wirsing reports that, according to a senior Indian military participant in the negotiation, the Pakistan military "wanted a solution when Zia was in power. But when Benazir took power . . . the Pakistan Army changed its tune and now 'won't allow Benazir to get a settlement.' "

Benazir Bhutto's government was undoubtedly weak and beset with serious problems.[36] Unable to manage domestic and international pressures, and increasingly mired in scandals of corruption and nepotism, the Bhutto government subsequently lost elections to an alliance of Islamic Democratic opposition led by Nawaz Sharif. Her attempts to scale down the training and the sanctuary extended to the Kashmiri separatists had run into stubborn opposition by Pakistan's army and its intelligence agencies.

Zafar Meraj, a Kashmiri journalist in Srinagar who enjoyed excellent connections in the militant movement, wrote in the *Kashmir Times* on February 10, 1989, that President Zia-ul-Haq and the late Air Marshall Rahim Khan had given permission to establish training centers for Kashmiri militants in different parts of Pakistan. But upon assuming office, Benazir Bhutto had tried to close them. She had sacked the chief of the Field Intelligence Unit, who was the link between Kashmiri youth and the Pakistan Army and had coordinated the whole program to destabilize the Indian part of Kashmir. When she tried to remove another senior officer involved in Kashmir, the Pakistani generals turned stubborn and refused to abandon the program. Bhutto backed down and eventually gave up the effort. Clearly, the Pakistani army and its intelligence units were unwilling to relinquish their control over foreign policy.[37] Nor were they particularly happy about her Indian initiatives.[38]

In retrospect, several initiatives that Rajiv Gandhi took underline his attempts to regain a measure of relational control over Pakistan. The willingness to keep on with the dialogue on Siachen suggests that he wished to delink the Siachen (undoubtedly an issue of small strategic importance but great symbolic significance) from events in Kashmir. The idea was to expand the area of agreement with Pakistan. If this could be achieved and if Benazir Bhutto proved successful in scaling down ISI's support for Kashmiri militants, Gandhi's hand would be strengthened against the insurgents in Kashmir. In that event, he would have the freedom to employ greater coercion to crush the militancy. Alternatively, he could emulate the earlier Punjab and Assam accords and offer the JKLF, a package of economic and political reforms to address their complaints. A third possibility was to adopt a two-track policy and employ both force and diplomacy to isolate the intransigent dissidents while a deal could be struck with the willing militants for peace in Kashmir. Mrs. Gandhi had tried something similar when she sent Rasgotra to Islamabad in May 1984. The failure of that mission eventually led to the assault on the Golden Temple. The failure of Siachen talks also led to enormous escalation in tension that, according to some observers, brought the two countries disturbingly close to a war.

It is not surprising that India and Pakistan should pursue their military buildups unrelated to the vicissitudes in Punjab and Kashmir, or to fluctuations in Indo–Pakistani tensions. The five rounds of talks on Siachen and the two brief episodes of a sincere search for peace—one immediately after Rajiv Gandhi assumed office in 1985 and the second soon after Benazir Bhutto was elected in 1989—did not slow down the expanding military budgets, and the quest for nuclear and missile capabilities. Gandhi had approved a five-year integrated defense plan designed to build a modern fighting force for India that would equip the Indian military with state-of-the-art weapons systems. He increased the defense budget by nearly 5 percent annually during his five years in office. Earlier, India had successfully tested the short-range missile "Prithvi" and had embarked on developing the medium-range missile capability before the end of the decade. Pakistan had negotiated the transfer of missiles from China and stepped up its development of nuclear capabilities.

The acquisition of weapons and arms did not increase the margin of safety for either India or Pakistan. It linked, instead, the nuclear issue to the dispute over Siachen and Kashmir, and these two to failures to contain the Sikh and Kashmiri nationalism within India's sovereign borders. Punjab and Kashmir were, in turn, inseparable from the growing international pressures on India to sign the NPT (Nuclear Nonproliferation Treaty) and to grant Kashmiris the right of self-determination. The United States was in the forefront to expand the NPT to include India and Pakistan and had begun to wield pressure through threat of trade sanctions and criticism of human rights violation, to get India to sign its nonproliferation initiative.[39]

Throughout the 1990s, Indo–U.S. relations fluctuated in response to the American stance on the NPT and Kashmir. The Bush administration which seemed to support India's contention that Kashmir should be solved within the framework of the Simla agreement had in response to Pakistan's continued efforts to develop nuclear capabilities, terminated economic and military assistance to that country in 1991. The Clinton administration, seemed to however see the Simla framework as inadequate and insensitive to the new realities on the ground, i.e., the uprising in Kashmir. It quietly encouraged the impression that the United States could act as a mediator and facilitate representation for the Kashmiris in a dialogue between India and Pakistan.

These seeming reversals in the United States stance were highly disturbing to the Indian leaders, mainly because the United States stance on Kashmir appeared to be the continuation of Pakistani and Kashmir demands for a plebiscite. At a press conference, Robin Raphel hinted that the United States had reservations regarding the instruments of accession of 1947 because India had not held a plebiscite in accordance with those instruments. It seemed that the United States had not only overturned the legitimacy of the Simla pact but undermined the entire structure of India's legal and political claims to Kashmir by questioning the 1947 India Independence Act and the subsequent consent by the maharajah to merge with India. Although these statements were later explained as misquotes by the media and commentators, India was made aware of the ways in which the U.S.-led new world order might threaten her territorial and national unity. In any event, the uprising in Kashmir had unraveled what Nehru (through the Delhi agreement) and then Mrs. Gandhi (in the Simla agreement) had tried to secure for the nation state of India: its territorial and political integrity.

While international pressures steadily mounted, the Congress party, already weakened from within, faced a formidable challenge from an alliance of opposition parties that had formed a National Front coalition under the leadership of Janata Dal party leader V. P. Singh. It is significant that Singh had served as defense minister and finance minister in the Rajiv Gandhi government and had quit in 1987 to lead the Janata Dal against the Congress. The V. P. Singh government lasted about ten months. But this was the second time since Independence that a non-Congress coalition government had come to power by a protest vote. The Singh coalition government proved even more vulnerable to international pressure, as India's total helplessness during the 1990 Gulf crisis was to demonstrate, than the faltering government of Rajiv Gandhi it had replaced.

For most of its time in office, the National Front government remained preoccupied with domestic problems, although in those months, the world as one had known it since the end of World War II was being dramatically transformed. The Soviet Union had collapsed, the Cold War had abruptly ended, and the United States had remained the only truly global single military power on earth. These changes had shaken the traditional premises of India's foreign and domestic policies. How was India to pursue nonalignment in a world without military alliances? How was she to insist on bilateralism when multilateral solutions were becoming the norm, supported by a growing number of powerful Western states? How was India to argue for the sanctity of its sovereign boundaries in Kashmir/Siachen, when a whole phalanx of human rights organizations were clamoring against India's denial of self-determination to its ethnonations?

These questions would have daunted even a strong and confident leadership in New Delhi. National Front leaders were hardly that. The V. P. Singh-led National Front was perhaps the weakest government to be elected to office since 1947! It could not cope with the domestic turmoil in Punjab and

Kashmir. It could not respond with vigor and confidence to the changing balance of regional and international power in the world. The main problems were its minority status and its abject dependence on parliamentary support from ideologically opposite political forces. The National Front could survive only with the help on the right from the Bharatiya Janata party, and on the left from the secular Socialist and Communist parties. The Bharatiya Janata party was the preeminent Hindu nationalist party that had emerged as a formidable force in the 1980s. The socialist and communist parties had little in common with the BJP. The Singh government had to perform not only the traditional task of balancing India's ethnonations with its supranational state (because it was only then that it could maintain some control over the situation) but also the task of balancing its left coalition partners with its Hindu nationalist supporters, represented by the BJP. That was the only way the National Front coalition could survive.

Such a government could not be expected to pursue a bold and confident policy. The Punjab problem thus languished, although Prime Minister Singh was presented with a window of opportunity in March 1990 when he could have held assembly elections and begun the process of healing wounds that had been festering since the collapse of the 1985 pact between Rajiv Gandhi and Akali Dal leader Longowal. Singh later admitted that he had been too timid and had lost a valuable opportunity to begin the process of normalization in Punjab.

But the more serious challenge for the National Front government came in Kashmir. On December 9, 1990, three weeks after Singh was sworn in, militants of JKLF kidnaped the daughter of the new home minister, Mufti Mohammed Syeed (a Kashmiri) and threatened to kill her if the government did not release five top militant leaders incarcerated in a Srinagar jail. The government capitulated, and this "moral" victory gave the independence movement the fillip and the legitimacy that it had so far lacked."[40]

V. P. Singh blamed the Abdullah/Congress coalition government for failing to contain the violence, forced Farooq Abdullah to resign, placed the state under direct rule from New Delhi, and launched a massive crackdown on the separatists. In Kashmir, these steps triggered a spate of antigovernment protests that were without precedent. By mid August 1990, more than 1,000 people had been killed in the uprising.

Kashmir's descent into chaos and violence brought India and Pakistan close to contemplating war in the early 1990s. Throughout May 1990, the Indo–Pakistan border was a source of tension. According to Seymour Hersh, who interviewed American, Pakistani, and Indian officials, the Indo–Pakistani confrontation of spring 1990 could have precipitated a nuclear conflict. Hersh's narration of events, particularly his characterization of these tensions for being "close to the brink of nuclear exchange," are denied by Indian officials. But no one denies that both countries were zealously watching each other for any signs of a preemptive attack.[41]

The end of the Cold War and the Soviet withdrawal from Afghanistan in 1988 did not diminish tension in Indo–Pakistani relations. In fact, these had intensified and reversed the Indocentric structure of relations that New Delhi had tried to establish at the conclusion of the Bangladesh war. In 1990, India and Pakistan were aware that the next war would not be confined to Kashmir nor possibly to conventional weapons. Even if it were fought by conventional means, war could result in immense damage because both countries were well supplied with large amounts of sophisticated weapons. And there was no guarantee that a war would end the Kashmir dispute even if the outcome was decisive, as it had been in 1971.

India's relational control over Pakistan had eroded not because the Soviet Union had intervened militarily in Afghanistan, nor had it diminished because Pakistan had achieved a measure of parity in weapons with India. India had also modernized its armed forces and spent substantial amounts of money on strengthening its own war machine. In a prolonged war it would hold decisive advantage over Pakistan; a short war would tilt the balance in favor of Pakistan. Rather, relational control had been lost because India's supranational State had failed to balance its own interests against the claims of Kashmiri and Sikh ethnonationalism. India had failed to defuse the ethnic upsurge among its overlapping nationalities. It had failed to prevent or curb separatist violence which steadily escalated beyond control. These failures were rooted in the growing inability to co-opt, represent, or, share power with its ethnonations. They had unraveled the interlocking balance of forces that safeguarded India's territorial sovereignty and unity of the supranational State.

The events of the 1980s had recast the security narrative in India and Pakistan. The perception of strength and vulnerability in one capital had become part of the strategic assessment in the other. In the early 1990s, Indian leaders weighed the balance of threats in relations to Kashmir and Pakistan as follows:

1. The uprising in Kashmir presents Pakistan with the first serious opportunity to alter the strategic status quo in South Asia since the emergence of Bangladesh in 1971. Pakistan is likely to resurrect its two-nation theory by pointing to the insurgencies in Kashmir and Punjab, and arguing that these

are also the two regions where non-Hindus constitute a majority. It was not an accident then that "Hindu" India was engaged in brutally suppressing a revolt in these regions.[42] Secessionist demands in Punjab and Kashmir gave Pakistan an undue ideological and psychological leverage with which to undo India's stability and security.

2. The 1971 defeat had demoralized the Pakistani army but by 1989 it had fully recovered from this blow. The Pakistani army was imbued with a new sense of purpose and as such posed a formidable challenge to India. It had a new "Islamic" image of itself and had acquired a large volume of modern arms and weapons, that in the event of an Indo–Pakistani war could inflict serious damage on India. The neighboring Islamic states of Afghanistan, Iran, and those of Central Asia, provided Pakistan with an additional advantage. These could be persuaded to act as a safeguard for Pakistan, and provide it with what Pakistani General Mirza Aslam Beg had described as the added "strategic depth." The Pakistani army had successfully moved from its earlier posture of defense to a new posture of "offensive defense" against India. Such a strategy enabled it to threaten India, deter it from military action, while Pakistan fomented separatist revolts in Punjab and Kashmir. The Pakistan army could then launch a preemptive attack and take the offensive into Indian territory. Pakistan would no longer have to confine itself to a defensive option to protect its urban centers (as it had done in the 1965 wars) nor did it have to depend on distant countries such as the United States for protection.[43] Pakistan's enhanced military strength, its induction of "new equipment plus the availability of missiles and nuclear capability," and its newly acquired strategic depth, had narrowed the margin of safety for India.

3. Pakistan had used China to counterbalance India and although China's stance on Kashmir was neutral, one could not rule out a close strategic relationship based on their shared desire to contain India in the region. Pakistan's ties to the United States were strained because of the differences over the nuclear issue. But Pakistan had a formidable ally in the United States on the question of human rights violations in Kashmir and Punjab. Pakistan was an important regional ally for the United States in opening channels of communication and influence to a hostile Iran and a chaotic Afghanistan. In contrast, India could not, as it had in the past, count on any solid and unstinted Soviet support on the regional issues.

4. It was true that Pakistan's inability to curb the drug traffic, its diminished strategic importance in the American scheme of things because of the end of the Cold War, and its relentless quest for nuclear weapons, had altered the equation between the United States and Pakistan, but Pakistan's disad-

vantage was not necessarily a gain for India. India also faced growing pressures from the United Nations and the United States to grant Kashmiris
some form of self-determination and admit third-party mediation to settle
the dispute over Kashmir. India could offset these pressures somewhat by
making concessions on the transfer of missile technology and sale of fissionable materials, but it could not, in the ultimate analysis, give up its option to
go nuclear, at least not as long as China continued to expand its nuclear capabilities. Nor could India permit third-party mediation in Kashmir since that
would mean losing further control over the distribution of power between
and among India's overlapping nationalities. These nationalities were already
a hostage to the militant organization based in Pakistan and supported by
Jama'at forces in that country.

   5. India was certainly vulnerable to the new "Islamic factor" in the region.
The Islamic revolution in Iran had demonstrated that in tackling external
pressures, size did not necessarily equal strength. The global transformation
of the 1990s had strengthened the legitimacy of the right to self-determination, whether that right was claimed by nationalities based on religion or on
ethnicity. Pakistan's case for a plebiscite in the Indian-occupied Jammu and
Kashmir had international support. The ferment in Kashmir needed to be
viewed therefore within the frame of ferment in the "strategic crescent" of
the Islamic region that began at the borders of Israel, and stretched through
Iran and Afghanistan to Kashmir. Although this did not represent a formal
alliance of forces, or a sweep of Islamization, it was a dangerous ideological
trend that had already begun to echo in India as evident in the 1993 bomb-
ing of the Bombay stock exchange, the destruction of the Babri Masjid before
that, and the increasingly frequent occurrence of Hindu–Muslim riots all
over India. The Islamic mobilization had led to the 1992 JKLF's march across
the Indo–Pakistani border, and terrorist occupation of the Hazaratbal and
Chirar-e Sharif shrines in Kashmir. It was also evident in the growing popularity of the Hindu nationalist interpretation of the events. The party of the
Hindu nationalists, the BJP, had found its ranks greatly swelled by the public
reaction to Pakistan's role in Kashmir and Punjab.

   6. These developments had destroyed the supranational State's impartial
image and diminished its political authority. The prolonged turmoil in both
Punjab and then Kashmir and the exodus of Hindus, particularly from
Kashmir, had further weakened the secular Indian state and whittled away
public faith in democracy. State repression in Kashmir and Punjab, not to
mention other unstable parts, had become more acceptable to the Indian
public while anxiety over the nation's unity had become magnified.

7. Given the balance of threats and opportunities in the 1990s, India had little choice but to build up its military strength, persuade the United States to restrain Pakistan in Kashmir, improve relations with China by expanding cooperation in the United Nations, diversify its sources of military supplies and foreign trade, and persuade the ethnonationalist leaders in troubled regions to negotiate a settlement with New Delhi.

The most remarkable feature of this security narrative was the continuity in India's perceptions and policies. The end of the Cold War, the changes in the governments in New Delhi, even the growing array of weapons and expanding capabilities–nuclear and/or conventional–had not altered the nature of India's regional concerns, at least not in any fundamental way. Its military strength had expanded but so had its sense of vulnerability to internal threats, particularly those that emanated from its overlapping nationalities. The turmoil in these regions undermined India's autonomy and prevented it from taking a risk for peace. Instead, its leaders acquired additional arms and militarized the borders in Kashmir and Punjab. By the middle of the 1990s, India had deployed over half a million troops and security personnel in and around Kashmir. It had fenced off long stretches of the Indo–Pakistani border to prevent Sikh and Kashmir militants from crossing over from Pakistan. Symbolically speaking, this was the most obvious attempt to build back India's collapsed frontiers.

As the autonomy of India's central state diminished, it lost the power to set the security agenda in the region, to control the pay off of actions by Pakistan, or of the separatist factions belonging to its overlapping Kashmiri ethnonation. In militarily capabilities, Pakistan was comparatively weaker but it had overturned the structure of relational control New Delhi had painstakingly established at the conclusion of the Simla summit. Pakistan was a threat in the 1990s, mainly because India could not regain the political initiative in Kashmir and restore the interlocking balance that could safeguard its territorial unity from subversive intervention from across its international borders. That such subversion had the potential to unravel communal and ethnic bargain on which India had been founded only added urgency to the search for hardened political boundaries. This quest pointed to the central security objective of India—making its territorial boundaries congruent with its sovereign nation-state.

Chapter 9

❦

The Past As Prologue

Looking Ahead

Is India a hegemonic state seeking dominance in South Asia or is it a defensive state facing serious challenges to its territorial unity and international security? In the 1990s, both descriptions of India's regional posture—dominant and defensive—seemed accurate. Such a characterization has been rejected here and a third perspective is proposed instead, based on a domestic analysis of India's regional policy. The purpose is to examine nation-building and international relations in post—colonial nations within a single coherent framework of analysis. More specifically, it is to understand how ethnically motivated domestic conflicts, particularly those that emanate from the overlapping character of ethnic nationality, become internationalized and shape a state's security perceptions and policies. The focus has been on the growing nexus between domestic ethnic conflicts, particularly those that emanate from India's overlapping nationalities, and external security concerns posed by two neighboring states, Pakistan and Sri Lanka. Even a superficial glance at South Asia's ethnic demography shows why Indian leaders should see, in Pakistan's support for the separatists in Punjab and Kashmir, an attempt to weaken India from within. It is not difficult to understand why Sri Lanka should accuse India of using the overlapping Tamil nationality as an excuse for military intervention in that country. The purpose here is to however get at the deeper connections between the Indian state and its role in the region.

The past decade has shown that ethnonationalism is a highly disruptive global force, with immense potential for dissolving sovereign boundaries, precipitating war and intervention, and destroying territorial and political unity of established nation-states. In the 1990s, internationalization of ethnic conflicts have led to inter-state tensions in several parts of the world and engulfed even long-established older nation-states of Europe. The foremost question in this decade is the continued viability of the territorial nation-states. Are they doomed to failure? Are the future states likely to consolidate around ethnically compact cultural nationalism or disintegrate altogether under the pressure of global market and interdependence? The collapse of the Soviet state and the proliferation of ethnic wars across the globe seem to suggest that. A closer examination of the Indian scene, however, suggests the opposite: that such a collapse is not inevitable. I do not pretend to know the full answers to these questions. I have, however, delineated some possibilities, through successes and failures in India, for the future of multinational states.

In recent years, scholars have paid increasing attention to the nexus between India's domestic and foreign policies. Two broad explanations have been given for it. The first might be referred to as the pluralist explanation of regional hegemony. The second might be described as the neo-Marxist perspective of regional hegemony. The pluralist hegemony explanations portray the Indian state as a weak/strong entity that concentrates power at the apex to compensate for its progressive weakening within, brought on by the shortsightedness and greed of its leaders. Undemocratic tendencies within India become hegemonic policies abroad, and repression of ethnic nationalities extends beyond the borders and becomes military intervention in the region.

There is no denying that the 1980s saw a growing concentration of power and an arbitrary use of coercion by Indian leaders. But neither adequately explain the course of India's regional policy as the proponents of pluralist hegemony seem to do. Such explanations tend to ignore the larger contradiction in leaders' responses. The concentration-of-power thesis does not explain why Indira Gandhi, who was at the height of her power in 1972, did not push for de jure division of Kashmir after the 1971 war. Did her counteroffer of a friendship treaty to Pakistan in the early 1980s reflect an authoritarian bent of mind? The pluralist hegemony thesis confuses the quantum of regulatory power (ability to structure the "rules of the game") with its concentration. A state may substitute coercion for compromise because its traditional political base has eroded and it has lost the moral authority to resolve conflicts. Mrs. Gandhi was not eager to storm the Golden Temple. But that action was the result of events that had demonstrated the previous erosion of the supranational State's power to impartially negotiate, co-opt, represent, and to speak for the rival communities in Punjab. A similar situation faced Rajiv Gandhi soon after the spectacular signing of the Punjab accord in 1985. Yet, decision-making power was greatly concentrated throughout the 1980s. Such concentration created an illusion of authority and led some analysts to argue that eventually that development led to a policy of military intervention in the region. The flaw in this argument lies in mistaking capabilities for motives for policy.

Economic factors are important to ethnic and religious identity formation, but they do not explain when and why such identities refuse to "nest" within the territorial India. The neo-Marxist perspectives of India's regional policies, notably in the context of military solutions applied in Bangladesh, Kashmir, Punjab, and Sri Lanka, are misleading. Ethnic identities are not identical with class categories. The Sikh nationality is divided internally into castes and sects. Some of the castes and sects are mutually antagonistic, as evident in Bhindranwale's attacks on the Nirankaris. The same is true of Tamil and Kashmiri nationalities. The neo-Marxists have tried to get at this cultural content by analyzing conflicts in terms of communal divide (i.e., the Hinhu/Muslim antagonism) and by arguing that the Hindu interest was blatantly reflected in the predatory state policies of the Indian bourgeoisie. From assertion of Indian hegemony to Hindu hegemony and interventionism in the region, however, requires an intellectual leap that is difficult to sustain in face of contrary evidence. Did the same causal chain lead to intervention in Sri Lanka? There, the armed extension of the "Hindu state," the IPKF, engaged in a bitter fight with Sri Lanka's Tamil militants, who happen to be Hindus! This confrontation, which never should have occurred from the neo-Marxist perspective, earned such hatred from the LTTE leaders for Rajiv Gandhi, that they finally assassinated him in 1991. Class conflict is not then a fitting framework for analyzing India's regional policy and the impact of its overlapping nationalities.

From the perspective of the suppressed ethnic nationalities, this dialectics of class and religion makes even less sense. The Sikh nationalists do not make Hindus the focus of their animus. That place has traditionally belonged to the central state of India, and not to an antagonistic class. It is true that militant religious preachers such as Bhindranwale talked about the Bania-Brahmin (caste/class) conspiracy in New Delhi but such references were not central to their demands. The principal line of conflict in India does not separate the elite from the subalterns, the coalition of rich and privileged on the one hand and the masses of working and peasant classes on the other. It is between the supranational State and its diverse nationalities. This is especially evident when we look at the impact of overlapping nationalities on India's security concerns.

I have, therefore, rejected both the Marxist and pluralist explanations of domestic/foreign policy connections of the Indian state. I have rejected also the expansionist/defensive, either/or analysis of India's regional policy. I have argued that the balance of power schema is misleading because it has generally stressed accumulated capabilities as a measure of power and ignored the transactional dimension of power.

Conventional theories have assumed that the conceptual frame applicable to international relations of early nation-states can be extended to explain behavior of third world countries such as India, and that foreign policy, in this instance India's policies, can be separated from the course of domestic conflicts. Such a separation seems highly artificial even in the well-established nation-states in the West; it is totally misleading in India's case. India does not possess the presumed characteristics of the Western nation-states—hardened boundaries and well-integrated, and relatively stable, domestic institutional structures. In sharp contrast to European integration strategies, India pursues a distinctly different method of national unification. It appears to possess attributes of a single unified nation-state, but it is still struggling to be one. The biggest obstacle to building a European-style nation-state is the absence in India of any congruency between its cultural and its territorial boundaries. It has compelled Indian leaders to separate adverse linkages between domestic and external policies, or at least, control the ways in which such connections are forged. This is why India has pursued nonalignment, opposed military alliances in South Asia, and attempted to insulate the region from extraregional forces. This is not to suggest that every security decision India makes is born out of ethnic considerations, or that all ethnic conflicts are a result of external interference. However, their increasing importance to relations among South Asian states cannot be ignored.

To understand the impact of overlapping nationality on the formation of policy toward Pakistan and Sri Lanka, we need a scheme that does not lock us into a single dimension of dominance and subjugation or to an index of power measured as comparative military strength, size, and technological advance, i.e., accumulated capabilities of a state. Instead, we need a transactional concept of power that at once looks inward at the configuration of domestic forces and outward at the distribution of international power. We need a frame that builds on the idea that large and heterogeneous countries such as India might not traverse the path to unification furrowed by the early nation-states, that the incongruity between their nation and territory might not be a temporary but an enduring condition of their existence, and, that such conditions require for us to depart from the conventional ways of thinking about security, sovereignty and legitimate defense.

Two key concepts were offered: relational control and interlocking balances. In this study, relational control is defined as an ability to affect not only the outcomes of events but the very relations of convergence and conflict that produce such outcomes. Relational control permits India's leaders to maintain an interlocking balance of interest between its central state and nesting nationalities, and to balance these against international threats from the neighboring countries. To this end, India has used persuasion, coercion, sanctions, and military intervention. India is not a status quo or a defensive state in South Asia, nor is it committed to a single goal of dominating the region and reducing neighboring states to be its satellites.

What did Indian leaders seek to balance when they sought relational control? It has been suggested that they sought to balance the concept of the historic state against their goal of building a modern state. This is one dimension of interlocking balances. The historic state does not refer to any specific empirical state of the past. Rather, it refers to an abstracted principles of unity and governance drawn from the "reading" of the past, what one might call the "invented" or imagined model of territorial unification and governance for India. This "imagined" unification pattern required overarching authority based on a universal ideology that retained a degree of impartiality between India's heterogeneous segments, a layered order that permitted accommodation of India's ethnic nationalities, and regional autonomy to local elite and communities that were territorially coherent enough to lay claims to a separate state. The first provided the supranational State of the past a degree of autonomy; the second acknowledged prior claims of cultural and local customs and traditions; and the third made inherent tendencies toward pluralism to "nest" within the overarching political order.

Historians have debated the extent of centralization under such empire states of the past. Some have rejected the claims of sovereign control exercised by such states; others have asserted that centralization took place periodically throughout Indian history. The validity of these conflicting views is less important to the problem of an interlocking balance than the fact that India's founding leaders believed in the existence of a historic state. The conflicting nationalities—the Sikhs, the Tamils, and the Kashmiris—also believed in it, if only to argue that the state had oppressed them in the past.

These narratives of oppression, or brave defense of the ethnic "nation" against overwhelming odds, were grist to the mill of Sikh, Tamil, and Kashmiri ethnic identity. These two conflicting interpretations of history, one espoused by the supranational State and the other by the ethnic nationalities (the Sikhs, Kashmiris, Assamese, Tamils, Nagas, and Nepalis), reflect contests over identities, homelands, and primary habitats. These contests have to be reconciled and absorbed within the scope of India's modern nation-state, which meant making the state correspond with the Indian nation. Modern India is not possible without integrating diversity; diversity however, permanently tugs at the quest for a unified India.

If one dimension of interlocking balances seeks to make the "historic state" congruent with the modern agenda of the nation-state, the second dimension requires reconciliation on a different time-line basis. It requires accommodation of conflicting claims to legislative power, public offices, and popular votes. This is the more traditional stuff of politics. It is here that we can see the exercise of interlocking balance: representation and co-optation, coercion or persuasion. The ability to co-opt and represent specific ethnic interests depends on the extent to which the central leaders are perceived as genuinely impartial amidst rival communities. In the early years of Independence, the Akali Dal had several times merged with the Congress; many top Akali leaders were absorbed into the Congress. A large section of the Sikh community regularly voted for the Congress during the Indira Gandhi and Nehru years. The early consolidation of Dravidian nationalism established a somewhat different relationship between New Delhi and Tamil Nadu. When the Congress lost legislative majority in Tamil Nadu, the central leaders (Indira Gandhi and Rajiv Gandhi) became reconciled to a junior partnership role and a limited leverage in the Tamil politics. Punjab and Tamil Nadu therefore represent two separate modes of interlocking balance. In the former, the Congress attempted to replace the Akali Dal; in the latter, it accommodated to the dominance of the Dravidian parties.

The early consolidation of Kashmiri nationalism under Sheikh Abdullah and the National Conference dictated a strategy similar to the one followed in Tamil Nadu. But several security considerations intervened to create a third distinctive pattern of integration. After the first Indo–Pakistani was of 1947, the dispute over accession, the pattern of infiltration and subversion across the border, the attempt to incite pro-Pakistani "Islamic" sentiments in Kashmir, and the progressive incorporation of the Kashmir dispute into a common U.S.–Pakistan front against the Soviet occupation of Afghanistan, Indian leaders were convinced that Kashmir would remain the weak spot in

India's defense. The domestic implications of the dispute over Kashmir were equally serious. Kashmir was the first line of defense against internal disintegration and communal violence. India's secular commitment, its leaders argued, depended on upholding the sanctity of the cease-fire line and territorial status quo in Kashmir. It is only in this context that the political responses to developments within the Indian state of J&K become intelligible.

If developments within Kashmir and beyond had shaped New Delhi's response to Pakistan, the fear of losing control over Kashmir forged its perceptions of events in and around Kashmir. These undermined the initial arrangement of Kashmir's integration within India, an arrangement that required retaining Kashmir's special status in the Indian union intact, permitting the National Conference (a regional party) to govern the state while forestalling the Kashmiris forging an "Islamic" connection to Muslims in India or in Pakistan. As the political authority of the supranational State declined so did the sanctity of article 370. Strained relations with Pakistan in the 1980s led directly from the fears produced by the erosion of the interlocking balances implicit in article 370.

The inside-out logic of India's security permits us to get at the complex interweaving between Sikh and Kashmiri nationalism on the one hand, and the vacillating course of India–Pakistan relations, on the other. The quadrangle link of events in Tamil Nadu, Jaffna, New Delhi, and Colombo similarly explains the twists and turns in India's relations with Sri Lanka during the past decade. India's responses in Punjab, Tamil Nadu, and Kashmir do not show a relentless drive toward regional hegemony. Instead, they point to a series of balancing acts, all designed to safeguard the autonomy of India's supranational State. It shows that the path to modernity is not linear but configurative or recursive. Indian leaders are frequently required to take a zigzag course: in the horizontal direction to accommodate competing ethnic nationalism, before they move forward toward greater national integration. This distinctive route to modernization suggests a degree of caution about taking the boasts and pronouncements of Indian leaders at face value and interpreting these as a proof of regional hegemony. Raju Thomas calls this the "Rodney King" complex: anxiety for status and a nagging sense that India has not received its due as a major regional power. More significantly, it suggests that India's security perceptions are likely to differ from those of the more fully integrated nation-states in the West. This is evident in the generalized and domestic orientation of security threats.

For instance, the most outstanding threats to India in the 1990s were: geopolitical threats from Pakistan and China both in terms of rival conventional and nuclear capabilities; threats emanating from low intensity conflict and subversion sponsored by hostile neighbors; threats to political stability from mismanagement of ethnic, caste, and religious conflicts; tension and violence resulting from demographic pressures generated by refugees or large-scale migration from the neighborhood; and the growing nexus between illegal cross-border flow of drugs, money, arms, and domestic strife. One can hardly miss the domestic and inward orientation of these threat perceptions. The debate over the Siachen glacier dispute illustrates this clearly.

The conflict with Pakistan over the glacier was not only very specific but also confined to the area of dispute. A large number of defense experts believed that compromise regarding Siachen was unlikely to jeopardize India's northern borders. The main reason why the dispute remains unresolved (although Rajiv Gandhi came close to it in 1989) is because India tends to see it as a layered, even symbolic, problem. Indian officials argue that although the territorial security might not be at stake, an unconditional compromise on Siachen might be taken as a sign of weakening in New Delhi. This might embolden Pakistan in Kashmir. They fear the domestic fallout from a compromise with Pakistan. The notion of the threat then extended inward. Security policies were shaped by perceptions of a more generalized sense of vulnerability peculiar to heterogeneous nation-states that could not afford to take their unity for granted.

There is no cool assessment of comparative advantage in size, weapons, and preparedness in this notion of threat; rather, it reflects an anxiety about losing control over balance of domestic and external relations. And in some ways, India's central leaders are not wrong. Most observers agree that the perception of a weakened India after Nehru's death precipitated the war in 1965. Commentators have also pointed out that V. P. Singh's accommodating stance toward the Kashmiri militants (who were fully backed by Pakistan by then) intensified cross-border subversion and insurgency in Kashmir. The National Front government had come to power pronouncing absolute faith in regional autonomy and good-neighbor relations but had retreated from that promise because of uncontrolled violence in Kashmir. Even if Pakistani and Indian leaders wanted to back off from the near-confrontation in Kashmir in 1994, they dared not do so. Hindu nationalists, Islamic extremists, and other opportunists stood ready to exploit the slightest sign of "weakness" by elected officials in both countries. These fears go a long way in explaining why the military exercises Operation Brasstacks triggered countermobilization of Pakistani forces across the border; why President Bush

sent Robert Gates posthaste to the region in 1992; and why Bush thought the
situation between India and Pakistan might precipitate a nuclear conflict.
While turmoil in Punjab had raised temperatures prior to the military exercises, the outbreak of insurgency in Kashmir had congealed the fears of an
imminent crisis in 1990.

At a deeper level, the "generalized" threat perception reflects New Delhi's
declining ability to effect the interlocking balance between itself and its nesting nationalities—the fear that such a balance might collapse altogether
because of factors beyond its control, i.e., democratic pressures generated
by expansion in the electorate, changes in the distribution of income, and
strengthening of religious and ethnic separatism. This explains the persistent
sense of vulnerability and the enduring anxiety for India's unity. Frequently,
such anxieties are combined with the opposite sentiment, i.e., an exaggerated confidence in India's size, economy, and weaponry.

The objectives of relational control and interlocking balances is, however, inherently limited. Desire to structure regional relations, influence the
"rules of the game," or acquire leverage over the distribution of regional military and diplomatic power does not mean an ever-widening circle of Indian
dominance. Nor is there a direct and immediate correspondence between
capabilities (military and economic) and actual power. This is evident in the
case of Sri Lanka. By almost any conventional index of power, India was
superior to Sri Lanka in the 1980s. However such superiority did not tempt
Mrs. Gandhi to punish Sri Lanka's departure from the nonaligned stance.
India undertook no military exercises to intimidate Sri Lanka, no talk of
intervention, economic sanction, or withdrawal from trade and diplomatic
intercourse. In focusing so exclusively on the unequal terms contained in
the letter appended to the 1987 Indo–Lanka pact, many experts have lost
sight of the fact that Rajiv Gandhi was reluctant to get militarily involved in
Sri Lanka, that the pact had not envisaged war with the LTTE or a long stay
in Lanka, and that President Jayewardene wanted the protection and superior firepower of the IPKF to insure his own and his party's political survival. Admittedly, India's Sri Lanka policies do not pass the test of morality
or good-neighbor behavior. But the issue here is not that. It is whether
Indo–Lanka relations in the 1980s reflect an Indian attempt to reduce
Colombo to the status of a satellite.

India's involvement in Sri Lanka during the 1980s was no unraveling of a
Machiavellian blueprint for Lanka's subjugation. There was no grand plan.
India's response had been gradual, piecemeal, and shaped by a cluster of
domestic, political, and strategic considerations. Rajiv Gandhi signed the

1987 pact because he wanted to minimize the fallout of the ethnic fratricide in Sri Lanka, lend Indian troops to tilt the military balance in favor of Colombo, and instill confidence among the Tamils that India would stand as a guarantor to the devolution plan contained in the pact. He wanted to foreclose the possibility of any extraregional military involvement (mercenaries, the PLO, Israel, or China) in the Lankan civil war. The commitment of the IPKF in 1987 and the extension of training and arms to the militants before that were spawned by the fear that the civil war would drive warring rivals to the arms of those hostile to India's security.

If New Delhi did not provide arms and money, it might lose leverage over the militants, and the latter would in all likelihood turn to other sources of arm supplies, as Colombo had done before the 1987 Indo–Lanka agreement. This would be more dangerous for India than the risks it would bear in sending the IPKF to support the pact. Although India had the military capabilities to permanently occupy the northern part of Sri Lanka, it never had any intention of doing so, not because India feared being branded as a regional bully but because it wanted to prevent the emergence of Eelam. New Delhi did not want a separate sovereign Tamil Eelam that might act as a magnate to the 50 million Tamils in southern India. The logic of relational control and the balance of interlocking interests on which India based its policies ruled out permanent occupation. The National Front government subsequently ended the IPKF operations because Sri Lanka wanted India to leave and public opinion had turned against the IPKF's continued presence in Sri Lanka.

The strategy of an interlocking balance also requires Indian leaders to "ethnicize" economic and political conflict, and define them not as class or religious but ethnic challenges. This is a double-edged weapon. On the one hand, it can localize the conflict but it can also make them intractable because the state legitimizes their ethnic identity. This is particularly so when a weakening central state is unable to prevent ethnic spillover beyond its borders or to other parts within India.

The first two decades after Independence—the Nehru years—were characterized by the creation of the supranational State, based on relational control and an interlocking balance of interests. India created political institutions, introduced planning for economic development, held regular elections, designed mechanisms to layer power, and granted autonomy to its ethnically compact communities. If this required a ban on the activities of the Communist party of India and of the extremist Hindu organization, the Jan Sangh, then Prime Minister Nehru did not hesitate to do so. In the international sphere, nonalignment guided India's policy. Nehruvian nonalignment

was internationalist in pronouncement and intent. It strove hard to break
away from the stereotype of passivity attributed to it by the West. Nehru
renounced responsibility for people of Indian origin in neighboring states,
and accommodated demands for linguistic-ethnic states. He sought to "ethnicize" conflicts—through Kamaraj Nadar in Tamil Nadu, Pratap Singh
Kairon in Punjab, and Sheikh Abdullah in Kashmir—so that interlocking balances between these regions and the supranational State could be preserved.
Such a bargain between its nationalities and the state gave the latter a degree
of leverage over developments in India's vicinity. Nehru wanted India to be
a modern nation-state, but he was aware of the profoundly divergent path his
India would have to take from that followed by the West.

India's strategic analysts have faulted Nehru for neglecting India's security
and sacrificing it on the altar of internationalism. The question here is not
whether Nehru was right or wrong. He was obviously mistaken in his assessment of China's intentions and responses. He might have overreacted to
Pakistan and missed opportunities to forge a settlement with President Ayub
of Pakistan. I do not want to advocate policies but rather get at the deeper
logic behind their formulation. Nehru's perceptions of India and the region
around it were rooted in his understanding of India's domestic compulsions
and pointed to economic development, not defense. One might argue that he
could have reversed these priorities, given the Congress's comfortable legislative majorities and his almost unchallenged leadership of the Congress,
the government, and particularly of India's foreign policy. But such concentration of power in a single leader did not mean restoring the boundaries of
the British Raj.

Similarly, the weakening of the Congress edifice had a serious impact on
India's external balance. This was evident in the humiliating dependence on
American aid for food, the pressure to devalue the rupee, and the general
sense of helplessness that gripped Indian leaders in the 1960s. Indira Gandhi
watched in consternation the disturbing Soviet attempt to take a more evenhanded approach to Indo–Pakistani conflicts. The first few years of her
tenure show a gradual departure from the Nehruvian strategy, i.e., greater
readiness to ethnicize conflicts (creation of the Punjabi Suba) in order to gain
autonomy for the supranational State (splitting the Congress and regaining
control over state Congress committees). Relational control was eventually
restored in 1972 with the Bangladesh war, Congress scoring a resounding
victory in the 1972 Assembly elections.

Many scholars have regarded the 1971 war in Bangladesh as a turning
point in India's bid for hegemony. This interpretation has gained in retrospect

because of the subsequent expansion in India's military power. Although the war had neutralized the Pakistani threat for a while, India reaped no enduring advantage from it in Kashmir or Bangladesh. The gains of the victory were more visible within India, in Indira Gandhi's ability to restore a balance of interests in Kashmir which continued relatively undisturbed until Sheikh Abdullah passed away in 1982. Despite Congress's subsequent defeat in 1977, the arrangements of 1975 held intact, preserving the balance between Kashmiri nationalism and India's supranational State.

Mrs. Gandhi had successfully executed her version of the "ethnic" strategy. It had rested on the military intervention in Bangladesh and exercise of relational control. She had established a new precept: India would use its military capabilities to structure interstate relations in South Asia in order to protect itself from war and turmoil in a neighboring state. She had used the Bengali ethnic nationalism against Pakistan's appeal to Islamic nationalism. She did not permit Bengali nationalists, whether in West or East Bengal (Bangladesh) to override India's conduct of the 1971 war. But she could not have anticipated with any certainty the outcome of the war. Motives behind actions must be therefore separated from its outcome. The most one can say is that anticipation of a particular outcome can influence motive, but it is only one among several factors that compels a state to act. As it turned out, Congress's spectacular victories in the 1971 and 1972 elections proved ephemeral.

The Janata government that replaced the Congress(I) also did not last long. It lacked coherence and stability; it could not handle the balance of interlocking interests between India's diverse nationalities and its supranational State. Nor did Janata forge a distinctive path in the sphere of foreign policy, although one might have expected it to do so. It is difficult to know how much of a difference the Janata might have made had it coalesced as a genuine and powerful alternative to the Congress.

By the time the Congress and Mrs. Gandhi were reelected in 1980, the logic of India's federal unity had altered dramatically. By the 1970s, a legislative majority in the central parliament could not be guaranteed without gaining electoral majorities in the state assemblies. Some states were, of course, more important than others (i.e., Uttar Pradesh) but the center's growing dependence on them could not be disputed. An increasingly fragmented and hollow political party, which the Congress(I) had become by the 1980s, could hardly win in local assemblies without also denying local parties a share in power. Its attempts to "ethnicize" tensions in Punjab and Kashmir had disastrous consequences. Its "ethnic" maneuvers—playing one ethnic community against another and pitting one ethnic faction against another ethnic faction—destroyed gradually the basis on which Sikh and Kashmiri nationalism had found space within the Indian union.

Indira and Rajiv Gandhi violated that most sacred of all founding rules of India's unity: never divide Kashmir and Punjab on the basis of religion. Their mistakes were apparent in the unleashing of Bhindranwale in Punjab, in the blatantly pro-Hindu rhetoric during the 1983 assembly election campaign in J&K, and again in the 1985 elections when Rajiv Gandhi sought to appease Hindu and Muslim communal constituencies by first overturning the court decision on Shah Bano and then granting concessions to the Hindu nationalists over Babri Masjid in Ayodhya.

Congress leaders argued that India's supranational State was safer in the hands of Congress nationalists such as Mrs. Gandhi and Rajiv Gandhi than in the hands of BJP or weak coalition governments such as the Janata and its subsequent reincarnation, the National Front. The Gandhis were not only firmly committed to the principle of secularism, but required to preserve Congress's subcontinental spread, which depended on preventing total identification with any single ethnic or religious community. The Congress, they argued, had to hold the secular center against votaries at the extremes.

That such reasoning influenced Rajiv Gandhi was evident in his actions during his first two years in office. He had given virulent anti-Sikh speeches in the 1985 elections but had moved with dispatch to sign the Punjab pact with Longowal in 1985. Even in their most politically compelling moments, then, Indian leaders sought to preserve the image of impartiality. This became increasingly difficult as the Congress began to decline. The subsequent juggling between rival ethnic constituencies destroyed the image and undermined the autonomy of the supranational State.

Increasing polarization within Punjab, Kashmir, and Tamil Nadu did not help either. The Congress lacked leaders who could effect partial integration of these ethnic nationalisms into the mainstream; the nationalities lacked leaders who could unify the community to demand redress within normal political channels. Ethnic leaders fought among themselves for the coveted prize, the office of the state's chief minister. Quarrels between Farooq Abdullah and G. M. Shah destroyed the National Conference's ability to control events in Jammu and Kashmir; fights between Tohra, Prakash Singh Badal, and Longowal destroyed Akali control of events in Punjab. Each tried to outdo the other by appealing to the exclusionary rather than the syncretic legacy of their ethnic history. And what they had unleashed soon spiraled beyond their control.

Pakistan's extension of sanctuaries and arms to Punjab and Kashmir insurgents showed that failure to contain ethnic disaffection softened India's national borders. It spurred unfriendly neighbors (that share such nationalities) to push India's sovereign frontiers inward. The same could be said about the effects of India's support for the Tamil militants. The scale and extent of such clandestine support by India and Pakistan to their respective ethnic clients also underlines the growing abilities of each state—one allegedly hegemonic, another allegedly at the receiving end of such hegemonic ambitions—to breach national boundaries and internationalize domestic conflicts. India, however, did not seek to permanently alienate northern parts of Lanka. In contrast, Pakistan seeks to wrest Jammu and Kashmir from India. Pakistan also seeks to internationalize India's ethnic conflicts; India seeks to confine them to the region to regain relational control and insulate South Asia.

Two additional caveats need to be noted before we discuss the future of the relational control and interlocking balance strategy. First, I do not attempt a moral judgment on leaders or their policies, nor do I seek to fix the blame for violence and war. Historians might argue as to who was more communal, the Akali Dal or the Congress; or who had better claims on Kashmir, India or Pakistan. No one, however, denies that the Akali Dal and Kashmiri pandits frequently resorted to communal rhetoric and that their respective ideologies were rooted in the negative definition of the self: "Hum Hindu nahin" (We are not Hindus) and "We are Hindus first and Kashmiris next." The Congress, whether as a movement or as a government, was likewise committed to winning elections and insuring political survival. It too resorted to unethical methods, which became increasingly perverted after it started losing legislative majority at the center and control of important states in northern India. None of these developments are disputed. My purpose is to get past the notion that every ethnic upsurge is the voice of the oppressed; to refute the "pathos of minorities" that has marked much that is written on the subject of identity politics. Ethnically based liberation movements are not necessarily democratic. The violence in the name of Eelam is unlikely to emancipate the Tamil masses. The democratic credentials of Khalistanis are highly suspect. Interesting though these questions are, they do not fall within the scope of this book.

Second, attempts to establish relational control does mean constraint over full and free exercise of independence by India's neighbors. Such constraints are selective, episodic, and limited to specific situations. They are also rooted in the logic of political events inside India. Many scholars see India's opposition to military alliances, insistence on bilateral resolution of disputes, and rejection of third party intervention in South Asia as an attempt to establish India's unchallenged dominance over the region.

I have argued that such dominance, if one must use that term, is selective. The projection of India's power is meant to restore relational control, not make an independent neighbor into a satellite and move on to the next victim in the region. The pattern of brief intervention and withdrawal, of pressure that is often followed by indifference, underlines the sporadic exercise of India's military power. Sri Lanka is a case in point. India's size and military superiority did not insure the success of the 1987 pact with Sri Lanka. A non-state actor such as the LTTE was able to frustrate the militarily more superior IPKF. The resurrection of the Kashmir dispute and its internationalization by Pakistan during the 1980s (in spite of agreements made eight years earlier in Simla) also shows this. India's expanding military power might make instruments of violence more lethal, but they do not necessarily make them more effective.

What then is the future of relational control and interlocking balance between India's ethnic nationalities and its supranational State, at least insofar as it will shape India's regional policy? What are the prospects for this model of national security in the 1990s and beyond, and how will it shape India's relationships with its neighbors? The answers depend on which version of the Indian nation-state survives the challenges of the post-Cold War world and how well its proponents can do the two things that are important to India's stability and security: construction of an overarching ideological order, and reconciliation of India's diverse nationalities (particularly the overlapping nations it shares with neighboring states) with its supranational State.

India's ability to retain a degree of relational control and affect a domestic balance between its central state and nationalities will depend on which vision succeeds in capturing popular power and imagination. At least two competing visions are likely to shape the future of South Asian security. For the sake of brevity let us call these "unity through centralization" and "unity through decentralization."

One version of the centralization model was espoused and implemented by Jawaharlal Nehru. His choice was made against solutions offered by K. M. Pannikar, who advocated a unitary State and strong defense, and those offered by ethnic leaders such as Master Tara Singh of the Akali Dal and Ramswami Naicker of the DK. These leaders had advocated that India become a subcontinent of several separate nations or a loose confederation. The 1980s have brought to the forefront yet another version of "unity through centralization." This is the resurgent vision of the Hindu nationalists, represented by the Bharatiya Janata party and its family of Hindu organizations, the "Sangh Parivar."

The other alternative vision, "unity through decentralization," was put forward first by the Janata coalition government, which lasted from 1977 to 1979. The more coherent and expanded articulation of this vision came twelve years later during the brief rule of the National Front government.

Briefly, the Congress stood for centralization of political power; the National Front stood for a progressive decentralization based on accommodation of regional and local autonomy and devolution of a large degree of power to communities. The BJP version of the centralized polity envisages unifying the Indian nation-state on the basis of a Hindu majority. It wants to homogenize the "Hindu" masses and erase differences of caste, ethnicity, and language. The term "Hindu" has two meanings for the Hindu nationalists: Hinduism as culture and as a religion. These have to be combined to determine the scope of the Indian nation: its territorial scope, its genealogical antecedent, and its culturally defined identity. Sikhs, Jains, and Buddhists could qualify as Hindus since all three religions were born in India. This is not the case with Islam. The Muslims can belong to India provided they assimilate. The Hindu nationalists do not claim that Muslims be excluded from India but insist that Muslim give their absolute and undivided loyalty to India. Implicit in this is the notion that their loyalty is somehow suspect.[1] The Hindu nationalists then echo the thesis of "separate and equal" nations of Hindus and Muslims that created Pakistan.

The Hindu nationalist version of unification is based on the acceptance of political and cultural centrality of "Hindu Rashtra" or Hinduness.[2] This is why the BJP favors replacing separate personal laws (for the Muslims and Hindus) with a uniform civil code. The Congress model of unification, at least before it became distorted in the later years, had rejected this definition and premised its vision on territorial nationalism and the composite culture of India. In this, unity was to be achieved by transcending ethnic and caste divisions and not by denying or eliminating these. The Congress model of unification favors the present federated arrangements because it permits the state to separate cultural and religious identities from political identity. Indian Muslims, defined as Indians first and Muslims second, can be regarded then in ethnic and regional terms. (i.e., Uttar Pradesh Muslims, Andhra Muslims, Muslims in Assam and the northeast). All can be separated from Muslims in Kashmir. This strategy of segmentation permitted the Indian state to safeguard its autonomy by affecting a series of balances that "ethnicize" regional differences and preclude division of class or religion.

In contrast to the Congress and BJP model of national security, the "decentralization" model is based on the reasoning that concentration of power at the apex leads to authoritarianism, which in turn leads to violence and insurgency. According to the model, the best way to preserve India's unity is to devolve power to regional and local entities and govern through consent and consensus. Such a polity, the decentralizers argue, will be more stable because India's heterogeneous nationalities will have a stake in its unity.

In foreign policy, the Hindu nationalist vision centers around establishing Hindu Rashtra's unchallenged dominance over the region because in its reading of history, India's cultural scope stretches from Afghanistan to Sri Lanka. This is not a model of interlocking balances, nor a selective and discrete application of pressure. There are no internal mechanisms as in the strategy of relational control to restrain a Hindu Rashtra's expansionist tendencies. Balances are not required in the "Hinduized" India because it is defined as a homogeneous nation that will reclaim what the Hindu nationalists believe is the cultural scope of the Hindu civilization.

This extreme strand of Hindu Rashtra ideology also seeks to make the nation and state congruent (undeniably a modernist impulse) which would include the present states of Pakistan and Bangladesh. The more moderate strand of this thinking is ambivalent about extending the borders of the Indian state but favors a tough, almost belligerent posture toward Pakistan. It advocates abolishing Article 370, which had been put in place to protect J&K's special status within the Indian union. Kashmiri Muslims are to be assimilated into the Rashtra and so pave the way to peace in Kashmir.

India can never be a homogeneous country. Its heterogeneity is irreducible. Should the BJP come to power, it would have to alter its doctrine to accommodate to this reality. Once in power, a BJP government (many have argued) would have to tone down its rhetoric and settle down to choices constrained by poverty and pluralism. What this means is that the BJP would have to abandon its vision and adopt some version of interlocking balances and relational control. On the whole however, the prospects for balancing the historic state against the modern state do not look promising under a BJP government. This is because the BJP is likely to be intolerant of the competing narratives of nationalities—Sikh, Kashmir, or Tamil and several others—that want to tell a separate story of their origins and evolution. Because of their objectives and ideology, the Hindu nationalists are ill-prepared to effect a balance between India's "Hinduized" supranational State and its nesting nationalities. The prospect under a Congress government appears equally dismal, at least so long as its political decline continues unchanged.

The Janata and National Front governments lasted only a short time. One could then claim that their potential for operationalizing the premise of "unity through decentralization" was never fully realized. The difficulties in implementation of this vision were evident in the collapse of the National Front coalition government in 1990. It could not secure a legislative base to anchor the new balance the NF had promised between the supranational State and its overlapping or troubled nationalities. Punjab festered and Kashmir went out of control. National Front government's helplessness in the face of the increasing flow of arms, money, and men from across Pakistan into Kashmir and Punjab showed that Pakistan could not be deflected from its purpose in Kashmir by promise of good relations. Promises of autonomy and arrival of a more tolerant government at the center did not convince the JKLF to lay down arms and negotiate with New Delhi. The IPKF withdrawal from Sri Lanka did not prevent Sri Lankan militants from illegally using Tamil Nadu as a sanctuary. The National Front did not have a fallback position in the event Sri Lanka again sought support from governments unfriendly to India. The "decentralization" inherent in the coalition nature of the National Front had made the government more vulnerable to ethnic separatism. The Front's dependence on the Karunanidhi government to control the Eelam groups had ended in disaster. The Tamil Nadu government could not control the Lankan groups or the security problem they had created for India.

The question remains whether a strong and permanent political base for the decentralization model would have improved its prospects for effecting successful interlocking balances. The answer is not clear. It is possible that a future coalition government with a comfortable legislative majority in state assemblies and in the central parliament might succeed. But then it might not look too different from the 1960s versions of the Congress. The Indian polity shows an inherent tendency towards pluralism and must be reconstituted again and again on a continuous basis. This make-over might have a different face each time but the process cannot be eliminated, at least, not without endangering India's security. India needs a strong center in which strength is the ability to defuse domestic conflicts, retain overarching control over the nation, and channel ethnic nationalism into regular processes of democratic politics. By the same token, the supranational State needs strong regional and local leaders who can represent and integrate ethnic demands into the national agenda for unity and modernization. Then only will India gain ability to forestall adverse fallout from overlapping nationality and control transborder conflict.

I have not made recommendations for or against relational control. The argument here is not that the IPKF should have remained in Sri Lanka. Nor is this a plea for a strong state. What is being stressed is that India's security dilemmas arise from the attempt to carve out a territorial nation-state from a heterogeneous historical empire state. The overlapping nationalities are at the nexus of this endeavor insofar as they challenge India's territorial and cultural identity. The dilemma posed by the overlapping nationalities is not easily amenable to solutions based on decentralization, or progressive centralization. This is because the question imposes the tyranny of two choices. There is a third choice based on interlocking balance between a strong center and a strong local seat of power. The former guarantees integration and security while the latter insures that these do not scuttle the autonomy of the nesting nationalities. The whole enterprise creates genuine autonomy for the supranational State and strengthens its hand against transborder conflicts. For India, the balance of interlocking interests and relational control are more than strategies of power; they are the conditions for its unified existence.

India is not alone in the kinds of problems it faces nor are the dangers emanating from overlapping nationalities unique to the South Asian subcontinent. Many countries in the world, notably Russia and its environs, South Africa and its region, and China and its neighboring states, face such dilemmas. In these regions, the political and cultural boundaries do not coincide as they do not in South Asia. The legitimate sovereign space of a state is then ambiguous. Do these countries have the right to protect themselves from the spillover effect of ethnic conflict in a neighboring country? How do we separate domestic from international security? Does the presence of ethnic overlap change the definition of legitimate intervention?

India had argued, in 1971 and in 1987, that it had no alternative but to intervene. There were circumstances preceding these interventions however that raised questions about Indian claims. There was also the fact that India was superior in size, economy, and military capability. Each intervention was preceded by clandestine support to ethnic dissidents that demanded a separate state. Although the Indian support was not the cause of the conflict, it had influenced the course of events in each instance. By the same token, in neither intervention were Indian policy makers tempted by territorial gain. India withdrew from each place when the crisis had passed, or, as in case of Sri Lanka, it was asked to leave.

While the Indian government subscribes to the conventional sanctity of sovereign space, its security interests extend beyond this space. Can countries like India, Russia, South Africa, or China live within their present boundaries? The answer to that question will always remain ambiguous as long as there are restless overlapping nationalities and transborder conflict. The concept of sovereignty has to accommodate these alternative interpretations of what is, and is not, legitimate defense. According to established international norms, military intervention is justified only in the instances of genocide or in self-defense. Both reasons were used by the Indian government in justifying its military intervention in Bangladesh and Sri Lanka. In case of Sri Lanka in 1987, intervention was by invitation. We need to ask whether this just-cause doctrine of intervention can answer the dilemma created by overlapping nationalities.

These questions have acquired added significance in the 1990s because of the collapse of the Soviet Union, the end of the Cold War, and the strengthening of demands worldwide for self-determination, democracy, and human rights have eroded the sanctity of national sovereignty. Today's territorial states confront challenges to their right to define "national" identity and to govern the regions that nesting ethnic nations claim as their homelands. These conflicts are partly caused by the spread of democratic ideas and demand for self-determination among previously nesting nationalities. The nation-state is a much weakened entity today than before. There is a supreme irony here: countries like India that are late modernizers have to struggle to become integrated nation-states, but precisely when their efforts might be bearing fruit, the world has changed course and made such a quest relatively unimportant.

Today trade and human rights transcend national borders. And the world seems less concerned with upholding the sanctity of sovereign rights. It is not clear how these contrary trends will get reconciled, but one thing is clear: they demand a redefinition of security and legitimate scope of ethnic self-determination. This book is an exploration of the operational logic of their interconnections, an exploration suggesting that stability and security of large and heterogeneous nation-states such as India is a matter of moving equilibrium between domestic autonomy and regional overlap, internal democracy and relational control.

Appendix

🌿

INTERVIEWS AND CONVERSATIONS

In Tamil Nadu, July-August 1986/1987:

A. Amrithalingam, The late President of TULF, favored in negotiations by Indira Gandhi. Later assassinated by the LTTE in Madras.

Yogeswaran, member of Parliament, Sri Lanka, later assassinated by Tamil militants.

Keethswaran and **Padmanabhan**, General Secretary and President of the EPRLF, Padmanabhan was later assassinated in Jaffna by the LTTE.

Balakumar, General Secretary of EROS.

A. Selvan, leader of the PLOTE.

Indian Tamil Leaders:

K. Karunanidhi, leader of the DMK.

Janardanan, prominent member of the AIADMK and resident expert on Tamil history in the party.

Nadamaran, leader of Tamil Nadu Kamaraj Congress.

Journalists Consulted on Sri Lanka–Tamil Nadu–New Delhi Connection, Summer 1988:

N. Ravi, editor (*Hindu*).

G. K. Reddy, resident editor in New Delhi (*Hindu*).

Sam Rajappa, chief reporter on Sri Lanka (*Statesman*).

Venkataramani, chief reporter on Tamil and Sri Lankan affairs (*India Today*).

Narayanan, editor, *Frontline* magazine

In Punjab:

Several **militant students** (who requested anonymity) at the Khalsa College, Amritsar. It was not clear if they were still students but they could be contacted at the Khalsa College through the underground network facilitated by **Gursharan Singh**, a Marxist publicist and playwright involved with street theater in Punjab.

Several **SGPC officers** at the Golden Temple, Amritsar, Winter 1986. Several **officials and leaders** of the various Hindu militant organizations such as the Shiv Sena, Bajrang Brigade, Rashtriya Suraksha Samiti based at the Durgyana Mandir, Amritsar, to protect the Hindu refugees from villages in Punjab. Amritsar, Winter 1986.

Journalists Consulted on Punjab/Kashmir:

Kuldip Nayar, author and commentator on Punjab politics, later Indian High Commissioner to the U.K.

P. S. Jha, syndicated columnist (*Hindu*).

Girilal Jain, editor, *Times of India*.

Bhabani Sengupta, scholar, journalist on South Asian politics.

Officials and Political Leaders:

Rajiv Gandhi, New Delhi, December 1989.

Inder Gujral, Foreign Minister, National Front government. New Delhi, several conversations during summers and winters of 1989, 1990, 1991.

Dinesh Singh, Rajiv Gandhi's personal emissary to Sri Lanka before 1987, an subsequently foreign minister in the Rao cabinet. New Delhi, December 1988; New York, summer 1994.

Julius Jayewardene, President of Sri Lanka. Colombo, June 1988.

Premadasa, Prime Minister. Colombo, June 1988.

Farooq Abdullah, former Chief Minister of J&K. New York, Fall 1994.

Prakash Singh Badal, prominent Akali Dal leader. Chandigarh, July 1986.

P. L. Vaishnav, then Chief Secretary of Punjab. Chandigarh, July 1986.

Julian Robiero, IG of Police in Punjab, permitted me to look through files of apprehended militants caught while crossing over from Pakistan. Chandigarh, December 1986.

S. S. Ray, then Governor of Punjab. New Delhi, December 1986.

J. N. Dixit, Ministry of External Affairs. New Delhi, December 1988

Jasjit Singh, Director, Indian Institute of Strategic and Defense Studies. New Delhi, January 1992.

S. K. Singh, Indian envoy to Pakistan and later Foreign Secretary. New Delhi, December 1992.

Muchkund Dubey, Foreign Secretary, National Front government. New Delhi, December 1992.

Notes

✦

1. Neither Hegemonic Nor Defensive: A Third Perspective on India's Security

1. Ashok Kapur, "The Indian Subcontinent: The Contemporary Structure of Power and the development of Power Relations," *Asian Survey* 28 (July 1988): 693–711. Also see his "Indian Security and Defense Policies Under Indira Gandhi," *Journal of Asian and African Studies* 22 (July and October 1987): 175–93.

2. Leo Rose asserts that the "basic principle underlying India's regional policy since 1947 has been its undeclared claim to hegemony in South Asia," in J. N. Rosenau et al., eds., *World Politics* (New York: Free Press, 1976), p. 214. Steve Cohen also supports the argument that India seeks dominance in the region. Stephen Cohen, *India: Emergent Power?* (New York: Crane, Russack, 1978). Surjit Mansingh takes a different view in her *India's Search for Power: Indira Gandhi's Foreign Policy, 1966–1982* (New Delhi: Sage, 1984). For recent writings on India's hegemonic ambitions, see Ross Munro, "Superpower Rising," *Time*, April 3, 1989, pp. 6–13; Brahma Chellany, "Passage to Power," *World Monitor* 3 (February 1990): 22–32.

3. Among early works on domestic and international policy connections, see Shashi Tharoor, *Reasons of the State: Political Development and India's Foreign Policy Under Indira Gandhi, 1966–1977* (New Delhi: Vikas, 1984); Nancy Jetly, *India–China Relations: The Study of Parliaments Role in the Making of Foreign Policy* (Atlantic Highlands, N.J: Humanities Press, 1979); J. Bandyopadhyaya, *The Making of India's Foreign Policy*, 2d ed. (New Delhi: Allied, 1980). Other standard works on foreign policy with the balance of power approach are A. G. Noorani, *India, The Superpowers and the Neighbors: Essays in Foreign Policy* (New Delhi: South Asian, 1985); Lalita Prasad Singh, *India's Foreign Policy: The Shastri Period* (New Delhi: Uppal, 1980); *India's Northern Security: Including China, Nepal, and Bhutan* (New Delhi: Reliance, 1986); *Janata's Foreign Policy* (New Delhi: Vikas, 1979).

4. Throughout this book, I have drawn on Nettl's definition of the state and its concept of variable "stateness." According to him, in the Hobbesian perspective, the State, is a "basic, irreducible unit, equivalent to the individual person in society." Although the concept of the state has been replaced by that of the nation-state, it has not changed the way in which "state" is used in current literature. "State as a Conceptual Variable," *World Politics* 20 (July 1968): 563.

5. According to Nettl, in the new states, the need to use foreign policy for the purposes of internal consolidation is even greater than that in earlier nation states of Europe. Ibid., p. 563.

6. There is extensive literature advocating caution in referring to third world countries as nation-states. Scholars have insisted on separating the state from the concept of the nation. Loyalty to the state is regarded as patriotism while allegiance to the nation is described as nationalism. Several authors talk about religious and territorial nationalism in connection with third world countries. Many of these countries are multiethnic, multilingual, multireligious societies in which territorial control is fiercely contested. For discussion of these issues see Connor Walker, *Ethnonationalism: The Quest for Understanding* (Princeton: Princeton University Press, 1994); Benedict Anderson, *Imagined Communities: Reflections on the Origins and Spread of Nationalism* (London: Verso, 1983); Ernest Gellner, *Nations and Nationalism* (Oxford: Blackwell, 1983); Nash Manning, *The Cauldron of Ethnicity in the Modern World* (Chicago: University of Chicago Press, 1989); James Mayall and Mark Simpson, "Ethnicity Is Not Enough: Reflections on Protracted Secessionism in the Third World," in Anthony Smith, ed., *Ethnicity and Nationalism* (Leiden, N.Y.: E. J. Brill, 1992), pp. 5–26. For discussion of conflict and collapse caused by imposition of the European models of political development on third world societies, particularly in their foreign policy see Steven David, "Explaining Third World Alignment," *World Politics* 43 (January 1991): 233–57. Mohammed Ayoob, "The Security Problematic of the Third World," *World Politics* 43 (January 1991): 257–84. Carolina Thomas, *In Search of Security: The Third World in International Relations* (Boulder, Colo.: Lynne Rienner, 1987); Edward Azar and Chung-in Moon, eds. *National Security in the Third World: The Management of Internal and External Threats* (College Park, Md.: Center for International Development and Conflict Management, University of Maryland, 1988).

7. For incorporation of the Indian economy into world capitalism see Sugata Bose, ed., *South Asia and World Capitalism* (New Delhi: Oxford University Press, 1991); Immanuel Wallerstein, "Incorporation of the Indian Subcontinent into the Capitalist World Economy," *Economic and Political Weekly* 21 (January 25, 1986): 28–39.

8. There is extensive literature on India's divisions based on religion and ethnicity. See Asghar Ali Engineer, *Communalism and Communal Violence in India: An Analytical Approach to Hindu–Muslim Conflict* (Delhi: Ajanta, 1989); Asghar Ali Engineer and Shakir Moin, eds., *Communalism in India* (Delhi: Ajanta, 1985); Sarbjit Johal, *Conflict and Integration in Indo–Pakistani Relations* (Berkeley: University of California Press, 1988); Imtiaz Ahmed, *India's Policy Fundamentals, Neighbors, and Post-Indira Development* (Dhaka: Bangladesh Institute of International and Strategic Studies, 1985); S. K. Dass, "Immigration and Democratic Transformation of Assam, 1891–1981," *Economic and Political Weekly* 15 (1980): 850–59; Maniruzzaman Talukadar, "West Bengal and the Bangladesh Liberation Struggle," *Indian Political Science Review* 14 (January 1980): 55–64.

9. This is one of the most fiercely debated questions among India's historians. Several studies have challenged the extent of political centralization under the Mughals and British claimed by earlier historians. For instance, the imperial unification thesis has been challenged by Burton Stein, *Peasant State and Society in South Asia* (1980); Nicholas Dirks, *The Hollow*

Crown: Ethnohistory of an Indian Kingdom (1993); Andre Wink, *Al Hind: The Making of the Indo–Islamic World* (1990); and Frank Perlin, "State Formation Reconsidered," *Modern Asian Studies*, 818, no. 3 (1985): 415–80. Burton Stein talks about the segmentary nature of the Indian state based on his work on south Indian kingdoms. André Wink and Frank Perlin have gone further and charged that the unity and centralization claimed by Mughal historians was illusory. Wink emphasizes the notion of "fitna," which he says governed relations between state and society, while Perlin talks about "watan" (civil society) as the dominant agency. These historians emphasize the prior existence and relative independence of civil society from the central state. Parallel work on the British and nationalist period has led subaltern theory historians to conclude that the nationalist version of unified India did not exist except in their imagination and that such nationalist claims reflected political bias because of slavish acceptance of Western modes of thinking. Inspired by the subaltern logic, Gyan Prakash writes in his "Writing Post-Orientalist Histories of the Third World: Indian Historiography Is Good to Think," in Nicholas Dirks, ed., *Colonialism and Culture* (Ann Arbor: University of Michigan Press, 1992), p. 359, that orientalist historians (which included scholars from Max Muller to nationalist historians such as Bipin Chandra, Beni Prasad, R. C. Majumdar) studied the ancient Indian empires and saw the modern nation state as the creation of these empires. Gyan Prakash points out that in *The Discovery of India*, Nehru reflects this thinking. Nehru's strategy was to document India's unity through her history. There can be no doubt that the "concept of India as essentially Sanskritic and Hindu—glorious in ancient times and then subjected to Muslim tyranny and degenerated in the Middle Ages that made it an easy target for British conquest—had, and continues to have, deadly implications in a multiethnic country such as India" (Prakash, "Writing Post-Orientalist Histories, p. 360). Similarly, Partha Chatterjee argues that in endowing autonomy and sovereignty to such a historical state, the nationalists were reaffirming the project of modernity.

However, sifting through these debates, I am led to believe that each, the centralization and decentralization (or regionalization) of power, reflected the authentic rhythm of Indian history. India's political history seems to represent a continuing, and often times shifting, balance between consolidation and disintegration. However, each integrative period left behind a legacy of new syncretic traditions. This is one reasonably well-supported proposition on which I have constructed the thesis of interlocking balance of interests between nations and the central state. This balance requires Indian leaders to accommodate domestic pulls and external pressures.

I owe a deep intellectual debt to Ronald Inden, particularly to the insights provided by his cameo study of the medieval Deccan state, the Rashtrakutas. See Ronald Inden, *Imagining India* (Oxford: Basil Blackwell, 1990). Here, he shows that excessive focus on centralization and decentralization misses an important historical fact: that Indian polity was made and remade by the interplay between kingship and caste groups as subject / citizenry. The kingship was often contested and operated on a sliding scale; it was not an absolute attribute. It would do Indian history considerable harm if it is constructed as a relentless march toward founding of centralized empires. Even when the state was centralized, it permitted considerable autonomy to local and regional forces, no matter how they might have been organized (whether as segments, regions, castes, or along modern formations of ethnicity and religion).

The opposite was also true. One must not overly stress the separation and distinctiveness of these groups. What is important for this study is the interplay, the continuing process of negotiation and contest. For a critique of the subaltern thesis see Jim Masselos, "The Disappearance of Subalterns: A Reading of a Decade of Subaltern Studies," *South Asia* 15 (1992): 105–25; Athar Ali, "The Mughal Polity: A Critique of Revisionist Approaches," *Modern Asian Studies* 27 (1993): 699–710. Among the subaltern theorists, see Partha Chatterjee, *The Nation and Its Fragments, Colonial and Post-Colonial Discourses* (Princeton: Princeton University Press, 1993).

10. It needs to be pointed out that there are other overlapping nationalities, i.e., in the northeast and Assam, as well as on the Nepal–India border, that have involved India with neighboring states, but these are not the subject of discussion here. Since Partition, there are no Sikhs in Pakistan. In this sense it is not an overlapping nationality. Punjab is however close to, and on the border of, India and Pakistan. It is well to remember that Sikhs constitute only 2 percent of the overall population of India; the Kashmir and Tamil nationalities are also not critical in numbers. But their location and the strength of their separatist sentiments make them potentially dangerous to India's unity and political integrity. In Kashmir, India has a special problem. Since it is the only Muslim majority province in India, Kashmir has become a test case of India's modernist and secular claim.

11. A schedule of interviews is included in the appendix.

12. U. S. Bajpai, ed., *India and Its Neighbourhood* (New Delhi: Lancers, 1986); A. P. Rana, *Imperatives of Nonalignment: A Conceptual Study of India's foreign Policy Strategy in the Nehru Period* (New Delhi: Macmillan, 1976); A. Appadorai and M. S. Rajan, *India's Foreign Policy and Relations* (New Delhi: South Asia, 1985); Ravi Rikhye, *The Militarization of Mother India* (Delhi: Chanakya, 1990); Jasjit Singh, *Maritime Security* (New Delhi: Institute for Defense Studies and Analyses, 1993).

13. Geraint Parry, "The Interweaving of Foreign and Domestic Policy-Making," *Government and Opposition* 28 (Spring 1993): 143–52; Imtiaz Ahmed, *India's Policy Fundamentals, Neighbors, and Post-Indira Development* (Dhaka: Bangladesh Institute of International and Strategic Studies, 1985); S. K. Dass, "Immigration and Democratic Transformation of Assam, 1891–1981," *Economic and Political Weekly* 15 (1980): 850–59; Chitra Tiwari, *Security in South Asia: Internal and External Dimensions* (Lanham, N.Y.: University Press of America, 1989).

14. Imtiaz Ahmed, *State and Foreign Policy: India, Role in South Asia* (New Delhi: Vikas, 1993) represents the neo-Marxist perspective on this question. The pluralist perspective is articulated in Bharat Wariawalla, "Personality, Domestic Political Institutions, and Foreign Policy," in Ram Joshi and R. K. Hebsur, eds. *Congress in Indian Politics: A Centenary Perspective* (Riverdale, Md.: Riverdale, 1988), pp. 245–70; "India in 1988," *Asian Survey* 29 (February 1989): 189–98; and "Price of Primacy," *Seminar* 358 (June 1989): 37–40. Also see Bhabani Sen Gupta, "India Doctrine," *India Today* (September 15, 1983). Conversations with Indian journalists and academics revealed a parallel controversy about India's role in South Asia. According to one view (held by Inder Malhotra and the late Girilal Jain, both highly influential journalists affiliated with the *Times of India* in the 1970s and 1980s) and S. D. Muni and Satish Kumar (both at the Jawaharlal Nehru University in New Delhi), India is a status quo power that simply wants to defend itself from encroachment. Others, notably at the Center for Policy Studies in New Delhi (Pran Chopra, Bhabani Sen Gupta, Nirmal Mukherjee) and at the Center for the Study of Developing Societies (notably, Rajni Kothari, Giri Deshingkar) see India's Congress leaders as arrogant and overly impressed with the importance of military strength. My discussions and interviews with these individuals were held on different occasions in the summer and winter of years between 1987 to 1992.

15. Bharat Wariawalla, "Personality, Domestic Political Institutions, and Foreign Policy," p. 260.

16. Imtiaz Ahmed, *State and Foreign Policy: India, Role in South Asia*, p. 234. Kautilya wrote the Arthasastra, an ancient text on power and rule at some time in the latter part of the fourth century. Metaphorically, Kautilya stands for the real politic or Machiavellian view in the Indian classical tradition of politics. The Arthasastra spelled out the principles for the conduct of external relations in which friendly and hostile states are organized in a concentric circle (known as Mandala) around the paramount king. A succinct study of Kautilya's "statecraft" can be found in George Modelski, "Kautilya: Foreign Policy and International System in the Third World," *American Political Science Review* 58 (September 1964): 549–60. Raju Thomas, *Indian Security Policy* (Princeton: Princeton University Press, 1986), p. 16, rejects the Mandala thesis as applied to India's external environment and points out that in the Mandala model, Sri Lanka, Burma, China, and Bangladesh would be India's enemies while Iran and Afghanistan would be friends. This has obviously not been the case.

17. Several scholars argue that centralization has led to a decline in the capabilities of the Indian state. See Atul Kohli, *Democracy and Discontent, India's Growing Crisis of Governability* (Princeton: Princeton University Press, 1990); Rajni Kothari, *State Against Democracy: The Search for Humane Governance* (New York: New Horizon Press); Robert Hardgrave Jr., *India Under Pressure* (Boulder, Colo.: Westview Press, 1984). There is no consensus on the autonomy enjoyed by India's federal units (i.e., Gujarat). Bhagwan Dua insists that the frequent use of Presidential Rule has reduced this autonomy to a farce. K. R. Bombwall rejects Dua's interpretation and argues that centralization is a temporary phenomenon, a mere legacy from the past. Brass argues regionalism and decentralization are the fundamental tendencies in the Indian polity. See Bhagwan Dua, "Presidential Rule In India: A Study in Crisis Politics," *Asian Survey,* 19 (June 1979): 626; K. R. Bombwall, *National Power and State Autonomy* (Meerat: Meenakshi Prakashan, 1978), p. 211.

18. See introductory remarks by Lloyd and Susanne Rudolph, *In Pursuit of Lakshmi: The Political Economy of the Indian State* (Chicago, London: University of Chicago Press, 1986); C. P. Bhambhri, *Politics in India, 1992–1993* (New Delhi: Shipra, 1993); Joel S. Migdal, *Strong Societies and Weak States: State Capabilities in the Third World* (Princeton: Princeton University Press, 1988).

19. Barry Buzan and Gowhar Rizvi, eds., *South Asian Security and The Great Powers* (London: Macmillan, 1986) analyze India's regional role on the premise that India is weak/strong, that is internally weak and militarily strong state. However they subsequently come to the surprising conclusion that internal changes in India have not altered the basic pattern of Indo–Pakistani relations. This is certainly not true in the short run. And even in the long run, domestic preoccupations have profoundly impacted on their relations. For counter arguments see Maya Chadda, "Why Detente Won't Happen," *Asian Survey* 26 (October 1986): 1118–36; and "Domestic Determinants of India's Foreign Policy in the 1980s," *Journal of South Asian and Middle Eastern Studies* 11 (Fall/Winter 1987): 21–36.

20. Mohammed Ayoob, "The Security Problematic of the Third World," *World Politics* 43 (January 1991): 270.

21. Even the Dalit (backward class and caste) women and minorities repeatedly voted for the Congress party and Indira Gandhi in particular. It is therefore difficult to find a clear line of conflict dividing the interests of the subalterns from those of political elites in Indian society. "Class" is a particularly problematic concept when applied to India, which is divided along several distinctive cultural identities. However, Imtiaz Ahmed argues otherwise, in his *State and Foreign Policy*, pp. 206–7.

22. Ibid., p. 205.

23. Tom Baumgartner, W. Buckley, and T. Burns, "Meta Power and Relational Control in Social Life," *Social Science Information* 14 (1975): 49–78.

24. Ibid., p. 49.

25. The flight of ten million refugees from East Pakistan led eventually to the 1971 war between India and Pakistan. The extension of political asylum to Tibetan refugees continues to bedevil India—China relations; the Chakma refugees from Bangladesh have created many tensions between India and Bangladesh; migration of Nepalis in and around Darjeeling has given rise to a militant movement for the creation of a separate Gorkhaland. Nepali migration to Bhutan and Sikkim has similarly embittered relations between Himalayan kingdoms. For a discussion of some of these and other instances of ethnic overlap see K. M. de Silva and R. J. May, eds., *Internationalization of Ethnic Conflict* (New York: St. Martin's Press, 1991); Sajal Basu, *Regional Movements: Politics of Language, Ethnicity-Identity* (New Delhi: Manohar, 1992), pp. 50–56.

26. Non-Marxists argue that in many instances the victims of domination also benefit from the relationship. In his analysis of British and American international policies, Robert Gilpin has shown how certain states under the sway of Pax Britannica achieved faster rates of growth than England did during its supremacy of such countries in the colonial period. On the other hand, the Marxist and neo-Marxist interpretations have focused on the class motives to determine the nature and scope of hegemony. For a lengthy discussion of available literature and their analysis see Robert Keohane, "Hegemonic Leadership and U.S. Foreign Economic Policy in the 'Long Decade' of the 1950s," in William P. Avery and David P. Rapkin, eds., *America in a Changing World Political Economy* (New York: Longman, 1982); Charles Kindleberger, "On the Rise and Decline of Nations" *International Studies Quarterly* 27, no. 1 (March 1983): 5–10; Kenneth Waltz, *Theory of World Politics* (Reading, Mass: Addison-Wesley, 1979). For Marxist interpretations see Immanuel Wallerstein, *Modern World System: Capitalist Agriculture and the Origins of the European World Economy in the Sixteenth Century* (New York: Academic Press, 1974); Fred Block, *The Origins of International Economic Disorder* (Berkeley: University of California Press, 1977).

27. Wallerstein has extended this concept to include hegemonism by international finance capital. When used in this way, the concept ceases to have a territorial connotation. However, this is only one, and a very particular, use of the term. Immanuel Wallerstein, "Incorporation of the Indian Subcontinent into the Capitalist World Economy," in Sugata Bose, ed., *South Asia and World Capitalism* (New Delhi: Oxford University Press, 1991), pp. 28–39.

28. Baumgartner, Buckley, and Burns, *Meta Power and Relational Control*, p. 49.

29. Paul Viotti and Mark Kauppi, *International Relations Theory* (New York: Macmillan, 1993), p. 45, write that "A State's influence or capacity to coerce is not only a function of accumulated capabilities but also a function of its willingness (and perception by others that it is so willing) to use these capabilities; and its control or influence over other states. Power can be inferred by observing the behavior of states as they interact with others. The relative power is best revealed by the outcomes of these interactions." The difference in power as a transaction and power as capability was glaringly visible in Vietnam where the U.S.'s huge preponderance of military strength did not match its unwillingness to use it.

30. For details on the provisions in the treaty see S. S. Bindra, *Indo–Bangladesh Relations* (New Delhi: Deep and Deep, 1982), pp. 19–22.

31. *Asian Recorder* 5, no. 51 (December 19–25, 1959): 3061.

32. Government of India, *Lok Sabha Debates*, 2d series, 35, November 27, 1959, p. 2231.

33. Government of India, *Foreign Policy of India: Text of Documents, 1947–59*, 2d ed. (New Delhi: Lok Sabha Secretariat, 1959), p. 17.

34. For instance, the narratives of Guru Gobind Singh's struggle against the Mughal rulers, forging of the Sikh Panth, and the order of the Khalsa in defense of the community acquired a particular poignancy during and immediately after the Sikh–Muslim riots of 1947. These same narratives were resurrected by Bhindranwale four decades later, in his struggle against New Delhi. This time the enemy was not the Muslims nor was it Pakistan, it was the "oppressive" Hindu India.

35. For instance, both the communities, Kashmiri Hindu and Muslim, claim equal rights to Kashmir.

36. For uses of Tamil history in Sri Lanka see Dagmas-Hellman-Rajanayagam, "Tamils and the Meaning of History," *Journal of South Asia* 3, no. 1 (1994): 3–25.

37. The other reason why Kashmiri disenchantment was transformed into an insurgency against New Delhi in the late 1980's was the growth of a class of educated but unemployed young people who emerged from the universities and technical schools to find that there were no jobs or careers. Their plight received no attention from the state or the central government. There was a similar component in the Punjab violence but Mrs. Gandhi focused on the Akali religious demands and neglected the economic ones throughout the early '80s.

38. The pre-eminent example is the Congress party's durable power sharing agreement with the AIADMK in Tamil Nadu.

39. The agreement to give trade concessions to aid Nepali industrialization and employment generation on a nonreciprocal basis in 1990 is a case in point. Earlier, before 1975, Nepal used to receive key materials like cement, steel, coal, and petroleum products at Indian domestic prices, which were much below the international prices. This arrangement was terminated by the government of Nepal in 1975.

40. Although India's global foreign policy posture is not the subject of this book, relational control also explains the conflicting perceptions of nonalignment within India and abroad. Abroad, it has been perceived as a response to the Cold War; at home, it is seen as the first line of defense that can block foreign interference. Since the end of the Cold War, many have begun to question the continued desirability of nonalignment. Since such threats did not end with the Cold War, and in some ways became even stronger, Indian leaders have argued that the idea still has value.

41. Organization of pro-Kashmir, Pro-Khalistani, and Pro-Eelam lobbies from among the expatriate residents in the United States and Canada is a case in point.

42. Walker Connor, "The Nation and Its Myth," *International Journal of Comparative Sociology* 33 (January 1992): 1–48; Paul Brass, *Ethnicity and Nationalism: Theory and Comparison* (New Delhi, Newbury Park, Calif.: Sage, 1991), *Ethnic Groups and State* (Totowa, N.J: Barnes and Noble Books, 1985); William Pfaff, *The Wrath of Nation: Civilization and Furies of Nationalism* (New York: Simon and Schuster, 1993); Elie Kedourie, *Nationalism in Asia and Africa*, 4th ed. (Oxford: Blackwell, 1993); Eric Hobsbawm, *Nation and Nationalism since 1780: Programme, Myth, Reality* (New York: Cambridge University Press, 1992), p. 112; Crawford Young, *The Politics of Cultural Pluralism* (Madison: University of Wisconsin Press, 1976); Andre Wink, *Islam, Politics, and Society in South Asia* (New Delhi: Manohar, 1991).

43. Paul Brass, *"Ethnic Groups and the State,"* p. 17.

44. Ibid., p. 20.

45. The premodernists point out that scholars such as Gellner have relied too heavily on print capitalism and spread of formal education as the means to forging nationalism (which according to Gellner and Hobsbawm create nations). Instead Michael Roberts, Gananath Obeyesekere, and Anthony Smith argue that it is possible to see national and ethnic consciousness, the we/they dichotomy even in premodern societies if one took account of oral traditional, folk theater, and generally the informal means of communications and their content. See Michael Roberts, "A Review Essay: Nationalism, the Past, and the Present: The Case of Sri Lanka," *Ethnic and Racial Studies* 16 (January 1993): 133–66. For this study, the origins of Sikh, Kashmiri, and Tamil nationalism are not particularly significant. Whatever their origin, they have been an important part of Indian history since the nineteenth century, and have shaped India's role in the region after independence.

46. John Breuilly, *Nationalism and the State*, 2d ed. (Chicago: University of Chicago Press, 1993), p. 1.

47. Generally, ethnic groups are more imaginative in making use of social space and transforming that into an arena of conflict. In contrast, the state relies on the legal, formal framework for a solution, and failing that, on coercion. See Sanjib Baruah's discussion of ethnic conflict in Assam in his "Ethnic Conflict as State-Society Struggle: The Poetics and Politics of Assamese Micro-nationalism," *Modern Asian Studies* 28 (July 1994): 649–71. The democratic and federal character of India requires a separation of culturally defined identities from political identities. Forging a unified nation state depends on absorbing the former and granting autonomy to the latter.

48. There is vast literature on the subject of the Indian state and its characteristics. For details see Pranab Bardhan, *The Political Economy of Development in India* (Delhi: Oxford University Press, 1984); Robert Hardgrave Jr., *India: Government and Politics in a Developing Nation* (New York: Harcourt and Brace, 1970); Zoya Hasan, S. N. Jha, and Rasheeduddin Khan, eds., *The State, Political Process, and Identity: Reflections on Modern India* (New Delhi: Sage, 1989); Rajni Kothari, *Politics in India* (Boston: Little Brown, 1970); *State Against Democracy* (Delhi: Ajanta, 1987); K. Mathew Kurien, ed., *India—State and Society: A Marxist Approach* (Bombay: Orient Longman, 1975); T. K. Ooman, *State and Society in India: Studies in Nation-Building* (New Delhi: Sage, 1991); Ravinder Kumar, "India: A 'Nation-State' or a 'Civilization-State,' " *Occasional Papers on Perspectives in Indian Development*, No. 8, Nehru Memorial Library, 1989; Susanne Rudolph and Lloyd Rudolph, *In Pursuit of Lakshmi*.

49. The early theorists of "state" focused on the question of how the institutions transplanted from the West onto the Indian soil—the liberal democracy, rational planning for economic development, and social engineering to modernize traditions—actually performed. W. H. Morris Jones juxtaposed political institutions of the Indian nation-state against traditional Indian social structures. In his view, India's achievements were impressive. Gunner Myrdal did not agree with him. He saw India as a "soft state" that had failed to fully modernize or ameliorate poverty.

50. J. P. Nettl, "The State as a Conceptual Variable," p. 562.

51. Ibid., p. 568.

52. Ibid., p. 590.

2. Forging Relational Control: Security in the Nehru Years

1. According to Ainslie Embree, debate about India's unity and diversity emerged clearly in the 1880s. He quotes Hobson Jobson: "no modern Englishmen, who had to do with India

ever speaks of a man of that country as an India": see Embree, "Indian Civilization and Regional Cultures: The Two Realities," in Paul Wallace, ed., *Region and Nation In India* (New Delhi: Oxford and IBH, 1985), p. 20. Also see John Strachey, *India* (London: Keagan Paul, 1888), pp. 5–8.

2. J. Pandian, *Caste, Nationalism, and Ethnicity* (Bombay: Popular Prakashan, 1987), p. 21.

3. According to British historian Vincent Smith, India's cultural unity was based on Hinduism. Ainslie Embree rejects this thesis. In his view, it is not Hinduism which has, tended to unite India, but one element of Hinduism, the Brahminical ideology that has unified the Indian civilization. Embree, "Indian Civilization and Regional Cultures," *Region and Nation in India*, p. 22.

4. Recent literature on nationalist history has deconstructed the Nehruvian worldview to demonstrate that in fact there was no such cultural unity, and no shared identity among Indians, and that Nehru's understanding was a self-serving exercise in legitimizing the claims of the dominant classes in Indian society. Second it is pointed out that the notion of an over-arching and impartial state masked the real intent of the nationalists: to justify hegemony of the nationalist bourgeoisie and subjugate the peasantry to this end. The main claim of the deconstructionist school of subaltern studies is that perspectives that are rival to their own— Nehruvian and left-nationalist—seek to legitimate the present Indian state and do not speak for the history of the subjugated subaltern classes of India. According to the Subaltern historians, the nationalist discourse is the discourse of the privileged. See Partha Chatterjee, *The Nation and Its Fragments: Colonial and Post-Colonial Discourses* (Princeton: Princeton University Press, 1958), p. 158. The subaltern viewpoint is not without problems. It is possible to question their categories and conclusions on several points. But for my purposes, the historical accuracy and hidden biases of the Nehruvian perceptions are less important than the fact that they dominated and shaped India's security policies in the first two decades after independence. Nehru's ideas and policies have produced prolific literature. Some of the useful sources are: S. Gopal, *The Mind of Jawaharlal Nehru* (Madras: Sangam Books, 1980); S. Gopal, *Jawaharlal Nehru: A Biography* (London: Cape, 1975–1984); for a view from the left see E. M. S. Namboodiripad, *Nehru, Ideology and Practice* (New Delhi: National Book Center, 1988); for a general critical view see R. C. Pillai, *Jawaharlal Nehru and His Critics, 1923–1947: A Study with Reference to the Ideas of Nehru, Gandhi, Subhash Chandra Bose, M. N. Roy, and Communists* (New Delhi: Gitanjali, 1986); for a positive assessment see M. J. Akbar, *Nehru: The Making of India* (London: Viking, 1988).

5. Jawaharlal Nehru, *The Discovery of India*, Centenary ed. (Delhi: Oxford University Press, 1989), p. 517.

6. Nehru, *Discovery of India*, pp. 251, 259, 276, 283.

7. Nehru discusses the Hindu Buddhist polity of Asoka Maurya and his Dharma policy as examples of such an universal order. He also talks about the pragmatism of the Islamic polity of the Mughals and the enlightened and tolerant approach pursued by the great emperor Akbar. The Mughal kings, as Nehru writes, had created a universal order based on absolute power (after the fashion of Persian and Mongol traditions that they had inherited) and combined this with the Hindu notion of the universal kings (the Chakravartin). Their belief in absolute power allowed them to override demands from the Islamic clergy while the ideal of the Hindu king required them to generally uphold and protect the existing social order. This kind of equidistance appealed to Nehru. Nehru blamed the British for India's subjugation and slavery, for the economic drain and degradation and poverty of its masses, and for setting one community against another in order to ensure their dominance. He does how-

ever credit them with territorial unity of India and for introducing ideas of equality and modernization, technological innovation and science, for building a uniform administration,
modern education, and generally providing impartial machinery for the adjudications of justice. For Nehru, this overarching ideological order symbolized India's civilizational unity.

8. He notes that the Mughal kings gave Rajput and Maratha feudatories considerable lat-
itude in local matters. The British, too, saw the wisdom in layering of political power. British
India consisted of regions that were directly under British administration and rule plus other
regions that were under the nominal sovereignty of princely rulers. The British authorities
represented the paramount power and symbolized the unity of the colonial state of India.
Once the British introduced limited franchise and electoral procedures, they also gave the
Sikhs and Muslims separate electoral representation. This was meant to honor their distinctive ethnic identity. Clearly, Nehru did not agree with upholding the extant social order just
as it was. He opposed caste and religious divisions and rejected authoritarian solutions.
Nehru hoped that traditional differentiation of caste and ethnicity would become less and less
significant as India developed and democracy took root. Indologists such as Drekmeier and
Heesterman have talked at length about the layered order and regional autonomy within the
ancient Indian polity. Charles Drekmeier, *Kingship and Community in Early India* (Berkeley:
University of California Press, 1962); J. C. Heesterman, "Power and Authority in Indian
Tradition," in R. J. Moore, ed., *Tradition and Politics in South Asia* (New Delhi: Vikas, 1979).

9. In a very interesting dissertation on the Hindu Muslim question, Nehru responds to
the charges of anti-Muslim bias in the Congress and talks about the democratic and representative nature of the movement. In contrast he talks about the Muslim League as a feudal
organization with a narrow vision and narrow popular base. He also condemns the Hindu
Mahasabha and Hindu extremists, and rejects politics in terms of a "Hindu" majority. These
were some of the elements of his universal order on which India's unity was to be constructed
and managed. Nehru, *Discovery of India*, pp. 386–87, 382–83.

10. Ibid., p. 61

11. Ibid., p. 62

12. Democracy, secularism, and federalism; modernization and nonalignment, were the
pillars of the modern Indian state. Although these concepts are now almost universally
accepted as the mark of a modern state, it is important to bear in mind that the historical
Indian model on which they were based was different from the model that spawned the modernist state in Europe. This difference has invested them with a different function than that in
Europe. Secularism meant not agnosticism but impartiality; liberal democracy did not establish preeminence of the individual but made room for communitarian rights. And whereas
Western federalism is largely an administrative or historical convenience, Indian federalism
is founded on the notion of ethnic autonomy.

13. *Constituent Assembly of India,* vol 3 (legislative debates), p. 1767.

14. See Harbans Singh, *The Heritage of the Sikhs* (New Delhi: Manohar, 1985), p. 302. In
1943, the Akali Dal had proposed a scheme for Azad Punjab or free Punjab in which the
Muslim majority areas would be detached and given to Pakistan. In the new province so created, the Hindus and Muslims would be evenly matched allowing the Sikhs to maintain a balance between the two. The Congress proposed a counter formula endorsing a commission to
demarcate contiguous districts in the northwest and northeast of India, followed by a
plebiscite. The Congress mixed ethnicity and democracy while the Akali and League leaders
defined their national habitat in religious terms.

15. *The Statesman* (Calcutta), July 7, 1943, reported Nehru's statement.

16. Panderel Moon discussed the events leading to partition and the demands before the Boundary Commission. See his *Divide and Quit* (Berkeley: University California Press, 1962), p. 35, n. 61. Also for an account of events leading to partition and the Akali response see, Hugh Tinker, "Pressure, Persuasion, Decision: Factors in the Partition of the Punjab," *Journal of Asian Studies* 36 (August 1977): 699.

17. It is noteworthy that the League had made overtures to the Akali Dal to keep Punjab united, but these negotiations failed. The Alkalis then urged the Boundary Commission to draw the line of partition that would leave the rich agricultural lands of Layallpur and Montgomery districts and the majority of the Sikh peasantry on the Indian side. In this also they failed. Lord Birdwood writes about his talks with Giani Kartar Singh, who he regarded to be the brain behind the Akali politics at the time. According to Birdwood, Kartar Singh had discussed the possibility of a separate Sikhistan with Jinnah in November 1943. See "India and Sikh Community," *Hindustan Times*, December 26, 1954. See also A. S. Narang, *Storm Over Sutlej* (New Delhi: Gitanjali, 1983), p. 67; Khushwant Singh, *The Sikhs* (London: Allen and Unwin, 1953), p. 259, n. 38.

18. P. D. Devanandan, *The Dravida Kazhagam: A Revolt Against Brahminism* (Bangalore: Christian Institute for the Study of Religion and Society, 1960), pp. 9–10. At the December 1938 Justice party convention, it was resolved that Tamilnad should be made a separate state, loyal to the British Raj and "directly under the Secretary of State for India." In the provincial elections held two years previously, the Congress had defeated the DK. Attempts to introduce Hindi in Madras province only further angered Ramaswamy Naicker and his supporters.

19. For details of the integration of princely states see H. V. Hodson, *The Great Divide: Britain, India, and Pakistan* (London: Hutchinson, 1969); Nicholas Mansergh, ed., *The Transfer of Power, 1942–1947* (London: Her Majesty's Stationary Office, 1970–83), 12 vols. provides the British official records bearing on partition and integration; V. P. Menon, *The Story of Integration of Indian States* (New York: Macmillan, 1956) provides an authoritative account of the events from the Indian nationalist perspective.

20. Menon, *Integration of the Indian States*, p. 126.

21. For the nationalist account of the events in Hyderabad and its final incorporation in the union, see ibid., pp. 314–90.

22. Menon describes how the prodding by the Razakars made the Nizam increasingly intransigent. The nizam's advisers told him that due to the troubles in Kashmir and other places, India was very weak and that the nizam could depend on the friendly Muslim countries, meaning Pakistan. Hyderabad radio announced that thousands of Pathans would march on India if she were to use force on the nizam. Menon, *Integration of Indian States,* p. 348.

23. In his first presidential address to the Muslim Conference Abdullah said, "The object of the Muslim Conference was to . . . secure responsible government." Mohibul Hassan, "Islam in Kashmiri Past and Present Perspective," in A. A. Saroor, ed., *Islam in Modern World: Problems and Prospects* (Srinagar: Iqbal Institute, Kashmir University), p. 190. The Muslim Conference was riven by struggle for power between the Mir Waiz Mohammad Yousuf Shah and Sheikh Abdullah. Each accused the other of distorting or incorrectly interpreting Quran and Islam. This rivalry drove the sheikh to quit the Muslim Conference and establish the National Conference in 1938. For an account of the reform oriented ideology of the Kashmiri nationalism, see U. K. Zutshi, *Emergence of Political Awakening in Kashmir* (New Delhi: Manohar, 1986).

24. Addressing the annual meeting of the Muslim Conference on June 17, 1944, Jinnah said that "99 percent of Muslims who met me were of the opinion that the Muslim Conference alone was the representative . . . of State Muslims." This angered the sheikh. The Muslim Conference also adopted an ambivalent stance toward the "Quit Kashmir" agitation launched in 1946. Jinnah and the Muslim League felt that the agitation was a threat to their political future. In the manipulations that preceded the partition, the League, the Muslim Conference, and Maharajah Hari Singh of Kashmir found themselves momentarily united in their aversion to the sheikh and his socialist, secularist, and pro-Congress advocacy. Jinnah's speech is reported in *Dawn* (Karachi), July 3, 1946.

25. The British role in Kashmir's accession is fiercely debated by students of South Asian politics, especially since the violent insurgency launched by various Kashmiri fronts in 1989. Recent publications by Alastair Lamb contend that Mountbatten had conspired with the Congress leaders, notably Nehru, to bring about Kashmir's accession to India. He builds his case on the basis of the India files in the official archives in London. The main reason why the British wanted Kashmir to accede to India were strategic ones in Lamb's view. India was larger and decidedly stronger of the two new countries in the region and was therefore better situated to watch developments in the Soviet Union, which Lamb suggests was the reasons behind British manipulation.

This argument is rejected by Prem Shankar Jha, based on close scrutiny of almost every piece of evidence used by Lamb, India files in London, and interviews with surviving officials and political administrators involved in the events of 1945–1948. Jha comes to exactly the opposite conclusion: that the British government in London and the foreign office were anxious for Kashmir to go to Pakistan. In a closely reasoned and undeniably persuasive study of actions and responses by Nehru and Patel, Mountbatten and the British officials in London, the Muslim League, and three principal contenders for power within Kashmir—Sheikh Abdullah, Maharajah Hari Singh, and leaders of the Muslim Conference, Jha successfully shows the weaknesses of Lamb's arguments.

Three additional issues complicate the succession debate: whether India intervened before the maharajah had signed the instruments of accession; whether this decision was in contravention of the popular sentiment; and whether the revolt against the maharajah was spontaneous or incited by Pakistan. See Prem Shankar Jha, *Kashmir 1947; Rival Versions* (New Delhi: Oxford University Press, 1995); Alastair Lamb, *Kashmir; A Disputed Legacy: 1846–1990* (Hertingfordsbury, Eng.: Roxford Books, 1991), pp. 101–48; also Alastair Lamb, *Birth of a Tragedy: Kashmir 1947* (Hertingfordsbury,Eng.: Roxford Books, 1994). The Muslim League launched an agitation for partition called Direct Action plan in August 1946. Communal violence soon spread to Punjab. The Unionist government, led by Shaukat Hyat Khan, collapsed, ending prospects for any accommodation between the Muslims, Sikhs, and Hindus in Punjab.

27. Nehru stated in February 1959 that he and others had never expected the terror and killings that took place after partition. "It was in a sense to avoid that we decided to partition. So we paid a double price . . . first, politically and ideologically; second, the actual thing happened that we tried to avoid. Quoted in Norman Palmer, *The Indian Political System* (Boston: Houghton Mifflin, 1961), p. 86.

28. See Ayesha Jalal's excellent study of the making of Pakistan, *The State of Martial Rule: Pakistan's Political Economy of Defence.*(Cambridge, Eng.: Cambridge University Press. 1990).

29. Quoted in Jaswant Singh, "A Backgrounder," in *Seminar* 301: 16–18.

30. The Constituent Assembly of India made a few symbolic concessions to Hindu sentiment such as banning cow slaughter but as Nehru wrote in the *Hindu*, September 13, 1950, p. 9, "The Government of a country like India, with many religions that have secured great and devoted followings for generations, can never function satisfactorily in the modern age except on a secular basis."

31. See Gopal, *Jawaharlal Nehru*, vol 2 (Cambridge: Harvard University Press, 1967), pp. 149–55.

32. On April 18, addressing the annual session of the All India States People's Conference, Nehru declared that any state that did not come into the Constituent Assembly would be treated as a hostile state. This speech provoked an immediate reaction from Liaquat Ali Khan, the leader of the Muslim League party in the Central legislature and the cabinet of the interim government, that the Congress had no right to coerce the states. They were free to choose according to the Cabinet Mission plan and that Pakistan recognized the right of rulers to make a choice to remain independent. The Muslim League had the Junagadh and Hyderabad princely states in mind and wanted to encourage their accession to Pakistan. But to forestall their incorporation in India, the League decided to take a narrowly legalistic position on this issue. See Menon, *Integration of the Indian States*, p. 78.

33. Nehru, *The Discovery of India*, p. 594.

34. Ibid.

35. Ibid., p. 309

36. The final shape was given to British India by Lord Dalhousie's Doctrine of Lapse—a device he used to legitimize wholesale annexation of princely states—in which the ruler did not have a natural born son and heir.

37. For the 1950s policy on ethnic demands see Joseph Schwartzberg, "Factors in the Linguistic Reorganization of Indian States," in Wallace, ed. *Region and Nation in India*, pp. 161–78.

38. Nehru thought the idea of a Punjabi Suba was "inviting disaster . . . for consequences similar to the earlier partition would follow . . . there is no doubt that it has grown up (the demand for Suba) not as a linguistic issue but as a communal issue." Quoted from Lok Sabha Debates by B. R. Nayar, *Minority Politics in Punjab* (Princeton: Princeton University Press, 1966), p. 52, n. 18,

39. As a chief minister, Partap Singh Kairon was more acceptable to the Akali Dal and the Sikh community than Bhimsen Sacchar, a Punjabi Hindu. Kairon was a Sikh and had been part of the Akali Dal before joining the Congress. On the language and Suba question Kairon adopted a middle position between the Hindu organization in Punjab and the Akali Dal. He recruited Sikhs, mostly former Akali Dal leaders to his cabinet and government, initiated a large number of agricultural projects that won him support of the Jat peasantry and isolated the Tara Singh faction in the Akali Dal which had since 1943 agitated (though sporadically) for a separate Sikhistan. With its support rapidly waning in face of Kairon's popularity, the Akali Dal muted its strident calls and eventually accepted the "regional formula" offered by the States Reorganization Commission. In 1956 Kairon brought about a merger between the Congress and the Akali Dal in Punjab. For discussion of Punjab politics in this period see B. R..Nayar, "Punjab," in Myron Weiner, ed., *State Politics in India* (Princeton: Princeton University Press, 1968). It is noteworthy that Nehru tolerated the scandals and corruption, rumors of bribery attached to Kairon and his political maneuvering. He overlooked these as long as Kairon was able to check the recalcitrant and disaffected elements in the Sikh community. See Joyce

Pettigrew, "A Description of the Discrepancy Between Sikh Political Ideals and Sikh Political Practice," in Myron Arnoff, ed., *Ideology and Interest: The Dialectics of Politics*, Political Anthropology Series, vol. 1 (New Brunswick, N.J.: Transaction Books, 1980), pp. 151–92.

40. As Kairon ethnicized the Congress in Punjab, Kamaraj Tamilized the Congress and the state administration in Tamil Nadu. He avoided appointing Brahmins to his cabinet. He also exploited the rivalry between Naicker and Annadurai, the two DK leaders, and persuaded the former to join the Congress. Naicker offered only a wavering support but his ambivalence helped to dampen the demand for a separate Dravidadesam. *Hindu* (Madras), February 2, 1956 and January 27, 1957 and V. P. Raman, "Politics in Madras," *Quest* 3, December 1957 and January 1958 discuss the struggle for ascendancy between the Kamaraj Congress and the DK and the DMK.

41. Imtiaz Ahmed, *State and Foreign Policy: India, Role in South Asia* (New Delhi: Vikas, 1993), pp. 176–82; Lamb, *A Disputed Legacy*, pp. 5–6, has argued that in Kashmir the Indian leaders had accepted the notion that the ruler could choose between India and Pakistan, but in Hyderabad where the ruler was Muslim they insisted on referring to the people.

42. Hodson, *The Great Divide: Britain, India and Pakistan*; Menon, *Integration of Indian States*, pp. 370–72, describes the deteriorating situation in Hyderabad. He talks about the Communist-Razakar alliance and gunrunning by Sydney Cotton, an Australian mercenary. The progressive militarization of the situation in Hyderabad, the Razakar insurgency led by Kasim Rizvi, a fanatic Muslim who appeared to have gained influence with the nizam, and the peasant agitation launched by the Communist party of India created a grave threat to the Indian security. He details the spillover of this violence to Madras and other neighboring states and points out that the Razakars were supplying the Communists with arms and weapons. Ahmed has ignored the significance of this alliance between these two ideological opposite elements. He has also not fully grasped the importance of the fact that India's emergent supranational State sought to prevent both Communists and Razakars from establishing a territorial base.

43. The nizam and his advisers were in constant touch with the Muslim League leaders and Jinnah. Pakistan offered to present the nizam's case to the United Nations; the nizam consulted Jinnah at various points in negotiations with New Delhi. Menon, *Integration of Indian States*, pp. 328–69.

44. Prem Shankar Jha, *Kashmir 1947: Rival Versions of History* (New Delhi: Oxford University Press, 1996). Here his arguments and conclusions are cited from the draft of the manuscript.

45. Lt. Gen. L. P. Sen, DSO, *Slender Was the Thread: Kashmir Confrontation 1947–48* (Bombay: Orient Longman, 1969), p. 297. General Sen was leading Indian forces across the Uri River and was ordered to turn back and rearrange his troops to a holding operation mode. His account details the enormous odds facing the Indian armed forces and also the fact that they could have marched on and prevented partition of Kashmir. Orders from New Delhi had halted all further moves.

46. See R. S. Singh and Champa Singh, *Indian Communism: Its Role Towards Indian Polity*, (New Delhi: Mittal, 1991), p. 67.

47. A. Appadorai and M. S. Rajan, *India's Foreign Policy and Relations* (New Delhi: South Asian, 1985), p. 37.

48. Ibid., p. 63

49. Nehru said at the Asian Relations Conference on March 22, 1947, that India had been used as a pawn in the great power game; now that it was independent, it would stand on its

own and guard its freedom to make decisions according to its interests. Appadorai and Rajan, *India's Foreign Policy and Relations*, p. 35.

50. See Ashok Kapur, "The Indian Subcontinent: The Contemporary Structure of Power and the Development of Power Relations," *Asian Survey* 28 (July 1988): 694.

51. See *Transfer of Power Documents*, vol. 9, no. 34, the letter from Pethick Lawrence to Wavell on November 13, 1946. And vol. 8, no. 248, for the letter from P. J. Griffiths, a former Indian Civil Service (ICS) officer and the head of European Association in Bengal to Wavell urging him to base his future calculations on the Muslim League rather than on the Congress.

52. At the Bandung Conference Nehru enunciated the policy of Panchsheel or noninterference. See Government of India publication *The Asian-African Conference*, Indonesia, Djakarta, April 24, 1955, no. 9, pp. 2–6. It is noteworthy that until 1957, India's defense expenditure remained well below 2 percent of the net national product. See Lorne J. Kavic, *India's Quest for Security: Defense Policies, 1947–65* (Berkeley: University of California Press, 1967), p. 221.

3. Narratives of Ethnic Nations: The Sikhs, Kashmiris, and Tamils

1. As Walker Connor has pointed out, in nationality formation what ultimately matters is not what is but what people believe is. "A Nation is a Nation, is a State, is an Ethnic Group, is a . . .," *Ethnic and Racial Studies* 1 (October 1978), pp. 377–400. James Mayall and Mark Simpson identify five conditions that are generally present in the transformation of a group from a community into a nation, particularly one advocating separatism. These are: where an ethnic group is treated differently by the colonial power; where post-colonial government is intolerant of ethnicity and seeks to monopolize power; where confessional difference provide a rallying point for the community; where regional rivalry provides support for ethnic separatism from the outside. The fifth condition is negative. The authors believe that political economy of the ethnic community is important but secondary to the nationality formation. See Mayall and Simpson, "Ethnicity Is Not Enough: Reflections on Protracted Secessionism in the Third World," in Anthony Smith, ed., *Ethnicity and Nationalism* (New York: Brill, 1992), pp. 9–10. A. Jeyaratnam Wilson, in his "The Politics of Ethnicity and Ethnonationalism in South Asia," *Contemporary South Asia* 2 (1993): 327–29, identifies four stages by which a nesting community within a nation-state becomes a separatist nationality. Also see Paul Brass' seminal chapter on nationality formation in *Ethnicity and Nationalism: Theory and Comparison* (New Delhi: Sage, 1991), pp. 41–68.

2. These stages are drawn from Brass' analysis of ethnic identity formation, *Ethnicity and Nationalism*, pp. 22–23.

3. Urmila Phadnis, *Ethnicity and Nation-Building in South Asia* (New Delhi: Sage, 1989), pp. 80–81.

4. See Dietrich Reetz, "Ethnic and Religious Identities in Colonial India (1920s–1930s): A Conceptual Debate," *Contemporary South Asia* 2 (1993): 109–22. As pointed out in chapter 1, scholars do not agree whether ethnic identities are primordial or modern. For the purposes of this study this debate is less important than the fact that such identities are present and have been reinforced by the responses of the two supranational authorities that preceded the modern independent government in 1947. It is not without significance that both the Muslims and Sikhs were granted separate electorates by the British. This officially acknowledged their claims to a distinctive historical identity. It bestowed on the successor state of independent India, a

legacy of separatist claims. The central state in New Delhi, whether it was presided over by the Mughal kings or the British administrators, played an important role in such identity formation.

5. A short list of useful sources for the Sikh identity formation would have to include: W. H. Mcleod, *The Evolution of the Sikh Community: Five Essays* (Oxford: Clarendon Press, 1976); Rajiv Kapur, *Sikh Separatism: The Politics of Faith* (London: Allen and Unwin, 1986); Richard Fox, *Lions of Punjab: Culture in the Making* (Berkeley: University of California Press, 1985); J. S. Grewal, *From Guru Nanak to Maharaj Ranjit Singh: Essays in Sikh History* (Amritsar: Guru Nanak Dev University, 1972); Kenneth Jones, "Communalism in Punjab: The Arya Samaj Contribution," *The Journal of Asian Studies* 26 (November 1968); K. L. Tuteja, *Sikh Politics, 1920–1940* (Kurukshetra: Vishal, 1984); M. J. Akbar, *India: The Siege Within* (New York: Viking, 1985). For a Marxist interpretation see T. G. Jacob, *Chaos in Nation formation: Case of Punjab* (New Delhi: Odyssey Press, 1985); and Avtar Singh Malhotra, "In the Name of Brotherhood of Ordinary People," *World Marxist Review* (February 1984): 44–47. For a short but succinct history of Sikh identity formation see M. S. Dhami, "Communalism in Punjab: A Socio-Historical Analysis," *Punjab Journal of Politics* 9 (January–June 1985): 30

6. Harjit Oberoi, "From Punjab to 'Khalistan': Territorialism and Meta Commentary," *Pacific Affairs* 60 (Spring 1987): 31.

7. The text of the Anandpur Sahib Resolution and its three versions are reproduced fully in *Punjab: Context and Trends* (Chandigarh: Center For Research in Rural and Industrial Development, 1984), see the appendixes.

8. The pamphlet is quoted in Akbar, *India, the Siege Within: Challenges to National Identity* (New Delhi: Penguin, 1985), pp. 192–93.

9. Robin Jeffrey, " Grappling with History: Sikh Politicians and the Past" *Pacific Affairs* 60 (Spring 1987): 59.

10. Quoted from *Sant Sipahi*, June 1986, pp. 25–28. This is a monthly founded by Master Tara Singh and published from Amritsar. Translated for me by student informants in Amritsar.

11. Quoted in Joyce Pettigrew, "In Search of a New Kingdom of Lahore," *Pacific Affairs* 60 (Spring 1987): 15

12. Quoted in Pettigrew, "New Kingdom of Lahore," p. 17

13. Quoted in Pritam Singh, "Two Facets of Revivalism: A Defense," in Gopal Singh, ed., *Punjab Today* (New Delhi: Intellectual Publishing House, 1987), p. 174

14. Many observe that the Gurdwaras emerged as the nerve centers of the community during Ranjit Singh's reign and continued subsequently. The imperial endowments permitted the propagation of the Sikh faith and religious instructions. This created a strong base for a social and religious network in Punjabi society. But Ranjit Singh was a tolerant ruler and gave gifts and endowments to other religious establishments as well.

15. Kuldip Nayar and Khushwant Singh, *Tragedy of Punjab* (New Delhi: Vision Books, 1984), p. 20

16. Ranjit Singh Khalsa, Harminder Singh Sandhu, Harinder Singh Kahlon, *Why the Reconstruction of Shri Akal Takht Sahib* (in Punjabi) AISSF (Amritsar: Raxona Press, n.d.), p. 4. Translated for me by an official at the SGPC office.

17. Ibid.

18. Oberoi, "From Punjab to Khalistan," p. 36

19. The Arya Samaj like the Singh Sabhas, provided an organizational network for intracommunal solidarity, and its message was disseminated through magazines, newspapers, religious treatises, and commentaries.

20. A. S. Narang, *Storm Over Sutlej*, p. 86.

21. Jeffrey, "Grappling with History," p. 69.

22. Pettigrew, "New Kingdom of Lahore." p. 6

23. Rajiv Kapur, *Sikh Separatism: The Politics of Faith,* preface, pp. 12–13.

24. Protracted militancy and prolonged violence led to another attempted redefinition of the Sikh identity. During conferences held at Columbia University in April 1994, a number of participants argued that the Sikh faith had many elements in common with Islam and that the notion of a permanent animosity between Sikhs and Muslims was artificial, that Sikh antipathy to Muslims was a natural response to the trauma of Partition but that event was long past. Sikh history needed more objective reappraisal. It was implied that the Sikh antipathy toward Muslims and Pakistan had given the Indian government undue advantage against the Akalis and Sikhs in Punjab. But India had betrayed the Sikhs, it had reneged on the promises made on the eve of Partition. New Delhi's denial of autonomy to Punjab was thus part of the larger plan of Indian hegemony in the region.

25. Separatist and pro-Islamic discourses can be found in the writings, such as: Kashmir Liberation Cell, *Glimpses of the Resistance Movement in Indian-Held Kashmir* (Muzaffarabad: Azad Kashmir, 1989), p. 20; A. R. Minhas and Mushtahsan Aquil, eds., *Kashmir Cry Freedom* (Mirpur, Azad Kashmir: Kashmir Record and Research Cell, Arshid Books, 1991); Amanullah Khan, *Free Kashmir* (Karachi: Central Printing Press, 1970); a Kashmir Pandit version of history can be found in Jammu and Kashmir Sahayata Samiti, *Communal and Political Situation in Present-day Kashmir* (New Delhi: Suruchi Prakashan, 1991). On early history and tradition of Kashmir see P. N. K. Bamzai, *Kashmir and Power Politics* (New Delhi: Metropolitan Books, 1966); P. N. Bazaz, *Kashmir in Crucible* (New Delhi: Pampash, 1967); C. E. Bates, *Gazetteer of Kashmir and Ladakh: Compiled 1870–1872* (New Delhi and Jammu: Light and Life, 1980), K.M. Pannikar, *Gulab Singh: The founder of the Kashmir State* (London: Allen and Unwin, 1953); Sisir Gupta, *Kashmir: A Study in Indo–Pakistan Relations* (Bombay: Asia, 1966); Lord Birdwood, *Two Nations and Kashmir* (London: Robert Hale, 1956).

26. Balraj Puri in all his writings has delineated the complexity of Jammu and Kashmir's ethnic and regional divisions. He stresses that Kashmir is a mosaic of diverse linguistic and religious groups and cannot be understood exclusively in terms of Hindu-Muslim divide. See his *Jammu and Kashmir: Triumph and Tragedy of Indian Federalisation* (New Delhi: Sterling, 1981); *Simmering Volcano: Study of Jammu's Relations with Kashmir* (New Delhi: Sterling, 1983).

27. Lord Birdwood writes in his *Two Nations and Kashmir* (London: Robert Hale, 1956), p. 25, that "the delimitation of a line on the map of Central Asia which on political considerations enclosed a completely artificial area, a geographic monstrosity which then assumed the name of the land of the Jhelum valley, Kashmir."

28. U. K. Zutshi, in his *Emergence of Political Awakening in Kashmir* (New Delhi: Manohar, 1986), covers the transformation of Kashmiri people into a nation.

29. This period is covered by a vast amount of primary and secondary literature: *Correspondence of Jawaharlal Nehru,* edited by S. Gopal and published by the Jawaharlal Nehru Memorial Trust in two series; *Correspondence of Sardar Patel,* Durga Das, ed. (Ahmedabad: Navajiwan Press), and *The Transfer of Power, 1942–47,* Mansergh ed. Among secondary sources, in chapter 2 references have been made to Hodson and V. P. Menon. Other useful books are Major General Akbar Khan, *Raiders in Kashmir* (Karachi: 1970); Fazal Muqeem Khan, *The Story of the Pakistan Army* (Karachi: Oxford University Press, 1963). The last two provide a Pakistani view of the Partition and war.

30. For details of policy making during the 1956 war, see L. P. Singh, *India's Foreign Policy: The Shastri Period* (New Delhi: Uppal, 1966).

31. The Indo–Pakistan conflict is one of the most extensively studied topics in South Asia's international relations. For accounts of the 1960s and the second war, see S. Biswas, *The Three Weeks War* (Calcutta: M. C. Sarkar, 1966); Air Marshal Asghar Khan, *The First Round* (New Delhi: Vikas, 1979); General Muhammad Musa, *My Version of the War, 1965* (New Delhi: ABC, 1983); Sumit Ganguly, *The Origins of War in South Asia: Indo–Pakistan Conflict Since 1947* (Boulder and London: Westview, 1986).

32. See Y. D. Gundevia, *The Testament of Sheikh Abdullah* (New Delhi: Palit and Palit, 1974); also based on my interview with the sheikh's son and successor, former chief minister of J&K, Dr. Farooq Abdullah, June 1994, New York. Parts of this interview was broadcast on Channel 47 (New York) at the end of June 1994.

33. For a nationalist interpretations of Mughal, Pathan, and Sikh rule, see P. N. Bazaz, *Kashmir in Crucible*; Gull Mohd. Wani, *Kashmir Politics: Problems and Prospects* (Springfield, Va.: Nataraj Books, 1993).

34. U. K. Zutshi, *Emergence of Political Awakening in Kashmir*, preface, p. 11.

35. P. N. K. Bamzai, *Kashmir and Power Politics* (New Delhi: Metropolitan Books, 1966), pp. 18–19.

36. Gundevia, *Testament of Sheikh Abdullah*, p. 61.

37. The Jammu Mukti morcha (JMM), launched in March 1990, rejected the concept of regional autonomy for Jammu within the state of J&K. Instead, it demanded a separate statehood for Jammu within the Indian union as the only real solution to the ''43 years of ills inflicted'' on it by the valley Muslims and their National Conference representatives. The JMM accuses New Delhi of appeasing and pampering the separatist Kashmiri leadership. For a detailed exposition of the Kashmiri Hindu, particularly Jammu regional view see Hari Om, *Debacle in Kashmir* (New Delhi: Anmol, 1992), p. 107

38. Many observers have pointed out that Sheikh Abdullah and other National Conference leaders who took over from him were not immune to the lure of power and office, and they were willing to bend ideals for political expediency. The erosion of Kashmir's autonomy did not seem to unduly bother Sheikh Abdullah in 1975 when Indira Gandhi released him from imprisonment and installed him once again at the helm of affairs in Kashmir. Whether the basis of accession is accepted or rejected at any given time has depended largely on the gains anticipated by political leaders of the National Conference and the Jammu Hindus.

39. Rajesh Kadian, *The Kashmir Tangle: Issues and Options* (New Delhi: Vision Books, 1992), p. 13.

40. Gull Mohd. Wani, *Kashmir Politics: Problems and Prospects*, p. 114.

41. Barry Buzan, "New Patterns of Global Security in the 21st Century," *International Affairs* 67, no. 3 (1991).

42. Syed Ali Geelani, Mukadama-Ilhaq, quoted in Wani, *Kashmir Politics: Problems and Prospects*, p. 113.

43. In addition to Robert Hardgrave, Jr., *The Dravidian Movement* (Bombay: Popular Prakashan, 1965); M. R. Barnett, *The Politics of Cultural Nationalism in South India*; and E .F. Irschick, *Politics and Social Conflict in South India: The Non-Brahmin Movement and Tamil Separatism, 1916–1929* (Berkeley: University of California Press, 1969). Also see G. Palanithurai and R. Thandavan, *Ethnic Movement in India: Theory and Practice* (New Delhi: Kanishka, 1992); P. Meile,

"Mythology of the Tamils," *World Mythology*, P. Grimal, ed. (London: Hamlyn, 1965); S. T. Nayagam, *Tamil Culture and Civilization* (New York: Asia, 1973).

44. In the late eighteenth century Father Beschi became a renowned Tamil poet, in the nineteenth century Rev. Pope translated two major works, Kural and Thiruvasaham, into English. Rt. Rev. Caldwell undertook a comprehensive study of Tamil grammar and customs as well as of Dravidian languages in the nineteenth century. Similarly, Suryanarayan Sastri and U. V. Swaminath Aiyer wrote extensive commentaries on ancient Tamil literature. See J. Pandian, *Caste, Nationalism, and Ethnicity* (Bombay: Popular Prakashan, 1987), p. 61.

45. Irschick, *Politics and Social Conflict in South India*, pp. 292–95.

46. Sastri changed his Sanskritic name to a Tamil name and was known as Paritimal Kalaigar. Other Tamil leaders followed.

47. See Mohan Ram, "Ramaswami Naicker and the Dravidian Movement," *Economic and Political Weekly*, 9 Annual Number (February 1974): 217–24.

48. S. Piyasena and R. Y. Senadheera, *India, "We Tamils," and Sri Lanka* (New Delhi: Sri Satguru, 1987), p. 107.

49. Barnett, *Politics of Cultural Nationalism in South India*, p. 72

50. Ibid., p. 73

51. Robert Hardgrave, *India: Government and Politics in a Developing Nation*, 4th ed. (San Diego: Harcourt Brace and Jovanovich, 1986), p. 258.

52. J. Pandian, *Caste, Nationalism, and Ethnicity*, p. 37.

53. Ibid., p. 29

54. This was evident in my conversations (June 1986 and again in August 1988) with various Tamil Nadu leaders, notably K. Karunanidhi, the leader of the DMK. Trans. by R. Raghavan. I also talked with several leading journalists (Anita Pratap and Venkataramani of *India Today*), public officials in the field of arts and entertainment, Justice Gopalan and Vyjayanthimala, a former actress turned politician. Even everyday conversations about politics and Sri Lanka led to repeated references to the ancient kingdoms, Aryan hegemony, and the ancient heritage of the Tamil people.

55. The Sri Lankan civil war and its spill-over into Tamil Nadu has spawned a large body of work on the cultural and security dimensions of the Tamil connection across the Palk Straits. For the text and analysis of the TULF manifesto see Piyadasa and Senadheera, *India, "We Tamils," and Sri Lanka*, pp. 39–54; P. S. Suryanrayana, *The Peace Trap* (New Delhi: East-West Press, 1988); Sumanta Basu, *States, Nations, Sovereignty: Sri Lanka, India, and the Tamil Eelam Movement* (New Delhi: Sage, 1994).

56. Theda Skocpol, "Bringing the State Back In: Strategies of Analysis in Current Research," in Evans, Rueschemeyer, and Skocpol, eds. *Bringing the State Back In* (London, New York: Cambridge University Press, 1985), p. 8.

4. RESTORING RELATIONAL CONTROL: INDIRA GANDHI'S FIRST TERM

1. Shri Lal Bahadur Shastri's death was particularly unfortunate because it came just when, thanks to India's success in the 1965 war with Pakistan, his stature as the leader of the Indian people had become unquestioned. Therefore, the India government could not take advantage of the sharp increase in its autonomy to reestablish the Nehruvian model of relational control through co-optation.

2. It is often forgotten that the decision to oust opposition coalitions in states that the Congress had lost was a decision of the entire party, including the Congress "syndicate," the powerful group of organizational leaders headed then by K. Kamaraj. It was not made by Mrs. Gandhi alone. It is doubtful whether the party would have behaved any differently under another leader. The most that can be said is that the Congress's decline in 1967 would have been much less precipitous had Shastri lived longer. His own preeminence within the party would have tilted New Delhi toward power-sharing instead of confrontation. For a description of the decision making within the party, and especially the crucial significance of the instructions given to the chief minister of Madhya Pradesh by the party high command at this time, see Prem Shankar Jha, *In the Eye of the Cyclone: The Crisis in Indian Democracy* (New Delhi: Viking Press, 1993), ch. 2.

3. Shortly after the 1962 elections, the government passed the sixteenth amendment to the constitution, which required candidates contesting legislative seats to take an oath to uphold the constitution and the republic of India. The DMK officially gave up the idea of Dravidasthan and joined other regional parties in pledging allegiance to New Delhi.

4. The DMK won 41.2 percent of the vote and became the ruling party in Tamil Nadu. In the 1971 elections, it further improved its percentage of the popular vote. P. Spratt, *D.M.K. in Power* (Bombay: Nachiketa, 1971), p. 49.

5. Mrs. Gandhi sponsored bank nationalization, abolished privy purses for the princes, and appealed to the young, minorities, and women for votes. She encouraged the left factions within the Congress, and secured her personal control over the parliamentary board and Central Electoral Committee. These moves gave her effective control over who would or would not run on the party ticket and forestalled challenges from the old guard in the Congress party.

6. Mrs. Gandhi eased out the chief ministers of Rajasthan, Andhra Pradesh, Assam, and Madhya Pradesh in 1972, which made the prime minister the most important source of power, decisions, policy, and patronage.

7. A whole host of grievances welded into a demand for Mrs. Gandhi's resignation: unkept promises to ameliorate poverty, continuing shortages of food and essential goods, lack of jobs, and rampant corruption. Under J. P. Narayan's leadership the protest became an organized movement and spread to other parts of India, particularly to the Hindi belt states of Bihar and Uttar Pradesh. There are several excellent accounts of the causes and consequences of national emergency of 1975. For a political economy oriented explanation, see Prem Shankar Jha, *India: A Political Economy of Stagnation* (New Delhi: Oxford University Press, 1980); the three-volume *Interim Report* of the Shah Commission of Inquiry, 1978; Robert Frykenberg, "The Last Emergency of the Raj," in Henry Hart, ed. *Indira Gandhi's India: A Political System Reappraised* (Boulder, Colo.: Westview Press, 1976), pp. 37–67; Michael Henderson, *Experiment with Untruth: India Under Emergency* (Columbia, Mo: South Asia Books, 1977); Kuldip Nayar, *The Judgement* (New Delhi: Vikas, 1977)

8. For the latest study of this war see Richard Sisson, *War and Secession: Pakistan, India, and the Creation of Bangladesh* (Berkeley: University of California Press, 1990); for India's role see Sucheta Ghosh, *The Role of India in the Emergence of Bangladesh* (Calcutta: Minerva, 1983). For a wider discussion of Indo–Pakistani conflict see Sumit Ganguly, *The Origins of War in South Asia* (Boulder, Colo.: Westview, 1994). For a Pakistani perspective see the account by Qutubuddin Aiziz, *Blood and Tears* (Karachi: United Press of Pakistan, 1974). A revisionist perspective on the events in the war can be found in the writings of Imtiaz Ahmed and

Maniruzzaman Talukadar. See Talukadar's *The Bangladesh Revolution and Its Aftermath* (Dacca: Bangladesh Books International, 1980).

9. Several scholars have portrayed the East and West Pakistan relations as a colonial and exploitative relationship in which East Pakistan always got the short end of the stick. See Subrata Roy Chowdhary, *The Genesis of Bangladesh* (New York: Asia Publishing House, 1972), particularly his first chapter entitled "East Bengal: A Colonial Status," pp. 1–22. For the opposite point of view see Akbar Khan Mohammed, *The Mystery of Debacle of Pakistan 1971, and Myth of Exploitation Since 1947, and Secret of the Covert War Unmasked* (Karachi: Islamic Military Science Association, 1972 or 1973).

10. *La Monde* (Paris), March 31, 1971.

11. Again, the Bangladeshi and Pakistani accounts differ on this point. According to Pakistani official history, killings of Pakistani officials and non-Bengali (Bihari Muslims) citizens of East Pakistan, with help from India, started first; the Awami League claimed that the attempts to crush the constitutional movement began before the Bengali police and armed forces defected to the Awami League.

12. According to the Indian government, by the end of August 1971 there were 8.2 million refugees from East Pakistan. Mrs. Gandhi remarked in October 1971 that nearly 13 percent of the population of East Bengal had already arrived in India as refugees. Government of India, *Bangladesh Documents* 2, no. 3, p. 251.

13. Indira Gandhi, *India and Bangladesh: Selected Speeches and Statements* (Delhi: Orient Longman, 1972), p. 29.

14. According to most scholars, the Bangladeshi resistance passed through five phases: March 26 to May 1971, when the resistance was spontaneous but uncoordinated; June to July 1971, which was a phase of initial organization and use of guerrilla tactics; August to September 1971, when these operations were stepped up; October to December 3, 1971, when the Mukti Bahini was scoring considerable success; and December 3 to December 16, 1971, when Indian armed forces and Mukti Bahini launched a joint operation to defeat Pakistan. For details see Chowdhary, *The Genesis of Bangladesh*, pp. 158–87.

15. For a detailed discussion of the military situation and the events that precipitated conflict see D. K. Palit, *Lightening Campaign* (New Delhi: Thomson Press, 1972).

16. Imtiaz Ahmed and Talukadar have already been mentioned. Leo Rose writes in J. N. Rosenau et al., *World Politics* (New York: Free Press, 1976), p. 215, that the basic principle underlying India's regional policy is its undeclared hegemony in South Asia.

17. Ahmed, *State and Foreign Policy* (New Delhi: Vikas, 1993), p. 248.

18. Ibid., p. 253.

19. See *Jugantar* (Calcutta) editorials on March 28 and April 11, 1971, and *Amrita Bazar Patrika*, editorials on April 6, 7, 19, 1971; *Economist* (London), April 24, 1971, quoted West Bengal's deputy chief minister as saying, "We in West Bengal recognize Bangladesh although the central government has not done so yet." Similar statements by high-level public officials and political leaders are to be found in various issues of the above two dailies published in Calcutta during this period.

20. Pran Chopra, "Where Do We Go from Saying Nothing?" *Hindustan Standard*, April 16, 1971; also see April 24, 1971.

21. Richard Sisson and Leo Rose, *War and Secession: Pakistan, India, and the Creation of Bangladesh*, p. 145.

22. Ibid., p. 145.

23. West Bengal had responded spontaneously to the deteriorating situation in East Pakistan. It organized demonstrations and sympathy strikes. There were mass pledges to express solidarity with the Bangladeshi struggle, the press got into gear and published articles and editorials urging New Delhi to stop the atrocities against East Bengalis. Observers list over ten large-scale organizations established in West Bengal to support the Bangladeshi resistance movement. *Hindustan Standard*, a newspaper from Calcutta, said in its editorial that "The artificial barriers that were raised in this part of the subcontinent 24 years back were down on the day, if not physically at least emotionally and spiritually, and split Bengals were temporarily united." April 1, 1971.

24. Jen-minh Jihn-pao wrote on April 11, 1971, that developments in East Pakistan were not a threat to India and that India was simply using the turmoil to advance its own expansionist designs. China extended its support to Pakistan against any foreign intervention. In the Chinese view, the Indian government, in league with the two super powers, was plotting intervention. *Survey of China's Mainland Press* 4882 (April 22, 1971): 109–10; *Peking Review* 114 (April 16, 1971): 7–8.

25. For the Soviet stance during the Bangladesh crisis, see Ghosh, *The Role of India*, pp. 156–81.

26. This question was fiercely debated at the time in India. See N. M. Ghatate, ed., *Indo–Soviet Treaty: Reaction and Reflections* (New Delhi: Deen Dayal Research Institute, 1972), pp. 63–64.

27. Rafiqul Islam, *A Tale of Millions: Bangladesh Liberation War 1971* (2d ed.; Dacca: Bangladesh Books International, 1981).

28. Ibid., pp. 237–42.

29. Both Maniruzzaman Talukadar and Imtiaz Ahmed have claimed this. Among Indian observers, Subrata Roy Chowdhary also suggests that with Indian help in weapons and logistics, the Mukti Bahini would have eventually defeated the Pakistani armed forces in Bangladesh. See Capt. S. K. Garg, *Spotlight: Freedom Fighters of Bangladesh* (New Delhi: Allied, 1984), p. 143.

30. Garg, *Spotlight*, p. 137. Garg's interviews with Indian and Bangladeshi military personnel involved in the war reveals that a large number of guerrillas lacked experience and training. Given the task of blowing up bridges and softening targets, guerrillas would often produce fake evidence of their success. This was partly because of the fear of Pakistani retribution and partly because they wanted to convince the Indian armed forces of their value to the overall struggle. It is true that the Mukti Bahini was beginning to come together as an effective force and inflict considerable damage on the Pakistani position, but that did not mean it could have forced Pakistan to surrender and accept unconditional independence of Bangladesh.

31. Garg notes that after Mujibur Rehman was assassinated, "tiger" Sidiqqi of the liberation war of 1971 had crossed into India with his 2,000 supporters in the fall of 1975. His purpose was to revive "Mujibism" in Bangladesh. The Indian government had met his request and provided funds via the RAW.

32. The text of the document signed at Simla can be found in S. S. Bindra, *Indo–Pakistani Relations: Tashkent to Simla*, (New Delhi: Deep and Deep, 1981).

33. Shashi Tharoor, *Reasons's of State: Political Development and India's Foreign Policy Under Indira Gandhi, 1966–1977* (New Delhi: Vikas, 1982), p. 73. The Bangladesh war is thus regarded by experts as a watershed event that expanded India's influence and power well

beyond her national borders. Even if one were to contend that the military intervention was in contravention of international law and the Charter of the United Nations, many argued that India had not cared that she violated them. Henry Kissinger saw the Bangladesh crisis mainly in this light. Kissinger described Mrs. Gandhi's handling of the Bangladesh war as "a strong personality relentlessly pursuing India's national interest with single-mindedness and finesse." Shashi Tharoor agrees with him.

34. Her principal adviser at this time was P. N. Haksar, a brilliant lawyer turned diplomat who had Marxist leanings. Haksar may have read too much into Bhutto's populism, and identified him as a kindred spirit.

35. For a recent discussion of this in the context of post-1990 insurgency, see A. G. Noorani, "Kashmir Issue-IV," *Statesman*, October 17, 1994.

36. Sheikh Abdullah's speech in the J&K legislative Assembly, 1975, quoted in Gull Mohd. Wani, *Kashmir Politics: Problems and Prospects* (Springfield, Va.: Nataraj Books, 1993), p. 84.

37. Mrs. Gandhi's statement to the Parliament, February 24, 1975, *Lok Sabha Debates* (New Delhi: Government Printing Press).

38. Quoted in N. N. Raina, *Kashmir Politics and Imperialist Manoeuvre: 1846–1980* (New Delhi: Patriot, 1988), p. 251.

5. EROSION OF THE SUPRANATIONAL STATE: INDIA UNDER INDIRA GANDHI AND RAJIV GANDHI

1. Although no one subscribes to a single cause theory of Congress's decline, some have argued that Mrs. Gandhi's personality—what they call her insecurity and paranoia—ultimately destroyed the Congress as an effective agent of democracy and development. Others see it as a phenomenon caused by an expanding electorate, maturing economy, and paradoxically weakening political institutions. India's journalists and publicists, politicians and some academics subscribe to the first view. At least two biographers of Mrs. Gandhi have refuted this charge. see Inder Malhotra, *Indira Gandhi: A Personal and Political Biography* (London: Hodder and Stoughton, 1989), and Mary Carras, *Indira Gandhi in the Crucible of Leadership: A Political Biography* (Boston: Beacon Press, 1979). For the deinstitutionalization thesis see Rajni Kothari, *Democratic Polity and Social Change in India* (Bombay: Allied, 1976), pp. 24–27; also see his "Where Are We Heading?" *Express Magazine*, November 29, 1981. In the latter, Kothari makes a powerful argument in favor of an institutional framework that is free of the cult of personality and politics of survival. Lloyd and Susanne Rudolph, *In Pursuit of Lakshmi: The Political Economy of the Indian State* (Chicago, London: University of Chicago Press, 1986), pp. 127–58, extend a similar argument although they are more interested in the political economy explanation of Congress's decline. Also see Paul Brass, "Pluralism, Regionalism, and Decentralizing Tendencies in Contemporary Indian Politics," in A. J. Wilson and Dennis Dalton, eds. *The States of South Asia: Problems of National Integration* (London: C. Hurst, 1982), pp. 223–64. The last two emphasize the inherently pluralistic and decentralizing tendencies in India's democracy.

2. "During the period from 1963 to 1969," writes Stanley Kochanek, "the passing of the old nationalist leadership eroded the effective power of the high command, and power in the Congress became more decentralized. District and state levels of the party operated with a considerable degree of independence, and there was a general dilution of power throughout the party structure." See Kochanek, "Mrs. Gandhi's Pyramid: The New Congress," in Henry

Hart, ed., *Indira Gandhi's India* (Boulder, Colo.: Westview Press, 1976), p. 110. Mrs. Gandhi responded to this by splitting the party and committing her wing of the Congress firmly to left-oriented programs. The combination of ideological revival, organizational control, and victory in the Bangladesh war brought Mrs. Gandhi and the Congress party spectacular victory in the 1972 Assembly elections. For discussion of this course of events and Mrs. Gandhi's political strategy, see Robert Hardgrave, Jr., "The Congress in India: Crisis and Split," *Asian Survey* 10 (March 1970): 256–62; and Mahendra Prasad Singh, *Split in a Predominant Party: The Indian National Congress in 1969* (New Delhi: Abhinav, 1981). Myron Weiner, in his "The Elections and the Indian Party System," *Asian Survey* 11 (December 1971): 1153–66, discusses the past split and struggle for power between Mrs. Gandhi and the opposition.

3. Hardgrave writes that Mrs. Gandhi sought "in direct appeal to the voters, to bypass the intermediary structures—the village notables and "vote banks"—that had been the base of the old Congress machine. Robert Hardgrave Jr. and Stanley Kochenek, *India: Government and Politics in a Developing Nation* (New York: Harcourt Brace, 1986), p. 207). The weakness of this approach soon became evident. Personal appeal could wane as it did by 1974 and eventually led to the imposition of "national emergency" in 1975. Accounts of these events and analyses can be found in several sources. For a political economy oriented explanation see Prem Shankar Jha, *India: A Political Economy of Stagnation* (Bombay: Oxford University Press, 1980); the three-volume *Interim Report of the Shah Commission of Inquiry, 1978*; Robert Frykenberg, "The Last Emergency of the Raj," in Hart, ed. *Indira Gandhi's India*, pp. 37–67; Kuldip Nayar, *The Judgement* (New Delhi: Vikas, 1977). A special issue of *Sunday* (Calcutta) 30, June-8 July provides a look back at the emergency.

4. Mrs. Gandhi may also have wanted to break the power of the chief ministers during her battle with the organizational leaders. This came to a head not over the party's economic policy, where they grudgingly let her have her way, but over the election of the president of India who, in India's complex system of indirect election, is elected by the sitting members of the parliament and all state assemblies. The chief ministers saw in Mrs. Gandhi's "rebellion" an opportunity to increase their independence by using Mrs. Gandhi against the central party organization. But Mrs. Gandhi had other plans. Having just escaped from bondage to the latter, she had no intention of becoming a vassal of the former. "Within eighteen months of the 1972 elections," write Hardgrave and Kochanek, "Six Chief Ministers had been eased out of the office and President's Rule imposed in four states. In relying heavily on personal charisma and populist politics, Indira Gandhi destroyed the boss-structure of the old Congress, but she did not replace it with an effective structure linking the Center with the local party units" (Hardgrave, *India*, p. 209). This, according to Joshi and Desai, led to "weak and attenuated party and lack of stable loyalty structure." Ram Joshi and Kirtidev Desai, "The Opposition: Problems and Prospects," *Economic and Political Weekly*, October 20, 1973), pp. 1913–22.

5. Mrs. Gandhi received a shock when three Madhya Pradesh by-elections in a row went against the Congress in March 1974.

6. The Congress(I) had won 43 percent of the vote, the Janata party got 19 percent, and the Lok Dal (a faction within the Janata coalition) won 9 percent. It is apparent from the various analyses of the 1980 elections that Mrs. Gandhi's victory was not solely because of the factionalism and divisions within the Janata government. A fair number of Congress seats were won with an absolute majority and a wide margin. Of the three candidates for the prime minister's position—Charan Singh, Indira Gandhi, and Jagjivan Ram—only Mrs. Gandhi enjoyed national stature, a fact that was not lost on the voting public. Even in Tamil Nadu,

where the Dravidian parties were well entrenched, Mrs. Gandhi's victory carried her DMK ally in a rout of the ruling AIDMK. Most studies of this election show that votes for the Congress and Mrs. Gandhi cut across caste, class, and ethnic lines. For instance, Jagjivan Ram had an appeal to the schedule caste vote, Mrs. Gandhi carried a substantial portion of this vote. See Myron Weiner, *India at the Polls, 1980: A Study of the Parliamentary Elections* (Washington D.C.: American Enterprise Institute, 1983); James Manor, "The Electoral Process amid Awakening and Decay: Reflections on the Indian General Election of 1980," in Peter Lyon and James Manor, eds., *Transfer and Transformation: Political Institutions in the New Commonwealth* (Leicester: Leicester University Press, 1983), pp. 87–116.

7. For a discussion of the impact of the corporate donation ban and the underground economy, see Prem Shankar Jha, *In The Eye of the Cyclone: Crisis in Indian Democracy* (Delhi: Viking Press, 1993), pp. 38–42.

8. See Rudolph, *In Pursuit of Lakshmi*, pp. 148–58, for an assessment of Rajiv Gandhi's record in the restoring democracy and party organization.

9. Brass comments that in the post-1967 India, to control the center it had become increasingly necessary to control the states. Brass, *Ethnicity and Nationalism: Theory and Comparison* (New Delhi, Newbury Park, Calif,: Sage Publications, 1991), pp. 171–72.

10. Atul Kohli, *Democracy and Discontent: India's Growing Crisis of Governability* (Cambridge: Cambridge University Press, 1990), p. 391.

11. B. A. V. Sharma, "Congress and Federal Balance," in Joshi and Hebsur, eds., *Congress in Indian Politics* (Riverdale, Md.: Riverdale Press, 1988), pp. 116–17.

12. N. T. Rama Rao, the leader of the Telugu Desam party, along with other opposition leaders was holding "opposition conclaves" with a single point program of defeating Indira Gandhi in the 1985 elections. Farooq Abdullah's fiery speeches at these conclaves infuriated Mrs. Gandhi. A bizarre touch to the opposition program was added when it became known that Rama Rao was dressing up as a women in the privacy of his home to propitiate the right gods who would hasten the day when he would be the prime minister! These shenanigans suggest that becoming prime minister was the main lure for the leaders of the opposition. In all likelihood, the opposition would have disintegrated had it won the 1985 elections. It is, however, equally true that Mrs. Gandhi was extremely suspicious of the opposition and by this time feared defeat in the 1985 elections.

13. For details see P. M. Kamath, "Politics of Defection in India in the 1980s," *Asian Survey* 25 (October 1985): 1049; Krishna Tummala, "Democracy Triumphs in India: The Case of Andhra Pradesh," *Asian Survey* 26 (March 1986): 379–89.

14. "Among other things," noted *India Today*, January 15, 1985, "this pointed to an enormous erosion in the BJP support."

15. See Atul Kohli, *Democracy and Discontent*, p. 78. Also see the *Times of India*, December 23, 1984; and the reports about an open letter by veteran RSS leader Nanaji Deshmukh, which offered support to Rajiv Gandhi in *The Indian Express* (Bombay), January 26, 1985.

16. The Congress posters asked a rhetorical question, "why should you feel uncomfortable riding in a taxi driven by a taxi driver who belongs to another state?" This was followed by more innuendos about the Sikhs: "they put a knife through the country and carve out a niche for their cynical, disgruntled ambition disguised as public aspiration. They raise a flag and give this niche the name of a nation. They show hatred and grow barbed-wire fences, watered with human blood."

17. *Hindustan Times*, December 13, 1984; *Indian Express*, December 26, 1984.

18. The latter showed turbaned assassins gunning down Mrs. Gandhi while the accompanying texts asked, "Will the country's border finally be moved to your doorstop?"The opposition parties failed to answer the barrage of criticism leveled at them.

19. *Times of India,* December 29, 1985.

20. Hardgrave, *India*, p. 234.

21. Sanjib Baruah, "Immigration, Ethnic Conflict, and Political Turmoil—Assam, 1979–1985," *Asian Survey* 26 (November 1986): 1191–92; also see Hiren Gohain, "Bodo Stir in Perspective," *Economic and Political Weekly* 24, June 24, 1989, p. 1377.

22. Bhagwan Dua, "India: Federal Leadership and Secessionist Movements on the Periphery," in Ramashray Roy and Richard Sisson, eds., *Diversity and Dominance in Indian Politics*, vol. 2 (New Delhi: Sage, 1990), p. 211

23. In 1991 the Congress was voted back into power in Assam, mainly because it made an alliance with Laldenga, a secessionist leader. Such a compromise had been anathema to Nehru. Paul Brass believes that such alliances are inherently dangerous. It might be argued, however, that in 1985, the Congress did not enjoy the kind of unchallenged dominance as it did in the first two decades after independence. Second, in Nagaland and Mizoram, in fact all along the northeast, Nehru's main response to secessionist challenges had been to send in the army. This had not neutralized the northeast, nor had it made India's borders more secure. For Brass's views on this question, see his *Politics of India Since Independence*, 2d ed. (New York: Cambridge University Press, 1994), p. 204.

24. Conversations with Sharad Pawar, the Congress chief minister in Bombay and with Murli Deora, an important Congress party machine politician from Bombay. Both these conversations took place in New Delhi in December 1987.

25. The opposition included Congress working president, Kamalapati Tripathi; Gundu Rao, the former chief minister of Karnataka; Madhav Singh Solanki, former chief minister of Gujarat; V. C. Shukla, a powerful minister in Mrs. Gandhi's cabinet; Jaganath Mishra, former chief minister of Bihar; S. S. Mohapatra, former Congress general secretary, and many others. See *Indian Express* and *Times of India*, June 1–3, 1986.

26. He made the first two ministers, which not surprisingly, reduced their access to him drastically, and began to pass critical remarks about some of his finance minister's actions in public.

27. "Why not simply dismiss Bhajan lal–and spare himself the odium of having one of the hard men of the Emergency, Bansi Lal, in his government?" asks James Manor. In answer Manor points out that "the Prime Minister can find no one else in Haryana party who could take over the state and withstand the subversive doings that could be expected from both Bhajan Lal and Bansi Lal. Rajiv Gandhi [was therefore] trapped by the wretched condition of his party there into perpetuating that very condition." Similar problems existed in other states as well. James Manor, "Parties and Party System," in Atul Kohli ed., *India's Democracy: An Analysis of Changing State-Society Relations* (Princeton: Princeton University Press, 1988), p. 96.

28. In October 1985, the defense ministry had tried to rid defense contracts of corruption and kickbacks by issuing an order banning middlemen from such deals. Defense firms abroad were allowed to appoint agents on a fixed remuneration to represent them, but agents, who worked for a percentage of the contract price were prohibited from even entering the ministry and defense establishments, let alone having a free run of them as they had formerly. This move was welcomed by the public.

29. Jha, *In the Eye of the Cyclone*, pp. 75–76.

30. *Far Eastern Economic Review*, April 30, 1987.

31. For details on the political controversy surrounding the Shah Bano case, see Asghar Ali Engineer, *The Shah Bano Controversy* (Delhi: Ajanta, 1987); also see John Mansfield, "Personal Laws or a Uniform Civil Code," in *Religion and Law in Independent India*, Robert Baird ed. (Delhi: Manohar, 1993); T. N. Ninan interviewed Rajiv Gandhi on the case, see *India Today*, May 31, 1986; also see Seema Mustafa, "Muslim Women Bill: Government's Dangerous Line in Lok Sabha," *Mainstream*, May 17, 1986. Progressive Muslims in India protested against Gandhi's appeasement of the most conservative interpretation of Sharia. Araif Mohammad Khan, a Muslim minister in Gandhi's cabinet, resigned. The government spokesman for the bill in the parliament, K. C. Pant, defended the bill as being fair and impartial and democratic. He also stressed the issue of the Hindu and Muslim "psyche" that had motivated the bill.

32. Ashutosh Varshney, "Battling the Past, Forging a Future? Ayodhya and Beyond," in Philip Oldenburg. ed., *India Briefing 1993* (Boulder, Colo.: Westview Press, 1993), p. 36.

6. From Protest to Militancy: Punjab and Kashmir

1. Notes for chapter 3 have already listed sources consulted for writing about the Sikh ethnonationalism and its evolution. For the post 1960s course of events the following additional sources were useful: Paul Brass, "The Crisis in Punjab and Unity of India," in his *Ethnicity and Nationalism: Theory and Comparison* (New Delhi, Newbury Park, Calif.: Sage, 1991), pp. 176–237. For a socioeconomic interpretation of the Punjab crisis and Sikh militancy see Brass, " Socioeconomic Aspects of the Punjab Crisis," in S. W. R. de A. Samarsinghe and Reed Coughlan, eds., *Economic Dimensions of Ethnic Conflict* (London: Pinter, 1991), pp. 224–39; Robin Jeffrey, *The Perils of Prosperity: India's Dilemma in Punjab* (Bedford Park, So. Aust.: Flinders University, 1985). For an excellent set of articles focusing on Sikh metacommentary, religion, and militancy, see the issue of *Pacific Affairs* 60 (Spring 1987); a steady stream of articles in the *Punjab Journal of Politics*; Gopal Singh, ed. *Punjab Today* (New Delhi: Intellectual Publishing House, 1987).

2. For a theological and cultural argument claiming Sikhs's right to a homeland, see Jaswant Singh Mann, ed. *Some Documents on the Demand for the Sikh Homeland* (Chandigarh: All-India Sikh Student's Federation and Manjit Publishing Co., 1970). Also Harjot Oberoi, "From Punjab to 'Khalistan': Territoriality and Metacommentary," *Pacific Affairs*, discusses the concept of homeland in Sikh narratives.

3. In the aftermath of Partition, the demographic complexion of Punjab was as follows: the influx of Hindu and Sikh migrants from western Punjab increased the urban population. Hindus still constituted 64 percent of the state's population; the Sikhs constituted about 33 percent but most of them settled in the rural areas. See Dhami, "Punjab and Communalism," *Economic and Political Weekly*: 33.

4. The chronological construction and analysis in this section draws on the voluminous work that is available on the electoral politics in Punjab, center-state relations, and the course of Akali politics from 1950 to 1980s. Some of the important ones are: Paul Brass, *Language, Religion, and Politics in North India* (Cambridge: Cambridge University Press, 1974), pp. 277–336; P. S. Varma, "Akali Dal: History, Electoral Performance, and Leadership Profile," in Gopal Singh, ed. *Punjab Today*, pp. 257–84; Robin Jeffrey, *What's Happening to India?* (London: Macmillan, 1986), pp. 36–45; Paul Wallace, "Religious and Secular Politics in

Punjab: The Sikh Dilemma in Competing Political Systems," in Paul Wallace and Surendra Chopra, eds., *Political Dynamics of Punjab* (Amritsar: Guru Nanakdev University, 1981).

5. The choice of Anandpur Sahib is highly significant. It was here that Guru Gobind Singh built his first string of fortresses and started the new community of the Khalsas. Starting from Anandpur, Gobind Singh defended the Sikh Panth against the alliance of Rajput chieftains and then Mughal armies led by Wazir Khan Sirhind. Anandpur Sahib is also one of the five Takhts from where Hukumnamas, religious edicts or instructions, can be issued.

6. See chapter 3, note 7.

7. M. J. Akbar, *India: The Siege Within* (London: Penguin Press, 1985), p. 179. In addition, for discussion of this debate, see K. R. Bombwall, "Sikh Identity and Federal Polity: A Critique of Akali Position," in Gopal Singh, ed., *Punjab Today*, pp. 156–63. Bombwall refers to the Anandpur Sahib resolution and writes that "any notion of 'preeminence' or 'paramountcy' of a particular social group is incompatible with the postulates of a secular and liberal democratic state which permits 'positive discrimination' only in favor of scheduled castes, including Sikh scheduled castes . . . in other . . . weaker sections. Happily Sikhs as such are neither backward nor weak." p. 160.

8. Akbar, *The Seige Within,* p. 179.

9. Quoted from the text of the October 16–17, 1973, resolution published in Pramod Kumar, et al. *Punjab Crisis: Context and Trends* (Chandigarh: Center for Research in Rural and Industrial Development, 1984), pp. 128–37.

10. Akbar, *The Siege Within*, p. 181.

11. The economic and political impact of the green revolution has been a subject of great controversy. According to one view, the introduction of new technology made the rich richer and the poor in Punjab poorer. See Pranab Bardhan, "Green Revolution and Agricultural Labour," *Economic and Political Weekly*, July 1970, special number. Later, in a note in *Economic and Political Weekly* (May 26, 1973) he had modified his early calculations about the severity of inequality caused by the green revolution. Francine Frankel, *India's Green Revolution* (Princeton: Princeton University Press, 1971), has also espoused a similar view though the focus there is on the political impact. She warns that the growing polarization of income and wealth caused by its concentration in the hands of prosperous farmers would lead to class tensions. For a more recent discussion on these views see Manohar Singh Gill, "The Development of Punjab Agriculture, 1977–1980," *Asian Survey* 23, no. 7 (July 1983); G. S. Bhalla and Y. K. Alagh, "Green Revolution and Small Peasants: A Study of Income Distribution in Punjab Agriculture," *Economic and Political Weekly* 7 (May 1982). A contrary view is offered by Lloyd and Susanne Rudolph, *In Pursuit of Lakshmi: The Political Economy of the Indian State* (Chicago, London: Universtiy of Chicago Press, 1986). They contend that economic benefits did trickle down to what they identify as the "bullock capitalists." These were neither Kulaks nor middle peasants but a strata below them that lived on the margins of the commercial and capitalist agricultural economy. Scholars, however, are agreed that the green revolution intensified political competition and strengthened ethnic and communal identities in Punjab. Based on exhaustive surveys and statistical evaluation of data correlating economic distribution with distribution of electoral votes among communal and secular parties, the Center for Research and Rural Development in Chandigarh concludes in *Punjab Crisis: Context and Trends*, pp. 49–72, that the rich Jat peasants prospered, built forward linkages, and branched out into agricultural trade as the green revolution matured, but they were thwarted in expanding these linkages further into industry and trade. This was because these sectors were dominated

by Hindu traders in Punjab. The lack of big industry in Punjab led to unemployment among educated youths, who in desperation turned to communal advocacy.

12. The coalitions were possible because the social bases of the Akali Dal and the Jan Sangh were distinct: the Akalis depended on support from some Sikh Jat peasants and traders while the Jan Sangh counted on Hindu and some Sikh traders, merchants, and urban professionals. Their separate communal agendas could not be reconciled even if they were united in opposition to the Congress. For a succinct discussion of these trends see *Punjab Crisis: Context and Trends*, pp. 63–72. Also see P. S. Varma, " Akali Dal," in Gopal Singh, ed., *Punjab Today*, pp. 270–79.

13. Since the reorganization of 1966, the Akalis had emerged as the main opposition to the Congress(I) in the now smaller Punjab. Formation of the Akali–Jan Sangh coalition governments between 1967 and 1972, though brief and tenuous, had created an alternative basis for legislative power. After 1967, control over state legislatures had become a prerequisite for stable power at the center. This further intensified the rivalry between the Akalis and the Congress(I) in Punjab. It was to be expected that the Akalis, who were (for economic reasons) the rising force in Punjab, would find themselves pitted against a Congress(I) made more nervous becasue of its declining strength in the country at large. Each had to, by the logic of national and local developments, compete with the other for votes and legislative majorities in Punjab. For an excellent analysis of the Akali Dal/ Congress(I) rivalry see A. S. Narang, *Punjab Politics in National Perspective: A Study of Democracy, Development, and Distortion*, 2d ed. (New Delhi: Gitanjali, 1986), chs 2, 3, 4,

14. In the 1977 general elections the Akali Dal had polled a higher percentage of votes than the Congress(I) and won nine Lok Sabha seats. However, they failed in the legislative Assembly elections, garnering only 17 seats against the Akali Dal, which, in alliance with the ruling Janata party and the Communist Party of India (Marxist), won 58 seats.

15. Giani Zail Singh (1972–77) marched from Anandpur Sahib to Damdama Sahib and named all the roads on the way after the gurus of the Sikh religion as well as Hindu saints. This seemingly evenhanded gesture was misleading, however, because in effect it heightened the already religiously charged atmosphere in Punjab.

16. The green revolution had thrown up a newly empowered stratum of peasant proprietors across North India, from Haryana to Bihar. See Vinay Kumar Malhotra, "Haryana: Territorial and River Water Claims," in Gopal Singh, ed. *Punjab Today*, pp. 254–380. The rise of the peasant proprietors was particularly evident in the rise of a new party, Bharatiya Lok Dal, led by Choudhari Charan Singh of Haryana. Common economic interests, however, had not resulted in forging a common political strategy. Sikh Jats in Punjab continued to support Akali Dal and confine their efforts mostly to promote the "Sikh" cause. The Bharatiya Lok Dal, which had unified the Hindu Jats in Haryana, West Uttar Pradesh, and north Rajasthan, had on the other hand given an increasingly "Hindu" tone to their political platform.

These developments presented the Congress(I) at the center with two challenges. First, the growing appeal of Akali Dal in Punjab and the Bharatiya Lok Dal in the Hindi belt states meant weakening control over areas critical to the continued dominance of the central state. The road to New Delhi wound its way through command of legislative majorities in the Hindi belt states. The six states included in the Hindi heartland have provided India with six prime ministers since Independence. These states accounted for nearly 42 percent of Lok Sabha seats. Rudolph and Rudolph, *In Pursuit of Lakshmi*, p. 180. Second, weakening control over these areas meant greater difficulties in harmonizing interstate conflicts—i.e., over redistribution of river waters or implementation of the Chandigarh award if these states passed out of Congress's hands.

There is another way in which Punjab politics became increasingly intertwined with developments elsewhere. The Jan Sangh and later the BJP (Bharatiya Janata Party), which constitutes the natural habitat of the militant Hindu nationalists, had successfully expanded their political appeal and organizational base all over North India. The Congress and the central state were vulnerable to charges by the Jan Sangh of granting special dispensation to the non-Hindu, non-Hindi-speaking minorities in Punjab. Ethnic peace could easily be disturbed by the Akalis as well as the pro-Jan Sangh elements in northern states of India.

17. Chand Joshi, *Bhindranwale, Myth and Reality* (New Delhi: Vikas, 1984); also see various articles by Joyce Pettigrew, in which she has interviewed Bhindranwale. Kuldip Nayar also relates his conversations with Bhindranwale in *The Tragedy of Punjab: Operation Bluestar and After* (New Delhi: Vision Books, 1984). These sources relate Bhindranwale's ideology with Akali politics and to the course of events (between 1977–1984) in Punjab.

18. For post-1978 politics in Punjab leading inexorably to the Operation Blue Star in 1984, see Satish Jacob and Mark Tully, *Amritsar: Mrs. Gandhi's Last Battle* (Calcutta: Rupa, 1985); Akbar, *The Siege Within*, pp. 173–201; Nayar and Singh, *Tragedy of Punjab*, pp. 30–114.

19. It is now well established that the Congress party aided and abetted Bhindranwale throughout these years and ignored his ruthless attacks on the Nirankaris. The Congress publicity machine projected Bhindranwale as the hero. On April 13, 1978, just a week before the attack on the Nirankaris, Sanjay Gandhi and Zail Singh helped Bhindranwale to form a new party, the Dal Khalsa, in which minor activists with known pro-Khalistani credentials were involved.

20. According to Satish Jacob and Mark Tully, Bhindranwale was arrested and charged with conspiracy to murder Jagat Nrain, but Zail Singh, who was home minister at that time, ordered his release. They report that Bhindranwale told them that in releasing him from the warrant, "the government has done more for me in one week than I could have achieved in year." Zail Singh thought Bhindranwale would be useful in bringing about the downfall of Punjab's then chief minister and his arch rival, Darbara Singh. See *Amritsar: Mrs. Gandhi's Last Battle*, pp. 70–71.

21. Jacob and Tully, *Amritsar: Mrs. Gandhi's Last Battle*, p. 82.

22. Quoted from my conversation with a militant Sikh student at Khalsa college in Amritsar, December 1986.

23. Quoted in Nayar and Singh, *Tragedy of Punjab*, p. 74.

24. I had long discussions with officials of the Bajrang Brigade at their office in the Durgyana Mandir in Amritsar in the summer of 1987. At this time there were 800 women and children taking shelter in the temple from militant activities in the villages around Amritsar. The Bajrang Brigade officials talked at length about building links with the Shiv Sena and other Hindu militant organizations in India. But in 1986 it was clearly a weak force with no grassroots organization or political mission beyond publicizing the suffering of the Hindus at the hands of Sikh "terrorists" in Punjab.

25. Apart from the Virat Hindu Sammelan (VHS) and Vishva Hindu Parishad (VHP), which are all-Indian organizations, in Punjab several Hindu organizations were established to counter Sikh militancy. For instance, Punjab Hindu Sangathan was born soon after the murder of Lala Jagat Nrain in September 1980; Hindu Suraksha Samiti, headed by Pawan Kumar Sharma, a youth Congress(I) activist from Patiala, was created in September 1982; the Hindu

Shiva Sena was established in Ludhiana around the same time. These were devoted to a right-revivalist agenda. Seven such Hindu organizations merged in May 1984 to form a Rashtriya Hindu Suraksha Sena (RHSS). The RHSS took the highly symbolic saffron flag and trident as its insignia.

On the Sikh side, the important militant organizations were: the Dal Khalsa committed to Khalistan; Babbar Khalsa, an offshoot of Akhand Kirtani Jatha, led by Sukhdev Singh; the Akhand Kirtani Jatha led by Bibi Amarjit Kaur, who had a falling out with Bhindranwale; Deshmesh Regiment, based in Anandpur Sahib and led by Sardool Singh, a mysterious figure of unknown background. There were several other cells and organizations with a hard-core group and small following. The main objective of these militant bodies was to dislocate the moderate Sikh leaders; pressure the central government through acts of terror; silence the voice of dissent (Nirankaris, Namdharis), undercut the police and army in Punjab, and evict the Hindus from Punjab.

26. Longowal declared a noncooperation program from June 3, 1984, with a view to stop the movement of food grains from Punjab. In launching demonstrations and marches he was trying to keep the Sikh movement for autonomy within the limits of constitutionally approved protests.

27. For details of the anti-Sikh riots in Delhi, see Uma Chakravarti and Nandita Haksar, *The Delhi Riots: Three Days in the Life of a Nation* (New Delhi: Lancers, 1987).

28. The text of the Accord is published in Gopal Singh, ed. *Punjab Today*, pp. 383–87. For comments and analysis on this, see D. P. Chaudhari," Punjab Accord and Haryana," pp. 343–54; Gobinder Singh, "Punjab Accord and Punjab Problem," pp. 327–42, in the same publication.

29. Bhajan Lal was initially supportive of the accord but soon he began to protest because he feared that control was passing into the hands of the Lok Dal (a rival political force in Haryana and the Hindi belt states in north India) regarding the river water and the Chandigarh issue. He therefore made an about-face and criticized Rajiv Gandhi at the Congress Centenary celebrations in December 1985 (where Rajiv had attacked the party machine) and stated that the canal water issue was a life-and-death issue for Haryana.

30. *Indian Express*, May 12, 1987

31. "Policy For Punjab," *The Statesman*, June 11, 1987

32. Information that has come to light only recently suggests that a step up in violence by the Pakistan-based militants was already in the works. In 1985, Pakistan's Inter Service Intelligence (ISI) had decided to use some of the extensive facilities created for training Afghan Mujahideen to train Sikh militants. See "Task Force on Terrorism and Unconventional Warfare," House Republican Research Committee: *The New Islamist International*, February 1, 1993, Washington D.C.

33. My discussions with Sushil Muni at his Jain Ashram in New Jersey, Summer 1989. Sushil Muni confirmed the details of Rajiv's strategy, the role of Darshan Singh Ragi, and the purpose of releasing Bhindranwale's nephew from jail. This stratagem failed because, first, the militants were fragmented and therefore undercut each other; second, the center bargained that it would meet demands of the militants (i.e., release of Sikhs falsely accused of terrorist activities, river waters, punishment of those involved in the Delhi riots) provided they negotiated with the center and ceased terrorist activities. Rode's credibility was however compromised the moment he was suspected of negotiating on behalf of the Rajiv government.

34. Writings on the Kashmir problem consulted for this section are: Ashutosh Varshney, "India, Pakistan, and Kashmir: Antinomies of Nationalism," *Asian Survey* 31 (November

1991): 997–1019; Robert Wirsing, *India, Pakistan and the Kashmir Dispute: On Regional Conflict and Its Resolution* (New York: St. Martin's Press, 1994); Raju Thomas, *Perspectives on Kashmir: The Roots of Conflict in South Asia* (Boulder: Westview Press, 1992); Rajesh Kadian, *The Kashmir Tangle: Issues and Options* (New Delhi: Vision Books, 1992); Jagmohan, *My Frozen Turbulence* (New Delhi : Allied, 1991); Sumit Ganguly, "Avoiding War in Kashmir," *Foreign Affairs* 69 (Winter 1990–91): 57–73. On the question of regional imbalances between Jammu and the Kashmir valley see Balraj Puri, *Simmering Volcano, A Study of Jammu's Relations with Kashmir* (New Delhi: Sterling, 1983); For a strategic view see Jasjit Singh, *India and Pakistan: crisis of relationship* (New Delhi: Lancer in Association with Institute for defense Studies and Analyses , 1990); Also see Raju Thomas, South Asian Security in the 1990s, The Prospects of War and Peace in South Asia Amidst Changes in the global and Regional Strategic Environments, *Adelphi Papers*, no. 278 (London: the International Institute for Strategic Studies, 1993).

35. On June 15, 1984, Mohammed Shafi, information minister of Kashmir, told a press conference that Sikh terrorists had never received training in "fortification and use of arms" and that Home Minister P. C. Sethi had himself confirmed on June 16, 1983, that no such arms training had been given in the Gurmat camps held in the state.

36. The Congress(I) was not reconciled, however, to losing legislative majority in Kashmir to the National Conference in the 1983 elections. In January 1984, the Kashmir Congress(I) launched a massive campaign to unseat the Farooq Abdullah government. This led to a three-way struggle for power in the Vale: between the Congress(I), the National Conference, and a whole phalanx of Muslim parties such as the Jama'at-e-Islami and the more moderate Awami Action Committee.

37. My interview with Professor Ralph Buultjens, New York, January 1994

38. My conversations with the late Girilal Jain (former editor of the *Times of India*), August 1988, in New Delhi, who made pointed references to Farooq's playboy tendencies, such as association with actresses and rich socialites.

39. "Kashmir Coalition: Will It Work?" *India Today*, November 30, 1986.

40. *The New Islamist International*, February 1, 1993, pp. 38–42.

7. COLLAPSING FRONTIERS: INDO–LANKA RELATIONS SINCE THE 1980S

1. On India–Lanka relations, the following sources were consulted. For Tamil–Sinhala conflict: K. M. de Silva, *A History of Sri Lanka* (London: Christopher Hurst, 1981); "Separatism in Sri Lanka: The 'Traditional Homelands' of the Tamils," in Premdas, Samarsinghe, and Anderson, eds., *Secessionist Movements in Comparative Perspective* (London: Pinter, 1990), covers the historical background for the civil war in the 1980s; Jonathan Spencer, ed., *Sri Lanka: History and the Roots of Conflict* (London: Routledge, 1990) is an excellent volume on cultural and sociopolitical dimensions of Sri Lanka's integration problem; A. J. Wilson, *Politics in Sri Lanka, 1947–1979* (London: Macmillan, 1979); and his *The Break-Up of Sri Lanka: The Sinhalese-Tamil Conflict* (London: Christopher Hurst, 1988); also see James Manor, ed., *Sri Lanka in Crisis and Change* (London: Croom Helm, 1984), for ethnic and national questions in Indo–Lanka relations. Urmila Phadnis, *Ethnicity and Nation-Building in South Asia* (New Delhi: Sage, 1989), provides the regional framework of ethnopolitics in South Asia. R. Coomarswamy, "Myths Without Conscience: Tamil and Sinhala Nationalist Writings in the 1980s," in Abeysekera and Gunasinghe, eds., *Facets of Ethnicity in Sri Lanka*

(Colombo: Social Scientists Association, 1987); and Richard Gombrich and Gananath Obeysekere, *Buddhism Transformed: Religious Change in Sri Lanka* (Princeton: Princeton University Press, 1990), provide insight into the politics of culture, religion, and ethnicity that divides Sri Lanka. S. D. Muni, *Pangs of Proximity* (New Delhi: Sage, 1993); Sumanta Bose, *States, Nations, and Sovereignty: Sri Lanka, India, and the Tamil Movement* (New Delhi: Sage, 1994), and to a lesser extent, Ravi Kant Dubey, *Indo–Lanka Relations:With Special Reference to the Tamil Problem* (New Delhi: Deep and Deep, 1993), provide scholarly overviews of the strategic issues and implications of Tamil ethnic overlap. In addition, P. S. Suryanarayana, *The Peace Trap: An Indo–Lanka Political Crisis* (New Delhi: Affiliated East-West Press, 1988); Mohan Ram, *Sri Lanka:The Fractured Island* (New Delhi: Penguin Books, 1989), provide a journalistic take on events. For accounts of Sri Lanka Tamil militant organizations and ideology, see M. R. Narayan Swamy, *Tigers of Lanka* (New Delhi: Konarak, 1994); Rohana Gunaratna, *Indian Intervention in Sri Lanka:The Role of Indian Intelligence Agencies* (Colombo: South Asian Network on Conflict Research, 1993), chs. 3 and 5.

In addition, my own interviews and discussions with Indian policy makers; journalists covering the events between 1983–1990; Prime Ministers Rajiv Gandhi and V. P. Singh; Presidents Premadasa and Jayewardene; Lanka's former Prime Minister Ranil Wikramasinghe; and militant leaders of the LTTE, EROS, and PLOTE provided invaluable insights about perceptions and motives of actors in the Indo-Lanka relations.

2. Imtiaz Ahmed, "Regional Hegemony in South Asia: The Indian State and Sri-Lankan Tamil's War of Liberation," in Emajuddin Ahmed and Abul Kalam, eds., *Bangladesh, South Asia, and the World* (Dhaka: Academic Press, 1992), pp. 76–101; Iftekhruzzaman, "The India Doctrine: Relevance For Bangladesh," in M. G. Kabir and Shaukat Hassan, eds., *Issues and Challenges Facing Bangladesh Foreign Policy* (Dhaka: Bangladesh Society for International Studies, 1989), pp. 18–43.

3. K. M. Pannikar, who favored making India a unitary instead of a federal state and building an iron ring around it, also argued for Sri Lanka and Burma to be regarded as part of India's strategic planning. See his *India and the Indian Ocean* (London: George Allen and Unwin, 1945). Ever since the appearance of this book, Pannikar has been repeatedly quoted to prove India's hegemonic designs on Sri Lanka. These writings have failed to mention that Nehru ignored Pannikar's suggestions. Nehru opted for a federal polity and disregarded naval defense. India's naval defense is beyond the scope of this book. It is enough to note here that since the 1970s, the Indian Ocean has acquired new importance for India's strategic planners. India wants to eventually acquire a blue water navy. Acquisition of capabilities is not however a proof of hegemonic designs. These have to be mediated by perceptions and objectives of international policy. Although K. Subrahmanyam and Jasjit Singh, both highly influential heads of the Indian Institute for Defense Analysis in New Delhi, advocated a strong military, their views on Sri Lanka echo the objectives of relational control spelled out in this chapter. The preceding conclusion is based on my interviews in December 1989 and 1993.

4. S. U. Kodikara, *Indo-Ceylon Relations Since Independence* (Colombo: Ceylon Institute of World Affairs, 1965), pp. 35–59.

5. For details of this period see H. S. S. Nissanka, *Foreign Policy of Sri Lanka Under Bandaranaikes* (New Delhi: Vikas, 1984).

6. If Sri Lanka had on its own "followed a policy of self-restraint and reassurance toward India, then she would not have felt the need to extract foreign policy concessions . . . by exchanging letters to that effect." The reference here is to the letters on strategic questions

attached to the Indo–Lanka accord of 1987. See Shelton Kodikara, ed., *South Asian Strategic Issues: Sri Lankan Perspective* (New Delhi: Sage, 1989), p. 102,

7. Although India extended her territorial waters boundary to 12 miles in 1967 (as did Sri Lanka), Indira Gandhi consented to Colombo's claim to the island of Katchcha Thivu, which otherwise falls within India's territorial waters. This 1974 Indo–Lanka agreement resolved conflicts of overlap of sovereign jurisdictions. This shows that as long as Sri Lanka's position was consistent with New Delhi's relational control, the Indian leaders were willing to make concessions in Lanka's favor.

8. S. D. Muni gives details of Western response to the overtures by President Jayewardene. *Pangs of Proximity*, pp. 51–58.

9. The 1983 ethnic eruption can be traced back to years of resentment and mutual animosities building up in Sri Lanka. These were a result of the growing force of Sinhala Buddhist and Tamil chauvinistic nationalism. The violent potential of the Sinhala nationalism became apparent during the election of S. W. R. D. Bandaranaike in 1956 and his subsequent assassination by a Buddhist fanatic. It was reflected in the passage of "Sinhala only" legislation of 1956 that blocked the Tamils from jobs and career opportunities and in extending Buddhism a constitutional status in 1972. When Lanka's two major political parties, the UNP and the SLFP, began to form governments without the parliamentary support or consultations with the Tamil political parties, the latter were increasingly marginalized. The Tamil community turned inward and began to redefine its political and ethnic identity in equally exclusionary terms. Once the process of social alienation and ethnic polarization began, normal channels of politics became inadequate to express the anger and resentment felt on both sides. Each community, the Sinhalas and the Tamils, then resorted to violence, which led to the tragic events of the 1983.

10. Shelton Kodikara, "Internationalization of Sri Lanka's Ethnic Conflict: The Tamil Nadu factor," in K. M. de Silva and R. J. May, eds. (New York: St. Martin's Press, 1991), pp. 107–15. Also see Suryanarayana, *The Peace Trap*, pp. 56–65.

11. Sinha Ratnatunga, *Politics of Terrorism: The Sri Lankan Experience* (Canberra: International Fellowship for Social and Economic Development, 1988), p. 164

12. Jayewardene visited Pakistan in March–April 1985 for a week.

13. My interview with former Foreign Secretary S. K. Singh, New Delhi, December 1992.

14. *The Times of India*, March 9, 1984.

15. Based on several conversations during 1993–94, with Stanley Kalpage, the Sri Lanka ambassador to the United Nations, and with J. N. Dixit, the Indian high commissioner to Colombo until 1989. Several Indian scholars have made much of this early Lankan quest for military assistance.

16. The Sri Lankan government had made available 1,000 acres of land next to the Katunayake airport for the American transmission facility. The proposed facility was to have had six transmitters, two of 250 KW each and four of 500 KW each.

17. Jasjit Singh, "The US Transmitters in Sri Lanka," *The Times of India*, March 6, 1985; also see James Manor and Gerald Segal, "Causes of Conflict: Sri Lankan and Indian Ocean Strategy," *Asian Survey* 15, no. 12, December 1985.

18. The Reagan administration had improved relations with India in 1982. Mrs. Gandhi's visit to the United States in 1982 was a success and the United States had opened up economic and technological, trade, and even military supplies to India, although differences over arms to Pakistan remained. Mrs. Gandhi was trying also to normalize relations with China although a better understanding on the border dispute was several years away.

19. My conversations with Hardip Puri, the desk officer in charge of the Lankan situation in the Ministry of External Affairs, July/August 1988, New Delhi.

20. The DK split and became the DMK; there were further splits that produced the AIDMK and the AIADMK.

21. It is necessary to consider the pressures of electoral competition on the DMK (led by Karunanidhi) and the AIADMK (led by M. G. Ramachandran). MGR was chief minister throughout Rajiv Gandhi's tenure as prime minister and was closely associated with various decisions regarding Sri Lanka, i.e., the December 19 proposals, the IPKF operations. Unencumbered by the responsibilities of office, the DMK on the other hand was able to take a more radical and pro-Eelam stance. This championing of the Tamil cause permitted the DMK to expand its public support and to cast doubts on the AIADMK's intentions by stressing MGR's close collaboration with New Delhi.

22. My interview with Karunanidhi, the DMK leader in Tamil Nadu, at his residence in Madras, summer 1986. Karunanidhi's responses to questions were translated for me by R. Raghavan, an active member of the Congress party in Madras.

23. *Lok Sabha Debates*, 38, 1983, col. 418; Also see the report of Mrs. Gandhi's statement in *The Times of India*, August 13, 1983.

24. In an interview in Madras during summer 1988, Balakumar, the leader of EROS, told me that though Mrs. Gandhi and President Jayewardene were suspicious of each other, their personal differences were "not the reason why India was trying to destabilize Sri Lanka." The militant leaders took a more objective view of the India–Lanka relations. In contrast to the Indian press views at that time, they argued that New Delhi supported them not because Mrs. Gandhi disliked Jayewardene but because of India's larger strategic interests. Balakumar gave three reasons why India had extended support to the militants: the spillover effect of Tamil nationalism; India's desire to prevent Sri Lanka from making alliances with countries unfriendly to India; and perhaps most importantly, the containment of ethnic conflict within the region. According to several other militant leaders that I interviewed between 1986 and 1988, Indira Gandhi had maintained firm control over their activities in Madras. This was done by making them dependent on Indian arms and threatening to withhold them when the Tamil militants proved recalcitrant. A. Selvan of the TELO told me during a conversation in 1986 that Sri Lankan militants had over 30 bases in India.

25. Between 1983 and 1984 both President Jayewardene and Prime Minister Premadasa had talked about India's contemplating a military intervention. See *Daily News* (Colombo), March 8, 1984; *Sun* (Colombo) May 26, 1984. Amrithalingam, the president of TULF (Tamil United Liberation Front) had speculated that India might consider a military option to settle the violence in Sri Lanka. For details see A. J. Wilson, *The Breakup of Sri Lanka: The Sinhalese-Tamil Conflict* (London: C. Hurst, 1988), p. 203.

26. For details on Indian diplomatic mediation, see Gurbachan Singh, "The Ethnic Problem in Sri Lanka and the Indian attempt at Mediation,' in Satish Kumar, ed., *Yearbook on India's Foreign Policy 1985* (New Delhi: Sage, 1987); P. S. Ghosh, *Cooperation and Conflict in South Asia* (New Delhi: Manohar, 1989), ch. 6.

27. No reliable information about the number of arms and training of cadres by India is available. There are educated guesses and conflicting estimates. My own information suggests that well into 1986, Indian efforts at supplying arms to Lankan militants remained haphazard and sporadic and that training was spotty. Many militant leaders ridiculed the Indian contribution. Balakumar told me that India taught them regular warfare while they taught them-

selves guerrilla warfare. According to PLOTE (A. Selvan) and EROS (Balakumar) leaders I talked to, India promised more than it delivered. They said about 1,200 or 2,000 cadres were trained until 1987. Rohana Gunaratna estimates a much more systematic and large training and supply operation than M. R. Narayan Swamy in their accounts of clandestine Indian support to the Tamil militants. Two points need to be noted. First, Indian willingness to support the militancy with safe sanctuaries and arms was aimed at precluding the guerrillas turning to other sources, i.e., other radical organization such as the PLO. Eros militants had contacted the PLO by early 1980. Second, it is important to note that Rajiv Gandhi turned the supplies on and off to correspond with his diplomacy. The militants therefore concluded that they had to develop alternative sources of funds and arms to insure the continuity of their operations. The Tamil Lankan expatriate community in the United States, England, and Canada was a crucial source of money for the militants. There is no doubt however that the main source of clandestine support was India.

28. According to Muni, the Sri Lankan argument that Indian support had precipitated the crisis of July 1983 is totally without foundation. Sri Lankan statements are based on assessments of U.S. intelligence analyst Tom Mark, who was known to be close to the Sri Lankan security establishment. Mark's analysis cannot be accepted as objective. A review of LTTE documents released later show that the RAW began to take a hand in the militant affairs only after September 1983. And at this stage, RAW was more interested in using the militants to gather information about movements of western naval activity in Trincomalee. Muni cites extensive corroborating evidence to support his contention. I was also told by Padmanabha and Keethiswaran, the two top leaders of EPRLF in 1986, that India had simply used the militant groups to its own end. They complained that the RAW became interested only when Jayewardene ignored Mrs. Gandhi's attempts to get Colombo to agree to the Annexure "C" proposals. These did not materialize until August 1983 and were rejected by both parties in September. Muni, *Pangs of Proximity*, p. 45.

29. The Annexure "C" envisaged far more autonomy for the Tamils than they had enjoyed before: greater devolution of power to the local bodies that would be controlled by the community, recognition of Tamil as a national language, proportional representation of ethnic minorities in the armed forces and police, and a national policy of land settlement that would maintain a demographic balance in ethnic terms.

30. At this time, Mrs. Gandhi seemed to favor PLOTE over other groups. The PLOTE therefore received a larger amount of training, weapons, and funds from Indian intelligence agencies. According to Selvan, the PLOTE leader in 1988, G. Parthasarathy had promised the group 700 Mausar rifles, 500 SMGs, 100,000 rounds of 7.92 rifle ammunition, and the same amount of 9 mm ammunition. Apparently these were never delivered. It was common knowledge, however, among the militant circles in Madras that Shekhar Master, an Indian army officer who had served in the Bangladesh war had trained the PLOTE cadres. My interview with Raja (obviously a code name), a PLOTE official in Madras, Summer 1989.

31. See *India Today,* July 15, 1985: 56. It points out that given the financial state of Sri Lanka, and the fact that its budget deficit was made up by foreign financing, declaration of a cease-fire was its only hope of convincing skeptical donors of continued aid.

32. *India Today*, July 15, 1985: 57.

33. As a punishment, India arrested thirty-eight Lankans in Tamil Nadu for smuggling 40 Kgs. of gold biscuits obviously meant to finance the struggle for Eelam. In the past, India had turned a blind eye to such clandestine operations. *India Today*, July 15, 1985: 57.

34. *The Times of India*, July 16, 1985.

35. Udayashankar, "Thimpu Talks on Lanka's Ethnic Problem: Round II," *Strategic Analysis*, 9, no. 8 (November 1985), p. 757.

36. Quoted in Mervyn de Silva, "Understanding the Slogans and Signs from Madras," *Lanka Guardian* 8, no. 9, September 1, 1985, p. 4.

37. "I agreed with him" says Mohandas, "the exercise had to be a Top Secret one and I would not be in a position to inform even MGR as to when and how I proposed to strike. . . . On 4th November, I informed the DGP (L&O) and the IGP (L&O) about the Chief Minister's instructions, with a request to keep it top secret. I particularly emphasized that we were against an enemy who were efficiently trained, in possession of sophisticated armaments, and ruthlessly motivated. I gave them a list of about 30 militant camps situated in the Madras city and 10 districts." K. Mohandas, *MGR: The Man and The Myth* (Bangalore: Panthers, 1992).

38. My interviews with Karunanidhi, Madras, July 1986. I met with Eros Leaders Balakumar, Selvan of PLOTE, Padmanabha and Keethiswaran of the EPRLF, in subsequent visits to Madras, summer 1986, 1987. All had offices in the suburbs of Madras. Karunanidhi's statements were translated for me by R. Raghavan.

39. Marguerite Johnson, "Island at War," *Lanka Guardian*, July 1986.

40. The *Lanka Guardian* of May 1, 1985, cited the interview Balasingham gave to the *Financial Times* in London.

41. My discussions with EPRLF and PLOTE leaders in 1986, with Lankan Tamil leaders and DMK leader Karunanidhi, revealed that Mrs. Gandhi had favored Sri Sabharatnam over other militant's leaders mainly because some of the most well-known and reasonable Tamil Lankan leaders had belonged to his group. In any case, TELO was the biggest beneficiary of India's intelligence agency's largess during 1983 and 1986.

42. The December 19 proposals, a second framework for negotiations, had been produced after considerable homework by the Indian diplomats, and use of the carrot-and-stick policy by the Indian Foreign Office. The Tamil Nadu chief minister had been involved every step of the way in this process. In fact, during the SAARC meeting at Bangalore in the fall of 1986, when Rajiv and Jayewardene had met to discuss the situation, MGR had been at hand. It was he who had persuaded Prabhakaran to fly to Bangalore and be available for consultations. When Prabhakaran had demurred, the Tamil Nadu government had immediately arrested all the Sri Lankan leaders and confiscated their communication and other facilities in Madras. MGR had played a critical role in conveying to the militants the line of policy emerging in New Delhi and the dire consequences that would follow should they jeopardize New Delhi's mediatory efforts. Similarly, he had been an important source of information for Natwar Singh and J. N. Dixit, latter the Indian high commissioner in Sri Lanka, about what was and was not acceptable to the LTTE.

43. Interview with Dinesh Singh, New Delhi, December 1988, an important member of the Rajiv cabinet and subsequently India's foreign minister in the Rao cabinet.

44. Nearly two hundred people were killed when a bomb exploded and there were other killings and bomb blasts on April 17 and 18. The Sri Lankan security forces were alleged to have killed 300 or more Tamil civilians and taken 6,000 young Tamilians in custody.

45. On May 26, 1987, the Sri Lankan armed forces launched "Operation Liberation," a full-scale assault by 8,000 men on the Vadamarachchi sector of Jaffna. India's High Commissioner Dixit met with President Jayewardene and conveyed to him the apprehension felt in New Delhi. The gist of the message, written on back of an envelope, focused on the

point that the armed offensive had altered the entire basis of Indo–Lanka understanding and that India would not accept such wholesale violence against the Tamils and that the Sri Lankan government should not do anything to force India to review its policies. This was an unmistakable warning by new Delhi. Based on my conversation with J.R. Jayewardene, Colombo, June 1988.

46. Prabhakaran also worried that his field commanders in Sri Lanka had gained an upper hand because of his prolonged absence from Jaffna. There were rumors that Kittu, his right-hand man had bypassed him and opened a line of communication with the Jayewardene government. This was told me by Padmanabhan, leader of EPRLF, during our discussions in Madras, July 1988.

47. President Jayewardene was however under tremendous pressure from the opposition parties and Sinhala chauvinists. These had staged many violent protests against his government and its inability to subdue the "terrorists." These events form the backdrop against which we can better understand Sri Lanka's reneging on the December 19 agreement.

48. The DMK had donated Rs. 100,000 from its party funds, while the Karnataka government sanctioned Rs. 5,000,000 toward the Tamil relief fund. *Times of India*, June 4, 1987.

49. Based on interview with President Jayewardene, Summer 1988. For additional corroboration see Muni, *Pangs of Proximity*, p. 101.

50. *The Island*, June 3, 1987.

51. See *Overseas Hindustan Times*, June 13, 1987.

52. Ibid., June 20, 1987.

53. For response from other countries to Jayewardene's requests, see Bertram Bastiampillai, "Ethnic Conflict in South Asia and Interstate Relations Especially in Relations to Sri Lanka," Kodikara, ed., *South Asian Strategic Issues*, p. 103.

54. My conversations with President Jayewardene in Colombo, June 1988. At the time of signing the pact, Jayewardene was facing an armed insurgency in the south. The JVP had escalated the acts of violence in the hope of toppling the Jayewardene government in Colombo. JVP chafed against the impotency of Sri Lankan security forces, saw the Tamils as outsiders, as a surrogate force of India, and Jayewardene as the wily politician unable and unwilling, for his own personal gains, to crush the separatist Tamils. In the JVP's political scenario, Jayewardene needed India to guarantee his continuation in power not only against the Tamils but also against the Sinhala people. In their view, the Pact had ensured that India and its armed forces would have a stake in the continuation of JRJ's political survival. In my interview with the president, Jayewardene rejected the JVP's interpretation of his personal motives but affirmed that at that point the pact was the only way to save Sri Lanka from chaos and disintegration.

55. Quoted in Rohana Gunaratna, *Indian Intervention in Sri Lanka* (Colombo: South Asian Network on Conflict Research, 1993), pp. 207–9.

56. The U.S. ambassador in Sri Lanka remarked to Pran Chopra that he hoped India would accept a great part of the responsibility, not so much financial as politico-administrative, for the reconstruction of Sri Lanka, once the civil strife had ended. See Chopra's articles "Fiasco in Palk Straits: Good Offices Cripples," *Indian Express*, June 17, 18, 1987

57. *Sunday Times*, New Delhi, February 11, 1990.

58. According to several reports, LTTE had surrendered only about 15 percent of its arms. See *India Today*, October 15, 1987, p. 49.

59. Jayewardene had stated in November 1987 that the merger would take place only after surrender of all arms, and resettlement of all those displaced by the violence. See *India Today*, November 15, 1987.

60. *Sunday Times* (Colombo), July 17, 1988.

61. In April 1988, J. N. Dixit and Natwar Singh, state minister for External Affairs, confirmed that India had promised Prabhakaran Rs. 5 million per month in order to help him transform the LTTE from a military to a peaceful democratic organization. Incidentally, only one payment was made because by the end of September 1987, New Delhi realized that Prabhakaran had no intention of keeping to the terms of the accord or to his September 28, 1987, agreement with Dixit. *The Hindu*, April 26, 1988; *India Today*, April 30, 1988; *The Sunday Observer*, April 18, 1988.

62. Sardeshpande, *Assignment Jaffna* (New Delhi: Lancers, 1992).

63. Throughout April 1988 to July 1988 the IPKF launched several offensives against the LTTE. The government of India ordered arrests of 72 LTTE cadres in Madurai and another 70 in Madras. This was in preparation for the scheduled elections in the newly merged provinces of Jaffna and Eastern in Sri Lanka. Despite these punishing actions the LTTE maintained its close links and support network in Madras.

64. Immediately upon assuming office, Premadasa asked India to withdraw the IPKF. Bradman Weerakoon, Premadasa's political biographer writes, "What irked Premadasa most was the realization that upwards of one-third of his country and two-thirds of its coastline were under the control of a foreign power, that is India." Bradman Weerakoon, *Premadasa of Sri Lanka: A Political Biography* (New Delhi: Vikas, 1992).

65. *The Hindu*, September 14, 1991.

66. Quoted from Gunaratna, *Indian Intervention in Sri Lanka*, pp. 294–95.

67. *India Today*, July 15, 1989, p. 29.

68. In support they pointed to the fact that the LTTE was provided with guns, vehicles, and ammunition by the Sri Lankan military.

69. In an interview in the summer of 1988, Premadasa told me that he disagreed with Jayewardene's solution to the problem. Even in 1988, well before elections catapulted him into the office of president, Premadasa thought India should be asked to leave; northern Jaffna could be written off to the Tigers; and although Lanka would not concede legal sovereignty to them, its security forces would concentrate on holding the situation in the Eastern province. Even if the conflict were to be prolonged, Premadasa believed that it would be on Colombo's own terms and free of India and Indian Tamils's foreign and ethnic agenda.

70. John Burns reported in the *New York Times*, September 24, 1995, that the LTTE had again entrenched itself deeply into the criminal and political world in Tamil Nadu. He cites several jailbreaks by arrested LTTE cadres, which Burns says could not have happened without the connivance of local politicians and the police. These jailbreaks were part of a wider pattern of complicity involving the Tamil Nadu state government and the LTTE rebels.

71. The Tamil Nadu coast of Tanjavar (that is closest to Jaffna) had become a base for the militant's activities. There were reported incidents of Tamil Nadu fisherman on the payroll of the militants. The *Hindu* reported that on January 20, 1990, near the village of Ramnad, the police had found huge caches of weapons including 88 AK-47 Chinese assault rifles, 64 nine

MM pistols, 40 LMGs, hand grenades, and several thousand rounds of ammunition. The arsenal also included a rocket launcher.

72. "Tigers or Man Eaters" *The Hindu*, August 12, 1990.

8. COLLAPSING FRONTIERS: INDO–PAKISTAN RELATIONS SINCE THE 1980S

1. See chapter 6, note 34 for literature consulted in writing this chapter. For a variety of interpretations of the emerging international environment and the Indian response, see Stephen Cohen, *South Asia After the Cold War: International Perspectives* (Boulder: Westview Press, 1993); Dennis Austin, *Democracy and Violence in India and Sri Lanka* (New York: Council on Foreign Relations Press, 1995).

2. In an article in the *Times of India*, April 4, 1995, P. N. Dhar, senior member of the Indian delegation at the 1972 Simla talks and a close adviser to Mrs. Gandhi, disclosed that Pakistani Prime Minister Bhutto had agreed to make the "line of control" dividing the two Kashmirs the de facto international boundary between India and Pakistan. Bhutto had promised Indira Gandhi that he would personally see to it that this line became endowed with "characteristics of an international border." According to Dhar, the Simla agreement "provided not only a mechanism for the solution of the Kashmir problem, but it also envisaged the solution itself." This was to consist of steps to open up communications and facilitate trade, cultural exchange, tourism, and movement of people between the two countries, essentially giving everyone a chance to get used to the idea of a new Indo–Pakistani relationship. The Pakistan occupied Kashmir was to become legally a part of Pakistan. Bhutto's party was to set up branches in Pakistan-occupied Kashmir in order to retain control while it was being thus absorbed. Even the public relations aspect of the process was carefully worked out . According to Dhar, "India would make proforma protests in a low key" but these were obviously for public consumption. The entire exercise was aimed at reconciling public opinion in both countries to the new border and to the final resolution of Kashmir's division. Dhar reports that Mrs. Gandhi asked Bhutto (after having clearly reiterated all the points of the agreement) "Is this the understanding on which we will proceed?" Bhutto replied, "Absolutely, Aap mujh par bharosa keejiye [You can trust me in this regard]." Dhar's April 1995 disclosure provoked a number of comments in the press. The timing of the disclosure is also noteworthy. In April 1995 Benazir Bhutto was about to visit with President Clinton and bring up the Kashmir and arms issues. Dhar was in a sense reminding her of the agreement her father had made to which she, as his young assistant, was a witness. Pakistani officials have denied any such understanding and those who were a part of the delegation at the time have remained silent. The other reason for the disclosure had to do with the growing pressure on India, particularly from the United States, to permit third-party mediation in Kashmir, a possibility foreclosed by the Simla agreement. A senior Clinton administration official, Robin Raphel, had told reporters in November 1993 that "we do not recognize the (1947) Instrument of Accession as meaning that Kashmir is forevermore an integral part of India." This statement was later explained as a misunderstanding by the U.S. State Department but that did not allay Indian suspicions. Dhar's statement was an attempt to reestablish the 1972 agreement as the true basis (and not the 1947 Accession) as the proper point of departure for future discussions on Kashmir. For comments on the Dhar statement in the Indian press see K. Subrahmanyam, "The Simla Pact: Lack of Strategic Thinking," *Times of India*, April 12, 1995; "Dhar's Disclosure Well Timed? *The Tribune*, April 7, 1995; I. K.

Gujral, "Bhutto–Mrs. Gandhi Accord: The Way Out in Kashmir," *The Hindu*, April 12, 1995. For a report on the Robin Raphel statement and reactions, see the special coverage by *India Abroad*, November 5, 1993.

3. G. S. Bhargava, *South Asian Security After Afghanistan* (Lexington, Mass: D. C. Heath, 1983), pp. 91–169.

4. Some scholars have argued that Pakistan's role in the overall U.S. strategy went well beyond being merely a line of defense and a conduit to the Afghan resistance. Francis Fukuyama had advocated in early 1980 that Pakistan (along with Diego Garcia) could be an entrepôt to preposition arms and equipment and to be a launching pad for U.S. forces assigned to the Persian Gulf. See *The Security of Pakistan: A Trip Report,* Rand Corporation, N 1584-RC, September 1980.

5. See Maya Chadda, *Paradox of Power: The United States in Southwest Asia* (Santa Barbara, Calif.: ABC-Clio, 1986), pp. 175–93. India was not alone in fearing a close collaboration between Pakistan and China. Congressman McCollum traced in his speech on September 12, 1994, the evolution of Pakistani ties with China and Iran. He saw a growing linkage between Pakistan's military buildup, India's response, Pakistan's wooing of China and Iran, acquisition of nuclear weapons, and mischief in Kashmir. "In the early 1990s, after coming to power, Ms. Bhutto redirected the Pakistani national strategy . . . in order to integrate it into the Trans-Asia Axis dominated by Beijing and Islamist Bloc dominated by Tehran." Congressman McCollum's sentiments reflected a fairly widespread anxiety about Pakistani nuclear capabilities. Several members of the Congress were convinced that the Chinese sale of ballistic missiles to Pakistan was meant to undermine U.S. influence. They were also convinced that sale of arms and nuclear capabilities emboldened Pakistan to support a terrorist insurgency in Kashmir and Punjab. McCollum points out that "with this in view, in February 1990, General Mirza Aslam Beg, then the Pakistani chief of army staff, went to Tehran. Beg returned from Tehran "greatly reassured." He quotes Beg as saying "with the support from Iran promised me, we will win in case of war over Kashmir." *Congressional Record*, 140, no. 126, September 12, 1994. These fears have turned out to be somewhat exaggerated. They continue to nevertheless occupy many members of the policy community in India and the United States.

6. *Pakistan Affairs* (Washington, D.C.: Embassy of Pakistan), April 1, 1986.

7. See Richard Cronin, *The United States, Pakistan, and Soviet Threat to Southern Asia: Options for Congress*, Library of Congress, Congressional Research Service, report no. 85–192 F, September 1985; also see S. A, Aiyar, "New U.S. Arms Aid to Pakistan," *Indian Express*, May 5, 1986.

8. Raju Thomas, "Indian Security Policy in the 1990s," in Hafeez Malik, ed., *Dilemmas of National Security and Cooperation in India and Pakistan* (New York: Macmillan, 1993), p. 116. Also see his "The Growth of Indian Military Power: From Sufficient Defense to Nuclear Deterrence," in Ross Babbage and Sandy Gordon, eds. *India's Strategic Future* (London: Macmillan, 1992), pp. 35–67. Also see Manoj Joshi, "Directions in India's Defense and Security Policies," pp. 67–94 in the same volume.

9. For an extremely well-informed and succinct discussion of the Indo–Pakistan military balance, see Raju Thomas, "Indian Security Policy in the 1990s," pp. 113–21. Also see Chris Smith, *India's Ad Hoc Arsenal: Direction or Drift in Defense Policy?* (Oxford: SIPRI, Oxford University Press, 1994), pp. 105–44.

10. Smith, *India's Ad Hoc Arsenal* , p. 128.

11. Ibid., pp. 128–30.

12. Ibid., p. 114.

13. My conversations with S. K. Singh in December 1992 (in New Delhi) and then again in June 1995 in New York.

14. K. Subrahmanyam writing in response to P. N. Dhar's disclosures (about the tacit understanding making the line of actual control the international boundary between India and Pakistan) castigates Indian leaders for depending on verbal agreements and not following through with Pakistan on the promises it had made. He perceives this as a failure of Indian diplomacy and lack of systematic foreign policy. *The Times of India*, April 12, 1995.

15. This is based on conversations with Inder Malhotra and Girilal Jain, over several summers in New Delhi. Both are reputable journalists and Girilal Jain was the editor of the *Times of India* and subsequently a respected columnist in the Indian policy community.

16. I was given a number of videos recording the damage to the Golden Temple and the number of arms and weapons captured from the terrorists after the June 6 assault. Subsequent interviews with militants in Amritsar in 1986 corroborated some of this but at that time the Pakistani role seemed to be marginal. It did provide some arms and a small amount of financial assistance as well as sanctuary. The last was perhaps the most important element in Pakistani involvement at that time. The Indian government however tended to greatly exaggerate the Pakistani role in an obvious attempt to shift blame for the armed action, an action which Mrs. Gandhi was reported to have regretted later.

17. Lt. General M. L. Chibber, "Siachen Solution Will Help India, Pak," *Times of India*, 13 June 1989. For a full account of his views see "Siachen—The Untold Story (A Personal Account)," *Indian Defense Review* (January 1990): 146–52.

18. The last culminated in mediation between the Tamil militants and Colombo and was taken up vigorously at the Thimpu meetings in Bhutan.

19. Statement by Yaqub Khan, Pakistan's foreign secretary, *Times of India*, June 9, 1985.

20. *Indian Express*, January 20, 1986. Romesh Bhandari, India's foreign secretary said on January 20, 1986, that had Pakistan agreed to the two conditions important to India, i.e., no foreign bases and commitment to solve problems within a bilateral framework, the Simla agreement could have been superseded by the new accord facilitating Mr. Gandhi's visit to Pakistan. India had wanted the visit to be a crowning event following normalization. Pakistan had insisted that the visit be unconditional. It must be pointed out that no one at this point could predict the course of the Afghan war. Pakistan did not want to make a promise it might have to break later. In any case, it had argued that the condition regarding bases violated its sovereign rights, not to mention the inordinate leverage India would gain over Pakistan.

21. Yaqub Khan told the National Assembly on October 29 that Pakistan would retaliate if Kahuta was attacked. This was in response to a frenzied public debate in the Pakistan press and Assembly on the question of nuclear parity with India. *Yearbook on India's Foreign Policy, 1985–86*, Satish Kumar, ed. (New Delhi : Sage, 1988), pp. 117–18.

22. Robert Wirsing, "The Kashmir Dispute: Prospects for Resolution," Hafeez Malik, ed., *Dilemmas of National Security and Cooperation in India and Pakistan*, p. 182.

23. This account is pieced together from my interviews with militant students at the Khalsa College in Amritsar and police files in Chandigarh during August 1986. I also had a conversation with Police Chief Rebiero in Chandigarh and following that with Sidharth Shankar Ray, then the governor of Punjab.

24. Human Rights Watch, Human Rights Watch Arms Project, 6, no. 10, *India: Arms and Abuses in Indian Punjab and Kashmir*, New York, September 1994, p. 15

25. According to the report by U.S. Congress Republican Research Committee, the Sikh, Tamil, and Kashmir liberation movements saw the Darra arms bazaar as their main source of weapons. The bazaar also provided Pakistan the ability to deny its government's involvement in sale of arms to the militants. See Task Force on Terrorism and Un-conventional Warfare, "The New Islamist International," Washington D.C., February 1, 1993, p. 39.

26. See, for example, John Ward Anderson and Molly Moore, "After the Cold War, U.S.–Pakistani Ties Are Turning Sour," *Washington Post,* April 21, 1993; Steve Coll, "India–Pakistan Wage Covert Proxy Wars," *Washington Post,* December 8 1990; James P. Serba, "Border Battle in Militaristic Pakistan, Struggle with India Bolsters Self-Identity," *Wall Street Journal*, December 28, 1990; the *Washington Post* also cited former ISI officials who claimed that Pakistani officials developed close ties to Indian Muslims who fought alongside the Mujahideen in Afghanistan, segregating them in special training camps, and providing assistance through them to the insurgents in Kashmir, Punjab, and Assam.

27. *Yearbook on Indian's Foreign Policy*, p. 29.

28. Several experts I talked to were of the view that military high command led by Sunderji had not fully appraised the prime minister of the scale of the exercise. For these analysts, the gap in communication underlines the growing political independence of the Indian military and its relative freedom from civilian supervision. Similar charges are heard about the level of spending and what these analysts characterize as bloated budgets for equipment and arms that India does not need. K. Subrahmanyam in his April 12, 1995, article in the *Times of India* has yet another take on the mounting tensions between India and Pakistan in the wake of the military exercise code named "Brasstacks." He says that the possibility of Pakistani-supported insurgency eventually leading to war was anticipated by the Indian military as far back as in 1986. The Indian armed forces "played a war game called 'Akhari Badla' (the final revenge), in which they . . . visualized fairly accurately what Pakistan would attempt." This was pub-lished subsequently in the *Indian Defense Review* as "Operation Topaq." Some of these papers that were actually about the war games set in 1990–91 were obtained by the Pakistani intel-ligence in 1986. So when the Indian "Brasstacks" exercises were undertaken, Pakistani lead-ers believed it to be the start of a real war. But neither the 1986 war games were real nor the reports believed by Pakistan in 1987. What followed was equally interesting. Subrahmanyam reports that Pakistan used its intelligence on the Akhari Badla and conveyed it to Rajiv Gandhi suggesting that the Indian army was carrying out studies on limited imposition of emergency in certain areas of the country to dictate its own agenda to India's civilian leadership. At the time, speculations were rife in New Delhi about a possible coup d'etat, the Napoleonic ambi-tions of army Chief of Staff Sunderji, and why Rajiv was never informed about the full scale of Operation Brasstacks. Most of this was exaggeration but it did reinforce the image of Rajiv's ineptitude, in contrast with another perception that saw him greatly enamored of high tech weapons and military power.

29. *Overseas Hindustan Times*, February 21, 1987; March 7, 1987.

30. A. G. Noorani, "Pakistan's Complicity in Terrorism in J&K: The Evidence and the Law," *Indian Defense Review*: 24–34.

31. Also see his interview in *Sunday* (Calcutta), March 18, 1990.

32. His statement appeared in a Srinagar Weekly *Chattan* in November 1988 and was republished in *The Statesman*, April 19, 1989.

33. See Jagmohan's *My Frozen Turbulence in Kashmir* (New Delhi: Allied, 1991).

34. Rajiv Gandhi told the Turkish president in July 1988 that "nothing could be more dangerous than by force of foreign arms to foist on the people of Afghanistan the kind of forces of reaction which Kamal Atatourk rejected when he established the Republic of Turkey." Gandhi was referring to the ascendancy of an Islamic fundamentalist regime in Kabul should the Najibullah government collapse. *Indian Express*, July 17, 1988.

35. "Agreement to Resolve Siachen Issue," *The Muslim* (Islamabad), June 18, 1989; also see "Breaking the Ice Over Siachen," June 18, 1989; "Army Officers to fix Positions," *The Hindu* (Madras), June 18, 1989.

36. There was the rising incidence of fratricidal ethnic conflicts in the province of Sindh, and frequent threats to Benazir Bhutto's authority from the military and rebellious local leaders of the influential province of Punjab. The Soviet withdrawal from Afghanistan had thrown the entire U.S.–Pakistan strategic consensus into doubt. There was increasing pressure from Washington on the nuclear question. Bhutto's own party, the PPP, was bogged down in a serious struggle for power with the MQM, the rival party in Sindh.

37. President Bush had dispatched Robert Gates to South Asia to prevent confrontation, which many in the United States feared might lead to use of nuclear weapons. Arif Niazi wrote in the *Nation* that "the Gates Mission had confirmed that the information [regarding Pakistan's running of 31 camps for the Kashmiri militants] was supplied by Pakistani officials." According to the *New York Times*, June 17, 1990, an offcial U.S. source claimed that Pakistan had already closed down 31 training camps for Kashmiri terrorists and subversives.

38. Selig Harrison, a senior associate of the Carnegie Endowment for International Peace wrote in the *Washington Post*, April 23, 1990, that "Evidence obtained in Pakistan as well as from Indian and American intelligence sources indicated that some 63 Pakistan-operated camps have been functioning at various times during the past two years, roughly half located in Azad Kashmir and half in Pakistan. At least 11 have operated continuously." He further stated that Pakistan had diverted some of the rocket launchers and Kalashnikov rifles from U.S.-supplied Afghan aid stockpiles. This was confirmed by Javid Mir (a JKLF militant leader) in an interview in *India Today*, March 15, 1990. The Arms Control Report of Human Rights Watch and the Republican Task Force Report confirmed the establishment of these training camps, the subsequent closure of half of them, and the removal of some to the tribal agency area far from Kashmir.

39. After the Soviet withdrawal from Afghanistan, the most critical concerns for the United States in South Asia were stability and nuclear proliferation. Both India and Pakistan were nuclear threshold states with growing arsenals of conventional weapons and missile technology. The Bush and then the Clinton administration had therefore proposed a variety of formulas to secure India's and Pakistan's signatures on the NPT. India has resisted these pressures and argued that the NPT is discriminatory. India pointed to China and argued that as long as Beijing's nuclear arsenal was not on the negotiating table, New Delhi would not discuss nonproliferation, though it promised not to export such technology to another country. Pakistan pointed at India and argued that it could not sign the NPT as long as India refused to sign. India has been however anxious about the impact these differences have had on Indo–U.S. relations and has tried to win American goodwill by signing agreements preventing export of missiles and missile technology and production of fissionable materials as well as protocols on chemical and biological weapons. The entire nuclear controversy, as it was playing out in early 1990s, is laid out in a brief but highly informative publication entitled *Preventing Nuclear Proliferation in South Asia* (New York: Asia Society, 1995).

40. Prem Shankar Jha, *In The Eye of the Cyclone: The Crisis in Indian Democracy* (New Delhi: Viking Press, 1993), p. 6.

41. The possibility of an Indo–Pakistani war had again raised its head when the JKLF had insisted on crossing the international frontier in February 1992. I was in New Delhi at the time for a seminar on India and China's foreign policy organized by the Nehru Memorial Museum and Library. This occasion provided me with access to a whole range of foreign and defense officials in New Delhi. They confirmed that a conflict was only a hair's breadth away. A large number of them commented, however, that nothing could be achieved in Kashmir by going to war with Pakistan. It would not solve the political problem in Kashmir and perhaps that is why a war will be avoided. According to M. A. Niazi, President Zia, sometime before his death, also had worried about Kashmir precipitating a conflict with India. *The Nation*, May 31, 1990. But that had not deterred him from continuing to secretly support the pro-Khalistani and Kashmiri separatist elements across the border.

42. Pakistan has tried to replace the "unreliable" JKLF with the Hizbul Mujahideen, who were more compliant and militant about Islam. This was meant to give Pakistan better control of the liberation struggle in Kashmir. According to Maleeha Lodhi, former editor of *Muslim*, the Kashmiri movement was being transformed, "with its symbolism changing from the secularism of Amanullah Khan's JKLF to the Islamic slogans of the newer, younger militants." The Hizbul Mujahideens advocated Kashmir's accession to Pakistan. The Jama'at-e-Islami in Pakistan was openly collecting funds for the "Jihad in Kashmir" and Azad Kashmir 's Premier Rathore had secured a fatwa (edict) from the religious authorities that some Rs. 430 million Zakat fund could be used on this jihad. *The Muslim*, November 20, 1990. Pakistan officials vigorously denied their involvement in Kashmir and Punjab. They have argued instead that Azad Kashmir was an autonomous entity. The organization of the "liberation struggle" from there was independent of the Pakistani government and without the knowledge and help from it. In any case, they claimed, it was a spontaneous and natural response by oppressed Kashmiri Muslims to Indian occupation. In view of mounting evidence of such an involvement from a diversity of sources, this claim become increasingly harder to sustain. Pakistani officials at the highest level finally conceded to John Ward Anderson of the *Washington Post*, in an article published May 16, 1994, that not only were Kashmiri insurgents being supported by private organizations such as the Jamaat in Pakistan, but that the ISI too was involved in training Kashmiri freedom fighters, although on a smaller scale than in 1992.

Mushahid Hussain, a Pakistani columnist of international repute, vividly described the strategic underpinnings of Pakistan's policy and by implication the dangers to India. Writing in the *Frontier Post*, May 18, 1991, he pointed out that, "Compounding the problem" for India "is a security nightmare that defines the Kashmir insurgency as an increasingly Islamic movement and views its close proximity to Punjab as creating a 'security opening' to India's jugular in the North West vis-à-vis Pakistan and China."

43. Mushahid Hussain, "Pakistan Can Rely on a Safe Rear Now" *Times of India*, January 8, 1990.

9. THE PAST AS PROLOGUE: LOOKING AHEAD

1. The term "Hindu" denotes the "nation"; "a person who regards this land–from the Indus to the seas as his fatherland (*pitrubhumi*) as well as his holy land (*punyabhumi*)." Moreover, because the Hindu nationalists insist that Indian nation is also the holy land of the Hindus

(*punyabhumi*), the supposed distinctions between culture and religion are hard to maintain. V. D. Savarkar, *Hindutva*, 6th ed. (Bombay: Veer Savarkar Prakashan, 1989), pp. 110–13.

2. The Hindu nationalists range from diehard ideologues committed to forced "Hinduization" of India to moderates willing to confine their goals to parliamentary methods and political persuasion.

Index